Frommer's®

MAINE
COAST

5th Edition

Updated by Brian Kevin

FROMMER'S STAR RATINGS SYSTEM

Every hotel, restaurant, and attraction listed in this guide has been ranked for quality and value. Here's what the stars mean:

★   Recommended
★★   Highly Recommended
★★★ A must! Don't miss!

AN IMPORTANT NOTE

The world is a dynamic place. Hotels change ownership, restaurants hike their prices, museums alter their opening hours, and busses and trains change their routings. And all of this can occur in the several months after our authors have visited, inspected, and written about, these hotels, restaurants, museums and transportation services. Though we have made valiant efforts to keep all our information fresh and up-to-date, some few changes can inevitably occur in the periods before a revised edition of this guidebook is published. So please bear with us if a tiny number of the details in this book have changed. Please also note that we have no responsibility or liability for any inaccuracy or errors or omissions, or for inconvenience, loss, damage, or expenses suffered by anyone as a result of assertions in this guide.

CONTENTS

Facing page: Late fall foliage is ablaze with color in Maine, as some lobstermen begin to hang up their buoys for the season. *Below:* Watching a Downeast summer sunrise over Tenant's Harbor.

A LOOK AT
THE MAINE COAST

There's a reason they call it Vacationland. Season after season, you can't turn a corner in coastal Maine without stumbling into some postcard-perfect New England tableau. Stately federal architecture, stoic fishermen on wharves, lighthouses proud against (Winslow) Homeric weather-beaten shores. In these hinterlands of Yankee country, eccentricity and bohemian funk have made inroads in a culture of modesty and taciturnity, so expect splashes of local color: lurid lobster buoys dangling from tree limbs like psychedelic lichen; front-yard art installations cobbled together from life's flotsam, gaudy flea markets edging Route 1 like God's own yard sale. And yet, for all the seaside human carnival, you'll never want for a quiet pocket of deep forest or sublimely dignified shoreline. It's a multiverse of overlapping ecosystems, from rounded coastal mountains to finger-like tidal inlets, the domain of everything from prehistoric horseshoe crabs to the occasional lumbering moose. Those guys look pretty good on the postcards, too.

Mooses flirt in Baxter State Park (p. 262), one of the state's best spots for hiking, climbing, and nature-watching.

PORTLAND AND THE SOUTHERN COAST

Maine's largest city, Portland manages to feel urban and hip without losing its historic harbor town character. See p. 82.

A vintage sign welcomes visitors to charming Kennebunkport (p. 70), full of boutiques, colonial B&Bs, and shingled summer mansions.

Ogunquit's main beach (p. 69) stretches for three long sandy miles, with room for every-one to spread a towel.

Ramping up the city's cultural cachet, the Portland Museum of Art (p. 101) would be outstanding in a community 5 or 10 times Portland's size.

The Portland Sea Dogs, a AA Red Sox farm team, play at delightfully old-timey Haddon Field. See p. 103.

A craft beer mecca, Portland has many hangouts like Gritty McDuff's Brew Pub in the Old Port (p. 107), with live music and the house brew on tap.

Summer family fun in the Kennebunks (p. 70) inevitably at some point involves an encounter with a crustacean.

Near York's popular beaches, Nubble Light (p. 59) is one of the world's most photographed lighthouses.

Rocky headlands protect Ogunquit's tiny Perkins Cove (p. 69), offering sweeping sea views and an escape from the harbor village's often-thronged gift shops and seafood shacks.

MIDCOAST

At low tide, horseback riders take a seaside canter at Popham Beach State Park (p. 127), one of the few sandy strands in the rockbound lower Midcoast.

The touch tank at the Maine State Aquarium (p. 136) in West Boothbay Harbor gives kids a hands-on encounter with tidal zone marine life.

On Penobscot Bay, shady Castine (p. 170) is a classic New England village. Walking tours begin on the town green at the Castine Historical Society.

Boats are the only way to reach remote, picturesque Monhegan Island (p. 141), beloved by landscape artists; rent a bike or kayak to explore once you're here.

A Midcoast classic: The Wiscasset seafood stand Red's Eats (p. 134), where in summer the hungry patiently wait in line for up to 45 minutes to taste the succulent lobster roll.

Life seems to slow down on the rural Harpswell Peninsula (p. 127), off the tourist-developed track. In winter, locals walk their horses to pasture.

From sloops to windjammers, Boothbay Harbor (p. 135) sailboats can be booked for tours, excursions, or lessons.

Opened in 2006, the Penobscot Narrows Bridge offers 360° views from the world's tallest bridge observatory (p. 170).

South of Rockland, the Owls Head Transport Museum (p. 154) displays vintage planes, trains, and automobiles – a fun rainy-day option.

Not into outlet shopping? Freeport's other attractions include the hiking trails of Wolfe's Neck Woods State Park (p. 120).

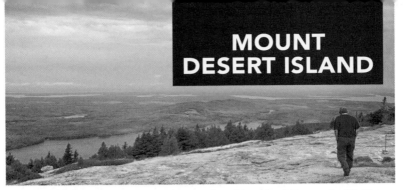

MOUNT DESERT ISLAND

A must-see stop along Acadia National Park's 20-mile Park Loop Road: The summit of Cadillac Mountain, the island's highest peak, with its breathtaking views. See p. 192.

Another scenic way to explore Mount Desert Island—paddle a canoe around one of its peaceful backwoods ponds. See p. 228.

In contrast to the rest of this bucolic island, the town of Bar Harbor fairly bustles, especially by the waterfront. See p. 207.

A LOOK AT THE MAINE COAST

Downtown Bar Harbor (p. 207) retains the strollable charm of its late 19th-century heyday.

Afternoon tea with popovers is a summer ritual at the Jordan Pond House (p. 192) in Acadia National Park

On the "quiet side" of Mount Desert Island, villages such as Somesville reward exploration.

Bass Harbor Light keeps watch from a stony crag at the island's southwest tip.

Flotillas of sea kayaks set out from Bar Harbor every day in summer, to explore Mount Desert Island's rocky shores. See p. 220.

The Abbe Museum (p. 218) in Bar Harbor has a top-rate collection of Native American artifacts, like this birchbark canoe. It's Maine's only museum affiliated with the Smithsonian Institution.

DOWNEAST & SIDE TRIPS

Youngsters dig in the clam-rich mudflats of Cobscook Bay State Park (p. 244), one of Maine's hidden jewels.

Along the Downeast coast, the vast Maine Coastal Islands Wildlife Refuge (p. 240) protects a host of shorebirds and seabirds, like this quizzical puffin.

At West Quoddy Head, the easternmost point of the U.S. is marked with this jaunty lighthouse, welcoming ships into Lubec harbor.

Near the lighthouse, walking trails lace through the dim coolness of a coastal forest in Quoddy Head State Park (p. 245).

On a day trip from Lubec to Canada's Campobello Island (p. 247), you can ramble in Franklin D. Roosevelt's boyhood footsteps along the surf-dashed shore of Herring Cove Provincial Park.

Across the state line in Portsmouth, New Hampshire (p. 250), an interpreter demonstrates colonial-era cooking in one of more than 40 historic buildings of the open-air museum Strawbery Banke.

The popular Chimney Pond (p. 272) hiking trail affords some stunning vistas on the climb up Mount Katahdin, Maine's highest mountain, in Baxter State Park.

Flowing along Baxter State Park's southern border, the wild west branch of the Penobscot River offers some of the most exhilarating whitewater rafting in the eastern U.S. See p. 272.

THE BEST OF THE MAINE COAST

Humor columnist Dave Barry once suggested that Maine's state motto should be changed to "Cold, but damp," thereby emphasizing its two primary qualities. That's cute, but it's also sort of true. Spring here tends to last just a few days or weeks (in its place, Mainers refer to "mud season," the period from, say, mid-March to June); November features bitter winds alternating with gray sheets of rain; and the long winters often bring a mix of blizzards and ice storms.

Ah, but then there's summer. Summer on the coast of Maine brings osprey diving for fish off wooded points, fogs rolling in poetically from the Atlantic, and long, timeless days when the sun rises well before visitors do. (By 8am, it can already feel like noon.) Maine summers offer a serious dose of tranquility; a few days in the right spot can rejuvenate even the most jangled city nerves.

The trick is *finding* that right spot. Route 1 along the Maine coast is mostly an amalgam of convenience stores, tourist boutiques, and restaurants catering to bus tours. The main loop road, single beach, and most popular mountain peaks in Acadia National Park tend to get congested in summer. And arriving without a room reservation in high season? Simply a bad idea.

On the other hand, Maine's remote position and size often work to your advantage. The state has an amazing 5,500 miles of coastline, plus 3,000 or so coastal islands (admittedly, some of these are nothing more than rocks). With a little homework, you can find that little cove, island, or fishing village that isn't too discovered yet, book your room well in advance, and enjoy coastal Maine's incredibly lovely scenery without sweating any of the last-minute details.

Getting to know the locals is fun, too. Many are fishermen (as opposed to the farmers who colonized the rest of New England) and other seafaring folk, or the descendants of such, and today's coastal Mainers—even the transplanted ones—exhibit a wry, dry sense of humor and a surprising gregariousness. (There's a Bait's Motel in

Searsport, complete with worm-hanging-off-its-hook motif, for instance, and a tiny street called Fitz Hugh Lane in Somesville.) And fishermen's stories, of course, are the stuff of legend. Take the time to get to know some folks, and you'll smile a lot more.

Basically, your main challenge when planning a vacation in coastal Maine boils down to this: Where to start? Here's an entirely biased list of destinations—some places I enjoy returning to time and again. Places like these, I'm convinced, merit more than just a quick stop; instead, they're worth a detour or an extended stay of a few days to a week.

THE best AUTHENTIC EXPERIENCES

o **Spread a Towel on York's Short Sands Beach** (Southern Maine): Bring the family and embrace the giddy un-self-consciousness of summer boardwalk culture. Sunbathe while a kid tosses a Frisbee over you. Pump quarters into skee ball in the Fun-O-Rama arcade. Eat four different kinds of saltwater taffy in a day. See p. 60.

o **Do the Portland Beer Circuit** (Portland): A taproom tour in the country's beer-iest city is more than just a weekend of tasty hedonism—it's a window into what the new Portland is all about: a championing of indie and artisan culture, a respect for the town's working-class heritage, an embrace of Maine agriculture, a thoughtful repurposing of old and often dilapidated urban spaces. Plus a decidedly non-urban vibe that reminds you you're in a town of just 67,000 people (with a brewery for every 3,700 of them). See p. 108.

o **Embed on Monhegan Island** (Lower Midcoast): Don't just pop off the ferry for a day. Get a simple, rustic room on Monhegan (there is no other kind) and spend a few days learning its quiet trails, schmoozing with the artists and the lobstermen, watching the ferries and the weather come and go, and falling into the rhythm of life on Maine's most enchanted island. See p. 141.

o **Get Off the Pavement in Acadia** (Mount Desert Island): Acadia National Park's elaborate trail network is a 120-mile museum to both MDI's natural history and its human one. It's also the best way to avoid the crowds and soak up the beauty of these rounded seaside mountains. Lace up your hiking boots and pack a backpack. Leave your car at the trailhead in the morning, and don't come back until sunset. (Bonus points for doing this on skis in the winter.) See p. 181.

o **Pitch a Tent at Cobscook Bay** (Downeast Coast): Camping here, you'll be centrally located to explore both Eastport and Lubec (the two loveliest and Downeast-iest of Downeast towns). Watching the 20-foot tides come and go outside your tent flaps is the best way to get attuned to the rhythm around which life revolves at the nation's northeastern tip. See p. 244.

THE best RESTAURANTS

o **The Black Birch** (Kittery; www.theblackbirch.com; © 207/703-2294): The rustic-adventurous gastropub that revitalized what is now one of New England's hottest dining scenes, it'd make this list for the to-die-for poutine alone. See p. 53.

o **Eventide Oyster Co.** (Portland; www.eventideoysterco.com; © 207/774-8538): A hip, contemporary distillation of the sea-to-plate heritage that makes Maine dining special. And among the most nationally lauded restaurants in a town crowded with foodie delights. See p. 92.

o **Duckfat** (Portland; www.duckfat.com; © 207/774-8080): Not the fanciest menu on this list, but that's part of what makes it great. Chef Rob Evans' superb sandwiches, Belgian fries, and crème anglaise milkshakes are worth the long waits. See p. 94.

o **Five Islands Lobster Co.** (Georgetown; www.fiveislandslobster.com; © 207/371-2990): A classic Maine lobster shack, and you can't beat the romance of Georgetown's working harbor and the evergreen-speckled islands dotting the horizon. Or the freshness of the bugs, pulled out some of the state's best lobstering grounds. See p. 123.

o **Primo** (Rockland; www.primorestaurant.com; © 207/596-0770): Melissa Kelly and Price Kushner create culinary magic on two floors of a century-old home at this storied Rockland bistro. Get out your credit card for fancy treatments of *foie gras,* scallops, duck, steak (and more) as well as outstanding desserts and a long, impressive wine list. See p. 151.

THE best HOTELS

o **White Barn Inn** (Kennebunk; www.whitebarninn.com; © 207/967-2321): This venerable inn has been world-class longer than most people reading this book have been alive. Sumptuous but not overwrought, country but not folksy, one of the best dining rooms around, and service for miles. See p. 77.

o **The Press Hotel** (Portland; www.presshotel.com; © 207/808-8800): Rarely do luxurious, historical, and fun all come together in one property, but this downtown hotel in the former *Portland Press Herald* headquarters really nails it. With clever nods to the golden days of newsprint (and great art around every corner), this place just has so much style. See p. 88.

o **Lincolnville Motel** (Lincolnville; www.lincolnvillemotel.com; © 207/236-3195). A throwback to the midcentury golden days of Maine tourism—and to the values that road-tripping families could expect back then. Super reasonable rates for a self-consciously stylish vintage motor court. No other lodging in this book offers a vinyl turntable and a stack of LPs as a standard amenity. See p. 159.

o **Balance Rock Inn** (Bar Harbor; www.balancerockinn.com; © **800/753-0494** or 207/288-2610): The property's pale blue outdoor swimming pool backs right up to the Atlantic, and the rooms are as elegant and comfortable as any in the state. You won't feel so cared for by a hotel staff anywhere else on Mount Desert Island. See p. 209.

THE best OUTDOOR PLAYGROUNDS

o **The Beaches of Southern Maine** (Southern Maine): The flat, white-sand beaches of southernmost Maine are gorgeous and perfect for playing Frisbee, walking, tanning, kite flying, and photography. Just watch your tootsies: That water's cold. See chapter 4.

o **Casco Bay's Islands** (Portland): Locals once called 'em the Calendar Islands for a reason: They claim there are 365 of these rocky islands dotting Casco Bay, in every shape and size. (I'd wager there are more than that, though.) Catch a mail boat from Portland harbor and see how many *you* can count. See p. 22.

o **Rocky Peninsulas** (Lower Midcoast, Upper Midcoast, and Downeast): Everywhere you go—from the Cape Neddick area to just south of Portland, from Harpswell to Georgetown, from Blue Hill to Boothbay to Schoodic Point—you'll find long fingerlings and headlands carved of sheer bedrock. Once these were mountaintops high above an ancient sea; now they comprise some of the East Coast's most beautiful scenery. Try some back-road wandering to find the best ones. See chapters 6, 7, and 9.

o **The Camden Hills** (Lower Midcoast): They're not huge, yet this run of hills comes with a bonus you'll only understand when you get to the top: eye-popping coastal vistas of boats, villages, and islands. In the winter, you can even toboggan-run from crest to valley. See chapter 6.

o **Acadia National Park** (Mount Desert Island): New England's only national park is also one of the most beautiful (and popular) in the U.S. Its rocky, surf-pounded coastline is the main attraction, but don't overlook the quiet forests and open summits of low mountains that afford stunning coastal views. Rent a mountain bike or horse-drawn carriage to explore further. See chapter 8.

o **The Appalachian Trail and Mount Katahdin** (North Woods): Well worth a detour inland, the nearly mile-high Mount Katahdin—Maine's highest peak—has an ineffable spiritual quality, rising abruptly from a thick blanket of North Woods forest. It's also the centerpiece of Baxter State Park, one of the last, best wildernesses remaining in the eastern U.S. The Appalachian Trail, which stretches 2,100 rugged miles from Georgia, winds uphill to the finish line here on Katahdin. The Trail's stretches in Maine traverse some of the most magnificent scenery in New England. See p. 262.

THE best SMALL TOWNS

- **York Village** (Southern Maine): Maine's oldest settlement has plenty of history and fine architecture; it's also got a set of beaches and a coastal trail nearby. Plus people just seem *friendly* here. See p. 48.
- **Camden** (Upper Midcoast): This seaside town has everything—a beautiful harbor; great Federal, Queen Anne, and Greek Revival architecture; and even its own tiny mountain range, affording great hikes with sweeping ocean views. With lots of elegant bed-and-breakfasts, it's a perfect base for explorations farther afield. See p. 154.
- **Castine** (Upper Midcoast): Soaring elm trees, a peaceful harborside setting, grand historic homes, and a selection of good inns make this a great spot to soak up some of Maine's coastal ambience off the beaten path. See p. 170.
- **Stonington** (Upper Midcoast): Maine's heritage as a fishing town is never more on display than it is in Stonington, the biggest town on little Deer Isle. You get a fair number of transplants here, too, who came for the views and stayed to paint pictures, paddle kayaks, do yoga, or set out for the little-glimpsed Isle au Haut. See p. 174.
- **Northeast Harbor** (Mount Desert Island): A single, sleepy main street anchors one of MDI's best little villages. Northeast has a waterside setting, sure, but also a mix of seafaring locals and art-loving summer folks, giving it an aura of a place that's still living life from a century ago. See p. 227.
- **Eastport** (Downeast): Now this is truth in advertising: You can't get any farther east in the U.S. than Eastport. You'd think this place would be a lonely outpost, but it's actually a thriving little hub of artistic culture, historic architecture, brawny fishing exploits, and briny eats. See p. 246.

THE best PLACES TO SEE FALL FOLIAGE

- **The Camden Hills** (Upper Midcoast): The surrounding countryside is full of blazing color, offset by gray-shingled homes and sailboats. See chapter 7.
- **Acadia National Park** (Mount Desert Island): This national park possesses some of the finest foliage in northern New England, all the more so because it's set right beside the dramatic, rocky coastline. See chapter 8.
- **Blueberry Barrens** (Downeast): One of Maine's least appreciated scenic treasures. Downeast Maine's vast wild blueberry fields turn a brilliant cranberry red each fall, setting the landscape ablaze with color. Wander the dirt roads northeast of Cherryfield, or just drive Route 1 between Harrington and Machias past an experimental farm atop (of course) Blueberry Hill. See chapter 9.

THE best COASTAL VIEWS

o **Hiking Trails on Monhegan:** While the village of Monhegan is clustered around the harbor of the same-named island, the rest of the 700-acre rock is comprised of picturesque wild lands, with miles of trails crossing open meadows and tracing rocky bluffs. See p. 143.

o **From the Deck of a Windjammer:** See Maine as many saw it for centuries—from the ocean, looking inland. Sailing ships depart from various harbors along the coast, particularly from Rockland and Camden. Spend between a night and a week exploring the dramatic shoreline. See p. 146.

o **Merchant's Row via Kayak:** The islands between Stonington and Isle au Haut, rimmed with pink granite and capped with the stark spires of spruce trees, are among the most spectacular on the entire East Coast. They're inaccessible by motorboat, but wonderful to explore by sea kayak. Some outfitters even offer overnight camping trips on the islands. See p. 178.

o **Acadia's Park Loop Road:** Forming the heart of Acadia National Park, this is New England's premier oceanside drive. Start along a ridge with views of Frenchman Bay and the Porcupine Islands, then dip down along the rocky shores to watch the surf crash against the dark rocks. Plan to do this 20-mile loop at least twice to get the most out of it. See p. 192.

o **From a Well-Located Rocking Chair:** Views are never better than when you're caught unaware—such as glancing up from an engrossing book on the front porch of an ocean-side inn and catching a great sunset or angle of light on the water. This book includes many hotels and inns on the water. A list of the best porch views in Maine could run for pages, but it would certainly include those gleaned from the **Beachmere Inn** in Ogunquit (p. 64), the **Black Point Inn** in Scarborough (p. 86), **Grey Havens** on Georgetown Island (p. 127), **East Wind Inn** in Tenant's Harbor (p. 148), the **Samoset Resort** outside Rockport (p. 149), the **Inn on the Harbor** in Stonington (p. 175), and the **Claremont** in Southwest Harbor (p. 122).

THE best DESTINATIONS FOR FAMILIES

o **York Beach** (Southern Maine): This beach town is actually a set of three towns; head for **Short Sands** with the kids, where they can watch a taffy-pulling machine, play video games in an arcade, ogle seashells in a trinket shop, or scarf cotton candy at a small amusement park. The **Long Sands** section is ideal for tanning, Frisbee tossing, or kite flying; nearby is Nubble Light (a scenic lighthouse) and a kid-friendly ice-cream shop. See p. 48.

o **Old Orchard Beach** (Southern Maine): This place has sort of a carnival atmosphere—there are french fries, hot dogs, and fried dough galore. Though it might be a bit much for stodgy adults who can't embrace the pure camp, the kids will probably love it. See p. 110.

- **Freeport** (Lower Midcoast). It's almost impossible to knock Freeport as a family vacation spot. We're talking about a town with loads of shopping, outdoor music in summer, about a half-dozen L.L. Bean stores (including nearly a whole floor focused on kids' outdoor wear), and tons of quick eats and chain hotels. Plus lobsters. Plus a souvenir shop with a moose theme. Heck, there's even a McDonald's—tastefully designed, of course. About the only thing this place *lacks* is a go-kart track and an Elmo theme park. And that's a good thing. See p. 113.
- **Monhegan Island** (Lower Midcoast): The mail boat from Port Clyde out to Monhegan is intriguing, the inns are a rustic overnight adventure, and the smallish island's scale is perfect for kids to explore, especially kids in the, say, 8-to-12-year-old range. See p. 141.

THE best PLACES TO REDISCOVER THE PAST

- **Sabbathday Lake Shaker Community** (New Gloucester): The last of the active Shaker communities in the nation, this was the only one that voted to accept new converts rather than die out. The 1,900-acre farm about 45 minutes outside of Portland has a number of exceptional buildings, including some from the 18th century. Visitors can view examples of Shaker craftsmanship and buy herbs to bring home. See p. 111.
- **Mount Desert Island & Bar Harbor** (Mount Desert Island): In the mid-1800s, America launched a love affair with nature and never looked back. See where it started, here amid surf-wracked rocks, where some of the nation's most affluent families erected vacation "cottages" with bedrooms by the dozen. The area still offers lessons on how to design with nature as accomplice rather than adversary. See chapter 8.
- **Portsmouth** (New Hampshire): This salty coastal city also happens to possess some of the most impressive historic homes in all New England. Start at **Strawbery Banke**, a 10-acre compound of 42 historic buildings, then visit some of the other grand homes in the surrounding neighborhoods. See p. 250.

THE MAINE COAST IN CONTEXT

Boiled down to its simplest facts, the Maine coast basically consists of two regions: southern Maine—"down there," also sometimes referred to as "Vacationland" or "not Maine"—and Downeast—"up there" or "the real Maine." The truth is, it's all "real Maine," although the two regions can seem as different as night and day. Broadly speaking, as you head north, the gourmet cuisine, fine cars, and luxury inns of the southern coast gradually give way to cottages, used cars tacked together with duct tape, and fried fish.

Maine's legendary aloofness is important to keep in mind when visiting the area, because getting to know the region requires equal amounts of patience and persistence. New England doesn't wear its attractions on its sleeve. It keeps its best destinations hidden in valleys and on the side streets of small villages. Your most memorable experience might be cracking open a boiled lobster at a roadside lobster pound marked by a scrawled paper sign, or exploring a cobblestoned alley that's not even on Google Maps. There's no Disneyland or Eiffel Tower here. This coast is the sum of dozens of smaller attractions; it resists being defined by a few big ones.

Of course, the natural elements here—the wind, the soft hazy light, the shining or roiling seas—always seem to have the greatest draw on the traveler. Rejuvenating as these elements are, they are also capricious. You're as likely to get a blue-sky day when the islands sparkle like coins in the harbor as you are 3 days of fog and spitting rain or snow. Maybe both in the same week. Attempting to understand this weather—just like trying to explore the coast as a regular tourist, hitting attraction after attraction—is pointless. It's better to just let the mood of each day catch you, cycling or driving a back road in search of something you've never seen before (a byway, an old house, a handmade sign advertising PIES). Or, if the weather's really nasty, stay inside and do crossword puzzles; paint a watercolor; listen to the Red Sox on the local radio station. *Now* you're getting the real Maine.

Some writers believe Maine's character is still heavily influenced by Calvinism, by such ideas as *nothing can change my fate* and *hard work is the only virtue*. It's hard not to agree, but Mainers aren't completely stone-faced—there are wonderful characters, smiles, and stories to be had in abundance here. You don't need to expect rock-hard mattresses and tasteless meals, either; as these pages demonstrate, spas, luxurious country inns, and restaurants serving London-class meals have arrived on the coastal Maine scene, displacing some of the boardinghouses and chowder houses of old. Be sure to visit these upscale places, but also set aside time to spend rocking in a chair on a simple inn porch, or wandering a rocky beach path unhurriedly. You'll be glad you did.

THE MAINE COAST TODAY

You might be on Monhegan Island, or traveling downeast along Route 1. You'll see a few houses and a few people. A store. A pickup truck. And you'll wonder, "What do these people do to earn a living, anyway?"

As recently as a few decades ago, the answer was almost always this: living off the land and water. They might have fished, harvested their own woodlots, or managed gravel pits, but *work* here usually fell into a category that was awfully close to that of *survival*. Of course, many still do three jobs, but hardscrabble work is no longer the only game in town. Today a coastal Mainer just as likely might be a former *New Yorker* editor, a farmer who grows organic produce for gourmet restaurants, or a financial consultant who handles his clients by fax and e-mail. And you'll find *lots* of folks whose livelihood depends on tourism, whether it's the lone tour guide, the high school kid working the local T-shirt shop, or the tow-truck driver hauling fancy cars around Mount Desert Island after they break down.

This slow change in the economy is but one of the big shifts facing Maine and New England. The most visible and wracking change involves development and growth; for a region long familiar with poverty, a spell of recent prosperity and escalating property values has threatened to bring to Maine that curious homogenization already marking suburbs and hip urban neighborhoods in the rest of the nation. Once a region of distinctive villages, green commons, and courthouse squares, parts of coastal Maine have come to resemble suburbs everywhere else—a pastiche of strip malls dotted with fast-food chains, big-box discount and home-improvement stores, and the like.

While undeniably convenient, this is nothing short of shocking to longtime residents. Coastal towns have long maintained their identities in the face of considerable pressure. The region has always taken pride in its low-key, practical

	Local Wisdom

	Welcome to Vacationland
	          —former Maine state slogan
	Maine: The Way Life Should Be
	          —former Maine state slogan

The Maine Coast

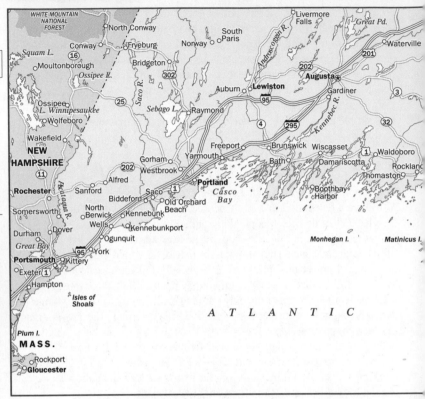

approach to life. In smaller communities, town meetings are still the preferred form of government. Residents gather in a public space to speak out about—sometimes forcefully—and vote on the issues of the day, such as funding for their schools, road improvements, fire trucks, or even symbolic gestures such as declaring their towns nuclear-free. "Use it up, wear it out, make do, or do without" is a well-worn phrase that aptly sums up the attitude of many longtime Mainers—and it's the polar opposite of the designer-outlet ethos filtering in.

It's not clear how town meetings and that sense of knowing where your town ends and the next one begins will survive the slow but inexorable encroachment of generic consumer culture. You see it already, as chain stores like Walmart and Banana Republic proliferate in places like the mall-heavy sprawl on Portland's fringes, the shopping outlets of Kittery and Freeport, and the Route 1 conglomeration near Bucksport and Ellsworth. In these spots, little regional identity can be found.

Meanwhile, the rest of coastal Maine is figuring out how best to balance the principles of growth and conservation—how to allow the economy to edge

into the modern age without sacrificing those qualities that make Maine such a distinctive place. Development is a hot issue, but it isn't white-hot—yet. Few locals have adopted the view that development should be allowed at all costs. On the flip side, few tend to think that the land should be preserved at all costs, either. They're not all that happy about rising property taxes and land prices—unless they happen to own a chunk of the coast, in which case they're probably putting up the for sale signs as we speak.

Pinching off all development would mean that the offspring of longtime Maine families would have fewer jobs, and that Maine would be fated to spend its days as a sort of quaint theme park. But if development continued unabated, many of the characteristics that make this place unique—and attract tourist dollars—would vanish. Will the Maine coast be able to sustain its tourism industry if it's blanketed with strip malls and fast-food joints, making it look like every other town in America? Unlikely. The question is how to respect the conservation ethic while leaving room for growth, but that question won't be answered anytime soon.

Maine: A Recent Discovery? Hardly!

Think Maine is your little secret get-away? Think again: This coast has seen wave after successive wave of visitation, beginning at least 3 centuries ago when European newcomers tried to settle it, only to be driven off by Native Americans. (It's also locally believed that Vikings may have touristed—er, pillaged?—the region even longer before that.)

By the early 19th century, the Maine coast had become well colonized and blossomed into one of the most prosperous places in all the United States. Shipbuilders constructed brigantines and sloops, using stout pines and other trees floated downriver from Maine's North Woods; ship captains built huge, handsome homes in towns such as Searsport, Kittery, Bath, and Belfast; and merchants and traders built vast warehouses to store the booty from the excursions, as well as their own grandiose homes.

Then things quieted down for a while, until landscape artists "rediscovered" Maine. In the mid-to-late 19th century, they brought in their wake a fresh influx of city dwellers from Boston, New York, and Philadelphia, seeking relief from the heat and congestion of the city. The huge, shingled seaside estates they built lined the coast in places such as Bar Harbor and Camden.

At the beginning of the 20th century, a newly moneyed emerging middle class (a third wave?) showed up to discover Maine yet again, building smaller, less expensive bungalows by the shore in places such as York Beach, Kennebunk Beach, and Old Orchard Beach. The next arrival? That's you, dear reader.

Complicating things, Maine's economy has been unpredictable, with tourism on the rise but few consistent trend lines. The mid-1990s saw a slump, then another in the wake of the housing bubble, and recent years have ushered in a steady uptick in visitors. Winners and losers in other sectors have been both predictable (service jobs are up, the paper mills keep closing) and surprising (real estate's anemic, small farms are booming). Through all the ups and downs, resourceful locals somehow found a way to buy and fix up farmhouses and keep their trucks running and dogs happy. Entrepreneurship has surged: Turn over a few stones, and it's remarkable how many self-owned enterprises you'll find along this coast.

One change is all but inevitable: Property values will continue to rise as city folks increasingly seek a piece of whatever it is that makes rural Maine special. Commentators believe this change, while welcome after decades of slow growth, will bring new conflicts. The continuing decentralization of the workplace has made it easier for telecommuters and info-entrepreneurs to settle the coast's more far-flung villages, clocking in via laptops and tablets. How might comparatively affluent newcomers feel about increased coastal development or growing numbers of tour buses cruising their quaint harborside streets? How will locals respond to all the new money—with envy, or with open arms? And how much will the state's priceless natural resources become stressed by increased tourism or development?

Change doesn't come rapidly to the Maine coast. But there's a lot to sort out, and friction will certainly continue to build, one waterfront condo at a time. One thing is for sure: It will be interesting to see how it plays out.

LOOKING BACK AT MAINE

Viewed from a distance, Maine's history mirrors that of its progenitor, England. This coastline rose from a sparsely populated, inhospitable place to a place of tremendous historical importance in a relatively short time, thanks to its tremendous natural resources (such as white pine trees for ship's masts, and endless schools of fish that could be caught offshore). For a time, Maine captured a good deal of America's overseas trade and became a legitimate industrial and marine powerhouse—not to mention a center of literary and creative thought and even fine art.

Don't believe me? That's because the party ended almost as suddenly as it began, when commerce and culture sought more fertile grounds to the west and south.

To this day, Maine refuses to separate itself from the past. When you walk through downtown Portland, layers of history pile up at every turn: punk-rock wannabes taking selfies in front of fine colonial church steeples; modern buses rolling through oceanview parks; elaborate mansions by world-class architects that speak to the refined sensibilities of the late Victorian era.

History is even more inescapable as you proceed up the coast and off the beaten track. Travelers in Downeast Maine—an overlooked, economically depressed area today—can still find clues to what Henry Wadsworth Longfellow called "the irrevocable past" in everything from stone walls running through the woods to the handsome Federal-style homes built by wealthy merchants.

Here's a brief overview of some historical episodes and trends that have shaped coastal Maine:

INDIGENOUS CULTURE Native Americans have inhabited Maine since about 7000 B.C. The state was inhabited chiefly by Algonquins and Abenakis, who lived a nomadic life of fishing, trapping, and hunting; they changed camp locations several times each year to take advantage of seasonal fish runs, wildlife movements, and the like.

After the arrival of the Europeans, French Catholic missionaries succeeded in converting many Native Americans, and most tribes sided with the French in the French and Indian War in the 18th century. Afterward, the Indians fared poorly at the hands of the British and were quickly pushed to the margins. Today, there are four nations of the Wabanaki in Maine: the Maliseet, Micmac, Penobscot, and Passamaquoddy. The Passamaquoddy administer two reservations in Downeast Maine; the relationship between the state and the tribes is sometimes turbulent.

THE COLONIES In 1604, some 80 French colonists spent winter on a small island on what today is the Maine–New Brunswick border. They did not care for the harsh weather of their new home and left in spring to resettle in present-day Nova Scotia. In 1607, 3 months after the celebrated Jamestown, Virginia, colony was founded, a group of 100 English settlers established a community at Popham Beach, Maine. The Maine winter demoralized these would-be colonists, as well, and they returned to England the following year. In 1614, Captain John Smith, of Jamestown fame, is said to have spent a Yule night off of South Bristol while exploring the Maine Coast, at the spot now called **Christmas Cove** (see p. 139).

The colonization of the region began in earnest with the arrival of the Pilgrims at Plymouth Rock in 1620. The Pilgrims—a religious group that had split from the Church of England—established North America's first permanent European colony, although it came at a hefty price: Half the group perished during the first winter. But the colony began to thrive over the years, in part thanks to helpful Native Americans. The success of the Pilgrims lured other settlers from England, who established a constellation of small towns outside Boston that became the Massachusetts Bay Colony. Throughout the 17th century, colonists from Massachusetts pushed northward into what is now Maine (but was then part of Massachusetts). The first areas to be settled—such as **York**, **Kittery**, and what's now known as **Cape Elizabeth**—were lands near protected harbors along the coast and on navigable waterways.

The more remote settlements came under attack in the 17th and early 18th centuries in a series of raids by Native Americans conducted both independently and in concert with the French. These proved temporary setbacks; colonization continued throughout New England into the 18th century.

THE AMERICAN REVOLUTION   Starting around 1765, Great Britain launched a series of ham-handed economic policies to reign in the increasingly feisty colonies. These included a direct tax—the Stamp Act—to pay for a standing army. The crackdown provoked strong resistance. Under the banner of "No taxation without representation," disgruntled colonists engaged in a series of riots, resulting in the Boston Massacre of 1770, when five protesting colonists were fired upon and killed by British soldiers.

In 1773 the most infamous protest—dubbed the Boston Tea Party—took place in Boston (and, at the time, Maine was still part of Massachusetts). Hostilities reached a peak in 1775 when the British, seeking to quell unrest in Massachusetts, sent troops to seize military supplies and arrest high-profile rebels John Hancock and Samuel Adams. The colonists' militia exchanged gunfire with the British, thereby igniting the Revolutionary War ("the shot heard round the world"). Hostilities formally ended in February 1783, and in September Britain recognized the United States as a sovereign nation.

While no notable battles were fought in Maine, a number of forts were established along the coast of Maine—first for the purpose of defending the British from the French, and then for the purpose of defending the new America from, well, the British. Many of these forts remain well preserved today, as state parks. Kittery's **Fort McClary** (p. 21) was garrisoned during the Revolutionary War; on the Pemaquid Peninsula, the **Colonial Pemaquid**

State Historic Site (p. 140) has a replica of a fort from 1692 (the replica itself is more than a century old).

FARMING & TRADE   As the new republic matured, economic growth in New England followed two tracks. Residents of inland communities survived by farming and trading in furs. On the Maine coast, however, boatyards sprang up anywhere there was a good anchorage, and ship captains made tidy fortunes trading lumber for sugar and rum in the Caribbean. Trade was dealt a severe blow following the Embargo Act of 1807, but commerce eventually recovered, and Maine-ported ships could be encountered everywhere around the globe. Entire towns such as **Searsport** (see p. 145), **Thomaston** (p. 43), and **Bath** (p. 120) developed almost solely as exclusive (at the time) hometowns for shipbuilders and the sea captains who stayed at sea for long months on these difficult journeys; many of their homes contained distinctive "widow's walks," from which their wives could watch for their returns.

The growth of the railroad in the mid-19th century was another boon. The train opened up much of the coast to trade by connecting Maine with Boston. The rail lines allowed local resources—such as timber from the Maine woods, floated downriver to the coast via log drives—to be much more easily shipped to markets to the south.

INDUSTRY   Maine's Industrial Revolution found seed around the time of the embargo of 1807. Barred from importing English fabrics, New Englanders simply pulled up their bootstraps and built their own textile mills. Other common household products were also manufactured domestically, especially shoes. Coastal towns such as Biddeford, Saco, and Topsham became centers of textile and shoe production. Today, however, industry no longer plays the prominent role it once did—manufacturing first moved to the South, then overseas.

TOURISM   In the mid– and late 19th century, Mainers discovered a new cash crop: the tourist. All along the eastern seaboard, it became fashionable for the gentry and eventually the working class to set out for excursions to the mountains and the shore. Aided by the dramatic paintings of the Hudson River School painters, Acadia and the downeast coast were suddenly lifted by a tide of summer visitors; this tourism wave crested in the 1890s in Bar Harbor. Several grand resort hotels from tourism's golden era, like Southport's **Newagen Seaside Inn** (see p. 131) and Rockland's **Samoset Resort** (see p. 149), still host summer travelers in the area.

ECONOMIC DOWNTURN   While the railways helped Maine to thrive in the mid–19th century, the train played an equally central role in undermining its prosperity. The driving of the Golden Spike in 1869 in Utah, linking America's Atlantic and Pacific coasts by rail, was heard loud and clear in Maine, and it had a discordant ring. Transcontinental rail meant manufacturers could ship goods from the fertile Great Plains and California to faraway markets; the coastal shipping trade was dealt a fatal blow. And the tourists, too, began to set their sights on the suddenly accessible Rockies and other stirring sites in the West.

Beginning in the late 19th century, Maine lapsed into an extended economic slumber. Families commonly walked away from their farmhouses (there was no market for resale) and set off for regions with more promising opportunities. The abandoned, decaying farmhouse became almost an icon for the Maine coast, and vast tracts of farmland were reclaimed by forest. With the rise of the automobile, the grand resorts further succumbed, and many closed their doors as inexpensive motels siphoned off their business.

BOOM TIMES During the last 2 decades of the 20th century, much of Maine rode an unexpected wave of prosperity. A massive real-estate boom shook the region in the 1980s, driving land prices sky-high as prosperous buyers from New York and Boston acquired vacation homes or retired to the most alluring areas. In the 1990s, the rise of the high-tech industry also sent ripples from Boston north into Maine. Tourism rebounded as harried urbanites of the eastern seaboard opted for shorter, more frequent vacations closer to home.

Travelers to more remote regions, however, will discover that some communities never benefited from this boom; they're still waiting to rebound from the early 20th-century economic downturn. Especially hard hit have been places such as Downeast Maine, where many residents still depend on local resources—lobsters, fish, farmland, maybe a bed-and-breakfast or crafts business on the side—to eke out a living. And, remarkably, it still works.

COASTAL MAINE ART & ARCHITECTURE

ARCHITECTURE You can often trace the evolution of a place by its architecture, as styles evolve from basic structures to elaborate mansions. The primer below should help you with basic identification.

o **Colonial** (1600–1700): The New England house of the 17th century was a simple, boxy affair, often covered in shingles or rough clapboards. Don't look for ornamentation; these homes were designed for basic shelter from the elements, and are often marked by prominent stone chimneys.

o **Georgian** (1700–1800): Ornamentation comes into play in the Georgian style, which draws heavily on classical symmetry. Georgian buildings were in vogue in England at the time, and were embraced by affluent colonists. Look for Palladian windows, formal pilasters, and elaborate projecting pediments. **Portsmouth**, New Hampshire (see p. 250), has abundant examples of later Georgian styles.

o **Federal** (1780–1820): Federal homes (sometimes called Adams homes) may best represent the New England ideal. Spacious yet austere, they are often rectangular or square, with low-pitched roofs and little ornament on the front, although carved swags or other embellishments are frequently seen near the roofline. Look for fan windows and chimneys bracketing the building. In Maine, excellent Federal-style homes are found throughout the region in towns such as **Kennebunkport, Bath**, and **Brunswick** (see chapter 6).

- **Greek Revival** (1820–60) and **Gothic Revival** (1840–80): These two styles—Greek Revival with its columned porticoes and triangular pediments, Gothic Revival with its mock turrets and castellations—didn't catch on in Maine as they did in other parts of the country, although a few examples can still seen here and there. Maine's late-19th-century tourist boom, however, perfectly coincided with the rise of . . .
- **Victorian** (1860–1900): This is a catchall term for the jumble of mid- to late-19th-century styles that emphasized complexity and opulence. Perhaps the best-known Victorian style—almost a caricature—is the tall and narrow Addams Family–style house, with mansard roof and prickly roof cresting. You'll find these scattered throughout the region. The Victorian style also includes squarish **Italianate** homes with wide eaves and unusual flourishes, such as the outstanding **Victoria Mansion** in Portland (see p. 101).
- **Shingle** (1880–1900): This uniquely New England style quickly became preferred for vacation homes on the Maine coast. Marked by a profusion of gables, roofs, and porches, they are typically covered with shingles from roofline to foundation.
- **Modern** (1900–present): Maine has produced little in the way of notable modern architecture; you won't find a Fallingwater (one of Frank Lloyd Wright's best-known works, near Pittsburgh), though you might spy a surprising modernist building somewhere on an enclave of wealth such as **Mount Desert Island** (p. 184) or **Cape Elizabeth** (p. 104)—if you can get past the security.

ART　New England is also justly famous for the **art** it has produced, particularly the seascapes painted on Cape Cod, along the coast of Maine, and by **Hudson River School** artists such as Thomas Cole and his student Frederic Church. Some of the other artists who have memorably painted New England landscapes and seascapes include **Winslow Homer** (1836–1910), **Fairfield Porter** (1907–75), **John Marin** (1870–1953), **Neil Welliver** (1929–2005), and **Andrew Wyeth** (1917–2009), he of the iconic *Christina's World,* painted in a coastal Maine field. To showcase these works, and the works of other local and traveling artists, there are a surprising number of excellent art museums and galleries in Maine, including the **Portland Museum of Art** (p. 101), the **Farnsworth Museum** in Rockland (p. 153), and the **Ogunquit Museum of American Art** in Ogunquit (p. 69). Consult individual chapters for more details on local art offerings.

COASTAL MAINE IN POPULAR CULTURE

BOOKS　Mainers have generated whole libraries, from the earliest days of hellfire-and-brimstone Puritan sermons to Stephen King's horror novels set in fictional Maine villages.

The tales of **Nathaniel Hawthorne** (1804–64)—a **Bowdoin College** alumnus (see p. 125)—captivated a public eager for native literature. His most famous story, *The Scarlet Letter*, is a narrative about morality set in 17th-century Boston; his numerous other books wrestled with themes of sin and guilt, often set in the emerging republic.

Another Bowdoin graduate, **Henry Wadsworth Longfellow** (1807–82), caught the attention of the public with evocative narrative poems focusing on distinctly American subjects. His popular works included "The Courtship of Miles Standish," "Paul Revere's Ride," and "Hiawatha." Poetry in the mid–19th century was the equivalent of Hollywood movies today—Longfellow could be considered his generation's Steven Spielberg (apologies to literary scholars). A tour of Longfellow's childhood home, the **Wadsworth-Longfellow House,** in Portland (see p. 102), opens a window onto his New England roots.

Henry David Thoreau's *The Maine Woods* explored Maine (although not the coast) in detail, at a time when few white men had yet penetrated the interior of the state—and there were still significant dangers involved in doing that. His canoe trip to **Mount Katahdin** (see chapter 10) was a genuine adventure.

Other regional writers who left a lasting mark on American literature include **Edna St. Vincent Millay** (1892–1950), a poet from **Camden** (see p. 154), and **Sarah Orne Jewett** (1849–1909), who wrote the indelible *The Country of the Pointed Firs* (you can visit her house in **South Berwick**—see p. 60). The best-selling *Uncle Tom's Cabin,* the book Abraham Lincoln half-jokingly accused of starting the Civil War, was written by **Harriet Beecher Stowe** (1811–86) while in **Brunswick** (p. 120). Though it isn't in Maine, New Brunswick's **Grand Manan Island** (see p. 281) claims **Willa Cather**, who summered there in the 1920s and 1930s.

The former *New Yorker* scribe **E. B. White** (1899–1985) wrote many fine, wide-ranging essays and books (including children's books such as the classic *Charlotte's Web*) about rural Maine from his perch in North Brooklin, near **Blue Hill** (p. 180), where he moved in 1939. You could do worse for an introduction to Maine than to pick up a copy of his essay collection, *One Man's Meat.*

Finally, Bangor, Maine (see p. 263), is still the home of **Stephen King,** who is considered not so much a novelist as Maine's leading industry.

FILM & TV   Maine is frequently captured through the lens of Hollywood, thanks in equal parts to its natural beauty and, probably, the unusually high numbers of actors and actresses (Oliver Platt, for example) who maintain vacation homes here.

Lillian Gish's 1920 silent film *Way Down East* was perhaps the first movie to bring cinematic attention to the region. Poignantly, Gish's last film, *The Whales of August* (1987), was set in a summer cottage on an island off the coast of Maine. Scenes from 1999's *The Cider House Rules*, which was set in Maine, were filmed on Mount Desert Island, and the 2005 HBO adaptation of Maine author Richard Russo's Pulitzer-winning *Empire Falls* was filmed all over the state. A host of horror films written by Maine's **Stephen King**—from *Carrie, Cujo,* and *The Dead Zone* down to a welter of TV miniseries—

make it sometimes seem like the only inhabitants of small New England towns are ghosts, creeps, and other supernatural forces. However, King also penned the short story upon which the wonderful flick starring Morgan Freeman and Tim Robbins, *The Shawshank Redemption* (one of my all-time favorites), was later based. The story and film are both based in Maine, though the prison and events are completely fictional.

EATING & DRINKING ON THE MAINE COAST

All along the coast you'll be tempted by seafood in its various forms. You can get fried clams by the bucket at divey shacks along remote coves and busy highways. The more upscale restaurants offer fresh fish, grilled or gently sautéed.

Live **lobster** can be bought literally off the boat at lobster pounds, especially along the Maine coast. The setting is usually rustic—maybe a couple of picnic tables and a shed where huge vats of water are kept at a low boil. Note that lobster prices in most Maine shacks vary, sometimes by a lot; it depends almost exclusively on the current year's take. (In a down year, you'll pay more.) There are two kinds of lobster, **soft-shell** and **hard-shell**. Many lobsters still have soft shells in the summer, because they've slipped off old ones and are still growing new ones back. People vary in their preferences, and some say the soft-shell lobsters have less meat. Not sure about that, but I'm a hard-shell man all the way. In fall and early winter, hard-shell lobsters become more numerous, and their price drops. The worst time to eat a lobster is probably spring, when the crustaceans are scarce, small, and overpriced. Put off that May feast; get a fish platter instead.

In summer small farmers set up stands at the end of their driveways offering fresh produce straight from the garden. You can usually find berries, fruits, and sometimes home-baked breads. These stands are rarely tended; just leave your money in the coffee can.

Restaurateurs haven't overlooked New England's bounty. Many chefs serve delicious meals consisting of local ingredients—some places even tend their own gardens. Some of the fine dishes I've enjoyed while researching this guide include curried pumpkin soup, venison medallions with shiitake mushrooms, and wild boar with juniper berries.

But you don't have to have a hefty budget to enjoy the local foods. A number of regional classics fall into the "road food" category. Here's an abbreviated field guide:

o **Baked beans:** Boston is forever linked with baked beans (hence the nickname "Beantown"), but they remain amazingly popular in Maine. A local Saturday-night church supper on the coast often consists of just baked beans and brown bread at "bean hole" suppers featuring the food. There's also a famous B&M baked-bean plant in Portland.

- **Lobster rolls:** Lobster rolls consist of some pretty basic fixings: fresh lobster meat plucked from the shell, mixed with just enough mayonnaise to hold it together, and served on a hot-dog roll (preferably buttered and grilled). There are fancier permutations in touristy areas, with stuff such as celery and onions mixed in, but you want this basic version: It's meatier and more succulent. You'll find the rolls almost everywhere along the Maine coast; expect to pay between $10 and $20 per roll (more in lean lobster-harvest years). One of the meatiest in Maine is served at **Red's Eats** (p. 134), a hot-dog stand by the side of the road in downtown Wiscasset. For info on where to find some of the best *boiled* lobsters off the pier, see "Pier, Beer & Lobster" on p. 225.

- **Moxie:** It's hard to imagine it now, but early in the 20th century, the Maine-made soft drink Moxie outsold Coca-Cola. Part of its allure was the fanciful story behind its 1885 creation: A traveler named Moxie was said to have observed South American Indians consuming the sap of a native plant, which gave them extraordinary strength. The drink was then helpfully "re-created" by Maine native Dr. Augustin Thompson. It's still very, very popular among old-timers in Maine, although some others say it tastes worse than cough medicine. Think Coke plus quinine, minus any sweetener.

- **Wild blueberries:** You sometimes get the feeling, traveling in Downeast Maine, that the entire state's economy would implode if anything ever happened to the blueberry crop; it's grown and harvested (and added to recipes) everywhere in these parts. Look for roadside stands and diners advertising pies made with fresh berries in mid- to late summer. Also note that the tiny wild blueberries (which grow on low shrubs, often on wind-swept rocks or hilltops) are tastier than the bigger, commercially grown high-bush variety you're probably familiar with.

Finally, no survey of Maine foods would be complete without a mention of the local beer. It seems you can't swing a lobster without hitting a craft brewery up here, and Maine brewers have a terrific reputation in the industry. The Maine Brewers Guild counted more than 70 members when this book went to print, with a few more due to come online. Popular brewpubs to hit include **Oxbow Brewery** (Newcastle); the **Maine Beer Company** (Freeport); and Portland's clutch of terrific mini-breweries—17, at last count, making it that U.S. city with the most breweries per capita (in your face, other Portland). See p. 108 for a Portland brewpub tour.

LIGHTHOUSES: A TOUR UP THE COAST

Unlike its neighbor Nova Scotia, Canada, Maine doesn't maintain, advertise, or market a "Lighthouse Trail." Various travel writers and bloggers have cobbled such itineraries together, though—which isn't surprising, since the state has some of the best lighthouses in the United States. Most were built of stone in the early to mid–19th century, and nearly all were automated in the

1960s or 1970s with very few exceptions. (Today no keepers live full time in any Maine lighthouses.) To see them all, you'd need to drive the coast bottom to top—in other words, follow the chapters of this book in geographical order—and also be in possession of a boat.

Let's forget about the boat for a minute and concentrate on those most easily seen by car; I've sprinkled references to Maine's most visible lighthouses throughout this guidebook, but henceforth, a quick primer on connecting the dots and seeing them one by one, beginning with the southern coast. (*Note:* If you're tacking on a side trip to Portsmouth, New Hampshire—described in greater detail in chapter 10—you've got a shot at even adding a few *more* lighthouses to your "seen-in-lifetime" list. See p. 260 for more on those.)

THE SOUTHERN COAST   Almost from the moment you cross the state line in Kittery, you're on the scent of our Lighthouse Trail. Make a beeline for Fort McClary Historic Park, about a mile and a half east from downtown Kittery on the back road to York (Route 103). From the park, overlooking Portsmouth Harbor, you can view squat, gray-granite **Whaleback Light.** It's not much to look at, though a private boat would help you get closer; public access to the lighthouse grounds is not permitted, however.

A few miles north of Kittery, detour off Route 1 to York Beach and head for Long Sands (see p. 60). Here, from the comfort of nothing more than a blanket or beach chair, you can—with good eyes—spy *two* lighthouses at once.

The first one, **Nubble Light** (p. 58), is obvious at the northern end of the beach. Sticking far out on a promontory, it's the archetypal Maine light. For a closer look, drive to the northern end of the beach and hang a right, then drive the winding cape road to the turnoff for Sohier Park (parking is free). Here, from a rock or bench, you can get almost close enough to the fabled light to touch it—don't try however; a dangerous narrow passage of water separates the viewing area from the rock-bound lighthouse. Snap a photo, then head up the hill for an ice-cream cone at Brown's, again keeping your gaze fixed on the lighthouse as you eat.

The other lighthouse visible from Long Sands, the tall, slim, ghostly **Boon Island light,** demands a perfectly clear day and binoculars or exceptional vision. Gaze out to sea, roughly in the middle of the stretch between both ends of crescent-shaped Long Sands, and its hazy outline may appear to you. Though nearly 10 miles offshore, the granite tower stands more than 13 stories tall—New England's tallest—which is why it can be seen.

Tiny, wind-swept Boon Island itself has an appropriately murky history: When a British ship ran aground here in 1710, survivors resorted to cannibalism for nearly 3 weeks to survive until a member of the party somehow sailed ashore and fetched help. Author Kenneth Roberts wrote a popular novel, *Boon Island* (1956), fictionalizing parts of this incident. Incredibly, the barren rock and its lighthouse was still inhabited as recently as 1978, when one of the worst winter storms in New England history destroyed all the outbuildings and part of the tower, where the keeper's family cowered for several days awaiting rescue. Soon afterward, it was automated.

It's a bit farther north to the next light. The small **Goat Island Light** lies just off the lovely hamlet of Cape Porpoise (see p. 81), north of Kennebunkport. (From Dock Square in the center of Kennebunkport, follow coastal Route 9 about 2½ miles north and east to find the village.) The light has a storied history, including its use as a Secret Service command post protecting the family compound of President George H. W. Bush; a keeper who did a 34-year stint of duty on the rock; a caretaker who died in a boating accident in 2002; and Maine's last lighthouse-keeping family, the Culps, who departed the light in 1990 and turned it over to automation and the care of the Kennebunkport Conservation Trust. The Trust maintains the 25-foot tower and keeper's house and plans to restore the property further in the future. Boat visits are welcome.

At the mouth of the Saco River, where the big river enters the Atlantic at the Biddeford-Saco line, the cute little **Wood Island Lighthouse** and its keeper's house still guard this passage—though you'd never know it, as the light's almost impossible to view, except by boat. The light has a rich history, however, including tales of ghosts, murder most foul, and a keeper's dog smart enough to ring bells by himself. The Friends of Wood Island Lighthouse (www.woodislandlighthouse.org) offer summertime boat tours to the island; otherwise, its premises can't be visited by the public.

GREATER PORTLAND Greater Portland contains perhaps the finest— and most visited and photographed—lights on the whole of the Maine coast.

To view **Cape Elizabeth Light,** the southernmost light in the Portland area, head straight for Two Lights State Park (p. 104). (There were previously two working lights here; one was phased out). The light-keeper's home is now privately owned, but this lighthouse has a rich lore, including daring rescues of shipwrecked sailors in the boiling, stormy sea and the work of painter Edward Hopper, who featured the light in several early-20th-century paintings. It is still an important signal on this rocky part of the coast. If you're hungry after viewing it, be sure to drop by the outstanding Two Lights Lobster Shack (see p. 95) for a bite, and also visit the small souvenir shack on the rocks.

Just to the north, **Portland Head Light** (p. 100) has lovely proportions, an 80-foot beveled tower, a handsome keeper's home (now a small museum), and a scenic position on a cliff before the horizon and the Atlantic. This is one of the very best lighthouses in Maine to view with the family—and one of the most popular and often photographed, as well. (Don't come here for solitude.) Hundreds of thousands of visitors come each year to the free park from which it can be viewed, just off Shore Road in Cape Elizabeth. There's also a gift shop.

From Portland Head Light, you can get a very good view of another lighthouse just offshore: the often-overlooked (probably due to its crude looks) **Ram Island Light,** built of Maine granite in 1905.

Next up, reachable by following South Portland's Broadway to its end, is the **Spring Point Light,** an amusingly shaped light that somewhat resembles a fire hydrant. But take it seriously: It guards the heavily trafficked passage between Portland Harbor and the so-called Calendar Islands, a passage critical to oil and freight transport into and out of Maine. The light is set out at the end of the narrow stone breakwater, and can be walked up to and viewed but not entered except during special open houses held periodically, when you may view the keeper's room, which is slowly being outfitted with period furnishings. There's a museum, the **Portland Harbor Museum** (www.portland harbormuseum.org; © **207/799-6337**), on the land side of the breakwater with plenty more information about the area. The light is also adjacent to both the pretty campus of Southern Maine Community College and the ruins of Fort Preble, good places for a picnic and a walk.

Nearby around the point, the Portland Breakwater Light—locally known as **"Bug Light"**—is a smaller, squatter version of the Spring Point light sitting on land that was once an important shipbuilding complex. A small, free city park surrounds the light.

FREEPORT TO MIDCOAST   From either Bath or South Freeport, you can take a boat tour to view the attractive high rock housing **Seguin Island Light** a few miles off Popham Beach. Contact Atlantic Seal Cruises (www.atlanticsealcruises.com; © **207/865-6112**), which runs weekly tours in summer, or the Maine Maritime Museum (www.mainemaritimemuseum.org; © **207/443-1316**; see p. 127), which offers periodic cruises past the light. Due to the heavy fogs that frequently move into this area, the house sports Maine's strongest (and most valuable) lens; it's 12 feet high, and has been operating since 1857, the same year the keeper's home and stone light tower were also constructed.

Smaller, weaker **Pond Island Light, Cuckolds Light,** the **Perkins Island Light, Ram Island Light,** and the mainland-based **Squirrel Point Light** are all located in the same general vicinity as Seguin, and they can also be viewed on the Maine Maritime Museum cruises or other charter runs from the Boothbay Harbor waterfront (p. 135). Squirrel Point's light can also be hiked to via a rough trail that begins off Bald Head Road in Arrowsic.

Also in Arrowsic, some of **Doubling Point Light**'s grounds are free to roam. To reach here, cross the huge bridge from Bath, make an immediate right onto Route 127 south, and follow signs to the Doubling Point Road turnoff on the right. The light is connected to the keeper's quarters by a long causeway, which is closed to the public. Two small related lights, known as the **Range Lights,** are housed in octagonal wooden towers near the Doubling Point grounds; these lighthouse grounds are also free to visit, and the towers are architecturally singular on the coast, though unsigned and a bit difficult to find. The Maine Maritime Museum's special lighthouse cruises (see above) often pass by this set of lights.

From the pier in Boothbay Harbor (see p. 135), it's easy to visit the handsome **Burnt Island Light** and its attractive complex of outbuildings: Catch an excursion from the pier, then settle in for one of the twice-daily summertime tours. Plan ahead, however; the tours take 2 to 3 hours apiece. Now owned by the state of Maine, the complex, still active as a navigational aid, is also home to a program of nature, arts, and even music courses—a real success story.

Before leaving Boothbay Harbor, you may wish to detour down the long peninsula to West Southport (take Route 27 to the turnoff for the village) to get a view of offshore **Hendricks Head Light,** now privately owned and beautifully restored.

Finally, there's the **Pemaquid Point** (in Bristol) and its museum and the **Marshall Point Lighthouse** (in Port Clyde) and its museum, both of which I describe in greater detail in chapter 6 (see p. 137 and p. 143). Offshore on Monhegan island (see p. 141), there's the **Monhegan Island Light** and *its* museum (open July–Sept; www.monheganmuseum.org; © 207/596-7003). It's well worth a look if you're out on the island, and makes a fine, fitting end to this section of our ad hoc lighthouse trail.

PENOBSCOT BAY   The Midcoast region harbors plenty of lights, though many are small and posted on offshore rocks, thus inaccessible (and unviewable) by car. However, the squat **Owls Head Light,** now owned by the Coast Guard and still active, sits on a promontory in Knox County Lighthouse Park (© 207/941-4014); it can be viewed by anyone who can wrangle a parking spot in the lot. (The light itself, though, is off-limits.) Interestingly, there's a long walkway and set of stairs connecting the keeper's house to the actual light, making this one of the most visually pleasing of all Maine's lighthouses.

The southernmost light of the two in the city of Rockland (see p. 146) is known as **Rockland Harbor Southwest Light,** and this light is fascinating: It's the only one in Maine that was built by a private citizen. A local dentist constructed the light as both an aid to ships and a kind of homage to the other Rockland light (see below), and it began blinking on and off in 1987; today it's an official navigational light and still privately held. From downtown Rockland, head south about 2 miles on Route 73 and hang a left onto North Shore Road.

The **Rockland Breakwater Light** sits at the northern edge of the harbor, sitting atop a handsome brick home about a mile out on a rugged stone breakwater; it's easily viewed from the Samoset resort complex (see p. 149), but the grounds are only open to the public during summer weekends.

Rockport's Marine Park is a good spot to look out at the attractive keeper's house and its **Indian Island Light;** however, the light itself no longer functions. Just north in Camden (see p. 154), the **Curtis Island Light** is quite attractive—it sits on a private island, now owned by the city—but can only really be seen well from the deck of a sightseeing charter or windjammer cruise leaving from the harbor. Just north of Camden in Lincolnville, stand on the ferry dock for a look at the **Grindle Point Light,** with its unusual squarish light tower—or, better yet, hop the ferry for an up-close look; it docks on Isleboro nearly beside the lighthouse. The light is part of a public park that includes a small museum built as a memorial to sailors.

Continuing north, pull off Route 1 at signs for Stockton Springs if you want a look at the tiny **Fort Point Light,** still active and now a state historic site. It's not the most impressive of the state's lights, however.

Castine (see p. 170) is already attractive enough, but the presence of the **Dice Head Light** makes it even more so. Besides the keeper's house (privately owned), the property features an unusual rough, conical stone tower (though the actual light is no longer atop this interesting structure). Simply follow Route 166 to its very end for a look. There's a foot trail to the water (with steps) that's open to the public, but be respectful of the keeper's house; it's private property.

There are three lighthouses on or just offshore **Deer Isle** (see p. 174), but one is no longer active and the other two can only be seen from a boat cruising off the island's back shore.

Finally, the **Robison Point Light** on Isle au Haut (see p. 178) is accessible to the public—in fact, this is the only lighthouse in Maine where you can sleep in the keeper's house (May–October). Contact the Keeper's House (www. keepershouse.com; ✆ **207/335-2990**) for current rates and availability; there's no phone and no electricity, but the owners will prepare a gourmet meal for you if you wish.

MOUNT DESERT ISLAND & DOWNEAST   Mount Desert Island and its surrounding islands (see chapter 8) are home to very few lights that can be visited or viewed by the public. One that can is the **Bass Harbor Head Light,** a famed symbol of Acadia National Park, on Mount Desert's western lobe, down Route 102A past Southwest Harbor. The complex includes a cylindrical light tower, simple keeper's house, triangular fog signal, and even a barn.

From Bass Harbor, head for another light that can be visited by the public: the **Burnt Coat Harbor Light** (also known as Hockamock Head Light). To get here, however, you'll need to catch a ferry from Bass Harbor to Swan's Island. The squared brick tower and keeper's home were built in 1872.

The downeast section of the Maine coast is rife with little ledges and lighthouses, often steeped in fog and usually off-limits to the public (and too far offshore or too indistinct to be seen anyway). The inactive **Winter Harbor Light** can be distantly glimpsed from the Schoodic Peninsula loop road (see p. 240).

The slim stone tower of the **Petit Manan Light** near Milbridge pokes an impressive 120 feet above the surrounding sea. However, it's off-limits and difficult to see anyway. You can get a better look at it while taking a tour of the Maine Coastal Islands National Wildlife Refuge (see p. 240).

Finally, there's the **West Quoddy Head Light** in Lubec (see p. 245), part of the state park of the same name, which is America's easternmost point. There's a museum on the lighthouse grounds, open daily from spring through Columbus Day. Check it out, then sit awhile to reflect on all you've seen on your lighthouse tour.

A LITTLE SOMETHING EXTRA   If you decide to begin your Maine coasting in Portsmouth, New Hampshire (see p. 250), you can take a side trip to the coast and glimpse a few more lighthouses. The cast-iron **Fort Point Light** (also known as Portsmouth Harbor Lighthouse), part of the state's Fort Constitution Historic Site (www.portsmouthharborlighthouse.org; © **603/436-1552**), is on Route 1B near the Wentworth by the Sea resort (p. 255). It can be viewed from the historic site—which is free to enter—from May through October, but can only be entered on Sunday open-house days during that season; admission is $4 for adults and $2 for children.

There's also the brick **White Island Light,** offshore in the Isles of Shoals and too far to be seen except when taking a cruise of the islands. Contact the Isle of Shoals Steamship Co. (www.islesofshoals.com; © **603/431-5500**) about periodic lighthouse cruises of the area.

For more on Maine's (and New Hampshire's) lighthouses and preservation efforts, contact the **American Lighthouse Foundation,** P.O. Box 565, Rockland, ME 04841 (www.lighthousefoundation.org; © **207/594-4174**).

THE GREAT OUTDOORS

While southern Maine has classic beach towns where the smell of salt air mixes with coconut oil and taffy, much of the rest of the Maine coast is unruly and wild. In parts it seems to share more in common with Alaska—you can see bald eagles soaring above and whales breaching below. In between these two archetypes, you'll find remote coves perfect for a rowboat jaunt and isolated offshore islands accessible only by sea kayak.

The best places for coastal adventure are often not the most obvious places—those tend to be crowded and more developed. You'll need to do a bit of homework to find the real treasures. A growing number of specialized guidebooks and outfitters can help point visitors in the right direction; some of the best are mentioned below.

Keep in mind that no other New England state offers as much outdoor recreational diversity as Maine. Bring your mountain bike, hiking boots, sea kayak, canoe, fishing rod, and/or snowmobile—there'll be plenty for you to do here.

If your outdoor skills are rusty or nonexistent, brush up at the **L.L.Bean Outdoor Discovery Schools** (www.llbean.com/outdoorsOnline/odp; © **888/552-3261**), which offers a series of lectures and workshops that run anywhere from 2 hours to 3 days. Classes are offered at various locations around the state, covering a whole range of subjects, including fly-fishing, outdoor photography, and first aid in the wilderness. L.L.Bean also hosts periodic (and popular) canoeing, sea-kayaking, and skiing festivals that bring together instructors, lecturers, and equipment vendors for 2 or 3 days of learning and outdoor diversion. Call for a brochure, or check the L.L.Bean website for a schedule.

LANDSCAPE IS not JUST SCENERY

The places you'll be traveling are not just scenery. They are the home to millennia of natural history (volcanoes, icebergs, polar bears, whales, and caribou, oh my!), as well as a deep human history (lobstermen, Vikings, and native Canadians fishing and hunting long before Europeans showed up). And the great part is, this story continues today: These layers overlap in fascinating ways to create the "place" that is now coastal Maine. Understand these creatures and landscapes you'll be interacting with *before* you get there, and you'll have a better trip—and become a more ecologically aware traveler with a deeper respect for what you're experiencing.

Pick up the books of Canadian author Farley Mowat; a locally written book on eastern Canadian geography, geology, natural history, or native Canadian culture (library book sales and local gifts shops are two great sources); or a novel by E. Annie Proulx. For information about the whales you'll be glimpsing (and how to respect them), visit the **Whale and Dolphin Conservation** organization (us.whales.org). For info on traveling lightly in general, see **Tread Lightly** (www.treadlightly.org) online.

BEACHES   Swimming at Maine's ocean beaches is for the hardy. The Gulf Stream, which prods warm waters south toward the Cape Cod shores, veers toward Iceland south of Maine and leaves the state's 5,500-mile coastline washed by a brisk Nova Scotia current, an offshoot of the arctic Labrador current. During summer, water temperatures along the south coast may top 60°F (16°C) during an especially warm spell where water is shallow, but it's usually cooler than that. Northeast of Portland a handful of fine beaches await— including popular **Reid State Park** (p. 127) and **Popham Beach State Park** (p. 127)—but rocky coast defines this territory for the most part. Maine's best beaches are found mostly between the New Hampshire border and Portland.

The southern beaches are beautiful but rarely isolated. Summer homes occupy the low dunes in most areas; mid-rise condos give **Old Orchard Beach** (p. 110) a mini-Miami air. Some of the best swimming beaches in the region are at **Ogunquit** (p. 62), which boasts a 3-mile-long sandy strand (some of which has a mildly remote character), and **Long Sands Beach** (p. 60) and **Short Sands Beach** (p. 60) at York. Long Sands has great views of the sea and a nearby lighthouse plus great walking at low tide (at high tide, the sand disappears completely), while Short Sands has a festive, carnival atmosphere. Both lie right on Route 1A. There are also a number of fine beaches in the greater **Portland** area; for a primer on the very best, see p. 104.

If you love swimming but aren't especially keen on shivering, head inland to the sandy beaches at Maine's wonderful lakes, where the water is tepid by comparison. A number of state and municipal parks offer access. Among the most accessible to the coast is **Sebago Lake State Park** (✆ **207/693-6613**), about 20 miles northwest of Portland; a small admission fee is charged.

BIKING   In southern Maine, **Route 103** and **Route 1A** offer pleasant scenery for bikers. Otherwise, I recommend bringing your bike to the bigger islands for car-free cruising. In Casco Bay, rustic **Chebeague Island** offers a pleasantly wooded excursion (the path cuts through forests to the sea), while more populous **Peaks Island** (p. 103) has a few cafes, more culture, and the advantage of a bicycle-rental shop near the ferry dock. Both are flat, and both are conveniently connected to Portland by Casco Bay Lines ferries. (Peaks is a much shorter ferry ride, if time matters.)

Serious mountain biking is also available in parts of coastal Maine, for those who like to get technical on two wheels. Your best bet is to consult area bike shops for the best trails, which are typically a matter of local knowledge.

The Maine Department of Transportation (DOT) publishes a list of more than 30 popular bike trips around the state; you can find some in the print *Maine Invites You Brochure* found at many chamber offices and rest stops, or log on to **www.exploremaine.org/bike** to get it. The Bicycle Coalition of Maine also keeps an exhuastive list of "Where to Ride" resources at www. bikemaine.org.

BIRDING   Birders from southern and inland states should lengthen their life lists along the Maine coast, which attracts migrating birds cruising the Atlantic flyway (there are warblers galore in spring) and boasts populations of numerous native shorebirds, such as plovers (including the threatened piping plover), terns, whimbrels, sandpipers, and dunlins. Gulls and terns are frequently seen; you'll see a surfeit of herring and great black-backed gull, along with the common tern. Less frequently seen are Bonaparte's gull, the laughing gull, the jaeger, and the arctic tern. For a recording of recent sightings of rare birds, call ℂ **207/781-2332**.

CAMPING   For information about state parks, many of which offer camping, contact the **Bureau of Parks and Lands** (www.campwithme.com; ℂ **207/287-3821**). To make camping reservations at most state park campgrounds, call during business hours on a weekday between February and early September (ℂ **800/332-1501** in Maine, or 207/624-9950).

Maine also has more than 200 private campgrounds spread throughout the state, many offering full hookups for RVs. For a guide to the private campgrounds, contact the **Maine Campground Owners Association** (www.camp maine.com; ℂ **207/782-5874**). Campsites get booked quickly for summer weekends, so call ahead for reservations.

CANOEING   For many outdoors enthusiasts in the Northeast, Maine is very alluring to serious paddlers. In fact, you can't travel very far in Maine without stumbling upon a great canoe trip. The state's best canoeing tends to be far inland and deep in the woods, true, but day paddlers can still find good trips at several lakes along the coast or in some of the protected bays. Two excellent sources of detailed canoeing information are the *AMC River Guide: Maine* and *Quiet Water Canoe Guide: Maine,* both published by the Appalachian Mountain Club (**www.amcboston.org**).

FISHING Anglers from all over the Northeast indulge their grand obsession on Maine's 6,000 lakes and ponds and its countless miles of rivers and streams. And deep-sea-fishing charters are available at many of the harbors along the Maine coast, with options ranging from inshore fishing expeditions for stripers and bluefish to offshore voyages in search of shark, cod, and pollock. Prices might typically range from $40 per person for day trips to $900 to charter an offshore boat for the day. Visitor information centers and chambers of commerce listed in this guide will be able to match you up with the right boat to meet your needs.

Saltwater fishing in Maine requires no license, if you're a passenger on a for-hire vessel. For freshwater fishing, nonresident **licenses** are $64 for the season or $23 for 3 days. One-, 7-, and 15-day licenses are also available. Fees are reduced for children (ages 12–15), and no license is required for those 11 and under. These licenses are available at many outdoor shops and general stores throughout the state or by mail from the address below. For a booklet of fishing regulations, contact the **Department of Inland Fisheries and Wildlife** (www.maine.gov/ifw; ℂ 207/287-8000).

GOLFING Many of Maine coast's best courses are private, but a few of these gems are open to the public. Kennebunkport's **Cape Arundel Golf Club** (www.capearundelgolfclub.com; ℂ 207/967-3494) is favored by a certain ex-president when he's in town. Other courses I like along the coast—nearly all of them wafted by sea breezes—include **Cape Neddick Country Club** in Ogunquit (www.capeneddickgolf.com; ℂ 207/361-2011), the **Kebo Valley Golf Club** in Bar Harbor (www.kebovalleyclub.com; ℂ 207/288-3000), the **Webhannet Golf Club** in Kennebunk Beach (www.webhannet golfclub.com; ℂ 207/967-2061), the **Riverside Golf Course** in Portland (www.riversidegolfcourseme.com; ℂ 207/797-3524), and South Portland's **Sable Oaks Golf Club** (www.sableoaks.com; ℂ 207/775-6257). But the best public course on the whole coast of Maine might be the **Samoset Resort Golf Club** in Rockport (www.samoset.com/golf; ℂ 207/594-1431): several holes run right alongside the Atlantic and past a mini-lighthouse. It's as scenic as golf gets.

HIKING Southern Maine's walks are not hikes but rather less-demanding strolls; many of these are a matter of local knowledge. Two fine pathways skirt the water in **York** (see p. 59), and even in **Portland** (see p. 102) you can saunter on well-maintained (and heavily used) recreational pathways along about 5 miles of tidal waters.

More serious hiking, however, is available as you get further north. **Camden Hills State Park** (see p. 160) has some 30 miles of hiking trails, including a 1000-foot climb to the ocean vistas atop Mount Megunticook. **Acadia National Park** (see p. 185) is a day-hiker's paradise, with trails like the Dorr Ladder Trail that ascend stone steps and ladders anchored to granite; mellower, but no less scenic shorefront footpaths, like the one around Jordan Pond; and breathtaking ridgewalks, like the trail over Acadia Mountain.

Serious backpackers hoping to tent it for a night or two will need to look inland—**Baxter State Park** (p. 262) in the Maine north woods is their Shangri-La, with 200 miles of backcountry trails crisscrossing the closest thing New England has to wilderness. An excellent resource for searching hiking trails by location and difficulty is **www.mainetrailfinder.com**.

SEA KAYAKING   Sea kayakers nationwide migrate to Maine for world-class sea kayaking. Thousands of miles of deeply indented coastline and thousands of offshore islands have created a wondrous kayaker's playground. Paddlers can explore protected estuaries far from the surf or test their skills and determination with excursions across choppy, open seas to islands far offshore. It's a sport that can be extremely dangerous (when weather shifts, the seas can turn on you in a matter of minutes), but can yield plenty of returns with the proper equipment and skills.

The nation's first long-distance water trail, the **Maine Island Trail**, was created here in 1987. This 325-mile waterway winds along the coast from Portland to Machias, incorporating some 200 state and privately owned islands (and mainland sites) on its route. Members of the Maine Island Trail Association, a private nonprofit group, help maintain and monitor the islands and in turn are granted permission to visit and camp on them as long as they follow certain restrictions (for example, no visiting designated islands during seabird nesting season). The association seeks to encourage low-impact, responsible use of these natural treasures, and joining is a good idea if you'll be doing some kayaking. The MITA guidebook, published annually, provides descriptions of all the islands in the network and is free with association membership (note that the guide is available only to members). For membership details, contact the **Maine Island Trail Association** (www.mita.org; ☎ **207/761-8225**).

The islands and protected bays around **Portland** make for great kayaking, as do the cliffs, parks, and beaches just south of the city—though surf can be rough at times. Make sure you're experienced enough to handle it.

For novices, a number of kayak outfitters take guided excursions ranging from an afternoon to a week. Outfitters include the **Maine Island Kayak Co.** on Peaks Island (www.maineislandkayak.com; ☎ **207/766-2373**) in the Portland area and **Maine Sport Outfitters**, located on Route 1 in Rockport (www.mainesport.com; ☎ **207/236-8797**).

Hiring a Guide

Guides of all kinds may be hired throughout the region, from grizzled fishing hands who know local rivers like their own homes to young canoe guides attracted to the field because of their interest in the environment. Alexandra and Garrett Conover of Maine's **North Woods Ways** (www.northwoodsways; ☎ **207/997-3723**), are among the most experienced in the region. The couple offers canoe trips on northern Maine rivers (including a Thoreau's Maine Woods trip), and are well versed in North Woods lore.

Maine has a centuries-old tradition of guides leading "sports" into the backwoods for hunting and fishing, although many now have branched out to include recreational canoeing and more specialized interests, such as birdwatching. Professional guides are certified by the state; you can learn more about hiring Maine guides by contacting the **Maine Professional Guides Association** (www.maineguides.org); the website features links to some of its members.

Elsewhere, contact the appropriate chambers of commerce for suggestions on local guides.

Guided Tours

Guided tours have boomed in recent years, both in number and variety. These range from 2-night guided inn-to-inn hiking trips to weeklong canoe and kayak expeditions, camping each night along the way. A few reputable outfitters to start with include the following:

○ **Backroads** (www.backroads.com; ✆ **800/462-2848** or 510/527-1555), has an extensive inventory of trips, including a 5-day bike trip from MDI to Rockland, following the contours of Penobscot Bay. This trip involves moderate physical challenge and nights in a few lovely hotels and inns.

○ **Country Walkers** (www.countrywalkers.com; ✆ **800/464-9255** or 802/244-1387) has a glorious color catalog (more like a wish book) outlining supported walking trips around the world. Among its Maine offerings: walking tours in Acadia National Park. Trips run 6 nights and include all meals and lodging at appealing inns.

○ **Maine Island Kayak Co.** (www.maineislandkayak.com; ✆ **800/796-2373** or 207/766-2373) has a fleet of seaworthy kayaks for camping trips up and down the Maine coast. The firm runs a number of 2- and 3-night expeditions each summer and has plenty of experience in training novices.

○ **Vermont Bicycle Touring** (www.vbt.com; ✆ **800/245-3868**), is one of the more established and well-organized touring operations, with an extensive bike tour schedule in North America, Europe, and New Zealand. VBT offers several trips in Maine, including a 6-day Acadia trip.

Local outdoors clubs are also a good source of information, and most offer trips to nonmembers. The largest of the bunch is the Appalachian Mountain Club (www.outdoors.org; ✆ **671/523-0655**), whose chapters run group trips almost every weekend throughout the region, with northern New Hampshire especially well represented.

SUGGESTED MAINE COAST ITINERARIES

3

Many travelers look at a coast-of-Maine trip as their only chance in a lifetime to see this part of the world. They try to race around the region seeing everything from Kittery to Portland to Acadia, plus even (maybe) a moose in the Maine Woods along the way . . . all in less than a week.

Trust me: That's nothing but a formula for disappointment—you'd end up seeing the inside of your windshield more than anything else. The coast of Maine doesn't lend itself to snap-a-photo tourism. Instead, it's best seen by moving slowly—on foot, in a canoe, on a bike, driving the back roads. The happiest visitors to this region tend to be those who stay more or less in one place or region, getting to know that place especially well through a series of carefully crafted day trips.

With that in mind, here are a few itineraries to use as a starting point; feel free to mix and match, improvise, or even devise your own. The first tour shows you the best of the entire Maine coast, but it takes up to 2 weeks to do right; the second tour whittles that down to a manageable week. I've also devised a tour geared toward traveling with families, plus two more guides to hopping your way up the coast: one for art lovers and a second for the most active travelers.

The Regions in Brief

Southern Maine From the state line at Kittery to, say, the Biddeford town line, Maine's southern coast features most of the state's best beaches and beach resorts.

Portland The state's largest and most vibrant city, Portland proper is home to fewer than 70,000 people, although the greater metro area—running roughly from Freeport down to the former mill towns of Saco and

Biddeford—has over 500,000. It's Maine's epicenter for shopping, adventurous dining, and arts and culture; the increasing "Brooklynization" of trendy Portland has earned it the (slightly derisive) nickname of "Portlyn."

Midcoast Maine Midcoast Maine begins, depending on whom you ask, somewhere around Freeport or Bath and ends at either Bucksport or

Ellsworth. In between, you'll discover more rocky headlands, bays, and coves than you ever dreamed existed, as well as quaint villages with names such as Blue Hill, Camden, and Rockport. For this book, I have broken this scenic region into two chapters: the Lower Midcoast, which extends from Freeport to the St. George peninsula, and the Upper Midcoast, which begins at Rockland and continues over the Penobscot River and up to the Acadia gateway town of Ellsworth.

Mount Desert Island A vacation paradise since the moneyed "rusticators" descended in the 19th century, Mount Desert Island is today home to one of the country's great public land parcels in Acadia National Park. On the fringes of the park, the fishing villages of MDI (as it's known to locals) have maintained their salty hinterland character for generations.

The Downeast Coast In Downeast Maine—which goes from the Ellsworth area all the way up the coast to the Canadian border—you'll find plenty of empty back roads and room to roam, not to mention rocky islands, foggy mornings, and lobster boats aplenty.

The Maine Woods Inland, north of Bangor, the Great North Woods of Maine could legitimately be called the Northeast's last bit of untrammeled wilderness. In chapter 10, I sketch out a side trip to this wilderness, as well as side trips to historic **Portsmouth, New Hampshire**, and across the Canadian border to a lovely slice of coastal **New Brunswick.**

THE MAINE COAST IN 2 WEEKS

Maine's coast tends to confound hurry-up tourists—there are simply too many dead-end peninsulas to backtrack along, and too many inlets cleaving the coast; you must sometimes drive great distances to get from one rocky, wave-beaten point to the next. Finding a home base or two and fanning out from there is the best strategy. Most of this route heads north along U.S. Route 1, which can be slow-pokey, at least in pockets, during high summer season. But take heart: You'll have more time to soak up the views, which are pretty good for stretches, particularly once you get north of Bath. This route supposes you're driving into Maine from the rest of America (there's only one way in, and that's from New Hampshire). If you're flying into Portland instead, consider making that town your home base for your first 4 days, exploring the southern coast on day trips—it's only a 40-minute drive from Portland to York.

Day 1: York ★★

Drive into Maine from the south on I-95, and head immediately for **York Village ★** (the first exit; p. 48). Spend some time snooping around the historic homes of the **Old York Historical Society,** and stretch your legs on a walk through town or the woods.

Drive northward through **York Beach ★★** (p. 48). Stock up on saltwater taffy at the Goldenrod (p. 55); stay near the beach.

From York, drive 20 miles north on the Maine Turnpike (I-95) or U.S. Rte. 1 to find:

Day 2: The Kennebunks ★★ & Ogunquit ★★

The Kennebunks are definitely worth a day if you enjoy blue-blood New England quaintness and luxury accommodations. There are some pretty fancy inns and bed-and-breakfast establishments in these parts. **Kennebunk** (p. 70), the lesser-known of the twin towns (they're separated by a slim tidal river), is a mixed bag of attractions, with the so-called **Wedding Cake House** ★, a very good public beach, a monastery (yes, really), and a natural-products factory store, among other things to see and do. Across the river in **Kennebunkport** (p. 70) you can stroll the leafy town, gawk at George Bush the elder's summer home (from a short distance away; those Secret Service guys mean business), and have a relaxed dinner at a fine restaurant. There is also a small shopping district and plenty of pleasure boats and yachts moored in the area.

While staying in the area, be sure to visit **Ogunquit,** a small town justly famous for its beaches, ocean views, and summery atmosphere. While there, stop in at the small but truly excellent **Ogunquit Museum of American Art** ★★★. If you're so inclined, hit the antiques shops lined up along Route 1 as you head northward. See p. 69.

From the Kennebunks, drive 27 miles north either on the Maine Turnpike (I-95, exiting onto Rte. 295 and following signs) or U.S. Rte. 1 to the Greater Portland area.

Days 3, 4: Portland ★★★

Plan to stay in **Portland** or on a nearby beach for up to 3 days, enjoying its hot-as-can-be culinary scene; shopping along the cobblestone streets of the Old Port; taste-testing chowder recipes and microbrewed beers; and just generally soaking up the salty air and atmosphere. Don't forget to take a walk along the **Eastern Promenade** ★★ or a day cruise on a local ferry. See p. 102.

From Portland, drive north 17 miles on I-295 or U.S. Rte. 1 to the Freeport area. There's a Maine state tourist information facility on Rte. 1 just north of Yarmouth, stocked with brochures and staff (daytime hours).

Day 5: Freeport & Surrounding Areas

Head north early to beat the shopping crowds in the outlet haven of **Freeport.** (You can't leave too early for **L.L.Bean**—it never closes!) See p. 118.

From Freeport, continue northward to **Brunswick,** home to **Bowdoin College** ★ (p. 125) and its two small but excellent museums. Then press a few miles farther north to atmospheric **Bath** ★, with plenty of ancient sea captains' homes, a shipyard, and the **Maine Maritime Museum & Shipyard** ★ (p. 127). Stay in a B&B in any of the three towns.

From Freeport, it's about 70 miles north on U.S. Rte. 1 to the Camden-Rockland-Rockport area; it can take up to 2 hr. in summer traffic congestion. Wiscasset (about halfway to Camden) and Damariscotta (off the highway, with a scenic river and a vibrant downtown) make nice stopping points along the way.

Days 6 & 7: Camden ★★ & Penobscot Bay ★★

Heading north from the Bath-Brunswick area, detour down to **Pemaquid Point** ★★ for a late picnic and to watch the surf roll in. Then head back to Route 1 and set your sights on the Camden-Rockland area, the

The Maine Coast in 2 Weeks

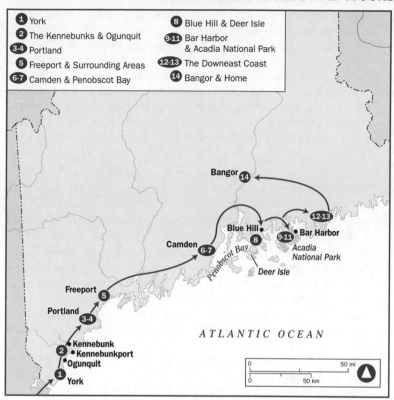

1. York
2. The Kennebunks & Ogunquit
3-4. Portland
5. Freeport & Surrounding Areas
6-7. Camden & Penobscot Bay
8. Blue Hill & Deer Isle
9-11. Bar Harbor & Acadia National Park
12-13. The Downeast Coast
14. Bangor & Home

Bangor 14

Blue Hill 8

Camden 6-7

Penobscot Bay

Deer Isle

12-13

Bar Harbor

9-11

Acadia National Park

Freeport 5

Portland

3-4

Kennebunk

2 Kennebunkport

Ogunquit

1 York

ATLANTIC OCEAN

0 — 50 mi
0 — 50 km

commercial heart of the **Penobscot Bay** region. **Rockland** ★ (p. 146), which comes first, is the more working-class half of the equation, though it's increasingly evolving into an arts destination. You'll find funky cafes, an excellent museum, and good restaurants. Nearby **Rockport** ★ (p. 164) is a tiny harbor town with superb views and an artsy main street. Finally, head a few miles north to wander around downtown **Camden** ★★ (p. 154), poking into shops and galleries, or hike up one of the impressive hills at **Camden Hills State Park** ★★. Hop a ferry to an island (North Haven and Isleboro are both great for biking), sign up for a daylong sail on a windjammer, or just spend a long afternoon unwinding on the deck of a local restaurant.

From Camden, drive U.S. Rte. 1 40 miles north to state Rte. 15, turn south, and drive 12 more miles to:

Day 8: Blue Hill ★★ & Deer Isle ★★

Have dinner and find accommodations in scenic **Blue Hill** (p. 180), an appealing mixture of a Maine fishing town with bookshops and restaurants is quite appealing. Also take a spin around the peninsula to even smaller towns such as **Blue Hill Falls** and **Brooklin,** where you'll see boatyards, old-fashioned general stores, and Maine ingenuity holding it all together. *This* is the real Maine.

Continue 18 miles south on Route 15 to **Deer Isle** (p. 174). The roads here are great for aimless drives, but aim anyway for **Stonington ★** at the far end of the peninsula. If distant **Isle au Haut ★★**, visible from the town docks, makes you pine for an offshore adventure, plan a boat trip for early the next morning; secure lodging in Deer Isle; and adjust your schedule accordingly. Otherwise, explore the area by car or sign up for a kayak tour with **Old Quarry Ocean Adventures** (p. 178).

From Stonington, backtrack 18 miles on Rte. 15 to Blue Hill, then follow Rte. 172 north 14 miles to U.S. Rte. 1. Follow Rte. 1 a short distance before bearing right onto Rte. 3 (follow signs to Acadia National Park). Continue 6 miles to the bridge to Mount Desert Island. Cross the bridge and follow Rte. 3 about 10 more miles to Bar Harbor.

Days 9, 10 & 11: Bar Harbor ★ & Acadia National Park ★★★

Bar Harbor is the most convenient base for exploring **Mount Desert Island ★★**, which is well worth at least 4 days on any Maine itinerary. Bar Harbor provides comforts and services such as a movie theater, souvenir shops, bike and kayak rentals, free shuttle buses fanning out all over the island, and numerous kinds of restaurants that other island towns don't have. Yes, it's a lot more developed (perhaps too much so) than the rest of the island, but think of it as a supply depot.

Hike, bike, boat, or do whatever you have to do to explore the island and this national park—in my humble opinion, one of America's finest. What it lacks in "bigness," it more than makes up for with intimate contact with nature. Options include taking a beginner's kayak trip down the eastern shore, a hike out to Bar Island, or a mountain bike trip along the scenic carriage roads built by the Rockefeller family: Only bicycles and horses are allowed on these roads, making them a good respite from the island's main roads, which—almost unbelievably—*do* get crowded in summer.

The scenic **Park Loop Road ★★** offers a good introduction to what's in store for you later (crashing waves, big mountains, drop-dead-gorgeous views). Make sure to buy a park pass that lasts more than 1 day.

While exploring the rest of the island, hit some of the towns off the beaten track, too. The fishing villages of **Northeast Harbor ★** and **Southwest Harbor ★★** have been transformed by tourism into small centers of art, music, and shopping, but they still have local grocery stores where fishermen slush in to shop for slickers and Wonder Bread.

On your last day, cap off your visit with a cold-water dip at Sand Beach and tea and popovers at **Jordan Pond House ★★** (p. 192). Maybe watch a sunrise from the top of Cadillac Mountain, take a quick last hike up The

Bubbles, or paddle a canoe on Long Pond. Or just enjoy one last lobster from atop a wooden pier before setting off back south.

From Bar Harbor, backtrack 20 miles to Rte. 1 on the mainland, then follow it up the coast about 17 miles to Rte. 186, a detour loop through the Schoodic Peninsula. (That drive will take you an hour, plus stops to look around or hike.) From Schoodic, it's another 65 miles to Lubec or 85 to Eastport.

Day 12 & 13: The Downeast Coast

Take a full day to work your way Downeast towards Eastport and Lubec. (Tell your motel or inn that you'll be arriving late.) Stretch your legs on the **Schoodic Peninsula** ★★ (p. 240), at **Tunk Mountain** (p. 242), or along the **Cutler Coast Trail** ★ (p. 243). On your second day, explore the rough-and-tumble towns at the tip of the Northeast, making time for **West Quoddy Head Light** ★★ in Lubec (p. 245) and the **Tides Institute & Museum of Art** ★★ in Eastport (p. 247). And maybe for one last lobster.

From either Eastport or Lubec, head inland towards Bangor on Rte. 9, the winding, woodsy, lonely road that Mainers call "the Airline." It's just over 2 hours to Bangor, without much reason to stop.

Day 14: Bangor ★ & Home

Once you've reached the inland city of **Bangor** (p. 263), it's worth grabbing lunch and strolling downtown a while. (It's doubly worth it you're a fan of horror writer Stephen King—his house is pretty obvious once you get downtown.) There are several museums in and around the city; it's the only place that passes for a cultural center in the vastly empty spaces of inland northern Maine, so stock up (and fuel up) while you've got the chance. If you're lucky enough to have *more* than 2 weeks to spend wandering Maine, hang a right at Bangor instead of a left and head into the "other Maine" of the north woods (p. 262).

From Bangor, take the Maine Turnpike (I-95) south 180 miles to the state line at Kittery. With no stops, it takes less than 3 hours.

THE MAINE COAST IN 1 WEEK

If you only have a week, but you still want to cover some ground, the trick is not to bite off more than you can chew. Skip Portland, as marvelous a city as it is, and speed past the crowded southern coast to focus on the Midcoast and Acadia. Refer to "The Maine Coast in 2 Weeks" above for fuller descriptions of each destination's offerings.

Day 1: The Kennebunks ★★ & Ogunquit ★★

Drive in from the south and head straight for the **Kennebunks** (p. 70). Even with a condensed itinerary, it's still worth your time to linger at the beaches and terrific museum in **Ogunquit** (p. 69).

The Maine Coast in 1 Week

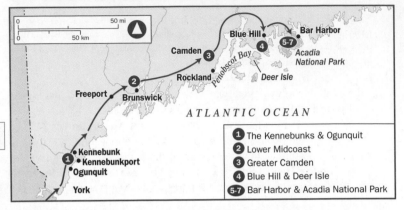

From the Kennebunks, drive 25 or so miles north on the Maine Turnpike (I-95), exit onto Rte. 295, and go another 22 miles to U.S. Rte. 1 at Brunswick. From there, follow Rte. 1 about 50 miles to greater Camden.

Days 2: Lower Midcoast

On your drive north from the Kennebunks, you may choose to stop in **Freeport** (p. 113) for a swing through the outlet stores, and/or detour through **Brunswick** (p. 120), **Bath** (p. 120), or the Harpwell Peninsula. Make **Rockland** ★ (p. 146) or **Camden** ★★ (p. 154) your home base for the next couple of nights.

Day 3: Greater Camden

Explore **Camden Hills State Park** ★★ (p. 164) on foot or mountain bike, and then make the art circuit in Rockland, with stops at the **Farnsworth Museum** ★★ (p. 153) and the **Center for Maine Contemporary Art** ★★★ (p. 153). Then take advantage of the great dinner options in either town.

From Camden, drive U.S. Rte. 1 40 miles north to state Rte. 15, turn south, and drive 12 more miles to:

Day 4: Blue Hill ★★ & Deer Isle ★★

Get a place to stay on the Blue Hill peninsula, check in early, and spend the rest of the day exploring **Blue Hill** (p. 180), **Castine** (p. 170), **Deer Isle** (p. 174), and **Stonington** ★ (p. 174). You'll spend a good amount of time behind the wheel today, but the driving's super scenic, and you can still sneak in an hour-long kayak tour off Stonington or a hike through the pretty **Holbrook Island Wildlife Sanctuary**.

From Stonington, backtrack 18 miles on Rte. 15 to Blue Hill, then follow Rte. 172 north 14 miles to U.S. Rte. 1. Follow Rte. 1 just a short distance before bearing right onto Rte. 3 (follow signs to Acadia National Park). Continue 6 miles to the bridge to Mount Desert Island. Cross the bridge and follow Rte. 3 about 10 more miles to Bar Harbor.

Days 5, 6 & 7: Bar Harbor ★ & Acadia National Park ★★★

Yep, even with a truncated schedule, it's still worth committing 3 days to Maine's only national park. **Bar Harbor** itself can eat up a day. Take time to stroll the busy town's shops, do some snacking, and maybe hop aboard a whale-watching tour. That leaves you 2 days to explore the **Park Loop Road** ★★, the trails, and the carriage roads of Acadia. See Chapter 8.

Heading back from Bar Harbor, skip the coastal route and take Rte. 1A about 30 miles between Ellsworth and Bangor. From Bangor, take the Maine Turnpike (I-95) south 180 miles to the state line at Kittery. With no stops, it takes less than 3 hours.

THE MAINE COAST FOR FAMILIES

Families would be wise not to attempt the whole swath of the coast in a week of travel—that's a too much time in the car. Instead, spend a few days wandering the cobblestones, shops, museums, and attractions of Portland, then focus on the surrounding towns, beaches, and attractions. This itinerary is designed so that you can have a home base anywhere within 30 miles of Portland. The beauty of it is that you could rearrange these days in any order.

Day 1: Portland

On Congress Square, begin exploring the city at two next-door museums: the **Portland Museum of Art** ★★★ (p. 101) and the interactive **Children's Museum of Maine** ★ (p. 98). Then, if your kids are good walkers, hoof it 7 blocks down to the cobblestoned streets of the **Old Port** ★★★ (p. 98), where you'll find shops, boats, and plenty of lunch options. For the afternoon, let off steam at the **Maine Narrow Gauge Railroad Co. & Museum** ★ (p. 100) with a (*very* slow) train ride tracing the foot of the cliffs framing Portland's east end.

Day 2: Portland

One of the don't-miss experiences of a Portland visit is a cruise around Casco Bay on a **Casco Bay Lines** (p. 103) ferry. You can take anywhere from a 20-minute run to a half-day mail-boat cruise. Two of my recommended destinations are **Peaks Island**—a favorite among stroller-pushing moms for its easy-to-cruise streets with Portland views—and **Long Island,** with an excellent beach. Once back at the port, head up to the **Eastern Promenade** ★★ (p. 102), a 68-acre hillside park with broad, grassy slopes and superb Casco Bay views. For more stupendous views, head up Congress Street to the distinctive shingled **Portland Observatory** ★ (p. 101), a National Historic Landmark built in 1807 to signal ship arrivals into the city's port. From the observatory, it's a 10-minute walk to the East End neighborhood, where **Duckfat** ★★★ (p. 94) has Maine's (New England's? the world's?) best milkshakes.

Day 3: Portland's Beaches

Cross the Casco Bay Bridge into South Portland. On your way out to the Cape Elizabeth beaches, stop by Fort Williams Park to see the **Portland Head Light** ★★ (p. 100), the state's most photographed lighthouse. Then continue down the shore on Route 77 to either **Two Lights State Park** ★★ (p. 104), with its long rocky beach and fun lobster shack, or **Crescent Beach State Park** ★★★ (p. 104), a mile-long sandy stretch with usually gentle surf. In season, if the schedule's right you can round off your Portland deep-dive with an afternoon or evening game at Hadlock Field, home of the **Portland Sea Dogs** ★★★ (p. 103), a minor-league club for the Boston Red Sox. Yankee fans, deal with it.

Day 4: Freeport

Dive into the busy shopping district in Freeport. Don't miss the sprawling **L.L.Bean** complex ★★★ (p. 118), obviously. Not up for a full day of shopping? Sign up for a day clinic with the retailer's **Outdoor Discover Schools**—maybe a 2½-hour kayaking clinic at Bean's Flying Point Paddling Center, just a 10-minute drive down the peninsula. Also in that direction, check out the seaside trails of **Wolfe's Neck Woods State Park** (p. 120) and a demonstration barnyard full of cute animals at **Wolfe's Neck Farm**.

Day 5: Inland

Head inland in the morning to visit the world's last remaining Shakers at the **Sabbathday Lake Shaker Community** (p. 111), with its museum, renowned crafts and furniture, and pastoral working farm. Get breakfast or lunch at the **New Gloucester Village Store**, the tiny hub of the tiny town, which has way better sandwiches and pizzas behind the counter than you'd expect. Then tour around glittery **Sebago Lake** before heading back to town, with maybe a stop for a dip at **Sebago Lake State Park** (p. 110).

Day 6: Old Orchard Beach

Slot this, the theme-park-iest day of your trip, for a weekday to miss the crowds. Spend the bulk of your day on the sand and the old-school carnival rides at **Palace Playland** at Old Orchard Beach (see p. 110). Indulge all the tacky stuff on the boardwalk, because it's worth it for the ambience; don't leave without trying the famous crinkle-cut taters at **Pier Fries.** End the evening with a double feature at the **Saco Drive-In** ★ in neighboring Saco (see p. 110).

Day 7: The Kennebunks

Start this day with one of two unmissable breakfasts: Either grab a stool at **Palace Diner** ★★ (p. 61) in Biddeford for tremendous updated diner chow or follow the coastal Route 9 from Biddeford to the Kennebunks to get farm/sea-to-table favorites at **The Wayfarer** (p. 77) in seaside Cape Porpoise. Then grab some blanket space at **Kennebunk Beach** ★★ or

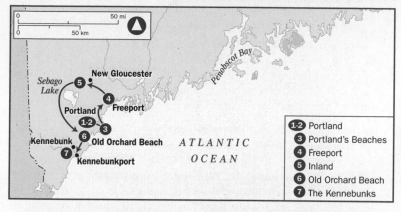

Gooch Rocks Beach ★★ (p. 81)—the latter's my pick, longer and better for strolling. In the afternoon, drop in on the **Seashore Trolley Museum** (p. 80) to catch a short ride on a handsomely restored streetcar, and then wander the shops at **Dock Square** (p. 71) and maybe tackle one last basket of fried seafood at the storied **Clam Shack** (p. 76).

THE ART LOVER'S MAINE COAST

This 6-day tour takes in some of Maine's best museums and gallery towns, with some extra attention to Rockland and its adjacent peninsulas, where a few of Maine's own artists did some of their best work. Note: This itinerary is designed to start on a Monday, to take advantage of various museums' open hours, free admission days, and scheduled programs (and give you Sunday to travel home). If your schedule doesn't quite match up, call ahead to verify hours and closures.

Our tour starts in Ogunquit and involves a drive north to Portland via Rte. 1. It takes about 2 hours, including a detour through Cape Elizabeth with time for a picnic lunch.

Day 1, Monday: Ogunquit to Portland via Cape Elizabeth

Start the trip in seaside Ogunquit, where the **Ogunquit Museum of American Art** ★★★ (p. 69) is that rarest of art-world finds: a great museum open on Monday. Ogunquit was a swingin' artist colony in the early 20th century, and the OMAA has pieces by **Walt Kuhn**, **Robert Laurent**, **Yasuo Kuniyoshi**, and others who used to frequent it. Show up right at 10am, when the museum opens, which will give you 1½ hours to explore before hitting the road for Portland. En route to Portland, you could stop off for a picnic lunch at **Two Lights State Park** ★★ (p. 104), where **Edward Hopper** painted his famous *Lighthouse at Two Lights* in 1929. (If you'd like to spend extra time in Ogunquit, skip Route 1 and Cape Elizabeth and take the I-95 toll highway to the city.)

Arrive at the **Portland Museum of Art** ★★★ (p. 101) by 2pm to hop in a van for a tour of the **Winslow Homer Studio at Prout's Neck**, offered on Mondays and Fridays in the summer (see p. 101). You'll be back at PMA with over an hour to explore the collection before it closes; then it's dinner and a well-earned rest in Portland.

From Portland, it's a 30-minute drive to Brunswick via Hwy. 295. From there, we're following coastal Rte. 1 to Bath and beyond.

Day 2, Tuesday: Brunswick and Bath,

Drive to Brunswick and the **Bowdoin College Museum of Art** ★★ (p. 125), with a wide-ranging collection that runs from Assyrian sculptures from the 9th century B.C.E. to midcentury modern furniture to interactive video installations. This jewel of a museum also holds work from big-shot Maine artists such as the **Wyeths, Marsden Hartley, Winslow Homer,** and **John Singer Sargent.** And admission is free. Get there before lunch, so there's time after to explore the historic campus, with many 19th-century buildings. Then it's off to Bath and the **Centre St. Arts Gallery**, 11 Center Street, a collective of a couple dozen regional artists with exhibits (by both members and guest artists) that change monthly-ish. From there, detour onto **Georgetown Island,** southeast of town, to see the landscapes painted by the "Seguinland" artists of the early 20th century (see p. 127).

Bath and Rockland are separated by 45 miles of Rte. 1, but there can be heavy traffic around Wiscasset in summer; give yourself plenty of time for detours.

Day 3, Wednesday: The Road to Rockland

Following Route 1 up the coast to Rockland, take time to wander the galleries in downtown **Wiscasset** ★★ (see p. 129), especially the **Wiscasset Bay Gallery,** which has works from many landscape painters—among them **Abraham Bogdanove** and Monhegan School of Art founder **Jay Hall Connaway**—who were drawn to Monhegan Island in the early 20th century. It's also worth a detour down to **Boothbay Harbor** ★ (p. 135), which has several excellent galleries. Among them **Gleason Fine Art** stands out for its contemporary collection of artists like Maine's **Eric Hopkins,** known for his bright aerial watercolors, and **Jessica Lee Ives,** best known for shimmering oil paintings of swimmers, boaters, fishermen, and all things wet.

En route to Rockland, before you pass through tiny **Warren**, call ahead to **Studio JBone** to see if you can tour the amazing scrap-metal sculpture garden.

The Maine Coast for Art Lovers

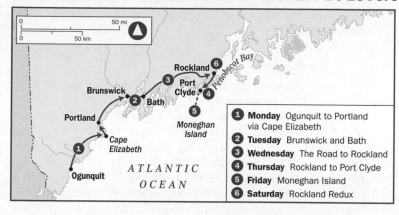

1. **Monday** Ogunquit to Portland via Cape Elizabeth
2. **Tuesday** Brunswick and Bath
3. **Wednesday** The Road to Rockland
4. **Thursday** Rockland to Port Clyde
5. **Friday** Moneghan Island
6. **Saturday** Rockland Redux

After settling into your Rockland digs (some nice new hotels here), head over to the **Farnsworth Museum ★★** (see p. 153), which has free admission on Wednesdays from 5–8pm throughout the summer. From **Alex Katz** to **Robert Indiana** (who did the 20-foot–high electric EAT sign on the museum's roof) to **N.C., Andrew, and Jamie Wyeth**, the Farnsworth collection features giants of Maine art, past and present.

Backtrack 5 miles along Rte. 1 to Thomaston, at the crotch of the Cushing and St. George peninsulas.

Day 4, Thursday: Rockland to Port Clyde

After breakfast in Rockland, head to Thomaston, your launch point for a day exploring two adjacent and little-visited midcoast peninsulas. First, follow the winding, bucolic River Road south towards **Cushing.** If it's open, detour on your way at the **Langlais Sculpture Preserve** (see p. 153), then turn right on Pleasant Point Road, and continue to Hathorne Point Road, following signs for the **Olson House** (see p. 153), the setting of Andrew Wyeth's renowned painting *Christina's World*.

Back to Thomaston for lunch, then head 20 miles south on Route 131 to spend the night in **Port Clyde** (see p. 143). Before supper, drop in on the **Barbara Prey Projects** gallery on Main Street. Once the town's public house and frequented by N.C. Wyeth, it's now a gallery space for one of Maine's most successful commercial painters.

Day 5, Friday: Monhegan Island

Hop the **Monhegan Boat Line** (see p. 141) ferry and spend a day and night discovering what once drew **Edward Hopper**, **Robert Henri**, **Rockwell Kent**, and others to Monhegan—along with gaggles of artists today. Hike the trails, duck into the small but impressive **Monhegan Museum** (p. 144), and fraternize with locals and tourists alike at the popular **Monhegan Brewing Company** (p. 144). You'll doubtless see some artists at their easels along the trail to stunning, weatherbeaten Lobster Cove; the gray house standing romantically against the waves belongs to **Jamie Wyeth**.

It's 18 miles back into Rockland from the Port Clyde ferry terminal, via Rte. 131 and Rte. 1.

Day 6, Saturday: Rockland Redux

After a ferry ride back to the mainland, make it a leisurely final day back in Rockland, where the downtown hops on Saturday afternoons and there are still plenty of galleries you didn't have time for on Wednesday. The best is the **Dowling Walsh Gallery** at 365 Main Street, where you can discover knockout contemporary Maine artists like **Greta Van Campen,** known for her design-influenced, geometric landscape paintings, and quasi-surrealist fine-art photographer **Cig Harvey.** Cap off a long week at the brand new **Center for Maine Contemporary Art ★★★** (see p. 153), a glittery mod building filled with rotating exhibits in any and every media. You might end the night with a movie or a show at the historic, gloriously restored **Strand Theater** (see p. 154)—it would have been 3 years old when Edward Hopper spent a formative summer here in 1926.

Come Sunday, allow 2 hours (with traffic) to backtrack to Portland via Rte. 1 and Hwy. 295. To reach the New Hampshire border and points south, give yourself 3 hours; traffic on I-95 can be a bear on summer Sundays, as folks head home.

OUTDOOR ADVENTURES ON THE MAINE COAST

You'll only see a portion of the coast following this 6-day itinerary, but you'll see it deeply. This is a trip all about minimizing time in the car and maximizing time in Maine's rugged outdoors, from mountain biking the Camden Hills to sea kayaking the Stonington Archipelago to hiking some of Acadia's more overlooked trails. Luckily, for all its wild corners, this stretch of coast still has plenty of great dining—and beer!—so you can stay, you know, fueled up.

Get yourself to Camden the night before this trip to make the most of the daylight on day one.

Day 1: Camden Hills Mountain Biking

Get a full-day mountain bike rental (with helmet, of course) from the helpful, knowledgeable folks at **Maine Sport Outfitters** (p. 163) and head for the hills. The Camden Hills offer an impressively varied 6-mile trail network at **Camden Snow Bowl** (p. 164) and the adjacent **Ragged Mountain Preserve.** The beginner's network is wooded and crisscrosses a shallow brook; trail names like Chutes & Ladders give you an idea of

Outdoor Adventures on the Maine Coast

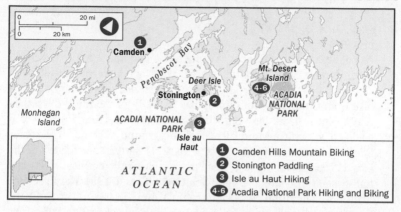

Camden

Penobscot Bay

Deer Isle

Stonington

Monhegan Island

ACADIA NATIONAL PARK

Isle au Haut

Mt. Desert Island

ACADIA NATIONAL PARK

ATLANTIC OCEAN

1 Camden Hills Mountain Biking
2 Stonington Paddling
3 Isle au Haut Hiking
4-6 Acadia National Park Hiking and Biking

what kind of bouncy fun you're in for. The New England Mountain Bikers Association prints a map you can pick up with your rental. Camden's Scottish **Drouthy Bear** pub, 50 Elm Street, is an NEMBA sponsor and pours a mean post-ride pint.

It's a (scenic) 2-hour drive from Camden to Stonington, following Rte. 1 over the Penobscot River, then following Rte. 15 south along the Blue Hill Peninsula and onto Deer Isle.

Day 2: Stonington Paddling

Some 60 islands, many of them tiny, make up the Stonington Archipelago in the glittering waters south of refreshingly proletarian **Stonington ★★** (p. 174). **Old Quarry Ocean Adventures** (p. 178) can rent you a sea kayak by the day or half-day or (even better for the inexperienced) lead tours; they'll even shuttle you out to the island of your choice. The islands are mostly edged by charismatic humps of exposed granite—quarrying them used to be big business here—and you're likely to spot eagles, osprey, harbor seals, and porpoises as you ping-pong from one to the next.

Day 3: Isle au Haut Hiking

The first mailboat out to **Isle au Haut ★★** (p. 178) leaves Stonington at 7am—catch it, and you'll have an 8-hour day on this gorgeous island outpost of Acadia National Park, strewn with silent, rugged trails (and very few visitors). Hike the Ridge Trail over the here-and-there exposed spine of the island for some great views of the Atlantic, and hang out in the horseshoe cove of Barred Harbor to spot sea ducks (and feel like you're the last person on Earth). Catch the 4:30pm mailboat back to Stonington and grab a patio table at **Aragosta** (p. 176), just steps from the dock.

From Stonington, follow Rte. 15 and then Rte. 172 through Blue Hill to Ellsworth, about an hour's drive. From there, Rte. 3 leads south onto Mount Desert Island and into Bar Harbor, another half hour in the car if the traffic isn't intense.

Day 4, 5 & 6: Acadia National Park Hiking and Biking

As public land in Maine goes, **Acadia National Park** ★★★ is the crown jewel (**Baxter State Park**, see p. 262, with mile-high Mount Katahdin, comes in a close second, but that's a trip for another itinerary). Rent a bike from **Cadillac Mountain Sports** (p. 220) for the full 3 days, then find a central home base on MDI, preferably out of Bar Harbor—you could do worse than **Mount Desert Campground** ★ at the tip of Somes Sound (p. 186) or **Acadia Yurts** ★ (p. 221) on the "quiet side" of the island. Then spend the next few days exploring the carriage roads and trail systems. If I have to suggest don't-miss hikes, I'll say **The Precipice Trail** ★★, **The Bubbles** ★, and **Acadia Mountain** (see p. 194 and 197). But what you really ought to do is take a map, a backpack full of snacks and water, and an open mind. Then head out onto the MDI roads and carriage roads each day with no particular destination, stopping to hike at whatever trailhead looks interesting.

If you're craving one last new campsite on Day 3, you could break camp, backtrack to Route 1 off the island, and drive 15 miles east to the **Schoodic Peninsula,** a much less visited section of Acadia, where you can pitch a tent at the new **Schoodic Woods Campground** ★ (p. 240) and have a new set of trails (biking and hiking) to explore.

Skip the coast on the way home. Backtrack to Ellsworth, then follow Rte. 1A 30 miles to Bangor, where you can pick up I-95 (with tolls, alas) for a quicker ride back to Portland (about 3 hr. total from Bar Harbor) or the New Hampshire border and points south (4 hr., or longer on a Sunday or a holiday).

SOUTHERN MAINE: KITTERY TO THE KENNEBUNKS

Tourist bureau statistics show that Maine's southern coast—stretching from the state line at Kittery to Portland—is the primary destination of most leisure travelers to the state. That's no surprise, given the number of day-trippers from the Boston metropolitan area who come up here in summer to enjoy its long, sandy beaches. Thanks to quirks of geography, nearly all of Maine's sandy shores occur along this stretch of coastline. In season, it takes some doing to find privacy or remoteness here, despite a sense of history in the coastal villages (some of them, anyway). Still, it's not hard to find a relaxing spot, whether you prefer dunes, the lulling sound of breaking waves, or a carnival-like atmosphere in a beach town.

Waves depend on the weather; during a good Northeast blow, they pound the shores, rise above the roads, and threaten beach houses built decades ago. During balmy midsummer days, though, the ocean can be gentle as a farm pond, its barely audible waves lapping timidly at the shore as the tide creeps in, inch by inch, covering tidal pools full of crabs, barnacles, and sea snails.

One thing all the beaches here share in common: They're washed by the chilled waters of the Gulf of Maine, which makes for, er, invigorating swimming. Though the beach season is generally brief and intense, running only from July 4th to Labor Day, the tourism season increasingly stretches into the stunningly colorful month of October, with most restaurants and hotels these days staying open to accommodate carloads of "leaf peepers."

The towns that border these beaches—Kittery, the Yorks, Ogunquit, and the Kennebunks—include some of the oldest English settlements in the New World and some bastions of New England Old Money. That patrician historicity makes for a funky cocktail when you mix it with the trappings of middle-class roadside tourism that spring up in the mid-20th century. These are the charming sort of towns where you can stroll a shady lane lined with 19th-century mansions, then turn the corner to find a low-slung hot dog stand with a line around the block.

KITTERY & THE YORKS ★★

Kittery is 60 miles N of Boston and 266 miles NE of New York City

Driving into Maine from the south, as most travelers do, you'll find that **Kittery** ★ is the first town to appear after crossing the big bridge spanning the Piscataqua River from New Hampshire. Once famous for its (still operating) naval yard, Kittery is now better known for its dozens of factory outlets and a hip dining-and-drinking scene that's recently sprung up in the old Foreside neighborhood.

"The Yorks," just to the north, are three towns that share a name, but little else. In fact, it's rare to find three such well-defined and diverse New England archetypes within such a compact area. **York Village** ★ is full of 17th-century American history and architecture in a compact area, and has a good library. **York Harbor** ★★ reached its zenith during America's late Victorian era, when wealthy urbanites constructed cottages at the ocean's edge; it's the most relaxing and scenic of the three. Finally, **York Beach** ★★ is a fun beach town with amusements, taffy shops, a small zoo, gabled summer homes set in crowded enclaves, a great lighthouse, and two excellent beaches with sun, sand, rocks, surf, surfers, fried-fish stands, and lighthouse views.

Just outside York Village, the protrusion of land known as **Cape Neddick** ★★ is an excellent back-road route to Ogunquit, *if* you can find it (go past the police station in Short Sands, then bear right at the sign for the Cape Neddick Lobster Pound).

Essentials
ARRIVING

BY CAR Kittery is accessible from either **I-95** or **Route 1,** with well-marked exits. Coming from the south, the Yorks are reached most easily by heading for (but not taking) the Maine Turnpike; follow I-95 to a point just south of the turnpike exit, then exit to the right ("last exit before tolls"). Coming from the north, pay your toll exiting the turnpike and then take the first exit, an immediate right.

BY TRAIN **Amtrak** (www.amtrak.com; *✆* **800/872-7245**) operates four to five Downeaster trains daily from Boston's North Station (which does not connect to Amtrak's national network; you must take a subway or taxi from Boston's South Station first) into southern Maine, stopping outside Wells, about 10 miles away from the Yorks. A one-way ticket starts at $15, and the trip takes 1¾ hours. From Wells, you'll need to phone for a taxi or arrange for a pickup to get to your final destination.

BY BUS The two chief bus lines serving the stretch of Maine between Portland and Kittery are **Greyhound** (www.greyhound.com; *✆* **800/231-2222**), which has service to Wells, and **C&J Trailways** (www.ridecj.com;

The Southern Maine Coast

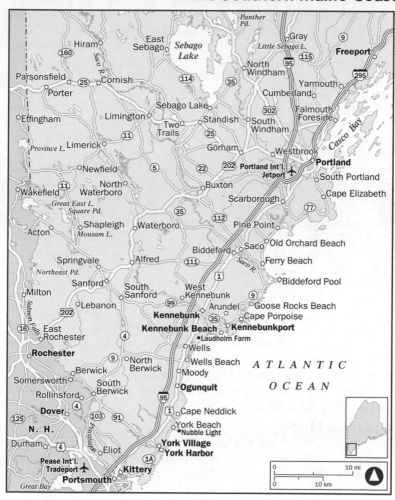

© **800/258-7111**), which runs a seasonal weekend service from New York to Ogunquit, Memorial Day through Columbus Day. Taking a Greyhound from New York City's Port Authority to Wells costs from $60 to $100 one-way and takes 7 to 8 hours; from Boston, figure on paying a fare of $12 to $30 one-way and a ride of 1¾ hours. A New York to Ogunquit trip on C&J Trailways runs $85 and takes 6 hours. Several competing bus lines also run regular buses daily from Boston's South Station to downtown Portsmouth, New Hampshire, which is very close to Kittery (you can actually walk over a bridge into Maine from Portsmouth). For more details, see the Portsmouth, New Hampshire, section of chapter 10 (p. 250).

VISITOR INFORMATION

The **Maine State Visitor Information Center** (✆ **207/439-1319**) operates at a well-marked rest area on I-95. It's full of info and helpful staff; has a pet exercise area and copious vending machines; and is open daily from 8am to 6pm in summer, from 9am to 5:30pm the rest of the year. (The vending machines and restrooms are open 24 hours a day.)

The **Greater York Region Chamber of Commerce** (www.gatewayto maine.org; ✆ **207/363-4422**) also operates another helpful **visitor center,** one that mirrors the shape of a stone cottage. It's across Route 1 from the Maine Turnpike access road (right beside the Stonewall Kitchen headquarters and café, see p. 55) on Stonewall Lane. In peak season, it's open Monday to Saturday from 9am to 5pm and Sunday from 10am to 4pm; from Labor Day through June, it's open Monday to Friday 9am to 4pm, Saturday from 10am to 2pm, and Sunday 9am to 1pm.

GETTING AROUND

From mid-June through Labor Day, a trackless **trolley** (a bus painted to look like a trolley) runs back and forth between Short Sands and Long Sands beaches in the Yorks, providing a convenient way to explore without having to be hassled with parking. Hop on the trolley (www.yorktrolley.com; ✆ **207/363-9600**) at one of the well-marked stops; it's $4 each way, $3 to sit on board for the entire loop without debarking. The trolley makes a circle through the Short Sands business district before heading out to Long Sands and proceeding all the way to the Libby's and Camp Eaton campgrounds at the far southern end of that beach, before turning around again. (It does not travel to Nubble Light, but if you want to see the famous lighthouse, debark the bus at Nubble Light Road and hoof it a little more than a mile out to the point.) The trolley operates from late June through Labor Day daily on the half-hour, from about 9:30am until around 10:15pm.

SPECIAL EVENTS

Swing through York in late July or early August, and you'll notice the sidewalks are even more packed than usual for the annual **York Days** festival, a week-and-a-half–long civic celebration with a slate of outdoor bands, a road race, fireworks displays, and the usual small-town revelry. Highlights include a sprawling, partially tented **craft fair** that takes over the York Beach baseball diamond on the festival's closing weekend and the **Christmas in July** ceremony out at Nubble Light, with the striking, island-bound lighthouse bedecked in holiday lights (plus a visit from Santa).

Where to Stay in Kittery & the Yorks

Airbnb rentals proliferate around Kittery and the Yorks, many of them right on the water. While there aren't many genuine bargains to be had, you're more likely to find last-minute lodging through online rental services than at the hotels, which fill up months in advance for peak season.

KITTERY

Portsmouth Harbor Inn & Spa ★★ This three-story brick manor, dating to 1879, manages to be surprisingly approachable. The small rooms are tastefully understated, with clawfoot tubs, wicker furniture, and antique furnishings. The common area downstairs stays stocked with cookies and sherry, and breakfasts are decadent, particularly the buttery baked goods that precede each morning's hot dish. Innkeeper Lynn Bowditch knows Portsmouth and Kittery intimately and delights in suggesting ambitious itineraries—cover all the ground she recommends and you'll have earned that hot stone massage at the adjacent spa.

6 Water St., Kittery. www.innatportsmouth.com. ⓒ **207/439-4040.** 5 units. May–Oct $190–$210 double and suite; Nov–Apr $170–$200 double and suite. Packages available. Rates include breakfast. **Amenities:** Spa treatments; massage; library; outdoor hot tub; free Wi-Fi.

THE YORKS

York Beach has a large supply of no-frills motels facing Long Sands Beach. Among those with simple accommodations are the **Anchorage Inn** (www.anchorageinn.com; ⓒ **207/363-5112**), the **Grand View Inn Motel** (www.grandview-york.com; ⓒ **207/363-3838** or 207/363-9815), and the **Sunrise Motel** (www.sunrisemotel.net; ⓒ **800/242-0750**), all directly across the highway from the ocean.

Dockside Guest Quarters ★ David and Harriette Lusty established this quiet retreat in 1954; more recent additions and new management (son Eric and wife Carol) haven't changed the friendly, maritime flavor of the place. Situated on an island connected to the mainland by a small bridge, the inn occupies nicely landscaped grounds shady with maples and white pines. A few of the rooms are in the cozy main house, built in 1885, but the bulk of the accommodations are in small, shared, town-house-style cottages added between 1968 and 1998 down by the water. These are simply furnished, but bright and airy; most have private decks overlooking the entrance to York Harbor. Several also have woodstoves, fireplace, and/or kitchenettes (though you do pay quite a bit extra for the kitchenette units and suites). The inn also maintains a simple restaurant (run by Philip Lusty, yet another son, and his wife, Anne), and offers personalized boat tours of the harbor from its own private dock.

22 Harris Island Rd., York Harbor. www.docksidegq.com. ⓒ **888/860-7428** or 207/363-2868. 25 units. $162–$263 double; $291–$350 suite. Rates include breakfast. Closed late Oct–Apr. 2-night minimum stay on weekends in summer. Packages available. **Amenities:** Restaurant; badminton; bike rentals; boat tours; croquet; rowboats; free Wi-Fi.

Union Bluff Hotel ★★ With its turrets, dormers, and porches, the Union Bluff looks like a 19th-century beach hotel—but it was actually built in 1989, replacing the previous (circa 1870) version of the hotel, which had burned down. Inside, the hotel is modern if bland; rooms have oak furniture, wall-to-wall carpeting, and small refrigerators. There are about 20 rooms in an annex next door, but the main inn's rooms and views are better—the best ones are the suites on the top floor, with beach vistas (and some Jacuzzis, fireplaces, and decks). It's amazing how low rates can plummet here midweek and off-season; but weekends, even before and after the summer, are quite expensive. The vibe is often festive, with families letting loose and a constant stream of wedding parties. The hotel's seafood-heavy restaurant is not half bad. Step outside and you're a half-block from Short Sands beach, T-shirt and shell shops, and a bowling alley and throwback arcade. The hotel assigns one parking spot for each room, which is great because parking is supertight in summer in Short Sands; but if you've brought an RV or second car, you'll need to use the big town parking lot adjacent to the hotel—bring quarters. Lots of quarters.

8 Beach St., York Beach. www.unionbluff.com. © **800/833-0721** or 207/363-1333. 71 units. Mid-June–Aug $89–$469 double and suite; rest of year $79–$289 double and suite. Packages available. **Amenities:** Restaurant; pub; free Wi-Fi.

York Harbor Inn ★★   Once known as the Hillcroft, the rambling York Harbor lords over the best views of York Harbor and the sea. It's also got some history of its own: the "Cabin Room" in the main building is made of original 1637 beams (once a sail loft) shipped over from the Isles of Shoals, and lanterns came from a trolley line that once ran along what is now the highway here. The basement pub has original hitching posts where travelers tied up horses as they drank. The handsome blue Harbor Crest building uphill is from the early 18th century, and contains wonderful tilework; another outbuilding dates from 1783. The main inn's 22 rooms are simplest, and are closest to the convivial basement pub. The adjacent Harbor Hill Inn contains the best units: all have Jacuzzis, gas fireplaces, heated bathrooms, CD players, and sea views, plus a hot tub out back. Nearby Harbor Cliffs is also a good choice, with breakfast included and a variety of room styles. The latest addition to this collection is actually the oldest building: the 1730 Harbor Crest Inn, a half-mile up the road, with wonderful common areas, porches, a variety of color schemes, king-size beds, big Jacuzzi tubs, and black-and-white tiled bathrooms.

480 York St., York Harbor. www.yorkharborinn.com. © **800/343-3869** or 207/363-5119. 61 units. Late June–early Sept $179–$379 double and suite; early May–late June & early Sept–Oct $149–$349 double and suite; Nov–Apr $129–$349 double and suite. Packages available. Rates include breakfast. Harbor Crest building is pet-friendly. **Amenities:** Restaurant; bar; free Wi-Fi.

CAMPING

Campers lack good options around here, but might head for **Dixon's Campground** (dixonscampground.com; © **207/363-3626**), which has a mix of wooded tent sites, RV sites, and yurts set back from busy Route 1 (just north of York proper) for $40 to $125 per night. Monthly (yes, monthly) rates are cheaper. There's a 3-night minimum on holiday weekends; it's open from early May through mid-September.

Where to Eat in Kittery & the Yorks
KITTERY

In the span of a few years, as the Foreside neighborhood has come into its own, Kittery has evolved from a bastion of traditional lobster pounds and fried seafood joints into one of New England's most diverse and happening food towns. In addition to the choices below, there's terrific Indian food at **Tulsi** (20 Walker St., ☎ **207/451-9511**) and outstanding sandwiches, breads, and pastries at the **Beach Pea Baking Co.** (53 State Rd., ☎ **207/439-3555**)—eat at one of the tables outside or on the front porch, if you can find an open one. If you want to go the traditional Down Easter route, **Chauncey Creek Lobster Pier** (16 Chauncey Creek Rd., ☎ **207/439-1030**] is the real deal, with lobsters fresh off the boat, brightly painted picnic tables, and a raw bar for clams and oysters. BYOB.

Anju Noodle Bar ★★ PAN-ASIAN Locals start filling this Foreside hotspot at lunch time, and the crowds don't let up until well after dark. The five varieties of kimchi are a draw, as are the sweet-and-spicy Korean and Japanese chicken wings. But really, everybody's coming for the ramen—big, fragrant bowls of wavy-thin noodles, bone broth, slow-roasted pork shoulder, and more, complex and savory and damn near medicinal. They're beautiful to look at too, each bowl a bright and colorful accent to the mod, wood-toned Anju dining room. The bar fills up at night, with patrons as likely to nurse a Maine craft beer as one of the offerings on the well-curated sake menu.

7 Wallingford Sq., Kittery. www.anjunoodlebar.com. ☎ **207/703-4298.** Small plates $7–$12; noodle bowls $13–$17. Sun–Thurs noon–9:30pm, Fri–Sat noon–10:30pm.

The Black Birch ★★★ GASTROPUB Assessing this boxy, bland former post office from the outside, you wouldn't imagine that there's regularly a line out the door by 5pm on weekends. But the magic's all inside: a long bar and tables made of reclaimed wood, 24 taps of ambitious regional beers and obscure imports, a turntable spinning classic vinyl, and a kitchen run by chef Jake Smith turning out totally indulgent and inventive comfort foods. Think deviled eggs stuffed with chorizo, tahini, toasted marshmallow, and more. Think deep-fried short ribs. Think the best poutine outside of Quebec, with duck confit on top and melted local cheese curds. Worth waiting in line for.

2 Government St., Kittery. www.theblackbirch.com. ☎ **207/703-2294.** Small plates $9–$12; dinners $11–$17. Reservations not accepted. Tues–Thurs 3:30–10pm; Fri–Sat 3:30–11pm.

Bob's Clam Hut ★ FRIED SEAFOOD Operating since 1956, Bob's manages to retain an old-fashioned flavor—despite now being surrounded on all sides by factory outlet malls, and with prices that have steadily escalated out of the "budget eats" category. It still does one thing very well: fries up plump and perfectly golden heaps of clams and other seafood, sides them with french fries and coleslaw in baskets, and puts them out with tremendous efficiency. Order at the window, get a soda from the machine, and stake out a

In 2011, a rewrite of Maine state law allowed the brewers of Maine's nascent craft beer scene to operate tasting rooms very much like bars, with unlimited pours of up to a pint. It's led to a craft-beer explosion in the Pine Tree State, and no region outside of Portland has benefited from the proliferation of tap rooms as much as the southern coast. A few of the standouts include Kittery's **Tributary Brewing Co.** (✆ **207/351-8162**), founded by venerable master brewer Tod Mott. The former post office full of picnic tables takes on a party vibe on the weekends—try the Mott the Lesser Russian Imperial Stout,

a legendary brew among beer geeks, based on a recipe Mott cooked up in a previous gig. The tap room at York's **SoMe Brewing Company** (✆ **207/703-0093**) has a sports bar feel, with a flat-screen usually tuned in to some New England team. The best pours at **Hidden Cove Brewing Company** (✆ **207/646-0228**) in Wells are the crisp, super quaffable, lower-alcohol brews like Cast-off Session IPA and the Summer Ale with lemon peel and honey. Aging barrels line a no-frills tap room that feels like a basement rec room you hung out in as a teenager.

table inside or on the deck (with its lovely view of, er, Route 1) while waiting for your number to be called. The food is surprisingly light, cooked in cholesterol-free vegetable oil; the onion rings are especially good. Fish-and-chips are also on the menu, and the lobster roll attracts foodie pilgrims from around the country. To ensure that your diet is irrevocably busted, Bob's also dishes up soft-serve ice cream: now, that's just overkill. But count us in.

315 Rte. 1 (west side), Kittery. www.bobsclamhut.com. ✆ **207/439-4233.** Sandwiches $4–$23; dinners $10–$35. Mon–Thurs, Sun 11am–7pm; Fri–Sat 11am–8pm.

THE YORKS

Besides the restaurants listed below, York Village harbors **Fazio's,** 38 Woodbridge Rd. (turn just before the town library; ✆ **207/363-7019**), a good Italian family restaurant with atmosphere. Directly on Long Sands in York Beach, **Sun & Surf** (✆ **207/363-2961**) has a takeout window proffering fried seafood and ice cream—but also a dining room with standout ocean views and an increasingly sophisticated menu that now incorporates steaks, salads, pastas, tuna, and lamb. For a quick bite, I like the **Long Sands General Store** (✆ **206/363-5383**), near the northern end of Long Sands beach, with pizzas, sandwiches, and other essential picnicking supplies.

Fox's Lobster House ★ SEAFOOD Fox's is unabashedly commercial, and charges more than it could, but so what? You're sitting outside, eating pre-cracked lobsters and breathing salt air, on a headland that would be worth zillions in real estate terms. Looking straight at Nubble Light. Fox's has been here since 1966, and I can see why: It delivers a pretty intensively "Maine" experience just a few miles across the state line. You can also dine inside, in a wood-and-nautical-themed dining room, where you can get platters including side dishes: a better deal for families, just without that great lighthouse view. There's an ice-cream window for kids as well.

8 Sohier Park Rd., York Beach. www.foxslobster.com. © **207/363-2643.** Lobsters $25 and up. May–June, Sun–Thurs 11:30am–8pm, Fri–Sat 11:30am–9pm; July–Aug, daily 11:30am–9pm; Sept–Oct, daily 11:30am–8pm. Closed Nov–Apr.

The Goldenrod ★ TRADITIONAL AMERICAN   Follow the neon to this beach-town classic—a York summer institution ever since it opened in 1896. It's easy to find: Look for visitors gawking through plate-glass windows at ancient machines hypnotically churning out taffy (millions of pieces a year). The restaurant, across from the candy-making operation, is low on frills but big on atmosphere: Diners sit on stout oak furniture around a stone fire-place or elbow-to-elbow at an antique soda fountain. Breakfast offerings are New England standards, and for lunch you can eat soups, burgers, and over-priced sandwiches. But what saves the place is the candy counter, where throngs line up to buy boxes of wax-wrapped taffy "kisses" (check the striping on each candy for its flavor; I'm a peanut-butter guy, myself), almond-pocked birch bark, and other penny-candy treats. The shakes, malts, and sundaes are on the sweet side.

Railroad Rd. and Ocean Ave., York Beach. www.thegoldenrod.com. © **207/363-2621.** Lunch and dinner entrees $5–$10. Memorial Day–Labor Day daily 8am–10pm (until 9pm in June); Labor Day–Columbus Day Sat–Sun 8am–3pm. Closed Columbus Day–Memorial Day.

Lobster Cove ★ SEAFOOD/FAMILY FARE   Right across the street from the pounding surf of Long Sands Beach, dependable Lobster Cove is a good choice when the family is too tired to drive far in search of a feed. And a "feed" is what you'll get here. Breakfast consists of standard, inex-pensive choices such as omelets, pancakes, and eggs Benedict. Lunch runs to burgers and sandwiches, but dinner is prime time, when a standard shore dinner of lobster, corn on the cob, clam chowder, and steamed clams is hefty and good. Lobster pie is an old-fashioned New England favorite. They also do lobster rolls, clam rolls, steaks, broiled seafoods, and

Jam Sessions in York

Need a souvenir but too weak with hun-ger to shop another minute? At **Stone-wall Kitchen's** flagship store, on Stonewall Lane (© **207/351-2712**)—just behind the huge tourist information complex at the corner of Route 1 and the access road leading to and from I-95 and the Maine Turnpike—you can sam-ple from among the company's delicious jams and spreads before tucking into a soup-and-sandwich special from the on-site deli. Then, hunger and birthday lists both satisfied in one fell swoop, keep browsing through a good selection of handy kitchen accessories: knives, lob-ster bibs, graters, and the like. Staff is friendly and helpful. It's open daily until 8pm; the cafe, though, closes at 3pm.

traditional Maine desserts such as wild blueberry pie and warm bread pudding with whiskey sauce.

756 York St., York Beach. ℂ **207/351-1100.** Main courses $7–$21. Mon–Thurs 8am–8:30pm; Fri–Sat 8am–9pm; Sun 8am–8pm.

Exploring Kittery

Kittery has become a shopping mecca thanks to the establishment of colonies of little factory outlet shopping malls clustered along both sides of U.S. Route 1, about 4 miles south of York. More than 100 of these outlets flank the highway, in more than a dozen strip malls. On rainy summer days, hordes of disappointed beachgoers head here and swarm the aisles; thus, parking can become tight on bad-weather days.

Since 2012 or so, the historic **Foreside neighborhood** has become Kittery's snug, hip town center. Once a rough-around-the-edges district catering to off-duty shipyard workers, Foreside now hosts a few of the state's most acclaimed bars and restaurants, plus indie-fied enterprises like eclectic arts venue **The Dance Hall** (www.thedancehallkittery.com; ℂ **207/703-2083**) and rustic-mod accessories boutique **Folk** (www.shop-folk.com; ℂ **207/703-2526**). It's a great few blocks where you can crush a craft beer or a cruller while mingling with student scenesters, young families, and Navy folks in their digital blues.

Nearby, the **Portsmouth Naval Shipyard** faces Portsmouth, New Hampshire. This active shipyard isn't open to the public for security reasons, but you can visit the **Kittery Historical & Naval Museum** (ℂ **207/439-3080;** www.kitterymuseum.com) to get a quick overview of maritime history. You'll find ship and sub models, lighthouse lenses, scrimshaw work, diving suits, and the like—plus muskets, utensils, and tools from another era. It's not a bad effort at all. From June through October, the museum's open Wednesday through Sunday, from 10am to 4pm; in the off-season, it's only open Wednesdays and Saturdays, with the same hours. Admission is $5 for adults, $3 for children, and $10 for a family. Find it by taking U.S. Route 1 to the Kittery traffic circle, then exiting for Route 236 south; that's Rogers Road. Continue to the end and Rogers Road Extension.

From Kittery, an attractive alternative route north to York follows winding Route 103 to the historic, lost-in-time village of **Kittery Point.** It's perfect for driving, though a bit busy and narrow for biking. Kittery Point homes seem to be just inches from the roadway and there are not one but *two* historic forts; both are parks open to the public.

Exploring the Yorks

York is split into several village centers, from colonial-era York Village to laidback York Harbor to the beach-town hubbub of York Beach. The best for walking around in is **York Village ★★**, a fine destination for those curious about early American history. First settled in 1624, the village opens several homes to the public.

TALE OF THE tags: KITTERY VS. FREEPORT

When visiting the Maine coast, many travelers only find time to shop once. Trouble is, there are *two* significant outlet centers on the southern coast—Kittery and Freeport. How to choose? Here's my quick take:

Generally speaking, **Kittery,** located at the southern edge of Maine, is best for the name-brand shopper who wants to hit a large volume of places in a short time. It's easier to do Kittery more quickly than **Freeport** because of the side-by-side arrangement of the various stores and the malls. Price tags tend to be lower in Kittery, too. The trade-off is the blandness of the experience: Each of these side malls offer vast parking lots and boring architecture, and you cannot safely walk from one mall to another—you need wheels.

In **Kittery,** the malls are clumped along Route 1 just a couple of miles north of the New Hampshire border. Though the area appears at first glance to be a conglomerated, single huge mall, in fact there are five or six distinct areas with separate entrances. Choose carefully before you make your turn. Among the best places to try among the various complexes are a **Gap** outlet, a **Samsonite** shop with knowledgeable sales help, a small but elegant **Coach** store, **Reebok** (I picked up swim trunks here for a fraction of the retail cost), **Polo Ralph Lauren, J. Crew** (good prices on sweaters), an **Orvis** sporting goods outlet, and a useful **Crate & Barrel** outlet. The pioneer-themed **Kittery Trading Post** is not all it's hyped up to be, but at least prices are low.

Information on current outlets is available from the **Kittery Outlet Association.** Call ✆ **888/548-8379** (which spells KITTERY, by the way), or visit the website at www.thekitteryoutlets.com.

There are also a couple of good places here to eat: **Bob's Clam Hut** (see p. 53), **Ben & Jerry's** for ice cream; or, for a sit-down meal, the **Weathervane,** a small New England fish-house chain that delivers value at moderate prices and is an excellent choice for families.

Finally, while visiting Kittery and the Yorks, don't forget that Portsmouth, New Hampshire makes a worthwhile side trip—in fact, if you're seeking culture, arts, coffee shops, and top-flight restaurants, you'll find a wealth of options on the New Hampshire side of the river. Best of all, it's just a half-mile from Kittery, or a few minutes' drive from the Yorks. I've described this city as a side trip in greater detail in chapter 10 of this book; see p. 250 for more details.

Museums of Old York ★★★ HISTORIC BUILDINGS York's local historical society oversees the bulk of the town's collection of historic buildings, some of which date to the early 18th century, and most of which are astonishingly well preserved or restored. Tickets are available to eight Old York–operated properties in all; one good place to start is at the **Jefferds Tavern** ★, across from the handsome **old burying ground** ★. Changing exhibits document various facets of early life. Next door is the **School House** ★, furnished as it might have been in the 19th century. A 10-minute walk along lightly traveled Lindsay Road brings you to **Hancock Wharf** (see box p. 250), next door to the **George Marshall Store.** Also nearby is the **Elizabeth Perkins House**, with its well-preserved Colonial Revival interiors.

John Hancock is justly famous for his oversize signature on the Declaration of Independence, his tenure as governor of Massachusetts, and the insurance company and tall Boston building that were named for him. What's not so well known is his involvement as a proprietor of York's **Hancock Wharf,** a failed 18th-century wharf-and-warehouse enterprise that went bust. Hancock never actually set foot on the wharf, but for years locals believed he used it to stash arms, contraband, and/or goods he didn't want taxed by those tax-happy British. It now appears that wasn't the case, but

it still makes for one of the many intriguing sites and stories in the **York Village** section of downtown York. (See Museums of Old York, p. 57, for more details on this neighborhood.)

Surprisingly, the wharf has a happy ending: It's more famous today than it was then, the only 18th-century warehouse still standing on the York River. It has been designated a National Historic Site, and the York Historical Society sometimes uses it to launch or receive the occasional historic boat passing through town.

4

Finally, there are two "don't-miss" buildings in the society's collection. The barn-red, hill-topping **Old Gaol ★★**, built in 1719 as a jail to hold criminals, debtors, and other miscreants, is said to be the oldest surviving public building in the United States; you can still see the dungeons. Just down the knoll from the jail, the bright yellow **Emerson-Wilcox House ★**, built in the mid-1700s and periodically added onto through the years, is a virtual catalog of architectural styles and early decorative arts.

207 York St., York. www.oldyork.org. ✆ **207/363-1756.** Admission per building $5 adults, $3 children 6–15; pass to all buildings $12 adults, $8 children 6–15. Museums open late May–Labor Day Tues–Sat 10am–5pm, Sun 1–5pm (some properties have shorter hours). Labor Day–mid-Oct open Thurs–Sun only; closed mid-Oct–late May.

Sohier Park ★★★ PARK/VIEW   The small peninsula known as Cape Neddick shoots off from York's beach areas, circles through beach views, and winds up here, at Sohier Park—a great place to look out onto **Nubble Light**, probably one of the ten most photographed lighthouses in the world. The light is especially lovely because it's set on a tiny island. The park is free; gaze at the lighthouse and snap pictures from the safety of a parking lot across the swift little inlet that separates it from the mainland. There are coin-operated looking-glasses to get a better view, and a small gift shop and information kiosk in the park. In high summer season, expect a parking lot jam-packed with RVs and motorcycles—watching the crowd is half the fun. There's also a lobster hut adjacent to the park, and an outstanding ice cream stand about 100 yards uphill from it. If you're coming to take photos, remember that the lighthouse is trimmed in additional white lighting twice a year—for a week during July's York Days festival and again from Thanksgiving through New Year's.

Nubble Rd. (off Long Sands Dr.), Cape Neddick. www.nubblelight.org. Free admission. Park open year-round, 24 hr.; welcome center and restrooms open daily May–mid-Oct, 7am–7pm.

WONDERFUL WALKS

A few local strolls will allow visitors to stretch their legs and get the cobwebs out of their heads.

York Harbor and York Village are connected by a quiet pathway that follows a river and passes through gently rustling woodlands. **Fisherman's Walk** ★ departs from below Edward's Harborside Inn, near the Stage Neck Inn. (There's limited parking at tiny York Harbor Beach.) Follow the pathway along the river, past lobster shacks and along lawns leading up to grand shingled homes. Cross Route 103 and walk over the **Wiggly Bridge** (said to be, not implausibly, the smallest suspension bridge in the world), then head into the woods. You'll soon connect with a dirt lane; follow this and you'll emerge at Lindsay Road near Hancock Wharf (see above). The entire walk is about a mile long and, depending on your pace, will take a half-hour to 45 minutes.

Also departing from near York Harbor Beach is the **Cliff Walk** ★★, a scenic little trail that follows rugged terrain along rocky bluffs and offers sweeping views of the open ocean as well as glimpses of life in some of the town's grandest cottages. The far end of this trail has been destroyed by ocean waves and has not been rebuilt; you'll have to retrace your steps back to the beach. The pathway is the perpetual subject of local disputes between the town and landowners seeking to limit access. The most recent developments limits traffic on the trail to the hours between sunrise and sunset, May 15 to October 15. Check signs for any new restrictions on trespassing before you set off.

Five miles northeast of town on appropriately named Mountain Road, some 5 miles of mostly wooded trails crisscross the **Mount Agamenticus Conservation Region**. It's a miniature wilderness bastion just minutes away from the din of Route 1, with 692-foot-tall Mount Agamenticus at its heart. The summit affords knockout views of the ocean on the one hand and New Hampshire's soaring Mount Washington on the other. Watch for migrating raptors, white-tailed deer, and even the occasional moose.

Finally, there's the small peninsula ending at an island capped by the scenic **Nubble Light** ★★★ lighthouse. This lighthouse, probably one of the most

---

Wheeling It to the Sayward-Wheeler House

If you'd like to get a taste of York's long history, but lack the stamina for the full-court Museums of Old York visit (p. 57), here's your best option: Stop by the **Sayward-Wheeler House** ★ at 9 Barrell Lane Extension in York Harbor, run by the group **Historic New England.** In this well-preserved merchant's home dating from 1760, you'll find booty (such as fine china) plundered during the 1745 Siege of Louisbourg, which routed the French out of Nova Scotia. But you'll have to do some planning: The home is open alternate Saturdays only, from June through mid-October; tours are given hourly from 11am to 4pm. Admission is $5 for adults, $4 for seniors, and $2.50 for students—but free if you join Historic New England. For more information, call the home (✆ **207/384-2454**) or the organization's home office in Boston (www.historic newengland.org; ✆ **617/227-3956**).

photographed in the world, is undeniably attractive—and absolutely free to view from the safety of a parking lot set across the swift little inlet that separates it from the mainland. There's little walking to be done, but this is a terrific spot for a picnic; walk a minute downhill and right on Nubble Road to **Dunne's Ice Cream ★★** for some of Maine's best homemade ice cream for dessert. (The lighthouse is lit up for the holiday season around Thanksgiving each year. If you happen to be here in late November inquire about the shuttle from Short Sands Beach out to the vantage point.) For information on additional lighthouses, see "Lighthouses: A Tour Up the Coast," on p. 20 in chapter 2.

On the Water

For a duck's-eye view of the local terrain, visit **Excursions Coastal Maine Outfitting Co.** in Cape Neddick (www.excursionsinmaine.com, © **207/363-0181**). This outfitter offers half- day, daily, and weekly sea-kayak rentals and tours—it costs $60 per adult for a guided half-day excursion, $50 for a child, for example—along the lovely local coastline. For more dramatic paddling, ask about sunrise, sunset, full-moon, and overnight kayaking trips. The shop is located on Route 1, between Ogunquit and York; go north 5 or 6 miles from York's information hut near the turnpike exit.

Beaches in the Yorks

York Beach actually consists of *two* beaches, **Long Sands Beach ★★** and **Short Sands Beach ★**, separated by a rocky headland. Long Sands has views of Nubble Light (see p. 58 above) and boats far out to sea; Short Sands, as the name suggests, is more compact and surrounded by quaintly appealing arcades, hotels, and grand summer homes.

Both beaches have plenty of room for sunning and Frisbees when the tide is out. When the tide is in, though, both become narrow and cramped. Short Sands fronts the honky-tonk town of York Beach, with its candlepin bowling, taffy-pulling machine, and video arcades. It's a better pick for families traveling with kids who have short attention spans. Long Sands runs along Route 1A, directly across from a line of motels, summer homes, and convenience stores. Parking at *both* beaches is metered in summer; pay heed, as enforcement is strict and you must feed the meters with quarters until 9pm, all 7 days of the week. (At the end of summer, though, they decapitate the meters—literally—and parking is subsequently free and plentiful until the next Memorial Day.)

Public restrooms are available at both beaches; other services, including snacks, are provided by local restaurants and vendors.

A Side Trip to South Berwick

It's tiny, it's not on the tourist map, and it's not on the coast, yet little South Berwick, Maine, provides a worthwhile detour back into Maine's colonial—and literary—history. Think about taking a few hours to explore it if raindrops happen to be pelting York Beach and ruining your beach outing.

SPOTLIGHT ON maine diners, PART #1

One thing you'll notice as you traverse the Maine coast is a preponderance of diners.

What gives? Ironically, the greasy spoons and dining cars that sprang up roadside during Maine's post-war auto tourism boom tend these days to be the haunts of fervent locals, who congregate daily in their kaffeeklatsches on the diner stools. Expect a steady stream of hunting caps, thick accents, doughnuts, eggs, and Red Sox or Patriots talk (depending on the season). You'd do well to sample one or two of them while on the road.

Heading north from York to Ogunquit along Route 1, you could easily blow right by the reddish-hut icon that is **Flo's Steamed Hot Dogs** (no phone) in Cape Neddick—a couple of miles north of York, in the middle of nowhere, at a bend in the road—without noticing. But if you crave a winner of a wiener, screech to a halt in the dirt parking lot and give it a whirl. You'll wait in the line, which resembles an assembly line: The steamed dogs here with the secret-recipe house relish are cheap ($2.50) and good, but they can only do them 50 at a time. If your dog's number 51, bring a paperback. There are only six seats, so you'll probably have to eat in the car, too. Come anyway. The hut is closed Wednesdays, and they don't take credit cards—what did you expect?

A little farther north, also on Route 1 but in Wells, the **Maine Diner** (© 207/646-4441) is a classic, though perhaps getting a little too famous for its own good. (They'll page you when a table is ready.) But worry not, there's a reason why they've just passed the "four million served" mark. The lobster pie and hot lobster roll are famous and delicious, as is a plate of baked scallops. Red flannel hash? Pot roast? They've got it—as well as the "Clam-o-rama," a sampler of clam items. They serve wine and beer here, too—very unusual.

In the working-class former milltown of Biddeford, **Palace Diner** (© 207/284-0015) requires you to veer a few blocks off Route 1 as you pass through town. The detour is rewarded by a throwback dining car with just 15 stools. On any given weekend morning, it's a safe bet that half are occupied by diners who've traveled from Portland or farther, brunch pilgrims who come for dishes like light and sweet challah French toast and the gut-buster deluxe breakfast sandwich—with egg, bacon, jalapenos, cheddar, and mayo on a perfectly griddled English muffin. The simple lunch menu of burgers, tuna sandwich, and fried chicken is similarly retro delish.

The two most important structures in town are the late-18th-century **Hamilton House,** 40 Vaughan's Lane (© **207/384-2454**)—a solid riverside home, with fine gardens and grounds—and its contemporary, the **Sarah Orne Jewett House,** 5 Portland Street (© **207/384-2454**), a 1774 Georgian where the famous Maine author lived. Her desk overlooks the village's main crossroads. Both homes are open to the public from June through mid-October, on slightly different schedules. Hamilton House is open Wednesday to Sunday from 11am to 4pm, while the Jewett House is open Friday through Sunday (same hours); tours are offered on the hour at each property. It costs $10 per adult ($9 seniors, $5 students) to visit Hamilton House, and $8 per person ($7 seniors, $4. students) to tour the Jewett House.

If you're looking for some nature, take the kids to **Vaughan Woods State Park** (✆ **207/384-5160**), down Oldsfields Road just off Route 236 (a bit south of the South Berwick town center). Set along the quiet Salmon Falls River, the park features picnic areas and a hiking trail through groves of old-growth pine and hemlock. It's open Memorial Day to Labor Day; the admission fee is $4 per non-Maine resident adult, $1 for seniors and children age 5 to 11.

For golfers, the outstanding **The Links at Outlook** golf course (www.outlookgolf.com; ✆ **207/384-4653**) on Route 4 is a fine, links-style track of bent grass fairways and greens. The greens fees for 18 holes will run you around $55 per person in high summer season; it's cheaper on weekdays, afternoons, and in spring and fall. Carts cost extra.

From York, South Berwick is quickly reached via Route 91 (which shoots west off Route 1 just south of the Maine Turnpike interchange for York). It's a ride of about 20 minutes.

4 OGUNQUIT

15 miles NE of Kittery

Ogunquit (Oh-*gun*-quit) is a busy little beachside town that has attracted vacationers and artists for more than a century. Although it's certainly notable for the abundant and elegant summer-resort architecture, Ogunquit is probably most famous for the 3½-mile white-sand beach, backed by grassy dunes, that dominates the town. This beach serves as the town's front porch, and most everyone drifts over there at least once a day when the sun is shining. As a bonus, a wonderful walking trail known as the **Marginal Way** begins at the beach, then climbs the cliffs above tide pools to great views back onto the sand and ocean.

Ogunquit's fame as an art colony dates from around 1890, when Charles H. Woodbury arrived and declared the place an "artist's paradise." He was soon followed by artists such as Walt Kuhn, Elihu Vedder, and Yasuo Kuniyoshi, not to mention Rudolph Dirks, author of the "Katzenjammer Kids" comic. (During the latter part of the 19th century, the town later found another sort of fame as a quiet destination for gay regional travelers; today, many local enterprises here are still owned by gay proprietors.)

Despite its architectural grace and civility, the town is narrow—there's only one main street—and can become seriously overrun with tourists (and their cars) during peak summer season, especially on weekends. If you don't like crowds, best to visit in the shoulder seasons or simply hit up another destination along the coast. Other advice: If you arrive early in the morning, stake out a spot on the long beach.

Essentials

ARRIVING

Ogunquit is right on U.S. Route 1, exactly midway between York and Wells—which means it's a long way to either of the nearest convenient turnpike exits. Take either exit 7 (York) or exit 19 (Wells) off the Maine Turnpike, a toll road.

Ogunquit

ATTRACTIONS ●
Leavitt Theatre **6**
Ogunquit Museum
  of American Art **22**
Ogunquit Playhouse **16**

ACCOMMODATIONS ■
Beachmere Inn **15**
Cliff House Resort & Spa **23**
Colonial Village Resort **1**
Dunes on the Waterfront **2**
Marginal Way House Hotel **13**
Nellie Littlefield House **10**
Riverside Motel **21**
Studio East Motel **5**
Terrace by the Sea **11**

DINING ◆
Barnacle Billy's **18**
Bread & Roses Bakery **7**
Cove Café **17**
Caffé Prego **12**
Egg & I **3**
Five-O Shore Road **14**
La Pizzeria **9**
MC Perkins Cove **20**
Oarweed **19**
Ogunquit Lobster Pound **4**
Village Food Market **8**

Proceed to U.S. Route 1 and follow it north from York or south from Wells, turning seaward (left if you're traveling south, right if you're coming from the south) at the confusing intersection at the center of town (see below) and follow Shore Road to reach Perkins Cove and the bulk of the shops, accommodations, and eateries. Or, for the best beach access, take the other prong of the intersection to Beach Street.

VISITOR INFORMATION

The **Ogunquit Welcome Center** (www.ogunquit.org; © **207/646-2939**), is on U.S. Route 1, just south of the village center. It's open daily from Memorial Day to Columbus Day (until 8pm on weekends during the peak summer season), and from Monday to Saturday during the off season. Helpfully, it has restrooms.

GETTING AROUND

Ogunquit's entrance is a horrid three-way intersection that seems intentionally designed to cause massive traffic tie-ups. Parking in and around the village is tight and relatively expensive for small-town Maine ($10–$25 per day in various lots). As a result, the town is best navigated on foot or by bike.

A number of trackless "trolleys" (℄ **207/646-1411**)—actually buses—with names like *Dolly* and *Ollie* (you get the idea) run all day from mid-May to Columbus Day between Perkins Cove and the Wells town line to the north, with detours to the sea down Beach and Ocean streets. These trolleys are very handy, and they stop everywhere. (There's a map of stops posted online at **www.ogunquittrolley.com**.) Rides cost $2 one-way (children under 10 $1.50); it's worth the expense to avoid driving and parking hassles and limits.

SPECIAL EVENTS

A pre-Halloween festival in late October, the **Ogunquit Fest,** offers 3 days of arts, crafts, costumes, and a parade; it's best for families with kids. Call ℄ **207/646-2939** for more information.

Where to Stay in Ogunquit

There are many family-owned budget- to moderately-priced motel operations around Ogunquit, especially along Route 1. Try the following three choices for a combination of affordability and amenities. The family-friendly **Colonial Village Resort** (www.colonialvillageresort.com; ℄ **800/422-3341**) on Route 1 is not a resort—but with two pools, a Jacuzzi, tennis court, free doughnuts, coin-op laundries, some weekly rental cottages and apartments, and free rowboats to cross the tidal river to the beach, it's almost a steal for families most of the year. Most rooms have kitchenettes. It's usually open from April until November, with double rooms starting as low as $65; summer rates, however, begin at around $120 per night. Just a few steps from Ogunquit's downtown crossing, the meticulously maintained **Studio East Motel,** 267 Main Street (www.studioeastmotel.com; ℄ **207/646-7297**) is open late March to early December, with peak-season rates running from $139 to $209 double. The rooms are basic, but all have refrigerators, telephones, TVs, and Wi-Fi, and there are a few two-bedroom suites. The quiet **Riverside Motel,** 50 Riverside Lane (www.riversidemotel.com; ℄ **207/646-2741**), has great marina views and Wi-Fi, as well as a convenient footbridge leading directly over the tidal inlet to Perkins Cove, which saves you the parking hassles and fees. Rooms here run $109 to $250 double, depending on the season.

Many locals don't mind getting out of town during the busy summers, so online rentals are plentiful. Try Airbnb and the like for short stays and **Seaside Vacation Rentals** (℄ **207/646-3232;** www.seasiderentals.com) or **Jean Knapp Rentals** (℄ **207/646-4548;** www.jeanknapp.com) to rent weekly.

Beachmere Inn ★★   In a town of motels, simple B&B's, and condos, the Beachmere excels. Operated by the same family since 1937, this quiet, well-run cliff-top inn sprawls across a scenic lawn where repeat visitors have reclined for decades. Nearly every unit gives you an amazing look up or down the beach, and all have kitchenettes. The original Victorian section dates from the 1890s and is the most fun; it's all turrets, big porches, angles, and bright beachy interiors. Next door is the modern Beachmere South, with spacious rooms and plenty of private balconies or patios—those on the end have absolutely knockout views. A new wing (Beachmere West) was added in 2008, with a small but nice little hot tub, exercise room, and children's play area; units in this wing have sitting rooms and bigger bathrooms. Larger groups traveling together should also inquire about several off-property cottages a short walk away. The inn is adjacent to the Marginal Way footpath, which is terrific for walks and beach access. The inn's now open year-round: you can rent snowshoes in winter to (carefully) stroll the path.

62 Beachmere Place, Ogunquit. www.beachmereinn.com. © **800/336-3983** or 207/646-2021. 53 units. June–Aug $190–$295 double, $360–$395 suite, $560 cottage; May and Sept–mid-Nov $90–$220 double, $200–$314 suite, $295–$424 cottage; mid-Nov–May $70–$125 double, $160–$215 suite, $260 cottage. Rates include continental breakfast. 3-night minimum in summer. **Amenities:** Lounge; beach access; children's play room; Jacuzzi; spa; restaurant; free Wi-Fi.

Cliff House ★★★ This complex of modern buildings, replacing a former grand hotel, completed a monster renovation and rebrand in 2016. Keeping up with the ever-expanding southern Maine tourism season, it's now a year-round resort, and it offers some of the best hotel-room ocean views in Maine: nearly a 360-degree panorama, in some cases. There are a number of different styles of rooms, but the overall vibe is clean seaside contemporary, with minimalist art on the walls, digital everything, midcentury-looking folding chairs, and crisp Cuddledown linens. A vanishing-edge pool fronting the sea does indeed seem to disappear into the blue yonder, and there's an upscale restaurant with knockout vistas. The spa and fitness facility, brand-new in 2016, dispenses a wide range of soothing treatments and exercise programs.

591 Shore Rd., Ogunquit. www.cliffhousemaine.com. © **207/361-1000** or 855/502-5433. 227 units. June–Aug $389–$639 double, $729–$1799 suite; Sept–Nov $279–$439 double, $729–$989 suite; Dec–May $209–$379 double, $579–$729 suite. Holiday rates are higher. Packages available. Dogs welcome for $100 fee. **Amenities:** Restaurants; bar; fitness center; Jacuzzi; indoor pool; outdoor pool; fire pits; room service; spa; free Wi-Fi.

The Dunes on the Waterfront ★★ This classic motor court (built circa 1936) has made the transition into the modern luxury age more gracefully than any other vintage motel I've seen. It has one six-unit motel-like building, but most of the rooms are in gabled cottages of white clapboard and green shutters; these have full kitchens and bathrooms. Plenty of old-fashioned charm remains in many of the units, with vintage maple furnishings, oval braided rugs, maple floors, knotty pine paneling, and louvered doors. Most of the cottages also have wood-burning fireplaces. The complex is set on 12 acres, wedged between busy Route 1 and the ocean, but somehow stays quiet and peaceful; Adirondack chairs overlook a lagoon, and guests can borrow a rowboat to get across to the beach.

518 U.S. Rte. 1, Ogunquit. www.dunesmotel.com. © **888/623-0244.** 36 units. $115–$390 double; $205–$575 cottage. Mid-June–mid-Sept 1-week minimum stay in cottages, 3-night minimum the rest of the year; July–Aug 2-week minimum stay in 2-bedroom cottages. Packages available. Closed Nov–late Apr. **Amenities:** Outdoor pool; watersports equipment rental; free Wi-Fi.

Cruising the Wells-Ogunquit axis, foodies will want to check out venerable **Congdon's Doughnuts Family Restaurant & Bakery ★★** (© **207/646-4219**) on Route 1 between the two towns. Clint and Dot "Nana" Congdon moved to Maine and opened a family style restaurant in 1945; Nana's sinkers proved so popular that she relocated the whole operation to Wells 10 years later and went into the doughnut business full-time. Chocolate-chocolate is ever-popular, but you can't go wrong with almost anything else among the dozens of choices—pillowy raised doughnuts; filled blueberry doughnuts; butter crunch, honey-dipped, sugar twist, and chocolate honey doughnuts . . . or one of the seasonal specials such as maple, apple, or pumpkin doughnuts. You can also eat diner meals here, most of which involve fried food and/or breakfast fare. Sure, they added a drive-through window a while back, but this place retains its original character (and that includes the local characters dining inside). The secret? They use lard. Yes, lard. Schedule the EKG now. Congdon's is open Thursday through Sunday, year-round from 6am to 3pm.

Marginal Way House Hotel ★

This simple, old-fashioned compound centers on a four-story, mid-19th-century guesthouse with summery, basic rooms and white-painted furniture; the whole complex is plunked down on a large, grassy lot on a quiet cul-de-sac, and it's hard to believe you're smack in the middle of busy Ogunquit. But you are: the beach and village are each just a few minutes' walk away. Room no. 7, despite its skinny twin beds, has a private porch and canopy and ocean views. The main building is surrounded by four more contemporary buildings that lack charm, but rooms here are mostly comfortable and bright; the "motel" building only has rooms with double beds, but the Wharf House has a cool quietude about it, enhanced by white linens and shady trees. Some units have little decks with views; all rooms have refrigerators and televisions, but none have phones. The property also maintains some one- and two-bedroom efficiency apartments (some have minimum stays); inquire when booking.

22-24 Wharf Lane, Ogunquit. www.marginalwayhouse.com. © **207/646-8801.** 30 units (1 with private bathroom down hall). Early June–Labor Day $129–$299 double; mid-Apr–early June and early Sept–mid-Nov $79–$209 double. $15 extra charge for more than 2 people (except kids under 3). Closed mid-Nov–mid-Apr. Pets allowed off season only; advance notice required. **Amenities**: Free Wi-Fi.

Nellie Littlefield Inn & Spa ★★

Of the many B&Bs and boardinghouses filling downtown Ogunquit, this might be the friendliest. The handsome 1889 home stands at the edge of the town's compact commercial district, and features elegant Queen Anne–style detailing. All rooms are carpeted and feature a mix of modern and antique reproduction furnishings; all have refrigerators. Rooms to the rear have private decks, although views are limited—mostly looking out on a motel next door. The most spacious room is the third-floor J. H. Littlefield suite, with a fireplace in both the bedrooms and living area, while the most unique unit is probably the circular Grace Little-field room in the upper turret, overlooking the street. The basement features a compact fitness room. Hospitality remains a strong selling point here.

27 Shore Rd., Ogunquit. www.nliogunquit.com. © **207/646-1692.** 8 units. June–Sept $139–$259 double; Mar–May and Oct–Dec $139–$169 double. Holiday rates higher. Rates include full breakfast. 2- to 5-night minimums depending on room and season. Weekends only Jan–Feb. No children. **Amenities:** Fitness center; Jacuzzi (few units); outdoor hot tub; spa; free Wi-Fi.

Terrace by the Sea ★ Overlooking Ogunquit Beach, this cluster of six modern buildings offers wide-open ocean views from many rooms. A land-scaped lawn dotted with deck chairs overlooks the water, while a boardwalk leads to the beach, a 5-minute walk away. There's also a nice heated outdoor pool, free Wi-Fi, and excellent customer service. Rooms of varying size and price range are simply furnished with colonial reproductions; eight rooms have kitchenettes, and many have private decks. Children ages 5 and under are welcome in the off season.

23 Wharf Lane, Ogunquit. www.terracebythesea.com. © **207/646-3232.** 61 units. Late May–Oct $87–$312 double; late Mar–late May and Nov–mid-Dec $76–$192 double. Closed Jan–Mar. **Amenities:** Outdoor pool, free Wi-Fi.

Where to Eat in Ogunquit

Excepting Portland, Ogunquit has got to be the latest-open-hours town in Maine: Amazingly, many places stay open until 10 or 11pm in summer.

Where the main Route 1 strip meets Perkins Cove Road, you'll find a tre-mendous variety of bakeries, coffee shops, markets, and restaurants. **Bread & Roses Bakery,** 246 Main St. (© **207/646-4227**), skillfully turns out cupcakes, peanut-butter-and-chocolate cake, raspberry mousse, cookies, and the like; there's outdoor seating as well. The **Village Food Market,** 230 Main St. (© **207/646-2122**), stocks good wines, ready-to-go meals, and staples, and it also has a small deli; try the house red-eye coffee.

There are also several lobster pounds packed into and around the little down-town, most of them seasonal; try the **Ogunquit Lobster Pound** (504 Main St.; © **207/646-2516**), **Oarweed** (65 Perkins Cove Rd.; © **207/646-4022**), or **Barnacle Billy's** (50 Perkins Cove Rd.; © **800/866-5575** or 207/646-5575). For a casual din-ner, friendly **La Pizzeria**, 239 Main St. (© **207/646-1143**), dishes out dependable sandwiches, meatballs, and pizza pies—plus it stays open later than just about anyplace else in Maine (usually until 11pm in summer). Like most places in town, though, it's closed in winter.

Breakfast in Ogunquit

Standout breakfast joints abound in Ogunquit. The excellent **Caffé Prego** (see p. 68) recently absorbed much of the menu and kitchen staff of the dearly departed Amore Breakfast, an Ogunquit institution for a quarter-century. Also check out the reliable **Egg & I,** 501 Main St. (© **207/646-8777**; no credit cards), and the little **Cove Café,** 4 Oar-weed Rd. (© **207/646-2422**), near Per-kins Cove.

Caffé Prego ★ ITALIAN BISTRO   Already beloved for its brick oven pizzas and classic pasta dishes like a rich Bolognese and veal saltimbocca. Caffé Prego added breakfast in 2016 after absorbing some of the staff and menu from a popular café down the road, the much-beloved Amore Breakfast. Expect variations on the eggs Benedict theme and a big slate of creative, yummy omelets. The outdoor seating area has lovely landscaping and over-looks the heart of town. Word to the wise: Caffé Prego is known for its des-serts, from more than 25 flavors of creamy, house-made gelato to airy and rich éclairs and tartufatas.

44 Shore Rd., Ogunquit. www.cafeprego.com. © **207/646-7734**. Breakfast items $7–$15. Sandwiches $10–$20. Dinner entrees $14–$24. Daily 7:30am–9:30pm. Closed late Oct to early Apr.

Five-O Shore Road ★★ NEW AMERICAN   A fine choice if you're looking for a meal you can brag about without spending a whole day's vaca-tion budget. Chef James Walter got a 2016 Chef of the Year nod from the state's restaurant association; his menu is eclectic in a brasserie/supper-clubby kind of way. You might order terrific steak frites or a roasted lamb loin, but also great clam chowder and pasta dishes. Of course, you can get a Maine lobster in season, too, perhaps served with shaved truffles and cream. There's also a cool cocktail lounge with a long list of creative martinis. It's like the Rat Pack wanted a casual coastal place to kick back in.

50 Shore Rd., Ogunquit. www.five-oshoreroad.com. © **207/646-5001.** Reservations strongly recommended in summer. Small plates $9–$18, main courses $20–$40. May–Sept Mon–Sat 5–9pm, Sun 10am–2pm and 5–9pm; call for hours outside peak season.

MC Perkins Cove ★★ SEAFOOD/NEW AMERICAN   Chef-partners Mark Gaier and Clark Frasier endeared themselves to Ogunquit (and picked up a coveted James Beard Award) with a groundbreaking, white tablecloth, farm-to-table restaurant called Arrows back in the '90s. It closed years ago, but not before "M" and "C" opened this sleek bistro on the best real estate in town. MC Perkins Cove manages to be fun rather than stuffy. Okay, no bath-ing suits are allowed in the dining room, but still: Expect big food, even on the "small" plates. Lobster rolls, chopped salads, calamari, oysters on half shell, and crab cakes give way to more sophisticated starters such as mussels in curry sauce, smoked trout rillette, and country ham paté. Entrees might include steamed lobster, sesame-encrusted trout, Kobe burgers, grilled tuna, hanger steak, or a piece of plank-roasted fish, plus one of the so-labeled "evil carbos" (cheesy mashed potatoes, onion rings, and so forth). Desserts are wonderful: brown-butter brownies with vanilla ice cream, burnt orange cara-mel, and candied orange peel; toffee pudding with bourbon caramel; a bit-tersweet chocolate cake with chocolate sauce and pistachio crème anglaise; or peppermint stick ice cream with cookies.

111 Perkins Cove Rd., Ogunquit. www.mcperkinscove.com. © **207/646-6263.** Reser-vations recommended. Lunch entrees $11–$25; dinner entrees $22–$34. Late May–mid-Oct daily 11:30am–9pm; rest of year closed Mon and Tues. Closed Jan.

Exploring Ogunquit

The village center is good for an hour or two of browsing among the boutiques, or sipping a cappuccino at one of the several coffee emporia. From the village, you can walk to scenic Perkins Cove along **Marginal Way ★★★**, a gorgeous mile-long ocean-side pathway that departs across from the Seacastles Resort on Shore Road. En route, it passes tide pools, pocket beaches, and rocky, fissured bluffs, all worth exploring. This is one of Maine's best public trails. The seascapes can be spectacular, but the Way can also get extremely crowded during fair-weather weekends or toward sunset. Early morning is a good time to avoid crowds.

Perkins Cove ★, accessible either from Marginal Way or by driving south on Shore Road and veering left at the Y-shaped intersection, is a small, well-protected harbor that attracts many visitors and is often heavily congested. A handful of galleries, restaurants, and T-shirt shops cater to the tourist trade from a cluster of quaint buildings between harbor and sea. (If teeming crowds and tourist enterprises are *not* the reason you came to Maine, steer clear of Perkins Cove.) An intriguing pedestrian drawbridge is operated by whoever happens to be handy.

Ogunquit Museum of American Art ★★★ MUSEUM   Not far from Perkins Cove, this is one of the best—and most beautiful—small art museums in the nation (that's not just me talking; the director of New York's Metropolitan Museum of Art said so, too). It's only open in summer and fall, however. Set back from the road in a grassy glen overlooking the rocky shore, the museum's spectacular view initially overwhelms the artwork as visitors walk through the door. But stick around for a few minutes—the changing exhibits in this architecturally engaging modern building of cement block, slate, and glass will get your attention soon enough. Its curators have a track record of staging superb shows and attracting national attention. The permanent collection holds work by seascape master Marsden Hartley and many members of the Ogunquit Colony, including Woodbury, Hamilton Easter Field, and Robert Laurent.

543 Shore Rd., Ogunquit. www.ogunquitmuseum.org. © **207/646-4909.** $10 adults, $9 seniors and students; children under 12 free. May–Oct, daily 10am–5pm.

Beaches in Ogunquit

Ogunquit's **main beach ★★** is more than 3 miles long, though its width varies with the tides. This beach appeals to everyone: the livelier scene at the south end near the town itself; the more remote and unpopulated stretches to the north, with their sand dunes; and the clusters of summer homes that lie beyond. The most popular access point is the foot of Beach Street, which runs into Ogunquit Village. This beach ends at a sandy spit, where the Ogunquit River flows into the sea; here you'll find a handful of informal restaurants. It's also the most crowded part of the beach. Less congested options are **Footbridge Beach** (turn on Ocean Avenue off Route 1 north of the village center) and **Moody Beach** (turn on Eldridge Avenue in Wells). Restrooms and changing rooms are maintained at all three beaches.

Ogunquit Arts & Entertainment

For evening entertainment, head for the **Ogunquit Playhouse** ★ (© 207/646-2402), a 750-seat summer-stock theater right on U.S. Route 1 (just south of the main town intersection) with an old-style look that has garnered a solid reputation for its careful, serious attention to stagecraft. The theater has entertained Ogunquit since 1933, attracting noted actors such as Bette Davis, Tallulah Bankhead, and Sally Struthers performing in shows like *A Chorus Line* and *Guys and Dolls*. Performance tickets generally cost in the range of $40 to $80 per person, and the season runs from May through December.

Anchoring Main Street, the humble **Leavitt Theatre** (www.leavittheatre.com; © **207/646-3123**), at 259 Main Street, dates to 1923; its arched marquee is something of a local landmark. Locals so adore the indie moviehouse and performance space that they scraped up $60,000 to save the place a few years back. On a rainy day, catch everything from first-run popcorn flicks to silent film festivals; live acts include nationally touring comedians, burlesque shows, and local rock bands. Did I mention the place serves beer and wine?

A Side Trip to Laudholm Farm

About 8 miles north of Ogunquit (bear right from Route 1 onto Route 9 just north of the beach town of Wells) is the **Wells Reserve at Laudholm** ★ (© **207/646-4521**), a historic saltwater farm owned by the nonprofit Laudholm Trust since 1986. The 1,600-acre property—locals just call it "Laudholm farm"—was originally the summer home of 19th-century railroad baron George Lord but is now used for estuarine research. The farm has 7 miles of trails through diverse ecosystems, which range from salt marsh to forest to dunes. A visitor center in the regal Victorian farmhouse will get you oriented. Tours are available, or you can explore the grounds on your own. Parking costs $5 per adult daily from Memorial Day through Labor Day, $1 per guest 6 to 16. You pay by donation the rest of the year. There's never an admission charge to the grounds or visitor center, and the 7 miles of trails here are open daily from 7am to dusk. The visitor center is open 10am to 4pm daily (closed weekends in the off season).

The farm is reached by turning east from Route 1 on Laudholm Farm Road at the blinking light just north of Harding Books. Bear left at the fork, then turn right into the farm's entrance.

THE KENNEBUNKS ★★

10 miles NE of Ogunquit

"The Kennebunks" consist of the side-by-side villages of **Kennebunk** and **Kennebunkport,** both situated along the shores of small rivers and both claiming a portion of rocky coast. The region was first settled in the mid-1600s and flourished after the American Revolution, when ship captains, boat builders, and prosperous merchants constructed imposing, solid homes. The Kennebunks are famed for their striking historical architecture and expansive beaches; make time to explore both.

Kennebunk & Kennebunkport

ACCOMODATIONS ■
Beach House Inn **18**
Captain Jefferds Inn **12**
The Captain Lord
    Mansion **11**
Franciscan Guest
    House **15**
Hidden Pond **3**
Kennebunk Inn **1**
The Lodge
    on the Cove **17**
Lodge
    at Turbat's Creek **13**
Maine Stay Inn
    & Cottages **10**
The Tides Beach Club **3**
White Barn Inn **16**
The Yachtsman Lodge
    & Marina **14**

DINING ◆
The Clam Shack **9**
Hurricane **7**
Nunan's Lobster Hut **4**
Pier 77 **4**
Toroso **2**
The Wayfarer **4**
White Barn Inn **16**

ATTRACTIONS ●
Dock Square **8**
First Families Kennebunkport Museum **5**
South Congregational Church **6**

A quick primer: Kennebunk proper is mostly clustered around Route 1, but it stretches towards the coast to the junction of Route 9 and Route 35, an area known as Lower Village. This is where you'll find the **White Barn Inn** (p. 77), **Toroso** (p. 77), and much of the town's hospitality infrastructure. Just across the Kennebunk River from the Lower Village begins Kennebunkport. But for the river, Kennebunkport's trim downtown, called Dock Square, is indistinguishable from the Lower Village, leading to frequent confusion about which town one is actually in (which is why Mainers tend to refer to both towns as a unit). On the north side of the river, Kennebunkport extends eastward to take in both million-dollar oceanfront homes (including the Bush family estate at Walker's Point) and the mellower (and scenic) fishing village of **Cape Porpoise** (see p. 81).

While summer is the busy season along the coast, winter has its charms: The grand architecture is better seen through leafless trees. When the snow flies, guests find solace in front of a fire at one of the inviting inns.

Essentials

ARRIVING

Kennebunk is just off exit 25 of the Maine Turnpike; follow signs east into town. You can also get here by taking Route 1 from York and Ogunquit. To reach Kennebunkport, exit for Kennebunk and continue through town on Port Road (Route 35) 3½ miles. At the traffic light, turn left and cross the small bridge.

VISITOR INFORMATION

The **Kennebunk-Kennebunkport Chamber of Commerce,** 17 Western Avenue (www.visitthekennebunks.com; © **207/967-0857**), can answer questions year-round by phone or at its offices in Lower Village beside the H.B. Provisions grocery store. The **Kennebunkport Information Center** (© **207/967-8600**), operated by an association of local businesses, is off Dock Square (next to Ben & Jerry's) and is open daily in summer and fall.

GETTING AROUND

Several higher-end inns in the Kennebunks offer free shuttles downtown. Otherwise, a local "trolley" (actually a bus) makes several convenient stops in and around the two towns and also serves the best of the local beaches; it picks up passengers about once per hour from 10am until 4pm (until 3pm in spring and fall). It's expensive, though: The fare comes in the form of a day pass costing $16 per adult or $6 per child. At least the pass includes unlimited opportunities to jump on and off the trolley during the day you are using it. Call © **207/967-3686** for more details, or check the trolley's schedule online at **www.intowntrolley.com**.

Where to Stay in the Kennebunks

Lodging in the Kennebunks tends towards the stately and upscale, and most of it is crowded around the mouth of the Kennebunk River, near the twin vacation epicenters of Lower Village and Dock Square. Since 2009, a chi-chi developer concern called the Kennebunkport Resort Collection has been reshaping—some would say elevating—the hospitality scene. KRC properties like **Hidden Pond** (p. 74), **The Tides Beach Club** (www.tidesbeachclub maine.com; © **800/632-3224**), and the **Lodge on the Cove** (www.lodgeonthe cove.com; © **800/879-5778**), among five other properties, offer boutique luxury at peak season rates that begin at $300 a night and spiral upwards from there. Some locals resent the gradual chic-ening of the Kennebunks, but there's no denying the attractiveness of the properties.

There are still some budget options in the Kennebunks, clustered away from the main tourism district, along Route 1 and the interstate in the mainland section of Kennebunk. A surprisingly reasonable choice inland is the **Kennebunk Inn** (www.thekennebunkinn.com; © **207/985-3351**), at 45 Main Street, set in a former private home built in 1799. Cozy doubles go for $220–$245 in July and August, $129–$180 in June and September, and even cheaper in the off-season. The in-house restaurant, **Academe**, is a known for its adventurous lobster applications—lobster pot pie, lobster "lo'Maine," and the like.

KENNEBUNK

Beach House Inn ★   This is a good choice if you'd like to be close to the people-watching, dog-walking action on and above Kennebunk Beach. The inn was built in 1891 but has been extensively modernized and expanded. The rooms here aren't necessarily historic, but most have Victorian furnishings and historic-feeling touches like wrought-iron bedframes, plus nice framed photographs of beach landscapes. Suites have panoramic views of the ocean. But the main draw here might be the lovely porch, where you can stare out at the pebble beach across the road and idly watch the bikers and in-line skaters. The inn has bikes and canoes for guests to use and provides beach chairs and towels.

211 Beach Ave., Kennebunk. www.beachhseinn.com. ℂ **207/967-3850.** 34 units. $129–$249 double; $200–$560 cottage and suite. Rates include continental breakfast. Packages available. 2-night minimum on weekends. Closed Jan–March. **Amenities:** Bikes; canoes; spa; fitness studio; free Wi-Fi in common areas.

Franciscan Guest House ★   This former dormitory on the 200-acre grounds of St. Anthony's Monastery is a unique lodging choice. The 60 or so rooms are basic and clean, with private bathrooms; guests can stroll the lovely riverside grounds or walk to Dock Square, about 10 minutes away. There's also a decent pool. It's not nearly as inexpensive as it used to be, though—the brothers have wised up to modern capitalism, and rates have escalated as a result. (They even have suites now.) Nevertheless, the place is still a fairly good bargain, especially given the fine walking trails and its position close to local beaches and restaurants.

28 Beach Ave., Kennebunk. www.franciscanguesthouse.com. ℂ **207/967-4865.** 60 units. $59–$179 double; $89–$249 suite. Rates include continental breakfast. Closed mid-Dec–mid-March. **Amenities:** Outdoor pool; free Wi-Fi.

White Barn Inn ★★★   As it has long done, the venerable White Barn goes the extra mile and sets a standard to which other resorts can only hope to aspire. This is arguably the state's best inn-style lodging, with its best inn dining (see p. 77). Upon checking in, guests are shown to a parlor and served a drink, while valets gather luggage and park cars. The atmosphere here is distinctly European, with an emphasis on service. Rooms are individually decorated in an upscale country style that's been recently recast to reflect the color schemes of the nearby sea. Many units have wood-burning fireplaces and Jacuzzis; renovations in 2016 include new double walk-in showers and marble tubs. Suites (in an outbuilding beside the main inn) border on spectacular, each with a distinct color theme and flatscreen television, whirlpool, or similar perks. There are plenty of other amenities such as fresh flowers daily, turndown service, an attractive spa, a lovely outdoor swimming pool, and complimentary afternoon scone service. A handful of cottages, on the Kennebunk River across the road, are cozy and nicely equipped with modern kitchens and bathrooms.

37 Beach Ave., Kennebunk. (¼ mile east of junction of rtes. 9 and 35). www.whitebarninn. com. ℂ **207/967-2321.** 26 units, 4 cottages. $290–$625 double; $440–$950 suite; $570–$1,160 cottage. Rates include afternoon tea. 2-night minimum weekends; 3-night minimum holiday weekends. **Amenities:** Restaurant, bar, free bikes; free canoes; concierge; conference rooms; outdoor heated pool; valet parking; room service; free Wi-Fi.

KENNEBUNKPORT

Captain Jefferds Inn ★   This 1804 Federal home is filled with fine antiques, and while it's a short walk to Dock Square, guests may need persuading to emerge from their rooms once they've settled in. Among the best is the Wiscasset, with a roomy sitting area and its own indoor garden. All of the units now have televisions, while the Arundel and Baxter both have whirlpool tubs. The price range reflects the varying room sizes, but even the smallest rooms—like the Katahdin, with views of the town—are comfortable and exceed the usual Maine B&B experience. Bright common rooms on the first floor offer nice lounging spaces. An elaborate breakfast is served before a fire on cool days, or outside on the terrace if good summer weather permits.

5 Pearl St. Kennebunkport. www.captainjeffersinn.com. ℂ **800/839-6844** or 207/967-2311. 16 units. Memorial Day–Oct $249–$439 double; rest of year $189–$352 double. Rates include full breakfast. 2-night minimum summer weekends. Packages available. Dogs in carriage house only, $30 per pet, by advance reservation. **Amenities:** Wine service; free Wi-Fi.

The Captain Lord Mansion ★★★   The Captain Lord is one of the most architecturally distinguished inns in Maine, housed in a pale-yellow Federal-style home on a shady lawn above the river. This is the genuine article, with grandfather clocks, Chippendale highboys, and a broad brick fireplace. There's also a conference room with a sofa and TV. Up the elliptical staircase are the rooms, furnished in splendid antiques and gas fireplaces. Among the best: the Excelsior, a large corner room with a massive four-poster bed, love seat, and a two-person Jacuzzi; the Hesper, with a big stained-glass window in the bathroom; and the Merchant, a spacious first-floor suite that pampers you with a large Jacuzzi and two fireplaces. Four rooms are in the Garden House annex, a gray clapboard home behind the main inn, where guests are served breakfast at a long table in the colonial-style kitchen; this building is less opulent but still well appointed.

6 Pleasant St., Kennebunkport. www.captainlord.com. ℂ **800/522-3141** or 207/967-3141. 20 units. $169–$389 double; $299–$599 suite. Rates include full breakfast. 2-night minimum weekends and holidays year-round (some holidays 3-night minimum). No children 11 and under. **Amenities:** Lounge; conference room; free Wi-Fi.

Hidden Pond ★★★   It's not easy to pull off crunchy carefree rusticity across a resort that costs more per night than many urban monthly rents. And make no mistake, Kennebunkport's Hidden Pond is trying extremely hard. The manicured organic farm in the middle of the wooded cottage campus? The rough-hewn Adirondack chairs surrounding the nightly bonfire? Even the cottages, with their riverstone fireplaces, screen porches, outdoor showers, and (would you believe) siding? It's an achievement for a place to seem this authentically bucolic and homespun when, in fact, you're surrounded by luxurious details and perks. The spa, the two heated outdoor pools (one is adults-only), and the vast weekly activity schedule (Pilates and yoga sessions, ice cream socials, watercolor clinics, mixology lessons) are among the reminders that this is a chi-chi resort and not some kind of bougie granola commune. The entrees at **Earth**, the on-site farm-to-table restaurant, are exquisite, and it's the nicest barn you'll ever have dinner in.

354 Goose Rocks Rd., Kennebunkport. www.hiddenpondmaine.com. © **207/967-9050.** 44 cottage units. $288–$869 1-bedroom; $508–$1629 2-bedroom. 3-night minimum Jul–Aug. Packages available. **Amenities:** Restaurant; bars; free bikes; beach shuttle; golf cart rentals; kids programs; fitness center; spa; two outdoor heated pools; free Wi-Fi.

Lodge at Turbat's Creek ★

This simple, clean motel isn't exactly a "lodge," but it does sit in a quiet residential neighborhood an easy 5-minute drive from Dock Square. It's a good value, if dated, in a town that usually gives you sticker shock. The grounds are attractive and endowed with Adirondack chairs; the inn also supplies free mountain bikes for guests who want to cruise to town, and there's a big, seasonally open heated pool as well. Rooms, on two floors, are standard motel size. They're decorated in rustic pine furniture and painted cheerfully. The continental breakfast can be taken outside, on the lawn, in good weather.

7 Turbat's Creek Rd., Kennebunkport. www.lodgeatturbatscreek.com. © **207/967-8700.** 27 units. $79–$169 double; holidays $89–$189 double. Rates include continental breakfast. Closed Dec–Apr. Pets allowed; inquire before arriving. **Amenities:** Free use of mountain bikes; heated outdoor pool; free Wi-Fi.

Maine Stay Inn and Cottages ★

Innkeepers Judi and Walter Hauer have maintained a strong sense of history in their 1860 home and its associated cottages. The decor in the main house is traditional, without going overboard (note the exceptional staircase in the main hall); the cottages, arrayed along the property's perimeter, skew a little more contemporary. Constructed during the 1950s, they've been thoroughly updated with small kitchens and fireplaces in all but a few rooms. Towels, umbrellas, chairs, and town parking passes make for easy beachgoing. The full breakfast is very good—it includes spinach frittata and fresh fruit—and can be delivered to most rooms if you like. Stressed? Most of the cottage rooms have Jacuzzis.

34 Maine St., Kennebunkport. www.mainestayinn.com. © **207/967-2117.** 18 units. $159–$450 double and cottage. Rates include full breakfast. 2-night minimum stay on weekends; 3 nights on major holiday weekends. **Amenities:** Free Wi-Fi.

The Yachtsman Lodge & Marina ★★

River views, proximity to Dock Square, and value are the selling points at this airy spot right off the marina. Nice touches abound, such as down comforters, granite-topped vanities, high ceilings, CD players, and French doors that open onto patios just above the river. While rooms are all standard motel size and on one level, their simple, classical styling is far superior to anything you'll find at a chain motel. And the service is seriously kicked up a notch.

59 Ocean Ave., Kennebunkport. www.yachtsmanlodge.com. © **207/967-2511.** 30 units. $109–$329 double. Rates include continental breakfast. 2-night minimum stay on weekends and holidays. Packages available. **Amenities:** Free bikes and canoes; free Wi-Fi in common areas.

Where to Eat in the Kennebunks

Those looking for a quick lobster have a couple of options in the Kennebunkport area, although the prices tend to be a bit more expensive than at other casual lobster spots farther north along the coast. **Nunan's Lobster Hut** (© **207/967-4362**), Route 9 north of Kennebunkport at Cape Porpoise (see p. 81), is a classic lobster shack, often crowded with diners and full of atmosphere, which helps make up for disappointments such as potato chips (rather than a baked potato) served with the lobster dinner. No reservations are taken, nor are credit cards accepted; it's open daily for dinner, starting at 5pm.

The Clam Shack ★ SEAFOOD   A Kennebunks institution, found right on the bridge separating the Lower Village from Dock Square, The Clam Shack's biggest claim to fame may be its lobster roll. Served on a round yeast roll (a break from the traditional split-top hot dog bun), the Clam Shack roll comes with butter, mayo, or both, complementing fresh-off-the-boat, saltwater-boiled lobster. And, crucially, they get the ratio right: plenty of meat with overwhelming the balance with the toasted bun. Light and fresh, the namesake fried clams are worth stopping for too (get 'em by the half-pint, pint, or quart).

2 Western Ave., Kennebunk. www.theclamshack.net. © **207/967-3321.** Sandwiches $5–$19; seafood baskets $16–$30. Daily 11am–8pm.

Hurricane ★ AMERICAN/SEAFOOD   The Kennebunks' fine-dining old guard, Hurricane hasn't missed a step in some three decades. Lunch might start with a cup of lobster chowder, small plates of carpaccio or mussels, a lobster Cobb salad, or oysters Rockefeller; the main course could be a Cubano sandwich or a "Maine Surf & Turf" burger (with lobster meat, natch). Local seafood shines among the dinner entrees, which run to such items as a Mediterranean-inflected, lobster-based cioppino, roasted garlic shrimp, or terrific seared scallops with quinoa. Finish with desserts such as vanilla bean crème brûlée, legit Maine blueberry pie, panna cotta, or s'mores.

29 Dock Sq., Kennebunkport. www.hurricanerestaurant.com. © **207/967-1111.** Reservations recommended. Main courses $22–$50; small plates $10–$17. Daily 11:30am–10:30pm weekends (9:30pm weekdays). Closed Jan–March.

Pier 77 Restaurant ★★ REGIONAL   Under the steady hand of owners Peter and Kate Morency—and thanks to Peter's training at the Culinary Institute of America and 20 years in top kitchens in Boston and San Francisco—Pier 77 has become that rare combination of a tourist destination and a locals' favorite in Cape Porpoise (see p. 81). Lunches skew toward slightly upscale comfort food such as barbecue, spaghetti and meatballs, cheddar burgers, and fried clams. At dinner it's again about traditional favorites (pasta, steak, and lobster), but there are also some slightly more adventurous dishes: housemade dolmas or a tomato-y seafood stew, for instance. The restaurant has racked up quite a few awards of excellence from *Wine Spectator*. Worth noting: a casual section of the restaurant known as the Ramp Bar & Grill stays open all day long, even between lunch and dinner service, offering lighter meals.

Kennebunk Beach is a fine spot for a picnic, with long sands and good waves. There are no shops on the beach, so before you go, pick up supplies at **H.B. Provisions** (© **207/967-5762**), in a grand old country store building near the Western Avenue bridge linking the two Kennebunks: it's very well stocked with local microbrews, baked goods, and groceries. Plus there's a deli fixing sandwiches and lobster rolls (those go fast).

77 Pier Rd., Cape Porpoise (Kennebunkport). www.pier77restaurant.com. © **207/967-8500.** Reservations recommended. Main courses lunch $14–$22, dinner $14–$32. Wed–Sun 11:30am–2:30pm and 5–8:30pm (Ramp Bar & Grill 11:30am–9pm).

Toroso ★★★ SPANISH TAPAS   New to the Kennebunks scene in 2016, Toroso is the hometown effort of chef Shannon Bard, whose Portland restaurant, Zapoteca, has been one of Maine's best since it opened in 2011. Here, in a dim, mod dining room with an open kitchen, Bard indulges her inner tapas purist, with a menu built around small plates of almost exclusively Spanish specialties. It's divided into a few entrees, a short selection of cold dishes, and a longer one of hot dishes: Standouts on the latter include oxtail-stuffed piquillo peppers and melt-in-your mouth lamb meatballs with sherry cream. The rotating selections of cheeses and charcuterie are also mouthwatering, deftly selected and exquisitely plated. Tap wines favor oenophiles who'd like to taste their way through a few glasses. Downstairs, the Salud Bistro does take-out soups, salads, sandwiches, and bakery goods.

149 Port Rd., Kennebunk. www.torosorestaurant.com. © **207/204-0544.** Small plates $8–$15; entrees $12–$29. Mon–Thurs 4:30–10:30pm; Fri–Sat 4:30–11pm; Sun brunch 11am–3pm, dinner 4:30–9pm.

The Wayfarer ★★ CONTEMPORARY DINER   Over the years this building has housed a long progression of mediocre seaside diners; not until owners Scott and Dee Lewis took over in 2013 was this cozy restaurant itself worth a detour to Cape Porpoise (see p. 81). Grab a table or a seat at the six-stool bar and tuck into Southern-tinged comfort food with contemporary twists. The place is probably most known for breakfasts, and the morning menu includes terrific benedicts (lobster/bacon/spinach, smoked salmon, corned beef hash) as well as biscuits and gravy with housemade sausage. High praise for the thinly sliced home fries. Lunch and dinner are, at turns, pubby and down-home classic: great fish and chips, sturdy burgers, meat loaf, chicken and waffles. Oh, and if the menu isn't homey and picnicky enough, the Wayfarer is BYOB.

2 Pier Rd., Cape Porpoise (Kennebunkport). www.wayfarercapeporpoise.com. © **207/967-8961.** Reservations recommended. Breakfast entrees $10–$15; lunch entrees $7–$15; dinner entrees $14–$31. Daily 7am–2pm, 5–9pm.

White Barn Inn ★★★ REGIONAL/NEW AMERICAN   The centerpiece of the White Barn Inn (see p. 73), this classy dining room—carved out of, yes,

Ocean Drive from Dock Square to **Walkers Point ★** and beyond is lined with opulent summer homes overlooking surf and rocky shore. You'll likely recognize the family compound of the former Presidents Bush right out on Walkers Point when you arrive. If it's not familiar from the time it has spent in the national spotlight, look for crowds with telephoto lenses. If they're not out, look for a shingle-style secret service booth at the head of a driveway. That's the place. There's nothing to do here, though, but park for a minute, snap a picture, and then push on.

a barn—attracts gourmands from far and wide. The space is half the fun, with its soaring interior and an eclectic collection of country antiques displayed in a hayloft; window displays are changed with the seasons. Chef Derek Bissonnette took over in 2015 from longtime chef Jonathan Cartwright, and he's continued his predecessor's traditions of changing up the menu frequently and privileging local produce, fish, and game: Recent options on the prix-fixe menu included a Guinea hen roulade with foraged mushroom risotto and a lobster fettuccini with carrot, ginger, snow peas, and cognic butter. Fresh, terrific intermezzo courses of fruit soups or sorbets are still a standard. The tasting menu is similarly seasonal, if a bit more exotic (think smoked bone marrow with bacon jam and chimichurri) and paired with selections from a first-in-class wine cellar. Service is astonishingly attentive and knowledgeable, capping the experience. A new, more casual bistro next door is meant to appeal to more casual diners (there's no dress code, for instance), but it's hard to beat the original dining room. Still one of Maine's best meals.

37 Beach Ave., Kennebunk. (¼ mile east of junction of routes 9 and 35). www.white barninn.com. ℂ **207/967-2321.** Reservations recommended. Fixed-price dinner $125; tasting menu $165 per person. Mon–Thurs 6:00–9:30pm; Fri 5:30–9:30pm. Closed 2 weeks in Jan.

Exploring Kennebunk

Inland, just off the turnpike, Kennebunk's downtown is a dignified, compact commercial center of white clapboard and brick. If you're a history buff, the **Brick Store Museum ★**, 117 Main St. (www.brickstoremuseum.org; ℂ **207/985-4802**) should be your first stop in town. The museum hosts showings of historical art and artifacts throughout the summer, switching to contemporary art in the off season. It also holds considerable local archives. The museum is housed in a former brick store plus three adjacent buildings, all renovated and re-polished. Adult admission costs $7.50, seniors $6, and kids age 6–16 $3. Half-hour **walking tours ★** of the downtown cost $5 per person additional. (They're a must, if you have time and interest.) The museum is open Tuesday to Friday 10am to 4:30pm, Saturdays from 10am to 1pm.

When en route to or from the coast, be sure to note the extraordinary homes that line Port Road (Route 35). This includes the famously elaborate **Wedding**

Cake House ★, which you should be able to identify all on your own. Local lore claims that the house was built by a guilt-ridden ship captain who left for sea before his bride could enjoy a proper wedding cake.

Exploring Kennebunkport

Kennebunkport is the summer home of former President George Bush (the elder), whose family has summered here for decades, and it has the tweedy, upper-crust feel that one might expect of the place. This historic village, whose streets were laid out during days of travel by boat and horse, is subject to traffic jams. If the municipal lot off the square is full, go north on North Street a few minutes to the free long-term lot and catch the trolley back into town. Or walk back—it's a pleasant walk of 10 or 15 minutes from the satellite lot back to Dock Square.

Dock Square has a bustling, mercantile feel to it, with low buildings of mixed vintages and styles. The boutiques in the area are attractive, and many feature creative artworks and crafts. But sometimes it gets a little overcrowded or tacky here. Kennebunkport's *real* attraction is found in the surrounding blocks and side streets, where the side streets are lined with one of the nation's richest assortments of Early American homes. These neighborhoods are especially ripe with examples of Federal-style homes; many have been converted to fine B&Bs (see "Where to Stay," p. 72).

First Families Kennebunkport Museum ★ MUSEUM   Situated on Maine Street at the head of Spring Street, this imposing Greek Revival house was built in 1853 with sturdy Doric columns and remains a Victorian-era dream. Known locally as "White Columns" or "the Nott house," for its long-time owners, the house remained untouched by the Nott family through the years and was donated to the local historical society with the stipulation that it remain forever unchanged. The period furniture, wallpapers, and rugs will amaze you if you're into that era. In-house tours run about 40 minutes, or from July through Columbus Day, you can take **walking tours** ★ departing from here—they're some of the best on the Maine coast.

8 Maine St., Kennebunkport. www.kennebunkporthistoricalsociety.com. ℭ **207/967-2751.** $10 adults, children free. Memorial Day–Columbus Day daily 10am–3pm.

St. Anthony's Franciscan Monastery ★ RELIGIOUS RETREAT/ GARDENS   Across the road from the White Barn Inn (p. 73), this monastery is a peaceful spot for walks through quiet grounds, chapels, and sculptures. The estate and property were purchased by Lithuanian Franciscans in 1947, who then added the grotto, statuary, and worship spaces. There's a section of sculpture from the Vatican Pavilion at the 1964/1965 World's Fair, as well as a chapel, an outdoor shrine, English gardens, statues, and a walking trail with some of the best river views in town. Park in the visitor's lot and be respectful of the grounds. If you like the calm vibe here, you can even stay overnight (see p. 73).

North side of Beach Ave., less than ½ mile from Lower Village and the intersection of Rte. 9 and Rte. 35, Kennebunk. Free admission. Daily dawn–dusk.

The Seashore Trolley Museum ★ MUSEUM   A short drive north of Kennebunkport is a little local marvel: a surreal scrap yard masquerading as a museum. Quirky and engaging, the museum was founded in 1939 to preserve a disappearing way of life, and today the collection boasts more than 250 trolleys and other transit vehicles, including specimens from Glasgow, Moscow, San Francisco, and Rome. Naturally, there's also a streetcar named *Desire* from New Orleans. Dozens of the cars still operate, and the admission charge includes rides on a 2-mile track. Other cars, some of which still contain early-20th-century advertising, are on display outdoors and in vast storage sheds. Head north from Kennebunkport on North St. for 1¾ miles; look for signs.

195 Log Cabin Rd., Kennebunkport. www.trolleymuseum.org. ⓒ **207/967-2800.** Admission $10 adults, $7.50 children 6–16, $8 seniors. Memorial Day–Columbus Day daily 10am–5pm; early May and late Oct Sat–Sun 10am–5pm. Closed Nov–Apr.

South Congregational Church ★★ CHURCH   To me, one of Kennebunkport's lasting images is the enormous clock face of this whitewashed, meetinghouse-style church (built in 1824), down a lane off Dock Square and close to the tidal river. The huge clock faces are the originals, and are made of wood (which is very unusual); they no longer keep the correct time, but this is still as lovely a church as you'll find in southern Maine. Inside, the simple spare theme continues but for some stained-glass work and an outsized, impressively columnar pipe organ—though it's only from 2004.

2 North St. at Temple St., just off Spring St., Kennebunkport. ⓒ **207/967-2793.** Office hours Mon–Fri 9am–2pm, Sun services 10:30am.

Beaches

The coastal area around Kennebunkport is home to several of the state's best beaches. Finding a parking spot is often difficult, however, and all beaches require a parking permit, which you can get at the town offices or from your hotel. The local trolley offers beach access (see p. 72).

Southward across the river (technically, this is Kennebunk, though it's much closer to Kennebunkport) are **Gooch's Beach** ★★ and **Kennebunk Beach** ★★. Head eastward on Beach Street (from the intersection of routes 9 and 35) past the White Barn Inn (p. 73) and in a few minutes you'll wind into a handsome colony of eclectic shingled summer homes. The narrow road continues twisting past sandy beaches and rocky headlands; this section is also well worth exploring for its summer mansions and golf course. Hard to believe, but it sometimes gets congested along this beach in summer; avoid the gridlock by exploring on foot or by bike. Very important, you *cannot park here* if you are not a resident—unless you've moseyed down to the police station on Route 1 and bought a temporary parking permit, which few summer visitors know to do. (Some local inns and hotels will give you a temporary day pass.] Again, if you can avoid bringing a car to the beach, do.

You can avoid the hassle by renting a bike and leaving your car at your inn or hotel. A good spot for rentals is **Kennebunkport Bicycle Company** (34 Arundel Rd.; ⓒ **207/385-4382**), which rents a variety of bikes by the half-day,

THE beach AT PARSON'S WAY

It's certainly one of the most attractive *approaches* to a beach in Maine, and Parson's Beach itself is lovely and much less crowded than others in the area. Find the beach by heading south on Route 9 from Dock Square in Kennebunkport, through the traffic light; just after you cross a marsh and the Mousam River, hang a left onto Parson's Beach Road.

You'll drive down a country lane lined with maples. At the end, there's limited parking, though you can also park on the north side of the highway if it's full. This is not the best beach on the southern Maine coast for swimming—it's rocky at the mouth of the river—but it's great for lounging and reading. Be on your best behavior here. (Don't trample the dunes, don't take stuff from the tide pool, and so on.) You have to cross private land to reach the beach, and signs ominously proclaim that access can be denied at any time if the landowner so chooses.

day, or week. There are also mountain bikes, along with kid trailers and baby seats. (Helmets and locks are free with rentals.) The bike shop is just north of downtown Kennebunkport: turn north on North Road, rather than following Route 9 north. A few hotels and inns in town also rent bikes to guests or even provide free bikes; ask when you book your room.

Goose Rocks Beach ★, north of Kennebunkport off Route 9 (watch for signs), is a good choice for those who like their crowds light and prefer beaches to beach scenes. You'll find an enclave of beach homes set amid rustling oaks just off a fine sand beach. Just offshore is a narrow barrier reef that has historically attracted flocks of geese, hence the name.

A Side Trip to Cape Porpoise

Cape Porpoise ★★ is a lovely little village, nearly forgotten by time, between Kennebunk and Biddeford. It makes for a superb day trip or bike ride. Beside a number of notable restaurants, such as **Pier 77** (p. 76) and **The Wayfarer** (p. 77), the village has a handful of shops, and even a postage-stamp-size library.

While here, think about packing a picnic and taking it to the rocks where the lobster boats are tied up; watch the fishermen, or train your binoculars on Goat Island and its lighthouse. Drop by **Bradbury Brothers Market** (✆ 207/967-3939) for basic staples, or the **Cape Porpoise Kitchen** (✆ 207/967-1150; www.capeporpoisekitchen.com) for gourmet-style prepared meals, cheeses, and baked goods.

Not in a picnic mood? Overlooking the sparkling water, the **Cape Porpoise Lobster Co.** (15 Pier Rd., ✆ 800/967-4268 or 207/967-4268) has some outdoor dining; most everything is served on Styrofoam plates, so beware of rogue winds that strive to dump your meal on your lap. It's open 9am to 7pm daily, from Memorial Day to late fall; no reservations are taken, but it does accept credit cards.

PORTLAND

Urban amenities, lively street culture, and a dense concentration of the East Coast's most lauded restaurants—all in a town you can bike end-to-end in 20 minutes. That's what draws transplants and travelers alike to Maine's biggest city (still fewer than 70,000 souls), which radiates out from a hammerhead-shaped peninsula extending into glittering Casco Bay. If you came to Maine for bucolic coastal seclusion, you might be tempted to drive right past on I-295, admiring the skyline at 60 miles an hour. But you'd be missing out on one of the country's most vibrant up-and-coming small metros.

5

Portland is worth at least an afternoon's detour, and even a weekend (or a week) isn't too much time to spend here. This historic city has plenty of charm—not only in the Old Port, with its brick sidewalks and cobblestone streets, but in several lovely residential neighborhoods of striking views and architecture. You can catch a quick ferry to an offshore island, browse boutique shops, snap photos of historic homes; crack lobsters, walk empty beaches, and pose beside lighthouses; and top off your day with top-shelf food and drink. (Portland is now a sort of culinary mecca, blessed with an uncommonly high number of excellent restaurants, craft breweries and distilleries, micro-roasteries, and so on for a city its size.) And there's a salty tang to local culture that you'll occasionally still glimpse in the waterfront bars and chowder houses.

Actually, it feels more like a large town than a small city. Strike up a conversation with a resident, and you're likely to get an earful about how easy it is to live here (this despite rents and home prices that have steadily risen with Portland's burgeoning cachet). You can enjoy acres of trails and parkland, see art-house movies, and get good Vietnamese or Thai food to go. Traffic isn't bad at all.

Like most New England cities, Portland has been forced to reinvent itself every couple of generations as economic and cultural trends overturn old paradigms. The city was a center for maritime trade in the 19th century, when a forest of ship masts obscured the view of the harbor. It's been a manufacturing hub, with locomotive factories, steel foundries, and fish-packing plants. It's been a mercantile center, with impressive downtown department stores and a slew of wholesale dealers. The post-recession years have seen a rapid wave of revitalization (or gentrification, depending who you ask) all across town. Drawn by its big-city perks and comparatively inexpensive standard of living, urban expats from other East Coast metros have descended on the Forest City (including enough creative-class former Brooklynites to engender the nickname "Portlyn"). Office space is in short supply these days, old warehouses and industrial properties are becoming sought-after real estate, and there's a brisk urban vitality that often eludes much bigger cities. A recent wave of immigration from Africa and Asia has given the place a shot in the cultural arm; Portland's art museum would be outstanding in a community five or ten times its size; new coffee shops seem to open daily; and a downtown arts college brings a youthful spirit to the streets. Best of all, there's always an offshore island to escape to when cruise ships on the waterfront unload a few too many fellow tourists for your taste.

ESSENTIALS

106 miles N of Boston and 317 miles NE of New York City

Arriving

BY CAR   Coming from the south by car, downtown Portland is most accessible by taking exit 44 off the Maine Turnpike (I-95, which is a toll road) into the city, then following I-295 (which is free) a few miles into town. Exit I-295 onto Franklin Arterial (exit 7), then continue straight uphill and downhill to the city's ferry terminal in the Old Port. Turn right onto Commercial Street and park. There's a visitor center nearby, and plenty to do within 10 minutes' walk. Get oriented here.

BY TRAIN   **Amtrak** (www.amtrak.com; ℂ **800/872-7245**) runs the daily Downeaster service from Boston's North Station to Portland (passengers from other cities must change stations from South Station to North Station in Boston via taxi or subway). The train makes five round-trips daily (time: 2½ hr.), for $20–$30 each way. Downtown is a short bus or cab ride or a drab 45-minute walk from the station, which is out on Thompson's Point (although a new recreational development in an old train repair facility has made Thompson's Point a destination itself—see p. 96).

BY BUS   Two big carriers, **Concord Coach** (www.concordcoachlines.com; ℂ **800/639-3317** or 603/228-3300) and **Greyhound** (www.greyhound.com; ℂ **800/231-2222**), provide bus service to Portland. The Greyhound bus terminal is at 950 Congress St., about a mile south of the downtown core. Greyhound runs buses from both Boston and New York City: from Boston, there are several buses daily (around 2 hr., $15–$30 one-way), while from New York there are two buses daily (8 hr., $33–$64 one-way). Concord Coach connects runs more than a dozen buses daily between Portland and Boston's Logan Airport (2 hr., $29 one-way; discounts for round-trips), plus two buses a day to NYC (6 hr., $69 one-way). Concord Coach's bus terminal is next to Portland's inconvenient Amtrak station (see "by Train," above) on Thompsons Point Road. City buses and taxis ferry you downtown from here.

BY PLANE **Portland International Jetport** (www.portlandjetport.org; ☏ 207/874-8877), airport code PWM, is the largest airport in Maine. It's served by flights from **American Airlines** (www.aa.com; ☏ 800/433-7300), **Delta** (www.delta.com; ☏ 800/221-1212), **Elite Airways** (www.eliteairways. net; ☏ 800/393-2510), **JetBlue** (www.jetblue.com; ☏ 800/538-2583), **Southwest Airlines** (www.southwest.com; ☏ 800/435-9792), and **United Express** (www.united.com; ☏ 800/864-8331). The airport got a significant expansion in 2011, and there are plans in place for further upgrades in 2018, but the terminal is still pretty easily navigated. A taxi ride to the city is about $30 with tip; some hotels near the airport and downtown will shuttle you to your digs for free. Ask when booking.

Visitor Information

The **Convention and Visitor's Bureau of Greater Portland** (www.visitport land.com) runs *four* tourist information centers around town. The main info center is on the Ocean Gateway Pier, just north of the Casco Bay Lines ferry terminal at the feet of Commercial St. and Franklin Arterial. Most of the year, it's open Monday through Saturday—but in July and August it's open 7 days a week. (It closes in February.) There's also a tourist information desk at the **Portland International Jetport** (☏ 207/756-8312), near baggage claim, open daily year-round, plus brochure kiosks at the Maine Mall in South Portland and at the Portland Transport Center at Thompson's Point (see "By Train," above; also see box on p. 96).

Portland's free weekly newspaper, the *Portland Phoenix,* and the monthly *Dispatch* both offer good listings of local events, films, nightclub performances, and the like. Copies are widely available at restaurants, bars, coffee shops, and convenience stores, and in newspaper boxes on curbs in the Old Port and around downtown.

City Layout

The city of Portland is divided into two areas: on-peninsula and off-peninsula. (There are also the islands, but more on that below.) Most travelers are destined for the compact peninsula, where the city's downtown area is located; most of Portland's cultural life and retail activity takes place here.

Viewed from the water, Portland's peninsula is shaped a bit like a swaybacked horse or the hammerhead on a shark, with the **Old Port** ★★★ lying in the middle near the waterfront. The peninsula's two main residential neighborhoods (Munjoy Hill and the West End) top gentle rises overlooking downtown. **Congress Street**, Portland's main artery of commerce, connects these two neighborhoods. The western stretch of Congress Street (roughly between Monument Square and State Street) is home to Portland's emerging **Arts District** ★, where you can find the handsome art museum, several theaters, the campus of the Maine College of Art (located in an old department store), and a calliope of restaurants and boutiques.

Parking

Parking is notoriously tight in the Old Port, and the city's parking enforcement is notoriously efficient. Several parking garages are convenient to the Old Port, and you can also park in some residential neighborhoods, often for a maximum of 2 hours. Read signs carefully for news of nighttime street-sweeping hours; you *will* be towed (don't ask how I know; I just do) if you run afoul of them.

Special Events

First Friday Art Walks bring Portlanders out along Congress Street (and spilling into the Old Port) early each month, even in winter. The sidewalk between Forest Avenue and Preble Street is a pop-up art fair with a pronounced indie/DIY aesthetic—a lot of the vendors are students at Maine College of Art, which also opens its galleries for the occasion. The streets are filled with buskers (and occasionally pretty sizeable roving bands), food trucks set up in the squares, and everything from coffee shops and bookstores to galleries and the Portland Museum of Art host openings and events. It's quite a scene in the summers. **Creative Portland** (www.creativeportland. com; © **207/370-4784**) puts out a monthly list of happenings.

The **Old Port Festival** (© **207/772-6828**) takes place in early June, when tens of thousands of revelers descend upon the historic Old Port section to herald the arrival of summer. Several blocks of the Old Port are blocked to traffic, and the throngs order food and buy goods from street vendors. Several stages provide entertainment, ranging from kids' singalongs to raucous blues. Admission is free.

WHERE TO STAY IN PORTLAND

In addition to the lodgings listed below, there are tons of chain hotels and motels in and around the city. Check around the Maine Mall (in South Portland) for the largest agglomeration; you'll find all the usual names there, in various price ranges; see p. 90 for a few suggestions.

If you're looking for something more central (and you should), Portland proper has options, but you'll pay for the privilege during high season. The city has a seasonal quandary on its hands when it comes to hotel rooms: Many rooms sit empty in the winter and spring, and you can score some great deals then, but during Portland's busy summers, reservations can be hard to come by and pricey, even after a spate of new hotel construction. Across the street from the main ferry dock in the Old Port neighborhood, the **Hilton Garden Inn** (65 Commercial St.; www.hilton.com; © **207/780-0780**) is convenient to restaurants, bakeries, and pubs—not to mention the islands of Casco Bay. You'll pay for the privilege of being in the heart of the waterfront, though: Double rooms mostly run from about $169 up to $449 per night. A couple of blocks inland, the **Holiday Inn by the Bay,** 88 Spring St. (www.innbythebay. com; © **800/345-5050** or 207/775-2311), offers great views of the harbor from about half the rooms, along with the usual chain-hotel creature comforts. Peak-season rates are approximately $210 for a double.

Portland is awash in Airbnb rentals at the moment, with everything available from couches to crash on to stately properties in the tony West End. As of this writing, however, the city is trying to crack down on seasonal rentals with new regulations, since rental properties (many owned by out-of-staters and seasonal residents) are pricing out locals and turning whole neighborhoods into patchwork ghost towns in the winter. So the thriving online rental market may take some hits in the near future.

Expensive

Black Point Inn Resort ★★   Just 10 miles south of Portland (about 15 minutes driving time from downtown), the historic Black Point Inn is a Maine classic. When new ownership took over the property back in 2007, the inn dispensed with one of its pools and all of the cottages, slashing the room count by more than two-thirds and giving the place more of a boutique feel than a resort vibe. The remaining rooms have been updated and upscaled. Situated on 9 acres with views along the coast both north and south, the inn was built as a summer resort in 1873 on the same attractive rocky point memorialized by landscape painter Winslow Homer. What remains is as elegant as ever, perhaps more so, and the expansive porch (with its constant sea breezes) thankfully remains. Dinner at The Point is a stately, white-tablecloth affair, while the pubbier Chart Room offers three squares and a killer outdoor seating area with beach views. Meal plans available.

510 Black Point Rd., Prouts Neck. (From U.S. Rte. 1 in Scarborough, turn onto Rte. 207 east.) www.blackpointinn.com. ℭ **207/883-2500.** 25 units. $330–$590 double; $500–$650 suite. Closed Nov–Apr. Packages available. **Amenities:** Restaurants; bar; free bikes and kayaks; fitness room; Jacuzzi; massage; heated outdoor pool; room service; sauna; private beaches; free Wi-Fi.

The Danforth ★★   In 2014, the owners of Camden's Relais & Châteaux property, the Camden Harbour Inn, took over this stately brick manor on the peninsula, and they've upped its status to "grand boutique inn," nicely balancing the elegant Federal architecture with splashy contemporary art and furniture that wouldn't look out of place in a modern art museum. Breakfast is served in a sunshiney dining room, and guests share common spaces such as an indoor herb garden, an old-school conservatory, and well-kept private gardens out back. The Victoria Mansion (p. 101) is just 2 blocks down the street, and the Old Port's only a 10-minute stroll. Fare at the adjacent restaurant, **Tempo Dulu ★**, is Indonesian fusion—unexpected, given The Danforth's old-school milieu, but a terrific dining experience nonetheless (great cocktails).

163 Danforth St. www.danforthmaine.com. ℭ **800/991-6557** or 207/879-8755. 9 units. July–Aug $349–$524 double; May–June and Sept–Oct $199–$279 double; Nov–Apr $179–$249 double. 2-night minimum on weekends. Rates include full breakfast. **Amenities:** Conservatory; garden; sitting room; restaurant; bar; free Wi-Fi.

Portland Hotels and Restaurants

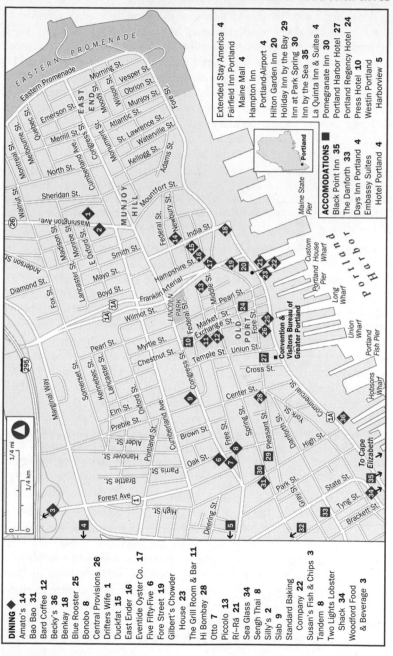

ACCOMODATIONS ■
Black Point Inn **35**
The Danforth **33**
Days Inn Portland **4**
Embassy Suites
  Hotel Portland **4**
Extended Stay America **4**
Fairfield Inn Portland
  Maine Mall **4**
Hampton Inn
  Portland-Airport **4**
Hilton Garden Inn **20**
Holiday Inn by the Bay **29**
Inn at Park Spring **30**
Inn by the Sea **35**
La Quinta Inn & Suites **4**
Pomegranate Inn **30**
Portland Harbor Hotel **27**
Portland Regency Hotel **24**
Press Hotel **10**
Westin Portland
  Harborview **5**

DINING ◆
Amato's **14**
Bao Bao **31**
Bard Coffee **12**
Becky's **36**
Benkay **18**
Blue Rooster **25**
Bonobo **8**
Central Provisions **26**
Drifters Wife **1**
Duckfat **15**
East Ender **16**
Eventide Oyster Co. **17**
Five Fifty-Five **6**
Fore Street **19**
Gilbert's Chowder
  House **23**
The Grill Room & Bar **11**
Hi Bombay **28**
Otto **7**
Piccolo **13**
Rí-Rá **21**
Sea Glass **34**
Sengh Thai **8**
Silly's **2**
Slab **9**
Standard Baking
  Company **22**
Susan's Fish & Chips **3**
Tandem **8**
Two Lights Lobster
  Shack **34**
Woodford Food
  & Beverage **3**

5

PORTLAND | Where to Stay in Portland

87

Inn by the Sea ★★★   Not so much an inn as a luxury retreat, Cape Elizabeth's best hotel has made the successful transition from relaxed seaside getaway to destination resort. Yet they've done it while retaining a wonderful sense of place: suites and dining areas emphasize Maine-themed art and foods, while summery gardens and ocean views tantalize through the windows. An expansive, lovely spa was added in 2008, as were a walk-in *cave,* fireplace rooms, and bi-level spa suites with double Jacuzzis. A further set of cottages (townhouselike suites) in an outbuilding add full kitchens and extra bedroom or bathroom space. Especially welcome is this inn's move toward green practices: It's the first hotel in Maine to burn biofuels, operate carbon neutrally, and employ printed-paper key cards. Recycled materials and low-flow toiletry also predominate. Need still more green? A walkway leads to one of Maine's best beaches.

40 Bowery Beach Rd., Cape Elizabeth. www.innbythesea.com. ⓒ **800/888-4287** or 207/799-3134. 57 units. July–Aug $579–$1040 suite (2-night minimum on weekends); May–June and Sept–Oct $370–$530 suite; Nov–Apr $200–$280 suite. Packages available. Pets welcome in some units. Breakfast plans available. **Amenities:** Restaurant; lounge; fitness room; Jacuzzi; heated outdoor pool; room service; sauna; spa; free Wi-Fi.

Portland Regency Hotel ★★★   Centrally located on a cobblestone courtyard in the middle of the Old Port, the Regency boasts one of the city's premier hotel locations. But it's got more than location—this is also one of the most architecturally interesting hotels in southern Maine. Housed in an 1895 brick armory, the hotel is thoroughly modern inside and offers attractive rooms, appointed and furnished with all the expected amenities. There are several types of rooms and suites, each fitted to the place's unique architecture; for a splurge, ask for a luxurious corner room with a handsome (non-working) fireplace, sitting area, city views out big windows, and a Jacuzzi. The small health club is one of the best in town (it includes a sauna and hot tub), and the downstairs level conceals a restaurant and a lounge.

20 Milk St. www.theregency.com. ⓒ **800/727-3436** or 207/774-4200. 95 units. Early July–late Oct $299–$359 double, $329–$509 suite; off season $149–$169 double, $189–$309 suite. Valet parking $20 per day. Some rooms allow pets $75 per day. **Amenities:** Restaurant; bar; free airport transfers; babysitting (with prior notice); conference rooms; fitness club w/ aerobics classes; Jacuzzi; room service; sauna; spa; free Wi-Fi.

The Press Hotel ★★★   If it's not the best urban lodging in Portland, it's certainly the most fun. The Press Hotel was constructed over the bones of the former headquarters of the *Portland Press Herald* newspaper, and there's a "golden days of journalism" theme throughout the building that's more fun than it sounds, from the art installation of vintage typewriters in the lobby to the wallpaper made of old headlines to the mod Inkwell bar. Rooms are clean and contemporary, done up in muted blues and grays, with vintage furniture, local art, and a really generous number of outlets and USB ports. The restaurant, **Union**, is one of Portland's best.

119 Exchange St. www.presshotel.com. ⓒ **207/808-8800**. 110 units. July–Aug $379–$499 double, $719–$799 suite; May–June and Sept–Oct $209–$299 double, $549–$619 suite; Nov–Apr $159–$199 double, $449–$539 suite. Packages available. **Amenities:** Free bicycles, art gallery; restaurant; bar; fitness room; room service; spa; free Wi-Fi.

Moderate

Embassy Suites Hotel Portland ★   Practically inside Portland's airport, this all-suite hotel gets very good reviews from business travelers. It's one of the best choices if you have a very late arrival or early departure, even if it won't win awards for innovative architecture. Business bonus: You can print remotely, for free, from all rooms.

1050 Westbrook St. www.hilton.com. © **207/775-2200.** 119 units. $119–$359 double. Rates include full breakfast. Pets allowed ($50 fee). **Amenities:** Restaurant; bar; conference rooms; fitness club; indoor pool; room service; sauna; free Wi-Fi.

Inn at Park Spring ★   This small, tasteful B&B is located on a busy downtown street in a historic brick home that dates back to 1835. It's well located for exploring the city on foot, and the friendly owners keep the place in good shape. Guests can linger or watch TV in a front parlor, or chat at the communal dining table in the adjacent room (communal breakfasts are a highlight—unless you're shy). The rooms are all corner rooms, and most are bright and sunny. Especially nice is Room 1, with its sleigh bed, hardwood flooring, and wonderful views of the historic row houses along Park Street, and periwinkle-hued Room 4, on the third (top) floor, which gets abundant afternoon light and is furnished with a king bed, big sitting room, and nice bathroom. The Portland Museum of Art and the city's children's museum (see p. 98) are only 2 blocks away, the Old Port a 10-minute walk.

135 Spring St., Portland. www.innatparkspring.com. © **800/437-8511** or 207/774-1059. 5 units. Jun–Oct $210–$255 double; off-season $105–$145 double. 2-night minimum weekends. Rates include full breakfast and off-street parking. No children 9 and under. **Amenities:** Free Wi-Fi.

Pomegranate Inn ★★   Located inside a 19th-century Italianate home in Portland's lovely West End, this is arguably the city's top B&B. Eight rooms feature individually distinct design touches, painted floors, faux-marble woodwork, and gas fireplaces. The carriage house room includes a private terrace whose sliding doors open onto a small garden, and breakfasts are a highlight. Also don't miss the flowery second-floor balcony and third-floor conservatory.

49 Neal St. www.pomegranateinn.com. © **800/356-0408** or 207/772-1006. 8 units. $199–$389 double. Rates include full breakfast. Packages available. Children 16 and older only. **Amenities:** Afternoon refreshments.

Portland Harbor Hotel ★★   Situated adjacent to Portland's busy bar scene on the corner of Fore and Union streets, this semicircular townhouselike structure—designed to fit in with the brick facades prevailing in the Old Port—appeals to the boutique crowd with its modern amenities. The interior courtyard throws off European ambience; large rooms are furnished with queen- and king-size beds and spacious work desks. Even the standard rooms are outfitted with armoires; duvets and down coverlets; deep bathtubs in granite-faced bathrooms; two-line phones; and big TVs. Deluxe rooms and suites add Jacuzzis and sitting areas, and some units look out onto a central garden area. The house restaurant, **Eve's at the Garden**, has a great patio in the summertime.

468 Fore St. www.portlandharborhotel.com. ℂ **207/775-9090**. 101 units. Mid-May–mid-Oct $289–$379 double, $369–$479 suite; off season $178–$189 double, $289 suite. Packages available. Valet parking in garage $20 per day. Some rooms allow pets $25 per day. **Amenities:** Restaurant; bar; babysitting; free bikes; concierge; fitness center; room service; free Wi-Fi.

The Westin Portland Harborview ★   Long known as the Eastland (the sign on the roof still proclaims this), this historic 14-story hotel off Congress Street reopened in 2013, after a $50-million renovation, as the Westin Portland Harborview. A few historic touches were saved, like the grand columns in the lobby and the ornately carved stairway to the ballroom, but the rooms are modern and efficient, if a little industrial cookie-cutter. The real selling points are the location, just off the heart of Congress Street, and **Top of the East ★,** the 14th-floor bar/lounge that's a Portland landmark for craft cocktails and views of the city.

157 High St. www.westinportlandharborview.com. ℂ **207/775-5411.** 289 units. Early July–late Oct $274–$380 double, $255–$446 suite; off season $115–$220 double, $168–$247 suite. Pets allowed. **Amenities:** Conference rooms; fitness club; restaurant; bar; free Wi-Fi in common areas ($10/day in-room).

Inexpensive

Budget travelers typically head for the chain hotels in the area surrounding the Maine Mall in South Portland, about 8 miles south of the attractions of downtown. The lowest-cost options include the **Days Inn** (461 Maine Mall Rd.; www.wyndhamhotels.com; ℂ **207/772-3450**). An **Extended Stay America** (2 Ashley Dr., Scarborough; www.extendedstayamerica.com; ℂ **207/883-0554**), a few minutes' drive south of the mall, features in-room kitchenettes; doubles start around $80 nightly in the off season, $140 in summer. In Portland proper, the **La Quinta** (340 Park Ave.; ℂ **207/871-0611**) doesn't have much of a view (there's a milk packaging plant across the street), but it's nicely located, just across the bridge from SoPo with a handy airport shuttle, and close to the Sea Dogs' ballpark and Thompson's Point (p. 96).

Fairfield Inn Portland Maine Mall ★   The Fairfield, on the southern edge of the Maine Mall's sprawl, is a good option for budget-minded families. The clean but basic rooms all have irons and ironing boards, there's a simple free breakfast in the lobby each morning, and parking's free and ample. You can practically walk to the mall (but don't). Note that there's no restaurant in the hotel.

2 Cummings Rd., Scarborough. www.marriott.com. ℂ **207/883-0300.** 118 units. $76–$259 double. Rates include continental breakfast. **Amenities:** Fitness club; Jacuzzi; outdoor pool; free Wi-Fi.

Hampton Inn Portland–Airport ★   Of all the hotels clustered around Portland's airport and mall, this is my top "family" pick. There's a pool, a free shuttle van to and from the airport, chocolate-chip cookies, an Internet terminal in the lobby, a pretty good included breakfast, friendly staff, and a quiet-ish location. Plus they'll bring cribs and highchairs as fast as you need 'em. Downtown is a 10-minute drive away, the Maine Mall a 30-second walk.

171 Philbrook Ave., South Portland. www.portlandhamptoninn.com. © 207/773-4400. 117 units. $89–$199 double. Rates include continental breakfast. Packages available. Pets allowed in some rooms. **Amenities:** Fitness club; indoor pool; free Wi-Fi.

WHERE TO EAT IN PORTLAND

Portland is nothing if not a city of creative cheap eats, so don't neglect local bakeries and coffee shops when trolling for quick or economical meals. My favorite bakery in New England, hands-down, is **Standard Baking Company** ★★, 75 Commercial St. (© **207/773-2112**; www.standardbakingco.com), across from the ferry terminal and behind the Hilton Garden Inn hotel. Allison Bray and Matt James bake some of the best sticky buns (with or without nuts) and focaccia I've tasted, plus top-rate breads, brioche, cookies, and more. There's good coffee, too. The bakery is open 7am to 6pm daily except Sundays, when it closes at 5pm.

Among the many coffee shops around the city, I frequent both **Bard Coffee** at 185 Middle Street (www.bardcoffee.com; © **207/899-4788**), open daily until 9pm except on Sundays, when it closes at 6pm, and **Tandem Coffee + Bakery** at 742 Congress Street (www.tandemcoffee.com; © **207/805-1887**), a former gas-station that now features beans from Tandem's East Bayside roastery, terrific pies (sweet and savory) from baker Brianna Holt, and a minimalist sipping space that encourages honest-to-god interaction (read: no outlets, no Wi-Fi; open 7am to 6pm, 8am to 6pm weekends).

For pizza, grab giant Sicilian slices from **Slab** (© **207/245-3088**; 25 Preble St.); adventurous toppings and a nice bar from **OTTO** (© **207/358-7090**; 576 Congress St., plus five other locations around greater Portland); or wood-fired beauties with local ingredients from **Bonobo** (© **207/347-8267**; 46 Pine St.).

Portland also claims to be the original home of the Italian sandwich—which may have been the original sub sandwich in America—and locals maintain the best example can still be found at the purported inventor of this creation, **Amato's,** 71 India Street (© **207/773-1682**), in what's left of Portland's Italian neighborhood.

Expensive

Central Provisions ★★ NEW AMERICAN   Small plates done right. Central Provisions made various national Best New Restaurant lists when it opened in 2014, and it's only upped its game since. The ever-changing menu skews way local and divies up simply: hot, cold, raw, and sweet. Maine tuna crudos are a mainstay on the raw menu, and they're typical of the restaurant's style: simple, fresh, flavorful, and elegantly plated. On a Friday night, this place is date-night central. Grab a seat at the long bar with the scenesters (on a bar stool made from Maine-forged iron and recycled burlap) or head to the basement for more of a rathskeller feel. There's a limited menu available late and between lunch and dinner.

414 Fore St. www.central-provisions.com. *C* **207/805-1085.** Small plates $8–$24. Lunch Tues–Sat 11am–2pm; dinner Sun–Wed 5–10pm, Thurs–Sat 5–10:30pm. Reservations not accepted.

Eventide Oyster Co. ★★★ OYSTER BAR/SEAFOOD   Maybe no restaurant is as emblematic of contemporary Portland dining as Eventide. The offerings are of the old-school Maine seafaring variety: a rotating selection of oysters (overwhelmingly local in season, many from the oyster mecca of the Damariscotta River), a brown-butter lobster roll that's a rich and inventive twist on the state's favorite proletarian treat, or a full-on clambake option, complete with a hardboiled egg nestled in a bed of rockweed. But the room is stylish and modern, with the raw bar occupying a huge hunk of gorgeous Maine granite, the accouterments are adventurous (think ginger and kimchi toppings on your half-shell), and the clientele (especially late) tends towards the young and urbane. Naturally, in this brunch-iest of New England towns, there's a Sunday brunch, with lobster benedict and salt-pork and beans. Eventide's a little on the dear side compared to no-frills oyster pubs on up the coast; it's also one of Portland's most fun dining experiences.

86 Middle St. www.eventideoysterco.com. *C* **207/774-8538.** Dozen oysters $29; sandwiches and small plates $7–$15. Brunch entrees $11–$16. Daily 11am–midnight; Sun brunch 11am–3pm.

Five Fifty-Five ★ NEW AMERICAN   When husband-and-wife Steve and Michelle Corry opened Five Fifty-Five in 2003, neither "small plates" nor "farm-to-table" were entrenched in the American foodie lexicon. The Corrys were instrumental in introducing both ideas to Northeast diners. Still, Five Fifty-Five's regulars love it for its large-plate signature dishes like truffled lobster macaroni-and-cheese, striploins and hanger steaks, hand-rolled pastas, and other maximalist stalwarts. Wine aficionados, take note: The wine list here is tops, one of the best in the entire state.

555 Congress St. www.fivefifty-five.com. *C* **207/761-0555.** Small plates $9–$15, main courses $20–$35. Daily 5–10pm; Sun brunch 9:30am–2pm. Reservations recommended.

Fore Street ★★ CONTEMPORARY GRILL   Fore Street has emerged as one of northern New England's most celebrated restaurants. Chef Sam Hayward routinely pops up in magazines like *Saveur* and *Food & Wine,* his restaurant was often in *Gourmet*'s 100 Best, and so forth. Hayward's secret is simplicity: local and organic ingredients are used where possible, and the kitchen avoids fussy presentations. The dining space centers around a busy open kitchen where a team of chefs constantly stoke the wood-fired brick oven and grill, which feature prominently in the culinary philosophy here. The menu changes nightly, but entrees might run to spit-roasted pork loin, grilled duckling, grilled marinated hanger steak, or a piece of pan-seared bluefish; the wood-roasted mussels are also a big hit. Finish with a dessert such as chocolate soufflé, hand-dipped chocolates, or gelati—these are often accented in summer by seasonal Maine berries or fruits. Though it can be difficult to snag a reservation here on summer weekends, management always sets aside a few tables each night for walk-ins. Get there early and grab one.

288 Fore St. www.forestreet.biz. ✆ **207/775-2717.** Main courses $26–$40. Sun–Thurs 5:30–10pm; Fri–Sat 5:30–10:30pm. Reservations recommended.

Piccolo ★★ ITALIAN   The cuisine of central and southern Italy takes center stage at this postage stamp of a restaurant (only about 20 seats) at the edge of the Old Port, where the ever-changing menu skews fresh and rustic: chef Damian Sansonetti plates up cavatelli with lamb neck ragout, grilled swordfish with beans and salsa verde, and other dishes his mom and grandma once made. Pastry chef Ilma Lopez is one of Portland's hottest culinary talents, and her airy Italian donut holes, called *zeppole*, are a highlight. The tasting menu on Sunday nights is as fun and daring as the tiny room is social—there's one 6:30 seating, and reservations are a must. At once cozy and sumptuous, Piccolo is my pick for the best date night in Portland.

111 Middle St. www.piccolomaine.com. ✆ **207/747-5307.** Main courses $19–$27. Wed–Sun 5–10pm; Sun brunch 10:30am–2pm. Reservations recommended.

Sea Glass SEAFOOD/AMERICAN CLASSIC   At the house restaurant of the lovely **Inn by the Sea** (p. 88), chef Andrew Chadwick sticks to white-tablecloth classics with a pronounced emphasis on sustainable seafood. Expect well-executed meat-and-potatoes entrees such as pork chops, short ribs, and duck breast, along with unexpected (and underutilized) seafood offerings like Atlantic ocean perch (red fish) and mackerel.

40 Bowery Beach Rd., Cape Elizabeth. www.innbythesea.com. ✆ **800/888-4287** or 207/799-3134. Entrees $22–$35. Breakfast Mon–Sat. 7–11am; lunch and dinner daily 11:30am–3pm and 5–9pm.

Moderate

BaoBao Dumpling House ★ ASIAN FUSION   Buzzy chef Cara Stadler opened this casual-hip dumpling depot as a more relaxed alternative to her much-praised and more formal Tao Yuan restaurant in nearby Brunswick. It's fun ordering a la carte off the inventive dumpling menu—options like shrimp and bacon, Kung Pao chicken and peanut, and lamb and black bean chili play around with classic formulas for the small, steamed bundles beloved in China and beyond. As befits the hangout vibe of the narrow, sparsely adorned dining room, BaoBao has a great bar, with a really well curated selection of Maine craft beers, a nice sake list, and some bracing house cocktails. Kids welcome.

133 Spring St. www.baobaodumplinghouse.com ✆ **207/772-8400.** Small plates $6–$12. Wed–Thurs 11:30am–10pm; Fri–Sat 11:30am–11pm; Sun 11:30am–9pm.

Benkay ★ SUSHI   Among Portland's sushi restaurants, Benkay is the hippest, usually teeming with a lively local crowd lured by the affordable menus. Chef Seiji Ando trained in Osaka and Kyoto; his sushi, sashimi, and maki rolls deliver a lot for the price, and there's a wide range of choices and combinations. Standard Japanese bar-food items such as tempura (deep-fried vegetables), *gyoza* (dumplings), teriyaki, *katsu* (fried chicken or pork cutlets), and udon (thick noodles) are also served. For dessert, consider the green tea ice cream: deliciously bitter . . . and good for you. Sort of.

2 India St. (at Commercial St.). www.sushiman.com. © **207/773-5555.** Main courses $10–$22. Mon–Thurs 11:30am–2pm and 5–9:30pm; Fri 11:30am–2pm and 5–11pm; Sat 11:30am–11pm; Sun 11:30am–9pm. Reservations not accepted.

Drifters Wife ★★ WINE BAR   A tiny wine bar in a tiny wine shop with amazing food put out by a tiny kitchen—everything about Drifters Wife is diminutive except its burgeoning reputation. *Bon Appétit* called it one of the country's 50 best new restaurants when it opened in 2016, and it's almost certainly the only entry on that list where the chef (Ben Jackson) is working only with two induction burners and a half-size oven. Nonetheless, Jackson turns out exquisitely plated (really, they're works of art) shareable portions of fresh local veggies and just-caught fish: maybe a head-and-all Atlantic mackerel with pistachio butter and fresh veggies, or chicken livers on toast with pickled egg and cucumbers. The wine list (like the picks at the surrounding Maine & Loire wine store) skews organic and biodynamic and additive-free.

63 Washington Ave. www.drifterswife.com. © **207/805-1336.** Entrees $13–$22. Tues–Sat 4–11pm. Reservations not accepted.

Duckfat ★★★ CAFE   James Beard-award-winning chef Rob Evans left the fine dining world years ago to open this beloved bistro serving hand-cut Belgian-style fries with curried mayo, truffled ketchup, and other gourmet sauces, plus amazing *poutine* (Canadian-style fries with cheese curds and gravy), esoteric panini sandwiches (house-smoked brisket or duck confit, anyone?), beignets, and to-die-for milkshakes (with crème anglaise). The beer list is impeccable, and there is always a wait. Don't let it deter you—no one in Portland doesn't like this place.

43 Middle St. www.duckfat.com. © **207/774-8080.** Entrees $8–$14. Daily 11am–10pm. Reservations not accepted.

East Ender ★★ NEW AMERICAN   The best brunch in town (in my opinion) nails a delicate balance of sweet, savory, and experimental in a room that's laid-back and welcoming. The plate of chicken and yeast-raised waffles will feed you for days, particularly if you are wise enough to also indulge in the house-made daily doughnut beforehand. Dinner is equally fun and exciting; the East Ender's schtick is serving comforty faves that are inventive on the margins, like grilled duck with sauerkraut and gruyere, or a patty melt with lobster (and bacon jam) instead of beef, or chili-lime Brussels sprouts. It's the kind of joint where you can wear a sport coat or a flannel shirt and not feel out of place either way.

47 Middle St. www.eastenderportland.com © **207/879-7669.** Dinner entrees $12–$18; lunch and brunch entrees $9–$15. Tues–Sat 11:30am–10pm; Sun 11am–9pm; Mon 11:30am–3:30pm.

The Grill Room & Bar ★ AMERICAN   Good food served unpretentiously. Chef Harding Lee Smith, a Portland native, left Back Bay Grill, one of Portland's legacy fine-dining establishments, to start his own local restaurant empire, including this mecca to meat. Most items are cooked on the open kitchen's wood-fired grills, but there's more than steak here: yummy seared-tuna sandwiches on ciabatta and thin-crust pizzas, for example. Of course, you can always get a steak (porterhouse, rib-eye, sirloin; the works) or a piece of grilled fish or chicken, and you're encouraged to do so: There's a card of tasty sauces running from "zippy" to "brandy cream" for your meat. The outdoor tables are ideal in summer, yet my favorite feature of the place is its bar area, with personable barkeeps, good beers on tap, and Red Sox on the flatscreen.

84 Exchange St. www.thegrillroomandbar.com © **207/774-2333.** Small plates and pizzas $7–$15; entrees $27–$51. Daily 11:30am–2:30pm and 5–10pm (Sun to 9pm). Reservations recommended.

Hi Bombay! ★ INDIAN   The best Indian food in town, steps from the Old Port: fiery vindaloos, great mango *lassi* shakes, good *shami korma, masala,* and *biryani* dishes—and superb puffed-up *poori* fried breads. Get chutney and yogurt on the side.

1 Pleasant St. www.hibombay.com © **207/772-8767.** Entrees $10–$17. Sun–Thurs 11am–9:30pm; Fri–Sat 11am–10pm.

Rí Rá ★ PUB   This Old Port chain eatery is styled after an Irish pub, though it's somewhat fancier than *real* Irish pubs. (Patriots and Red Sox are on the TV instead of soccer—sorry, "footie.") They've got the decor right, at least: the doors were imported from a pub in Kilkenny, and the back bar and counter are from other public drinking houses in County Louth. Upstairs beyond the pub is a dining room with a view of the docks; look for Irish breakfast all day, fish and chips, bangers and mash, shepherd's pie, and Guinness bread pudding, plus a few more upscale dishes such as crab-filled salmon, Derrybeg pork (which is glazed with apricot, mustard, and cider), and *boxty,* a scallion-potato pancake topped with parsley sauce and meat. It's a rowdy place on a weekend night, with good live music more often than not.

72 Commercial St. www.rira.com. © **207/761-4446.** Main courses $9–$20. Mon–Sun 10am–10pm; Sat–Sun 9am–10pm.

Two Lights Lobster Shack ★ SEAFOOD   This seasonal takeout shack, festooned in farm implements and plunked down on a piece of rock practically atop a Cape Elizabeth lighthouse, is one of my favorite places to direct the new-to-Maine tourist. Yes, it's touristy. But it's been here forever; locals aren't shy about heading out here for a bite; and you absolutely cannot beat the views. You're looking at a panorama of the Atlantic while you wait for the kitchen to cook you pre-cracked, steamed lobsters (order a platter, with coleslaw and blueberry cake included). You can also get clams. Eat in the homey dining room or out on the picnic tables, which are set right out there on the open rocks; troll through the gift shop next door; and don't forget to try or take home a whoopie pie for dessert.

225 Two Lights Rd., Cape Elizabeth. www.lobstershacktwolights.com © **207/799-1677.** Lobsters market priced. Late Mar to Oct daily 11am–8pm. Closed Nov to late Mar.

Woodford Food & Beverage ★ CONTEMPORARY DINER Not all the exciting dining around town is centered on the peninsula. Woodford F&B shares its building with a dry cleaner and a tanning salon, but the kitchen at this vinyl-boothed, formica-countertopped, family-friendly neo-diner turns out dishes every bit as ambitious as any reservations-only joint downtown. The menu's full of comforting brasserie options such as steak and fries, luscious deviled eggs, and a seriously rich croquet madame, but you can also keep it simple with a burger or bibb salad. Feels like a neighborhood place, but attracts diners from all over town.

660 Forest Ave. www.woodfordfb.com. © **207/774-1740.** Entrees $14–$28, brunch dishes $12–$14. Wed–Sat 5–10pm; Sun 11am–8pm; Mon 5–9pm. Reservations not accepted.

Inexpensive

Becky's ★ DINER This Portland institution resides in a squat concrete building at the not-so-quaint end of the waterfront. It's been written up in *Gourmet* magazine, but that's where the comparison to "fine dining" ends; this is a diner, Maine-style, complete with drop ceilings, fluorescent lights, and scruffy counters, booths, and tables. It opens early (4am) for the local fishermen grabbing a cup of joe and some eggs before heading out onto (or in from) the water; later in the day, it attracts high school kids, businessmen, and just about everyone else. The menu is extensive, offering what you'd expect: sandwiches, fried haddock, corn dogs, tuna melts, and milky bowls of chowder with just-caught fish. It's notable for its breakfasts, including more than a dozen omelets, eggs any way you want 'em, pancakes, French toast, and five types of home fries.

390 Commercial St. www.beckysdiner.com. © **207/773-7070.** Breakfast items $4–$11; lunch and dinner items $4–$17. Daily 4am–9pm (until 10pm in summer).

To the Point

The redevelopment of the formerly industrial **Thompson's Point**—which one local newspaper writer called "the biggest dump in Portland" as recently as 2011—is arguably a microcosm for the city's recent cultural (and physical evolution). A long, 19th-century brick warehouse that once served as a storage facility for trains today houses a fleet of indie/artisan ventures. There's a clowning and acrobatics school (with monthly cabaret performances) in **Circus Maine** (© 207/536-0768, www.circusmaine.org) and the Bigfoot-documenting **International Museum of Cryptozoology ★** (www.cryptozoologymuseum.com), not to mention the welcoming tasting room of the **Stroudwater Distillery** (© **207/536-7811**, www.stroudwater distillery.com), a Portland outpost of **Cellardoor Winery** (© **207/536-7700**, www.mainewine.com), and one of Maine's finest craft brewers (and most bangin' tap rooms) in **Bissell Brothers ★** (see p. 109). **Big J's Chicken Shack ★** (www.bigjschicken.com; © **207/747-4005**) serves terrific fried chicken and mouth-singing Nashville hot chicken to the crowds that hop from door to door on weekends, augmented by the occasional food cart outside. If none of that's enough to draw you to this out-of-the-way riverside post-industrial hotspot, a former railroad platform-shed hosts big-name concerts in the summer and a 10,000-square-foot ice rink in the winter.

PACKING A picnic

Portland and its surrounding area is so stuffed with picnic spots you might need a week to sample them all. For starters, don't miss the hilltop **Eastern Promenade** (p. 102), with expansive views of Casco Bay. The **Western Promenade** (p. 103), reached across town via Congress Street, has distant views of the White Mountains and often free musical performances in summer. For a tranquil water view, there's **Back Cove** (p. 102). Just a few miles north of Portland along Route 1 in Falmouth, the Maine Audubon Society's **Gilsland Farm**

Sanctuary (p. 102) is one of the best picnic spots I've found. And, of course, the beaches and parks in Cape Elizabeth (see "Hitting the Beaches," p. 104) are all superlative picnic spots. In metro Portland, make a quick fly-by of **Standard Baking Company** (p. 91) for great baked goods, sweets, and coffee. **Cape Elizabeth** has a few general stores good for stocking up prebeach; they're heavy on sodas, beer, and candy, but you can also score an Italian sandwich or an ice-cream treat at most of them.

Blue Rooster Food Company ★ SANDWICHES/GLOBAL Great sandwiches, although most locals stop in for the piled-high tater tots or the creative hot dogs, natural-casing franks served with pineapple and bacon, pickled ginger and wasabi mayo, cheese curds and gravy, BBQ and jalapenos, you name it. Not much seating in this counter-service joint, so best to park it on a bench somewhere in the surrounding blocks of the Old Port.

5 Dana St. www.blueroosterfoodcompany.com. © **207/747-4157.** Sandwiches and hot dogs $5–$12. Sun–Thurs 11am–6pm; Fri–Sat 11am–2am.

Gilbert's Chowder House CHOWDER/SEAFOOD Gilbert's is a very popular waterfront spot with tourists, and is nautical without taking the theme too far. The reasonable prices keep locals coming, too. The chowders are okay, if unspectacular; other choices include fried clams, haddock sandwiches, and various seafood you can order either broiled or fried. There's also a basic lobster dinner with corn on the cob and a cup of clam chowder. Limited microbrews are on tap, and they serve decent cheesecake for dessert, among other choices.

92 Commercial St. www.gilbertschowderhouse.com. © **207/871-5636.** Chowders $5–$14; sandwiches $5–$16; main courses $12–$22. Daily 11am–9pm.

Seng Thai Food 2 ★ SOUTHEAST ASIAN For Thai food, this funky, lowbrow corner eatery has been best in town for some 25 years, and it must be good—doctors at the nearby hospital show up for cheap eats. Most everything costs less than $15, the Thai iced tea is excellent, and the head chefs (sisters, apparently) are unfailingly friendly. The cashew-nut entree with pineapple is great; you can't go wrong with a standard order of pad Thai either. A good local bite.

921 Congress St. www.saengthaihousemaine.com © **207/780-0900.** Entrees $6–$16. Sun–Thurs 11am–9:30pm; Fri–Sat 11am–10pm.

Silly's ★ ECLECTIC   Silly's has long been the favored cheap-eats joint of hip (and, particularly, crunchy) Portlanders. Situated on a busy, commercial street near the Eastern Promenade, the interior is informal, bright, and funky, with mismatched 1950s dinettes and a hodgepodge back patio beneath trees. There's also an unhealthy fascination with Einstein here; like Einstein, the immense menu is creative. The place is noted for its roll-ups ("Abdullahs"), a series of tasty fillings piled into soft tortillas—try one with shish kabob and feta, or a "Diesel" made with pulled pork and coleslaw. The fries are hand-cut, the burgers big and juicy, and there's beer on tap. Vegans and vegetarians also flock to Silly's for wraps, noodle dishes, and monstrous salads, and the kitchen keeps a separate gluten-free fryer. Lots of fun, fruity cocktails and sangria by the pitcher keeps the mood pretty festive most nights.

40 Washington Ave. www.sillys.com. ☏ **207/772-0360.** Most items $8–$14. Wed–Fri 11am–9pm; Sat–Sun 9am–9pm.

Susan's Fish and Chips SEAFOOD   Zero pretense, zero frills, and what's arguably the best fried fish in a fish town. The stuff's fried up in a deliciously sandy, crunchy jacket that's never too heavy, but rather just right. Get fries, and put ketchup or vinegar on them. Or bring your *own* catch: They'll fry it! You've gotta love that.

1135 Forest Ave. www.susansfishnchips.com. ☏ **207/878-3240.** Entrees $8–$23. Daily 11am–8pm.

EXPLORING PORTLAND

Any visit to Portland should start with a stroll around the historic **Old Port** ★. Bounded by Commercial, Congress, Union, and Pearl streets, this area near the waterfront has the city's best commercial architecture, a mess of boutiques, fine restaurants, and one of the thickest concentrations of bars on the eastern seaboard. (The Old Port tends to transform as night lengthens, with crowds growing younger and rowdier.) The narrow streets and intricate brick facades reflect a mid-Victorian era; most of the area was rebuilt following a devastating fire in 1866. **Exchange Street** is the heart of the Old Port, with other attractive streets running off and around it.

Just outside the Old Port, don't miss the **First Parish Church** ★ (see p. 100) at 425 Congress Street, a beautiful granite meetinghouse with an impressively austere interior that has changed little since 1826. A few doors down the block, Portland's **City Hall** is at the head of Exchange Street. Modeled after New York City's, it was built from granite in 1909. In a similarly regal vein is the **U.S. Custom House,** 312 Fore Street near the Old Port. The fine woodwork and marble floors here date to 1868.

Portland's Top Attractions

Children's Museum of Maine ★ MUSEUM   The centerpiece exhibit in Portland's kids' museum is its camera obscura, a room-size "camera" located on the top floor of this stout, columned downtown building next to the

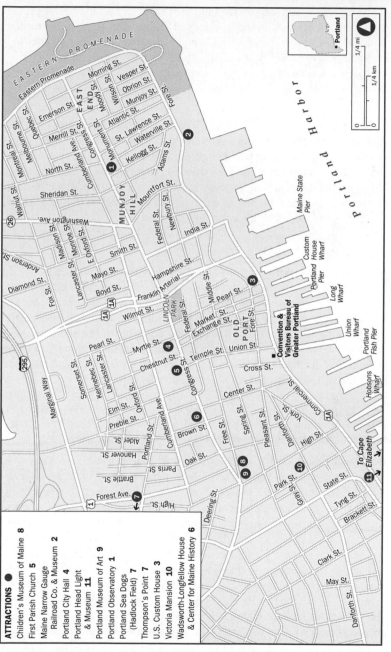

Portland Harbor

Portland

1/4 mi

1/4 km

EASTERN PROMENADE

Eastern Promenade

EAST END

Maine State Pier

Custom House Wharf

Portland Pier

Long Wharf

Union Wharf

Portland Fish Pier

Hobsons Wharf

Convention & Visitors Bureau of Greater Portland

OLD PORT

LINCOLN PARK

MUNJOY HILL

To Cape Elizabeth

ATTRACTIONS ●

Children's Museum of Maine **8**
First Parish Church **5**
Maine Narrow Gauge Railroad Co. & Museum **2**
Portland City Hall **4**
Portland Head Light & Museum **11**
Portland Museum of Art **9**
Portland Observatory **1**
Portland Sea Dogs (Hadlock Field) **7**
Thompson's Point **7**
U.S. Custom House **3**
Victoria Mansion **10**
Wadsworth-Longfellow House & Center for Maine History **6**

art museum. Children gather around a white table in a dark room, where they see magically projected images that include cars driving on city streets, boats plying the harbor, and seagulls flapping by. This never fails to enthrall, providing a memorable lesson in the workings of lenses. That's just one attraction; there are plenty more, from a simulated supermarket checkout counter to a firehouse pole to a mock space shuttle that kids pilot from a high cockpit.

142 Free St. (next to the Portland Museum of Art). www.kitetails.org. © 207/828-1234. Admission $10, or $2 from 5 to 8pm 1st Fri of each month. Tues–Sun 10am–5pm (open until 8pm 1st Fri of each month).

First Parish Church ★ CHURCH Portland's oldest continuously operating house of worship (continuous since at least 1674, believe it or not) is right here in the heart of the city, although the present-day structure was "only" built in 1825 to replace a previous wooden church building. Constructed of Maine granite quarried near Brunswick, Maine, it's a narrow, graceful counterpoint to the modern high-rises encircling it. The rough granite blocks and clock tower are topped by a surprisingly graceful spire.

425 Congress St. at Temple St. www.firstparishportland.org. © 207/773-5747. Admission free. Interior tours possible, by appointment.

Maine Narrow Gauge Railroad Co. & Museum ★ MUSEUM In the late 19th century, Maine was home to several narrow-gauge railways, operating on rails 2 feet apart. Most of these trains have disappeared, but this nonprofit organization is dedicated to preserving the examples that remain. There's a small fee for admission to the museum only, while a more expensive ticket also includes a short ride on the little train that putters along Casco Bay at the foot of the Eastern Promenade. Views of the islands are attractive; the ride itself is slow, but your kids will undoubtedly enjoy it.

58 Fore St. www.mainenarrowgauge.org. © 207/828-0814. Museum admission $3 adults, $2 seniors and children 3–12; train fare (includes museum admission) $10 adults, $9 seniors, $6 children 3–12, free for children 2 and under. May–Oct Sat–Thurs 9:30am–4pm, Fri 11:30am–4pm (trains run on the hour); closed Nov–Apr.

Portland Head Light & Museum ★★ LIGHTHOUSE A short drive south from downtown Portland, this 1794 lighthouse is one of the most picturesque in the nation. You'll probably recognize it from advertisements, calendars, or posters. The light marks the entrance to Portland Harbor and was occupied continuously from its construction until 1989, when it was automated and the graceful keeper's house (built in 1891) was converted to a small, town-owned museum focusing on the history of navigation. The lighthouse itself is still active, and therefore is closed to the public, but visitors can stop by the museum or browse for lighthouse-themed items in a gift shop. The surrounding grounds of Fort Williams Park are great for picnics; if you're traveling with kids, plan extra time for them to enjoy its two playgrounds and a brand new children's garden full of winding paths, hopscotch stones, and tunnels.

1000 Shore Rd. (in Fort Williams Park), Cape Elizabeth. www.portlandheadlight.com. © 207/799-2661. Free admission for grounds; museum admission $2 adults, $1 children

6–18. Park grounds open daily year-round sunrise–sunset (until 8:30pm in summer); museum daily Memorial Day–Oct 10am–4pm, weekends only mid-Apr–mid-May and Nov–early Dec.

Portland Museum of Art ★★★ MUSEUM

The modern main building of Portland's art museum, designed by I. M. Pei & Partners and opened in 1983, is an arresting red-brick presence on Congress Square, and it's top-rate by every standard. The museum features selections from its own fine collections along with a parade of touring exhibits. (Summer exhibits are usually targeted at a broad audience.) The museum, which began as the Portland Art Society in 1882, has over the years amassed particularly strong holdings of American artists with Maine connections, including Winslow Homer, Andrew Wyeth, and Edward Hopper, and it has fine displays of Early American furniture and crafts. The museum shares with Colby College the Joan Whitney Payson Collection, which includes wonderful European works by Renoir, Degas, and Picasso, among other titans. Recent special exhibitions have brought the art books of Henri Matisse, photographs from Maine's pioneering Rose Marasco, a retrospective of photorealist painter Richard Estes, and a juxtaposition of Warhol's *Mao* with the *Mona Lisa*. The museum's film series, shown on an auditorium big-screen, is a worthy substitute for the arthouse cinema Portland lacks. If you're into American masters, check out the tour of the **Winslow Homer Studio at Prout's Neck** in Cape Elizabeth, offered on Mondays and Fridays in the summer ($55, van trip from museum, call to reserve well ahead). Homer spent the last 26 years of his life there, staring at the rockbound coast and creating some of his most famous works.

7 Congress Square. (corner of Congress and High sts.). www.portlandmuseum.org. ⓒ **207/775-6148**. Admission $15 adults, $13 seniors, $10 students, kids 14 and under free; free admission Fri 4–8pm. Sat–Wed 11am–6pm, Thurs–Fri 11am–8pm; closed Mon–Tues from Columbus Day to Memorial Day.

Portland Observatory ★ MUSEUM/LANDMARK

Atop Munjoy Hill, above the Eastern Promenade, this quirky shingled tower dating from 1807 was originally built to signal the arrival of ships into port. Exhibits inside provide a quick glimpse of Portland's past, but the real draw is the expansive view from the top of the city and the harbor.

138 Congress St. www.portlandlandmarks.org. ⓒ **207/774-5561**. $10 adults, $8 seniors and students, $5 children 6–16. Daily Memorial Day–Columbus Day, 10am–5pm; last tour at 4:30pm.

Victoria Mansion ★ HISTORIC HOME

Perhaps no building in Portland is more famous than this imposing High Victorian manse, built from 1858 to 1860 of brownstone after plans by New Haven architect Henry Austin. This home, also known as the Morse Libby House, is the nation's premier showpiece of Victorian architecture. Details fill the interior, from wonderful and plentiful mural work to a grand staircase, gas-fueled chandeliers ("gasoliers"), Persian-style rugs hand-woven in Scotland, stained glass, nearly all the original furniture, and plaster work and cabinets by famed interior decorator

Gustave Herter. Yes, it's pricey and over the top, but a must-see for anyone serious about architectural history. The month of December is particularly lively here, with themed decorations, parties, tours, and special events.

109 Danforth St. www.victoriamansion.org. © **207/772-4841.** $15 adults, $13.50 seniors, $5 children 6–17, $35 family, free for children 5 and under. May–Oct Mon–Sat 10am–4pm, Sun 1–5pm; late Nov–early Jan daily 11am–4:30pm (Mon to 6:30pm). Tours twice per hour. Closed Nov and early Jan–Apr.

Wadsworth-Longfellow House ★★ HISTORIC HOME   This 18th-century, red-brick home is one of three structures containing the famous Portland writer Henry Wadsworth Longfellow's boyhood home, as well as one of the state's best historical archives: a history campus, if you will. This home was built by Gen. Peleg Wadsworth, grandfather of the poet, and is still furnished in early-19th-century style with some original furniture. Adjacent is the Maine History Gallery, a decent museum inside a former bank.

487-489 Congress St. www.mainehistory.org. © **207/774-1822.** $15 adults, $12 seniors and students, $3 kids 6–17. Wadsworth-Longfellow House May–Oct Mon–Sat 10am–5pm, Sun noon–4pm (tours on the hour); Nov–Apr Tues–Sat 10am–5pm.

WONDERFUL WALKS

The city's finest harborside stroll is along the **Eastern Prom Pathway ★**, which wraps for about a mile along the waterfront beginning at the Casco Bay Lines ferry terminal at the corner of Commercial and Franklin streets. This paved pathway is suitable for walking or biking, and offers expansive views of Casco Bay and its myriad (more than one for each day of the year) islands. Some have favorably compared this view with San Francisco's; even if that's stretching it a bit, you can't go wrong here watching the weather and light come and go. The pathway skirts the lower edge of the **Eastern Promenade ★★**, a 68-acre hillside park with broad, grassy slopes extending down to the water. Little East End Beach is also here, but the water is often off-limits for swimming (look for signs). The easiest place to park is near the beach and boat ramp. From downtown, head east on Congress Street until you can't go any farther; turn right, and then take your first left on the road down the hill to the water's edge.

The pathway continues on to **Back Cove Pathway ★**, a 3½-mile loop around tidal Back Cove, offering attractive views of the city skyline across the

---

Back to Nature

Just a few miles north of Portland along Route 1 in Falmouth, the Maine Audubon Society's **Gilsland Farm Sanctuary** is a lovely place to enjoy nature (and a perfect place for a picnic, if you're so inclined). Gaze out on grassy fields, wildflowers, and tidewater. Afterward, explore the society's intriguing displays, demonstration projects, and gift shops; this is clearly an organization that cares deeply about the state's natural resources. What the heck? Become a member while you're here.

The **Portland Sea Dogs** are a minor league Double-A team affiliated with the Boston Red Sox (a perfect marriage in baseball-crazy northern New England). They play through summer at **Hadlock Field** (217 Park Ave.; www. seadogs.com; © **800/936-3647** or 207/879-9500), a delightful small stadium near downtown that still retains an old-time feel despite aluminum benches and other updating; it's one of the better minor league parks at which I've ever attended a ballgame. Activities are geared toward families, with lots of entertainment between innings and a selection of food that's a couple of notches above basic hot dogs and hamburgers. (Try the tasty fries and sausages, and make sure you get a Sea Dog biscuit: local vanilla ice cream between two chocolate chip cookies.) You might even catch future pro stars. The season runs from around April until around Labor Day.

water, glimpses of Casco Bay, and a bit of exercise. The pathway is the city's most popular recreational facility; after work in summer, Portlanders flock here to walk, bike, jog, and windsurf (there's enough water 2½ hours before and after high tide). Part of the pathway shares a noisy bridge with I-295, and it can be unpleasant at a dead low tide; when the tides and the weather cooperate, however, it's a nice spot for a walk. The main parking lot is located across from Hannaford Plaza at the water's edge. Take exit 6 (Forest Ave. north) off I-295; turn right at the first light on Baxter Boulevard. At the next light, turn right again and park in the lot ahead on the left.

On the other end of the peninsula is the **Western Promenade** ★. (Follow Spring Street westward to Vaughan Street; turn right and then take your first left on Bowdoin Street to the Prom.) This narrow strip of lawn atop a forested bluff has sweeping views across the Fore River west to the White Mountains in the distance (you can just make out the massive outline of Mount Washington on a clear day). The airport, Maine Mall, and paper mill in the foreground may be less than scenic, but still, it's a great spot to watch the sun set. Around the Western Prom are some of the grandest and most imposing houses in the city that include a wide array of architectural styles, from Italianate to shingle to stick.

On the Water

Casco Bay Lines ★ BOAT TOURS Six of Casco Bay's islands have year-round populations and are served by scheduled ferries from downtown Portland. Except for Long Island, the islands are part of the city of Portland. The ferries provide an inexpensive way to view the bustling harbor and get a taste of island life. Trips range from a 20-minute (one-way) excursion to **Peaks Island** (the closest thing to an island suburb, with 1,000 or so year-round residents) to the 5½-hour narrated cruise (with a long lunch stopover) to **Bailey Island** (connected by bridge to the mainland south of Brunswick) and back. All of the islands are well suited for walking; Peaks Island has a rocky back shore that's easily accessible via the island's paved perimeter road

HITTING THE beaches

One of the supreme pleasures of visiting the Portland area is the opportunity to sample some of its many great beaches and lighthouse and ocean views. Even within Portland city limits, you can laze on the Eastern Promenade's tiny **East End Beach** (see p. 102) for free; the views are great, though swimming there is a judgment call—a wastewater treatment plant looms nearby, although after years of cleanup efforts, city officials claim it's safe for swimming. Across the bridge in South Portland, **Willard Beach ★** is a good neighborhood beach: small, with friendly locals, dogs, and tidal rocks to scramble over. There's plenty of parking here.

For the best of the out-of-town beaches and views, though, strike out for **Cape Elizabeth,** a moneyed bedroom community just south of the city. (From Portland's State Street, cross the Route 77 bridge going south, then follow signs.) You can choose from a trio of good beaches as you meander along **Route 77,** a lovely lane that occasionally recalls England with its sweeping views of marsh, ocean, or cultivated field. **Two Lights State Park ★★** (*(C)* **207/ 799-5871**) is impressively scenic, and has the advantage of a decent

lobster-and-seafood hut beside it: **Two Lights Lobster Shack ★**, open late March through October. The lobsters are smallish, lobster rolls meaty, clam chowder pretty good, and the views are sublime. Farther south on Route 77, **Crescent Beach State Park ★★★** (*(C)* **207/799-5871**) is a lovely mile-long curve of sand, reached by a walk through beach roses; it has ample parking, barbecue pits, picnic tables, and a snack bar. Both charge a fee from Memorial Day to Columbus Day.

The town-operated **Fort Williams State Park ★**, located on Shore Road in Cape Elizabeth just off Route 77, offers free access and sweeping vistas of craggy waves crashing onto dramatic rocks, as well as the much-photographed **Portland Head Light ★★** (see p. 100). Two to 3 miles farther south, turn left onto Route 207 for two more options: **Scarborough Beach Park ★**, on the left, another long strip of clean sand and dunes with changing facilities ($8 for access in summer) or—a bit farther along, on the right at the end of Ferry Road—quieter **Ferry Beach State Park** (*(C)* **207/283-0067**), which has good views south toward Old Orchard Beach (see p. 110).

(bring a picnic lunch). There's also a bike rental outfit a few blocks from the island's ferry dock. **Long Island** has a good hidden beach. **Cliff Island** is the most remote of the six-pack, with a sedate turn-of-the-20th-century character.

Commercial and Franklin sts. www.cascobaylines.com. *(C)* **207/774-7871.** Fares vary depending on the run and the season; summer rates $7–$12 round-trip. Frequent departures 6am–10pm.

Shopping

Aficionados of antiques and secondhand furniture stores love Portland. Good browsing can be enjoyed along Congress Street; try the stretches between State and High streets in the arts district, or from India Street to Washington Avenue on Munjoy Hill. About a dozen shops of varying quality (mostly low-end) can be found in these two areas.

More serious antiques hounds may choose to visit an **auction house** or two. Two or three times per week, you'll be able to find an auction within an hour's drive of Portland. A good source of information is the *Maine Sunday Telegram*. Look in the classifieds for listings of auctions scheduled for the following week.

For new items, the Old Port, with its dozens of boutiques and storefronts, is well worth browsing. It's especially strong in contemporary, one-of-a-kind clothing that's a world apart from generic stuff you'd find at a mall. Artisan and crafts shops are also well represented.

ANTIQUES AND VINTAGE ITEMS

Allen & Walker Antiques ★★ This is a great stop for New England, American, and Oriental items ranging from period oil paintings to antique furniture to sake sets . . . and much more. You just never know what you'll find here on a given day, and both Allen and Walker really know their stuff. 684 Congress St. ℭ **207/772-8787.**

Portland Flea For All ★★ Vintage, antique, and artisan goods rule the day at this consignment coop in Bayside, a beautiful potpourri of furniture, jewelry, vinyl, and unclassifiable (but always cool) old junk. Around 100 vendors. 585 Congress St. www.portlandfleaforall.com ℭ **207/370-7570.**

BOOKS

Print: A Bookstore ★★ An indie shop in the super-hip Munjoy Hill neighborhood, Print has all the bestsellers, plenty of more obscure titles, and a super knowledgeable staff. Moreover, they bring in great authors for readings and events. 273 Congress St. www.printbookstore.com ℭ **207/536-4778.**

Yes Books ★ Once owned by legendary local poet Pat Murphy (sadly deceased), this bookshop is about as well organized as an artist's bedroom, but so what? The first editions, philosophy, poetry, history, and prints here are amazing. 589 Congress St. ℭ **207/775-3233.**

CRAFTS AND ARTISANS

Abacus Gallery ★ A wide range of bold, inventive crafts of all varieties—from furniture to jewelry—is displayed on two floors of this centrally located shop. Even if you're not in a buying frame of mind, this is a great place for browsing. 44 Exchange St. www.abacusgallery.com ℭ **207/772-4880.**

Maine Potters Market ★ Maine's largest pottery collective has been in operation for 2 decades, and it's open daily. You can select from a variety of distinctive styles crafted by local potters; shipping is easily arranged. 376 Fore St. www.mainepottersmarket.com ℭ **207/774-1633.**

Green Design Furniture ★ This inventive shop sells beautiful mission-inspired furniture, crafted of cherry and other woods, that disassembles for easy storage and travel. "Green," by the way, isn't ecobabble: The owner's name is Doug Green. 250 Commercial St. www.greendesigns.com ℭ **866/756-4730** or 207/775-4234.

SHOPPING AT THE maine MALL

The big **Maine Mall** takes up a huge chunk of real estate near the Portland Jetport in South Portland (easily reached off the Maine Turnpike via its own exit). The options here are uniformly bland—this could be Anywheresville, America—and there are no outlet or factory stores; you'll pay full price, plus Maine state tax.

Still, if there's something reassuring about being able to bop among the likes of **Macy's, Bath & Body Works, Victoria's Secret, Pottery Barn,** the **Apple Store,** and **H&M,** then sitting down with a coffee and a book or CD at **Books-A-Million** (in its own free-standing building), you might enjoy it. There's not much

that's distinctive here, though the bookstore is very well stocked and the staff is helpful. Also check out the **Sports Authority** for low-priced sporting goods; watch for specials on exercise equipment, golf balls, camping gear, and the like.

Needless to say, there's a food court here, though it isn't very good. Consider dining at a nearby restaurant instead; a number of them surround the moatlike ring road that surrounds the mall and its acres of parking lots. Good choices include the **Sebago Brewing Company** for local beers and pub fare, or **Taj,** a respectable family-run Indian place with a lunch buffet to fuel your shopping spree.

FASHION
Amaryllis Clothing Co. ★ Portland's original creative clothing store, Amaryllis sells unique clothing for women, plus accessories such as lingerie, belts, and jewelry. It's as comfortable as it is elegant: Colors are rich, patterns are unique, and some items are designed by local artisans. 41 Exchange St. www.amaryllisclothing.com. *C* **207/772-4439.**

GOURMET
Harbor Fish Market ★★ One of Portland's several waterfront fish markets, it's worth visiting just to see piles of fish hard-working guys have pulled out of the bay. You can buy smoked fish for your bagels, and lobsters packed safely for 24 hours' worth of traveling. You can also buy picnic fixings. 9 Custom House Wharf (across from Pearl St.). www.harborfish.com. *C* **207/775-0251.**

LeRoux Kitchen ★ What's a touristy shopping area without a crack kitchen store? Nothing. And this is Portland's. You'll find kitchen gadgets, made-in-Maine food products, and a good selection of wines at this Old Port shop. 161 Commercial St. www.lerouxkitchen.com. *C* **207/553-7665.**

Stonewall Kitchen ★ Maine's homegrown Stonewall is a frequent winner at trade shows for its delicious mustards, jams, and sauces: ginger peach tea jam, sun-dried tomato and olive relish, maple chipotle grill sauce, and so on. Browse (and sample the goods) at its Old Port store, which also features frequent cooking classes. 182 Middle St. www.stonewallkitchen.com. *C* **207/879-2409.**

JEWELRY
D. Cole Jewelers ★ Jewelers Dean and Denise Cole produce lovely handcrafted gold and silver jewelry that's always attractive, and often surprisingly affordable. Browse through elegant traditional designs, as well as more

offbeat ones, at the bright, low-pressure shop; the staff is extremely helpful. 10 Exchange St. www.dcolejewelers.com. ℰ **207/772-5119.**

Folia Jewelry ★ Original, handcrafted jewelry by owner Edith Armstrong (and some of Maine's top designers) is nicely displayed at this tasteful shop in the heart of the Old Port. The rings are especially arty and nice. 50 Exchange St. www.foliajewelry.com. ℰ **207/761-4432.**

PORTLAND AFTER DARK
Bars & Music

Portland is usually lively in the evenings, especially on summer weekends when the testosterone level in the Old Port seems to rocket into the stratosphere, with young men and women prowling the dozens of bars and spilling out onto Fore Street and the surrounding alleys and streets.

Among the Old Port bars favored by locals are **Three-Dollar Dewey's,** at the corner of Commercial and Union streets (the popcorn is free); atmospheric **Gritty Cuff's Brew Pub,** on Fore Street at the foot of Exchange Street, where you'll find live music and a cast of regulars quaffing great beers brewed on-site; and the slightly rowdy Irish pub **Brian Ború,** on Center Street, with a rooftop patio. All three bars are casual and pubby, with guests sharing long tables with new companions.

Off the peninsula, check out **The Great Lost Bear** (540 Forest Ave., www. greatlostbear.com; ℰ **207/772-0300**), a venerable locals hangout with 50 to 60 beers on offer at any given moment, including many Maine-crafted brews. Some of the choicest ales are even dispensed from one of three cask-conditioned hand pumps. Every Thursday the bartender showcases a particular brewer or style—a good way to get educated about the nuances of good beer. To find the Bear, head about 2 miles out on Forest Avenue (*away* from the Old Port), or ask a local for directions.

Beyond the active bar scene, a number of clubs offer a mix of live and recorded entertainment throughout the year. As is common in other small cities where there are more venues than attendees, clubs tend to come and go, sometimes quite rapidly. Check the city's free weekly *Portland Phoenix* or monthly *Dispatch* for current venues, performers, and showtimes.

Both the *Phoenix* and the *Dispatch* are also good resources for concert schedules at **Thompson's Point** (www.thompsonspointmaine.com—see box p. 96), the **State Theatre** (609 Congress St., www.statetheatreportland.com), or the open-air stage at the **Maine State Pier** (www.waterfrontconcerts.com), a very cool place to see a summer outdoor show, with the smell of salt on the air and the ferries coming and going right next door.

Performing Arts

Portland has a growing creative corps of performing artists. Theater companies typically take the summer off, but it doesn't hurt to call or check the local papers for special performances.

let's get hopping: THE BEERS OF PORTLAND

Portland is unquestionably the beer capital of New England. Not just northern New England, but *all* of New England—and it holds its own against most of the rest of the country, too, with more craft breweries per capita than any American city. In general, Maine's craft brew scene is characterized by liberal pour laws that make tap rooms as popular as bars, plus a penchant for embracing (and reviving) Old World styles.

For starters, there's the granddaddy of Belgian-style beer in the U.S. Head west out Forest Avenue (off Congress Street) a few miles, then turn right on Riverside Street and take the next right into an industrial park. You'll come to **Allagash Brewing ★★** at 50 Industrial Way (www.allagash.com, ✆ **800/330-5385** or 207/878-5385), a legend of a craft brewer that's gained nationwide recognition for its Belgian-style white, double, and triple beers. Allagash offers daily tours from 11am to 4:30pm. The brewery is still crazy experimental—taps pouring at the spacious and rustic tap room include hard-to-find seasonal and limited release brews: wild-fermented beers, beers brewed with coffee or fruit or ginger, dry-hopped and barrel-aged beers, you name it. Still, it's the company's flagship brew, Allagash White, that holds a special place in many beer lover's palates. Founding brewer Rob Tod's Belgian white is as crisp and clean as an orange rind, and indeed he uses citrus peels in the mix, as well as coriander and other spices. It's an exquisite beer that helped kick off this country's craft brew revolution.

And while you're out here, don't miss three other topnotch brewers in the very same industrial park. Across the street from Allagash, at 1 Industrial Way, you'll want to try the milk stout or the slightly sour, easy-drinking Lawn Mower saison from **Austin Street Brewery** (✆ **207/200-1994;** www.austinstreetbrewery.com), then duck next door into **Foundation Brewing Company** (✆ **207/370-8187;** www.foundationbrew.com), which, for my money, brews two of the crispest, tastiest IPAs in New England, the so-very-floral Afterglow and the bit-more-of-a-wallop Epiphany. The two tiny tap rooms are a great hang in the summer, when the party spills onto picnic tables out front. Then keep going around the circuit to find **Geary's** (www.gearybrewing.com; ✆ **207/878-2337**) at 38 Evergreen Drive, often credited as New England's very first microbrewery. Geary's year-round beers rely on a British yeast strain that's a bit of an acquired taste, but the tap room also offers more diverse small-batch pours from the brewery's pilot series.

Portland Stage Company ★ The most polished and consistent of the Portland theater companies, Portland Stage offers crisply produced shows starring local and imported equity actors in a handsome, second-story theater just off Congress Street. About a half-dozen shows are staged throughout the season, which runs from about October to May. Recent productions have included *A Song at Twilight, Heroes, God of Carnage,* Shakespeare's *Julius Caesar,* and world premieres by playwright Tom Coash and bestselling Maine novelist Monica Wood. Performing Arts Center, 25A Forest Ave. www.portlandstage.com. ✆ **207/774-0465.** Tickets $35–$45 adults, discounts for students and seniors.

Head down to the East Bayside District to find two of Portland's buzziest brewers and most convivial tap rooms, a short walk from each other. **Oxbow Blending and Bottling ★** (www.oxbow beer.com; ✆ **207/350-0025**) is the Portland outpost of a farmhouse brewery headquartered up the coast, in Newcastle (p. 139). Its urban iteration pours super-crushable Old World farmhouse ales in a huge former warehouse decorated with an oh-so-Portland mix of b-boy graffiti and reclaimed barn wood. Though a bit hard to find (49 Washington Avenue, head into the alley next to the coffee shop), this place is a party on a Saturday night. **Rising Tide Brewing Company** (www.risingtidebrewing.com; ✆ **207/370-2337**) at 103 Fox Street has a great patio with lawn games and food trucks and excels at lower-alcohol brews. Its Maine Island Trail Ale, at just 4.3% ABV, is crispy, citrusy, and beloved by Mainers in summer.

Off the peninsula, beer lovers literally line up around the block at Thompson's Point (p. 96) when **Bissell Brothers ★** (www.bissellbrothers.com) releases cases of its newest batches. The 2,500-square-foot tap room (complete pinball, wall murals, and lofted hangout space) is often packed by noon with devotees of Bissell's bright, strong, often opaque ales. A mile away (along the bikeable Fore River Parkway Trail), in a former warehouse at 17 Westfield Street, **Bunker Brewing** (www.bunkerbrewingco. com; ✆ **207/613-9471**) is known for its easy-drinking flagship pilsner.

Incredibly, this list only scratches the surface of the more than 20 craft brewers operating in Greater Portland. You can taste a bunch at the Old Port's superb **Novare Res Bier Café** (4 Canal Plaza, www.novareresbiercafe.com; ✆ **207/ 761-2437**), a modern-day rathskeller with a bottle list 500 strong and an emphasis on obscure Euro imports. Come happy hour, the crowd is a mix of flannel-clad scenesters, tipsy businessmen, bemused out-of-towners, and salty types from down on the wharf. The best six-pack shopping is at the Bier Cellar (www.biercellar.com; ✆ **207/200-6258**), just off the highway at 299 Forest Avenue.

Both **Maine Beer Tours** (www.maine beertours.com; ✆ **207/553-0898**) and the **Maine Brew Bus** (www.themaine brewbus.com; ✆ **207/245-1940**) will shuttle you around from tap room to tap room (tour options vary widely, $40–$70 per person). For an exhaustive list of brewers and a map of the Maine Beer Trail, visit **www.mainebrewersguild.org**.

Portland Symphony Orchestra ★★ The well-regarded Portland Symphony, headed by Robert Moody, whose last season with the symphony will end in 2018, offers a variety of performances throughout the season (typically September to May), ranging from pops concerts to Mozart; half the orchestra are Mainers, the rest New Englanders, and all are talented. Summer travelers should consider a Portland detour the week of July 4th, when the "Patriotic Pops" is held (weather permitting) at the city's Eastern Prom. There are also special Christmas shows. 477 Congress St. www.portlandsymphony.com. ✆ **207/842-0800** for tickets, or 773-6128 for information. Tickets $32–$83, discounts for students and seniors.

SIDE TRIPS FROM PORTLAND

Old Orchard Beach ★

About 12 miles south of Portland is the unrepentantly honky-tonk beach town of Old Orchard Beach, which offers considerable stimulus for the senses (not to mention bikers, fried dough, and French Canadians aplenty). This venerable Victorian-era resort is famed for its amusement park, pier, and a long, sandy beach that attracts sun-worshipers from all over.

Be sure to spend time and money on the stomach-churning rides at the beachside amusement park of **Palace Playland** (www.palaceplayland.com; ✆ **207/934-2001**), and then walk on the 7-mile-long beach past the midrise condos that sprouted in the 1980s like a scale-model Miami Beach. The beach is broad and open at low tide; at high tide, space to plunk your towel down is at a premium.

In the evenings, teens and young adults dominate the town's culture, spilling out of the video arcades and cruising the main strip. For dinner, do as the locals do and buy hot dogs, pizza, and cotton candy—and be sure to save your change for the arcades.

Just outside of "OOB," as many Mainers call it, neighboring **Saco** has two often-mobbed waterparks, **Aquaboggan** (www.aquabogganwaterpark.com; ✆ **207/282-3112**) and **Funtown Splashtown USA** (www.funtownusa.com; ✆ **207/284-5139**). A more charming local institution is the **Saco Drive-In ★**, 969 Portland Road (www.sacodrivein.com; ✆ **207/286-3200**), a lovingly maintained al fresco theater with a throwback snack shop—you can usually count on a kid-friendly earlier show and something for the grown-ups after.

Old Orchard Beach is just off Route 1 south of Portland. The quickest route is to leave the turnpike at exit 36 in Saco and then follow I-195 and the signs to the beach. Don't expect to be alone here: Parking is tight, and the traffic can be horrendous during the peak summer months.

Sebago Lake ★★

Maine's second-largest lake is also its most popular. Ringed with summer homes, Sebago Lake attracts thousands of vacationers to its cool, deep waters.

You can take a tour of the outlying lakes and the ancient canal system between Sebago and Long lakes on the *Songo River Queen II* (www.songoriverqueen.net; ✆ **207/693-6861**), a faux-steamship berthed in the town of Naples. Operating from July through Labor Day, the 1-hour trips cost $15 for adults, $8 for children ages 4–12. Longer tours and group rates are also available for a little more money.

Or just lie in the sun along the sandy beach at bustling **Sebago Lake State Park** (✆ **207/693-6613**), on the lake's north shore—the park is off Route 302 (look for signs on the south side of the road, between the towns of Raymond and South Casco). This park has shady picnic areas, a campground, a snack bar, and lifeguards on the beach. It can be uncomfortably crowded on sunny summer weekends; it's best on weekdays. Bring food and charcoal for barbecuing at the shady picnic areas off the beach. (*Tip*: The park's campground has a separate beach, and you don't have to be camping there to enjoy it.; it's located a distance from the day-use area, but it is much less congested during good weather.)

Park admission costs $8 for non-Maine resident adults, $2 for nonresident seniors, $1 for children. Camping sites tend to book up early in the season, but call to check (© **207/693-6231**)—you might luck into a cancellation if you want a spot to pitch your tent.

Sabbathday Lake Shaker Community ★

Route 26, from Portland to Norway, is a speedy highway that runs past new housing developments and through hilly farmland. At one point, however, the road pinches through a cluster of stately historic buildings that stand proudly beneath towering shade trees. That's the **Sabbathday Lake Shaker Community** (www.maineshakers.com; © **207/926-4597**), the last active Shaker community in the nation. The world's two remaining Shakers living here today still embrace their traditional beliefs and maintain a communal, pastoral way of life. The bulk of the community's income comes from the sale of herbs, which have been grown here since 1799.

Tours are offered a half-dozen times daily from Memorial Day through Columbus Day (in other words, mid-May through mid-October), providing a look at the grounds and several buildings, including the graceful 1794 meetinghouse. Exhibits in the buildings showcase the famed furniture handcrafted by the Shakers and include antiques made by Shakers at other U.S. communes. You'll learn plenty about the Shaker ideology, with its emphasis on simplicity, industry, and celibacy. The tours begin at 10:30am; last tour starts at 3:15pm. After your tour, browse the gift shop for Shaker herbs and teas. The tour lasts 1 hour and 15 minutes and costs $10 for adults, $2 for children ages 6–12; it's free for children 5 and under.

The village is about 45 minutes from Portland, on Route 26 near the attractive village of **New Gloucester.** From Portland, head northwest out Route 26 (Washington Avenue, reachable from I-295, U.S. Route 1, and Congress Street). Or, from southern Maine, take exit 63 from the Maine Turnpike; after exiting, follow signs into the center of downtown **Gray** and follow signs for Route 26 north and into the village. Don't miss the farm stand, either, selling a wonderful array of dried herbs, flowers, and crafts farmed and crafted right on-site.

6

LOWER MIDCOAST: FREEPORT, THE BOOTHBAYS & PEMAQUID

Veteran Maine travelers contend that this part of the coast, the southern leg of what's long been known as the "Midcoast" (one word, please), is fast losing its native charm—it's too commercial, they say, too developed, too highfalutin' . . . in short, too much like the rest of the United States. These grousers have a point, especially along U.S. Route 1. But get off the main roads, and you'll swiftly find pockets of another Maine, with some of the most pastoral and picturesque meadows, hills, peninsulas, and harbors in the entire state.

Anchoring the south end of this section of the coast is **Freeport,** a shopping mecca with more outlet stores than you can shake a stick at. North of Freeport, get onto U.S. Route 1 in the lively college town of **Brunswick** (exit 28 from I-295). Going north, some highlights of the coastal route include the historic shipbuilding town of **Bath,** rich with Victorian architecture; riverside **Wiscasset,** the self-proclaimed "prettiest village in Maine"; a string of scenic oceanfront villages collectively known as **The Boothbays**; the rugged, rocky **Pemaquid** peninsula; and lost-in-time **Monhegan Island.**

Beyond local tourist huts and chambers of commerce, the best source of information for the midcoast region in general is found at the **Maine State Information Center** (✆ **207/846-0833**) just off exit 17 of I-295 in Yarmouth, which isn't really *in* the Midcoast—but you'll almost certainly pass through it to get there. This state-run center is stocked with hundreds of brochures, and is staffed with a helpful crew that can provide information about the entire state; it's particularly well informed about the middle reaches of the coast. It's open daily year-round, though not 24 hours—but the attached restroom facilities are always open.

FREEPORT

123 miles NE of Boston, 333 miles NE of New York City, and 17 miles NE of Portland

If **Freeport** were a mall (which is not all that far-fetched an analogy), L.L.Bean would be the anchor store. It's the business that launched this town to prominence, elevating its status from just another Maine fishing village near the interstate to one of the state's major tourist draws for the outlet centers that sprang up here in Bean's wake. Freeport still has the look of a classic Maine village, but it's a village that's been largely taken over by the national fashion industry; many of the old historic homes and stores have been converted into upscale factory shops purveying name-brand clothing and housewares at cut-rate prices. Banana Republic occupies an exceedingly handsome brick Federal-style home; a Carnegie library became an Abercrombie & Fitch pumping club music (oh, the inhumanity); and even the McDonald's is inside a tasteful, understated Victorian farmhouse—you really have to look for the golden arches.

While some modern structures have also been built to accommodate the outlet boom, strict planning guidelines have managed to preserve most of the town's local charm, at least downtown. Huge parking lots are hidden from view off the main drag, and as a result Freeport is one of the more aesthetically pleasing places to shop in New England—though even with these large lots, parking can be scarce during the peak season. Expect crowds.

Seeking the real Maine? Head at some point for **South Freeport,** which consists of a boat dock, general store, and lobster shack at the end of a finger of land reached via a numberless side road off U.S. Route 1.

Essentials

ARRIVING

Freeport is on U.S. Route 1, though the downtown is most easily reached via I-295 from either exit 20 or exit 22.

VISITOR INFORMATION

At the **Freeport Information Center,** at 23 Depot Street (www.freeportusa. com; © **207/865-1212**), you can pick up a map and directory of businesses, restaurants, and overnight accommodations.

Global Influence

Right across the road from the state information center in Yarmouth is the former **DeLorme Map Store,** open Monday to Friday from 8am to 5pm. The mapping company DeLorme was purchased by GPS giant Garmin some years back, and the new owners shut down what had been a store full of map and atlases.

They've kept the lobby open, though, so that visitors can drop in to get a look at Eartha, "the world's largest rotating and revolving globe." The 42-foot-diameter globe occupies the entire atrium and is constructed on a scale of 1:1,000,000, the largest satellite image of the earth ever produced. Far out.

SPECIAL EVENTS

One more fine reason to come to Freeport in summer is for the abundant free music performances that take over the village's Discovery Park from mid-June through Labor Day. Underwritten by L.L.Bean (of course), it's officially known as **Summer in the Park.** The performers in this summer concert series are eclectic—and impressively famous: In 2016, they ranged from Texas-based Grammy winner Lyle Lovett to New England chanteuse Grace Potter to Brooklyn hipster-folk trio The Lone Bellow. (Not to mention Maine's own folk icon, David Mallett.) Occasional food festivals, kids' events, and a well-loved Independence Day fireworks display add to the eclectic fun. Get a schedule by picking up a brochure at Bean's information desk or checking **www.llbean.com**: Search for Summer in the Park.

Where to Stay in Freeport

Freeport has more than 700 guest rooms, ranging from quiet B&Bs with just a few rooms to chain motels with several dozen. Reservations are strongly recommended during the peak summer season. Several new midrange chain hotels and motels south of town on Route 1 have helped accommodate the summer crush. In a pinch you might try the **Comfort Suites,** 500 Route 1 (© **207/556-5568**), or the adjacent **Super 8** (© **207/865-1408**). Both are simple, clean, and good enough for a night's rest.

Harraseeket Inn ★★   The Harraseeket is a large, modern hotel a short walk north of L.L. Bean on Freeport's Main Street. Despite its size, a traveler could drive right past and not even notice it—which is a good thing. A 19th-century home is the soul of the hotel, though most rooms are in annexes added in 1989 and 1997. Guests can relax in the dining room, read the paper in a common room while the baby grand player piano plays, or sip a cocktail in the homey **Broad Arrow Tavern** (with its wood-fired oven and grill, it serves dinner as well as lunch). Guest rooms are large and tastefully furnished, with quarter-canopy beds and a mix of contemporary and antique furnishings; some have gas or wood-burning fireplaces, around half have whirlpools, and some are even done up with wet bars and refrigerators. The big second-floor Thomas Moser Suite is a nod to the local furniture craftsman, with a pencil post bed, writing desk, dresser, and flatscreen TV in the bedroom, plus a sitting room with a modern sofa, lounge chair, coffee table, Bose stereo, and stone fireplace. Plus a soaking tub. This inn is especially pet-friendly, with doggy beds and treats for four-footed guests.

162 Main St., Freeport. www.harraseeketinn.com. © **800/342-6423** or 207/865-9377. 93 units. $158–$310 doubles; $262–$352 suites. Rates include full breakfast and afternoon tea. MAP rates available. Packages available. Pets welcome ($25/night per pet). **Amenities:** 2 restaurants; bar; concierge; indoor pool; room service; free Wi-Fi.

Maine Idyll Motor Court ★   Talk about a throwback: This 1930s "motor court" is a Maine classic, a cluster of 20 cottages scattered around a grove of oak and beech trees. It could have faded into oblivion, yet it hasn't:

The place is still good enough for a simple night's sleep. Most cottages come with a tiny porch, wood-burning fireplace (birch logs are provided), television, modest kitchen facilities (no ovens), and dated furniture. The cabins aren't especially large, but they're comfortable enough and kept clean; some have showers, while others have bathtubs, and a good number of the cottages have two bedrooms (one even has three bedrooms). Ask for a cottage with air-conditioning if that's important—a few units have it. Kids like the play area, while dog-walkers head for nature trails accessible from the property and picnickers fire up grill sets. The only downers are the spotty Wi-Fi service (it's best at the Maine office) and the sometimes drone of traffic: I-295 is just through the trees on one side, U.S. 1 is on the other side. Get past that traffic sandwich, though, and this place is a decent lowbrow value.

1411 U.S. Rte. 1, Freeport. www.maineidyll.com. ☎ **207/865-4201.** 20 units. May–Oct $69–$136 double. Rates include continental breakfast. Closed Nov–Apr. Pets on leashes allowed ($4/night per pet). **Amenities:** Playground; free Wi-Fi.

TALE OF THE tags: FREEPORT VS. KITTERY

While the outlet malls in **Kittery** (see box p. 57), down south near the New Hampshire border, are convenient for a blitz of name-brand shopping, **Freeport** is a different animal. The outlets here are crunched together along and interspersed around Freeport's busy Main Street. That makes driving around town a headache, as pedestrians and cars cruising for parking bring things to a constant halt, but it's more convenient once you're out of the car. My advice? Strap on your walking shoes, park anywhere you can find a spot—even in a distant satellite lot—and just resign yourself to a lot of hoofing it. Bring a portable dolly or luggage rack to carry packages if you're expecting to buy a lot.

Freeport's outlets generally offer a higher grade of product than Kittery's do, and the stores have a great deal more architectural (and corporate) personality, too. You will actually find local, small manufacturers here, not just the big guys, and inventive big brands that go beyond the usual. Price tags tend to be higher here than in Kittery, however.

You can troll **L.L. Bean**'s many stores (see p. 119), but even just sticking to Main Street you'll come across such finds as **Cuddledown of Maine**'s comfy pillows and comforters; the **Casco Bay Cutlery and Kitchenware**'s respected knife shop; **Abercrombie & Fitch**'s ever-young fashions, housed in a former Carnegie library; excellent bi-level **Gap** and **Banana Republic** outlets; the familiar **Polo Ralph Lauren** and **The North Face** outlets; and plenty more distinctive factory shops.

If you love shopping and you love quality, it's a genuinely enjoyable experience to stroll around here for a day, taking a snack of chowder or lobster (for restaurants, see below); pausing to assess your finds; grabbing a soda, grilled hot dog, or ice cream from a vendor; then planning dinner somewhere. Parking and traffic are negatives to consider, however—you may cruise a half-hour before finding an open spot (if you ever do).

Where to Eat in Freeport

Despite all the outlet glitz of Freeport, a couple of small-town restaurants have persisted. For a quick and simple meal, you might head to the **Azure Cafe ★**, 123 Main Street (www.azurecafe.com; ✆ **207/865-1237**), for hearty sandwiches and pasta. The **Lobster Cooker,** 39 Main Street (www.thelobstercooker.com; ✆ **207/869-5086**), serves daily seafood, sandwich, and chowder specials on an outdoor patio with views of the shopping hordes; go for salmon, lobster, or crab.

For yet another option, try the **Broad Arrow Tavern** at the Harraseeket Inn (see p. 114).

Gritty McDuff's ★ BREWPUB Spacious, informal, and air-conditioned in summer, Gritty's is an offshoot of Portland's original brewpub. It's a short drive south of Freeport's village center, and is best known for a varied selection of house-brewed beers like the unfiltered Black Fly Stout. The pub offers a wide-ranging bar menu of reliable salads, burgers, steaks, stone-oven pizzas, cheesesteak sandwiches, quesadillas, and pub classics such as shepherd's pie and fish and chips. There's a kids' menu as well.

187 U.S. Rte. 1 (Main St.), Freeport. www.grittys.com. ✆ **207/865-4321.** Reservations not accepted. Main courses $10–$17. Daily 11:30am–11pm.

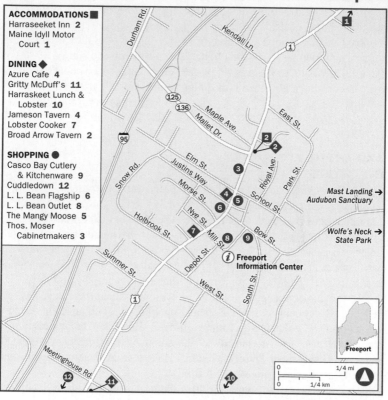

ACCOMMODATIONS ■
Harraseeket Inn **2**
Maine Idyll Motor
Court **1**

DINING ◆
Azure Cafe **4**
Gritty McDuff's **11**
Harraskeet Lunch &
Lobster **10**
Jameson Tavern **4**
Lobster Cooker **7**
Broad Arrow Tavern **2**

SHOPPING ●
Casco Bay Cutlery
& Kitchenware **9**
Cuddledown **12**
L. L. Bean Flagship **6**
L. L. Bean Outlet **8**
The Mangy Moose **5**
Thos. Moser
Cabinetmakers **3**

Mast Landing →
Audubon Sanctuary

Wolfe's Neck →
State Park

ⓘ **Freeport
Information Center**

Freeport

0 ————————— 1/4 mi
0 ————————— 1/4 km

Harraseeket Lunch & Lobster ★ LOBSTER Next to a boatyard on the Harraseeket River, about a 10-minute drive from Freeport's busy shopping district, this lobster pound's picnic tables get crowded on sunny days—although, with its little heated dining room, it's a worthy destination any time. Point and pick out a lobster, than take in river views from the dock as you wait for your number to be called. Advice? Come in late afternoon to avoid the lunch and dinner hordes—and don't wear your nicest clothes. This is roll-up-your-sleeves eating. You can also get fried fish, burgers, chowder, or an ice cream from the window. From Freeport, take Bow Street to South Street; continue on South Street to the South Freeport four-way intersection. Turn left at the stop sign and continue downhill to the water.

Main St., South Freeport. www.harraseeketlunchandlobster.com. ℂ **207/865-4888.** Lobsters market price (typically $10–$20). No credit cards. May–mid-Oct daily 11am–8:30pm. Closed Columbus Day–Apr.

Jameson Tavern ★ AMERICAN In a farmhouse right in the shadow of L.L. Bean (on the north side), Jameson Tavern touts itself as the birthplace of

Maine. And it really is: In 1820, papers were signed here legally separating Maine from Massachusetts. Mainers still appreciate that pen stroke today. The historic Tap Room is to the left, a compact spot of beer and casual food. The rest of the house contains the main dining room, decorated in a more formal, country-Colonial style. Meals here are either pubby or clubby: sandwiches, burgers, and fried seafood on the lighter side, prime rib and stuffed lobster on the heavier. What's new in this old place? A nice porch, open about half of the year (not in winter, obviously) for dining semi al fresco.

115 Main St., Freeport. www.jamesontavern.com. © **207/865-4196.** Reservations recommended. Main courses $10–$25. Tap room daily 11am–11pm; dining room daily 11am–9pm.

Exploring Freeport
THE STORES

Freeport has more than 140 retail shops spaced out between exit 20 of I-295 (at the far lower end of Main Street) and Mallet Road, which connects to exit 22. Some shops have even begun to spread south of exit 20 toward Yarmouth. The bulk of them are "factory" or "outlet" stores. If you don't want to miss a single one, get off at exit 17 and head north on U.S. Route 1. The bargains can vary from extraordinary to "huh?" Plan on wearing out some shoe leather and taking at *least* a half-day if you're really intent on finding the best deals.

The sometimes-changing rotation of national chains here has recently included Abercrombie & Fitch, Banana Republic, Gap, Calvin Klein, Patagonia, North Face, Nike, Orvis, Tommy Hilfiger, Cole Haan, among many others. You'll also find a number of high-end Maine brands represented, including Georgetown Pottery, chi-chi blankets from Brahms Mount, and beloved import emporium Mexicali Blues.

Stores in Freeport are typically open daily 9am to 9pm during the busy summer and close much earlier (at 5 or 6pm) in other seasons; between Thanksgiving and Christmas, they remain open late once more.

Casco Bay Cutlery & Kitchenware ★   Long known as Freeport Knife for its signature product, this store still sports a wide selection of knives for kitchen and camp alike, including blades from Germany, Switzerland, and Japan. Also find esoteric pots, pans, and gadgets from the likes of Le Cresuet, Peugeot, and Maine's Fletchers' Mill.

5 Depot St., Freeport. www.freeportknife.com. © **800/646-8430.**

Cuddledown ★   Cuddledown started producing down comforters in 1973, and now makes a whole line of products much appreciated in northern climes and beyond. Some of the down pillows are made right in the outlet shop, which also carries a variety of European goose-down comforters in all sizes and weights. Look for linens, blankets, moccasins, and home furnishings, too.

554 U.S. Route 1 (btw. exits 17 and 20), Freeport. www.cuddledown.com. © **207/865-1713.**

L.L. Bean ★★★   Monster outdoor retailer L.L.Bean traces its roots from the day Leon Leonwood Bean decided that what the world really needed was

One of the big reasons that L.L. Bean's flagship shop is such a tourist draw is that it's open 365 days a year, 7 days a week, 24 hours a day—note the lack of any locks or latches on the front doors. As such, it's a popular spot even in the dead of night, especially during summer or around holidays. Folks have been known to set out from New Hampshire at 1 or 2 in the morning to enjoy the best deals (and empty aisles) on their middle-of-the-night arrival. But **L.L. Bean's** campus doesn't stop at the flagship store. The **Hunting & Fishing Store** is connected to the flagship (indeed, you can walk from one into the other without realizing you've done so); it's the place for fly-fishing gear, hunting boots, and tons of other undeniably cool stuff—from freeze-dried camp food to hand-crank-powered LED flashlights (no batteries required), folding Adirondack chairs, 13-foot game-hunting perches, and a zillion lures, fly ties, buck knives, tent lines, and watercraft. L.L. Bean also maintains several a few nearby **satellite shops** stocking small, rapidly changing inventories of specialized goods. **The Bike, Boat & Ski Store,** just across the Freeport Village Station plaza from the flagship store, holds lots of canoes, kayaks, paddles, cycles, and helmets. Next to it is a huge **Home Store,** selling hand-crafted beds, sofas, and other furniture, plus home accessories (doormat, anyone?). Finally, Bean's **outlet shop** is just across Main Street in the new Freeport Village Station complex.

a good weatherproof hunting shoe. He joined a watertight gum shoe to a laced leather upper; hunters liked it; the store grew; an empire born. Today, L.L. Bean sells millions of dollars' worth of clothing and outdoor goods nationwide through its well-respected catalogs, and it continues to draw hundreds of thousands of customers through its doors to a headquarters building and several offshoots around town. The modern, multilevel main store is about the size of a regional mall, but it's very tastefully done with its own indoor trout pond, a fish tank that gobsmacks kiddos, a (famous) huge Bean boot outside, and taxidermy displays around every corner. Selections include Bean's own trademark clothing, books, shoes, and plenty of outdoor gear for camping, fishing, and hunting (and separate stores across the plaza house home goods and bike and ski gear—see box above). The staff at each store is incredibly knowledgeable—probably because Bean's policy is to encourage staff to take the gear home and try it out themselves so they can better advise their customers.

95 Main St. (at Bow St.)., Freeport. www.llbean.com. ✆ **877/755-2326.**

The Mangy Moose ★   A souvenir shop with a twist: Virtually everything in this place is moose-related. Really. There are moose wineglasses, moose trivets, moose cookie cutters, and (of course) moose T-shirts. And yet somehow, hokey as this notion sounds, this merchandise is a notch above what you'll find in most other souvenir shops around the state.

112 Main St., Freeport. www.themangymoose.com. ✆ **207/865-6414.**

Thos. Moser Cabinetmakers ★★ Classic furniture reinterpreted in lustrous wood and leather is the focus at this shop, which—thanks to a steady parade of ads in the *New Yorker* and a Madison Avenue branch—has become nearly as representative of Maine as L.L. Bean has. Shaker, Mission, and modern styles are wonderfully reinvented by Tom Moser and his designers and woodworkers, who produce heirloom-quality signed pieces. Nationwide delivery is easy to arrange. There's a good selection of knotted rugs made by an independent artisan, and a worthy gallery of rotating Maine-made art on site. Finally, don't miss the outlet annex and its samples, prototypes, and refurbished pieces; you can save big bucks here.

149 Main St., Freeport. www.thomasmoser.com. © **800/862-1973** or 207/865-4519.

BEYOND THE STORES

While Freeport is nationally known for its outlet shopping, that's not all it offers. Just outside of town you'll find a lovely pastoral landscape, picturesque picnicking spots, and scenic drives that make for a handy retreat from all that spending.

By car head east on Bow Street (down the hill from L.L. Bean's main entrance), and wind around for 1 mile to the sign for **Mast Landing Audubon Sanctuary ★** (© **207/781-2330**). Turn left and then right about ¼ mile into the sanctuary parking lot. A network of trails totaling about 3 miles criss-crosses through a landscape of long-ago eroded hills and mixed woodlands; streams trickle down to the marshland estuary. The 140-acre property is owned by the Maine Audubon Society and is open to the public until dusk.

Continue south on Wolfe's Neck Road, and you'll soon come to the 233-acre **Wolfe's Neck Woods State Park** (© **207/865-4465**). This compact, attractive park has quiet woodland trails that run through forests of white pine and hemlock, past estuaries, and along the rocky shoreline of the bay. Googins Island, just offshore and reached by following the park's Casco Bay Trail, has an osprey nest on it. This is a good destination for enjoying a picnic brought from town or for letting the kids burn off some pent-up energy—there are guided nature walks at 2pm daily during the summer. The day-use fee for the park is $6 per non-Maine resident adult, $2 for nonresident seniors, and $1 for children ages 5 to 11.

BRUNSWICK & BATH ★

Brunswick is 10 miles NE of Freeport. Bath is 8 miles E of Brunswick

Brunswick and Bath are two handsome, historic towns that share a strong commercial past. Many travelers heading up Route 1 pass through both towns eager to reach areas with higher billing on the marquee. That's a shame, for both are well worth the detour to sample the sort of slower pace that's being lost elsewhere.

Brunswick ★ was once home to several mills along the Androscoggin River. These have since been converted to offices and the like, but Brunswick's broad Maine Street still bustles with activity. (Idiosyncratic traffic patterns can lead to snarls of traffic in the late afternoon.) Brunswick is also home to **Bowdoin College ★★**, one of the nation's most respected small colleges.

Eight miles east of Brunswick, **Bath ★** is pleasantly situated on the broad Kennebec River and is a noted center of shipbuilding. Young professional émigrés have been attracted by its fine old houses, but it's still at heart a blue-collar town, with massive traffic tie-ups weekdays at 3pm when the shipyard changes shifts.

Essentials

ARRIVING

Brunswick and Bath are both on Route 1. Brunswick is accessible via exit 28 off I-95. If you're bypassing Brunswick and heading north up Route 1 to Bath or beyond, continue up I-95 and exit at the "coastal connector" exit in nearby Topsham (exit 31), which avoids some of the slower traffic going through Brunswick.

For bus service from Portland or Boston, contact **Greyhound** (www.greyhound.com; ✆ **800/231-2222**) or **Concord Coach** (www.concordcoachlines.com; ✆ **800/639-3317**).

VISITOR INFORMATION

The **Southern Midcoast Chamber of Commerce,** 2 Main Street in Topsham (www.midcoastmaine.com; ✆ **877/725-8797** or 207/725-8797), offers information and lodging assistance Monday to Friday from 8:30am to 5pm from its offices in downtown Topsham.

SPECIAL EVENTS

Note that **Christmas** is a big time in Bath: For a full month, from Thanksgiving to the holiday, downtown features fun window displays, a parade, and other events. Contact the local tourist office for more details.

Where to Stay in Brunswick and Bath

The most interesting lodging around Brunswick and Bath are stately B&Bs and inns that fall in with the two towns' historic vibes.

BATH

In Bath, the **Residence Inn By Marriot**, 139 Richardson St. (✆ **207/443-9741**) is great for long stays, with one- and two-room suites. It's a brand-new building, just opened in late 2015, and feels fresh and spotless.

Grey Havens ★ Located on Georgetown Island southeast of Bath, this gracefully aging 1904 shingled home with prominent turrets sits on a high, rocky bluff overlooking the sea. Inside, you can relax in front of a cobblestone fireplace before checking in. Guest rooms are as simple as you'd expect, with plain bathrooms; oceanfront rooms command a premium but are worth it for the views—if you're looking to save a few bucks, ask about an oceanfront room with its bathroom located across the hall. Guests can use the inn's canoes or bikes to explore the area. (There's a little stairway down to a tiny dock on the water, from which guests have reportedly caught whopping fish.)

A drawback? This inn has been only lightly modernized, so its character remains authentic—and its walls thin. The wonderfully big and (half-screened) porch is worth sitting on for a while, and the lounge features a big picture window. From U.S. Route 1, go south on Route 127 and then follow signs for Reid State Park for 11 miles; just after turning onto Reid State Road (also known as Seguinland Road), watch for inn on left

96 Seguinland Rd., Georgetown Island. www.greyhavens.com. ℭ **855/473-9428** or 207/371-2616. 13 units (2 with private hall bathrooms). $155–$325 double. Rates include full breakfast. 2-night minimum stay weekends. Closed Nov–Apr. No children 11 and under. **Amenities:** Restaurant; bar; free Wi-Fi.

Sebasco Harbor Resort ★

Sebasco is a grand old seaside resort fighting a mostly successful battle against time; some guests have been returning for 60 years, and spacious grounds remain the star attraction. Expect sweeping ocean views, a lovely seaside pool, and great walks, plus children's activities (including a kids' camp), a spa, and pancake breakfasts on the lawn. Most guest rooms are adequate, not elegant, although the resort has poured a pile of money into renovation. Small decks on many of the inn rooms are a plus. Better are the quirky rooms in the octagonal Lighthouse Building; most have TVs. There are also interior-court and lakefront cottages of various sizes (with up to 10 bedrooms), though some are very expensive—figure $1,000 and up per night (you read right) for primo lakeside digs. To get here, drive south from Bath 11 miles on Route 209; look for Route 217, then signs to Sebasco

29 Kenyon Rd., Sebasco Estates. www.sebasco.com. ℭ **207/805-2397**. 111 units, 22 cottages. Mid-June–Labor Day $169–$329 double, $229–$2,390 cottage; May–mid-June and Sept–Oct $139–$234 double, $189–$2,090 cottage. MAP rates also available. Rates do not include 10% resort service charge or state sales tax. 2-night minimum on weekends. Closed late Oct–early May. Pets allowed (some units). **Amenities:** Restaurants; bar; bike rentals; children's program; golf course; health club; pool; sauna; spa; tennis courts; hot tub; canoe and kayak rentals; sailing lessons; shuffleboard; bowling; free Wi-Fi.

BRUNSWICK

In Brunswick, **Best Western Plus,** 71 Gurnet Road (ℭ **207/725-5251**), is pet-friendly and a convenient hopping-off point for the Harpswell peninsula and islands to the south.

The Brunswick Inn ★

This handsome B&B in a rambling Federal-style house with a wraparound porch sits smack-dab in downtown Brunswick, facing the town green. Run by the enthusiastic and friendly Eileen Horner, it has been recently updated, and is positioned perfectly: within walking distance of Bowdoin College, a summer music theater, and restaurants lining Maine Street. Rooms are spacious, furnished in a country-modern style—some with wingback or wicker chairs, and all with attractive quilts; ask about the bright corner rooms, suites, and the Garden Cottage. The full breakfasts here are a highlight. Even better: A bar/lounge serves wine and microbrews before views of the park or a fireplace, with local acoustic musicians sometimes dropping by to play intimate sets.

10 Water St., Brunswick. www.brunswickbnb.com. ℭ **800/299-4914** or 207/729-4914. 15 units. $129–$229 doubles; $195 suites; $260–$299 cottage. Prices include full breakfast. **Amenities:** Lounge; free Wi-Fi.

The Daniel Inn ★★   The core of this boutique property is a 1819 Federal-style home, although serious recent renovations (the current owners took over in 2013) leave this place feeling as fresh and modern as any property in Brunswick. Rooms are sumptuous if snug, with flatscreen TVs, beautiful wooden bed frames, and thick comforters and drapes. Some have balconies, refrigerators, and two-person rain showerheads. The on-site bistro has pubby favorites and a really terrific beer, wine, and cocktail list (though it closes early if it's not seeing a lot of action). The giant lobby fireplace is a fine spot to chill with a drink. From Maine Street, turn right on Mason Street, then left on Water Street to cross an overpass above Route 1.

163 Danforth St., Brunswick. www.danforthinn.com. ℂ **207/373-1824**. 24 units. Mid-May–Oct $195–$329 double, $245–$329 suite; Nov–mid-May $124–$249 double, $154–$279 suite. Rates include breakfast. Some rooms accommodate pets (with $100 deposit). Packages available. **Amenities:** Free bikes; restaurant; bar; fitness center; Jacuzzi; sauna; free Wi-Fi.

CAMPING

One of the coast's best campgrounds, the **Chewonki Campground** ★ (www.chewonkicampground.com; ℂ **207/882-7426**) is located between Bath and Wiscasset. It occupies 50 acres overlooking a salt marsh and a confluence of lazy tidal streams. The 47 sites here are sizable and private; there's a nicely maintained pool with a sweeping view, and kayaks and canoes are available for rent. Campsites cost from $48 to $80 per night, which is at the quite high end of the camping price scale in Maine—yet it actually might be worth it. Drive 7 miles east of Bath on U.S. Route 1; turn right on Route 144, then take the next right past the airport and follow signs to the campground.

Where to Eat in Brunswick and Bath

Both downtown Brunswick and downtown Bath offer plenty of casual places to dine, ranging from burgers to barbecue and better. For informal fare, it's hard to go wrong at these cafes and restaurants.

BATH

If you've just got to have lobster, head for Five Islands Lobster Co. (see below), or continue north across the Route 1 bridge a few miles to **Taste of Maine** (ℂ **207/443-4554**), an overlarge tourist trap that nevertheless delivers the goods (read: lobster and fish), plus good marsh views.

Five Islands Lobster Co. ★★★ LOBSTER POUND   The drive alone makes this lobster pound a worthy destination. It's about 12 miles south of Route 1, down winding Route 127, past bogs and spruce forests with glimpses of the ocean. (Head south from Woolwich, just across the big bridge from downtown Bath.) Drive until you pass a cluster of clapboard homes, and then keep going until you can't go any farther. Wander out to the wharf (with great views) and place your order. This is a down-home affair, with local lobstermen coming and going on all aides. The adjacent snack bar purveys soda and side dishes; gather all your grub and settle in at a picnic table or a grassy spot at the edge of the dirt parking lot. But don't expect to be alone: Despite its edge-of-the-world feel, this beloved pound draws steady traffic and can actually get *crowded* on weekends.

1447 Five Islands Rd. (Rte. 127), Georgetown. www.fiveislandslobster.com. © **207/371-2990.** Prices vary according to market. Daily 11am–8pm June–Aug; shorter hours Sept to early Columbus Day. Closed Columbus Day–mid-May.

Mae's Café & Bakery ★ BREAKFAST/BRUNCH Great breakfasts served in a wonderful old house in downtown Bath. Try one of the creative benedicts, like housemade lamb sausage with feta and spinach, or the unexpectedly yummy Brussels sprouts and bacon hash. Locals line up to take out baked goods like the pecan-studded sticky buns and specialty cakes and pies.

160 Centre St., Bath. www.maescafeandbakery.com. © **207/442-8577.** Breakfast and lunch entrees $7–$15. Daily 8am–2pm. Closed Feb.

Solo Bistro ★ BISTRO Right on Bath's main drag, this bistro/slash/jazz club (live music on Fridays sometimes) is a locals' favorite for a date night. The menu is divided between creative small plates (soups, salads, seafood) and more substantial large plates (burgers, hanger steak, grilled fish, gnocchi, curry); desserts are especially well thought out. The decor here is cooler than cool, including minimalist, brightly colored chairs; Scandinavian birch tabletops; and the space's native, rough-hewn stone walls.

128 Front St., Bath. www.solobistro.com. © **207/443-3373.** Main courses $18–$27; 3-course prix-fixe menu $25 ($18 on Wed). Daily 5pm to closing.

BRUNSWICK

Enoteca Athena ★ MEDITERRANEAN Greek and Italian wines, renowned to obscure, are ostensibly the draw here, but the talent of chef-owner Tim O'Brien makes this smartly casual downtown destination much more than a wine bar. Perfectly executed gyros, chicken parmesan, and Grandma's spaghetti for the less-than-adventurous, and decadent bucatini with mushrooms and blue cheese or lamb ragu over frascarelli for the rest of it. Local seafood specials are a treat as well. In the summer, there's fine people-watching from the sidewalk tables up front.

97 Maine St., Brunswick. www.enotecaathena.com. © **207/721-0100.** Main courses $13–$22. Mon–Thurs 3:30–9pm, Fri–Sat 3:30–10pm.

Frontier ★ PUB/ECLECTIC FARE Taking up a significant chunk of a historic old mill looking out over the Androscoggin River dividing Brunswick and Topsham, this welcoming, mildly bohemian hangout has a great bar and a global menu that accommodates everything from kimchi to Bolognese to fish and chips to falafel. Friday night in here is a great cross-section of Brunswick: dating couples, families with little kids, packs of students quaffing beers a few tables over from their professors blowing off steam. After dinner, catch an indie movie or live music in the Frontier cinema, or just wonder around and enjoy all the local art on the walls.

14 Maine St., Brunswick. www.explorefrontier.com. © **207/725-5222.** Main courses $13–$25. Tues–Thurs and Sun 11am–9pm, Fri–Sat 11am–10pm.

Exploring Brunswick

Brunswick is increasingly a bedroom community for young professionals and families priced out of Portland and its immediate suburbs. Together with the Bowdoin College crowd, these folks keep **Maine Street** pretty hopping on a summer Saturday night, and their patronage helps Brunswick support a handful of really standout restaurants, not one but two indie movie theaters, a few funky book and record stores, and so on.

Collectibles buffs and aficionados of antiques malls should schedule an hour or so for **Cabot Mill Antiques,** 14 Maine Street (www.cabotiques.com; © 207/725-2855), located on the ground floor of a restored textile mill in downtown Brunswick. In the 15,000-square-foot showroom, more than 140 dealers purvey a wide variety of books, bottles, dolls, art, china, and porcelains. Quality is highly variable. The facility is open daily from 10am to 5pm (7pm on Friday).

Brunswick's main attraction, **Bowdoin College ★★,** was founded in 1794, offered its first classes 8 years later, and has since amassed an illustrious roster of prominent alumni, including Nathaniel Hawthorne, Henry Wadsworth Longfellow, President Franklin Pierce, and arctic explorer Robert E. Peary (see box p. 130). Civil War hero Joshua Chamberlain served as president of the college after the war. The campus green is well worth a short stroll. Sturdy little **Massachusetts Hall**, my favorite building, originally contained the entire college within its walls. **Winthrop Hall,** close by, was the first of the line of brick dormitories that march in a prim line away from **Hubbard Hall** (1934), a drippingly Gothic library. The steepled granite **chapel** is worth peeking inside if it's open—designed by Richard Upjohn, it's unmistakably the visual focal point of the campus.

Bowdoin College Museum of Art ★★ MUSEUM This domed building on Bowdoin's main quad is one of the best small museums in New England—and it's free. The grand rotunda entrance announces the building's presence: It was designed by the prominent architectural firm of McKim, Mead & White. Collections are small but superb. The holdings include a number of American artists—some with close ties to Maine such as the Wyeths, Winslow Homer, and other landscape painters—but there's also a significant collection of work from classic European painters, and plenty of modern art. The older, upstairs galleries have soft, diffused lighting from skylights high above; the basement galleries, which feature rotating exhibits, are modern and spacious thanks to a thorough redesign in 2008 by an Argentine architect, which brought in light, color, and style.

Inside Walker Art Bldg., Bowdoin College, Brunswick. www.bowdoin.edu/art-museum. © **207/725-3275.** Free admission. Tues–Sat 10am–5pm (Thurs to 8:30pm); Sun 1–5pm. Closed holidays.

Peary-MacMillan Arctic Museum ★★ MUSEUM While Admiral Robert E. Peary (Bowdoin class of 1887) is better known for his accomplishments—he "discovered" the North Pole at age 53 in 1909—Donald

MacMillan (class of 1898) also racked up an impressive string of Arctic achievements. You can learn about both men (and the wherefores of arctic exploration) in this tucked-away museum on the Bowdoin campus, just across the lawn from the college's fine museum of art (see p. 125). Why here? Admiral Robert Peary and non-admiral Donald MacMillan graduated from Bowdoin in consecutive years late in the 19th century. When they returned from their respective polar travels, the two men donated many items they collected to their alma mater. The front room features mounted animals from the Arctic, including some impressive polar bears. A second room outlines Peary's historic 1909 expedition, complete with excerpts from his journal, and another room includes varied displays of Inuit arts and crafts, some historic and some modern. Rotating exhibits focus on Inuit and First Nations art, scrimshaw, contemporary Arctic photography, and more. It's a compact museum that can be visited in about 20 minutes or so.

Inside Hubbard Hall, Bowdoin College, Brunswick. www.bowdoin.edu/arctic-museum. ℰ **207/725-3416.** Free admission. Tues–Sat 10am–5pm; Sun 2–5pm. Closed holidays.

Exploring Bath

First and foremost, Bath is a shipbuilding town. The first U.S.-built ship was constructed downstream at the Popham Bay colony in the early 17th century. In the years since, shipbuilders have constructed more than 5,000 ships hereabouts. Bath shipbuilding reached its heyday in the late 19th century, but the business of shipbuilding continues to this day; Bath Iron Works is still one of the nation's preeminent boatyards, constructing and repairing ships for the U.S. Navy. The scaled-down military has left Bath shipbuilders in a somewhat tenuous state, but it's still common to see the steely gray ships in the dry dock (the best view is from the bridge over the Kennebec) and the towering red-and-white crane moving supplies and parts around the yard.

Architecture buffs will find a detour to Bath more than worthwhile. (Look for the free brochure *Architectural Tours: Walking and Driving in the Bath Area,* available at information centers listed below.) The Victorian era in particular is well represented. **Washington Street,** lined with maples and impressive homes, is one of the best-preserved displays in New England of late-19th-century residences.

Front Street is the heart of Bath's compact downtown, on a small rise overlooking the river, and it's home to some remarkable Victorian commercial architecture—walk down the street slowly and try to count the brick buildings, but you'll lose track. There's also a clutch of shops, groceries, and eateries. Note especially the blond, stone Richardson-style **Patten Free Library** (at Summer Street)—its park features a gazebo, fountain, and perfect view of the Winter Street Church—and the bell tower on the big **City Hall/Davenport Memorial** (its correct name) at 55 Front Street, built in 1929 during the Great Depression with money bequeathed by a wealthy local merchant. Its bell, from 1802, was probably cast by Paul Revere. Stop by the **Centre Street Arts Gallery** (11 Center Street) to see works by regional artists.

Art lovers in particular will enjoy exploring **Georgetown Island**, southeast of town. During the early 20th century the island, together with the neighboring Popham Peninsula, was known as "Seguinland," a summer outpost for modernist artists like photographer Paul Strand, sculptor Gaston Lachaise, and painters Marsden Hartley and Marguerite and William Zorach.

Maine Maritime Museum & Shipyard ★ MUSEUM   On the shores of the Kennebec River, this museum (just south of the big Bath Iron Works shipyard) features a wide array of displays and exhibits related to boat building. In fact, the museum is housed in the former Percy and Small shipyard, which built some 42 schooners in the late 19th and early 20th centuries. (The largest wooden ship built in the United States—the 329-foot *Wyoming*—was constructed here.) The centerpiece of the museum is the handsomely modern **Maritime History Building**, housing exhibits of maritime art and artifacts. There's also a gift shop with a good selection of books about ships. The remaining property (closed on cold winter days) houses a fleet of displays, including an intriguing exhibit on lobstering and a complete boat-building shop. Kids enjoy the play area (they can search for pirates from the crow's nest of a play boat, for instance), and there's always something interesting tied to the docks on the river.

243 Washington St., Bath. www.maritimemuseum.org. © **207/443-1316.** Admission $15.50 adults, $14 seniors, $10 children 6–12. Daily 9:30am–5pm.

Beaches

This stretch of the Maine coast is better known for rocky cliffs and lobster pots than swimming beaches, with two notable exceptions, both south of Bath.

Popham Beach State Park (© **207/389-1335**) is located at the tip of Route 209 (head south from Bath). This handsome park has a long and sandy strand, plus great views of knobby offshore islands such as Seguin Island, capped with a lonesome lighthouse. Parking and basic services, including changing rooms, are available; rare birds are often seen here. Admission is $8 for non-Maine resident adults, $2 for nonresident seniors, $1 for children 5 to 11 in season. There are discounts in the off season.

At the tip of Georgetown Island, to the east, is **Reid State Park** (© **207/371-2303**), an idyllic place to picnic on a summer day and party with friends. Arrive early enough, and you can stake out a picnic table among the wind-blasted pines. The 1½-mile-long beach is great for strolling and splashing around. Services include changing rooms and a small snack bar. Admission is $8 for nonresident adults, $2 for nonresident seniors, $1 for children 5 to 11. To reach Reid State Park, follow Route 127 south from Bath and Route 1.

HARPSWELL PENINSULA ★★

13 miles S of Brunswick, 17 miles S of Bath

Extending southwest from Brunswick and Bath, the picturesque Harpswell region is actually three peninsulas, like the tines of a pitchfork, if you include the islands of Orrs and Bailey, which are linked to the mainland by bridges.

If a steamed lobster is what you want (and you do), several sprawling establishments specialize in delivering the crustaceans fresh from the sea. On the Bailey Island side of the Harpswell Peninsula, **Cook's Lobster & Ale House ★** (www.cookslobster.com; ⓒ **207/833-2818**) has been serving a choice of shore dinners since 1955 and is open year-round—no mean feat in a Maine winter—daily from 11:30am until 9pm in the summer, with a limited pub menu until 11pm, and Wed–Sun 11:30am until 8pm the rest of the year. The restaurant's deck is unbeatable on nice days. Past Harpswell down Route 123 at the *very end* of the point (great views), the popular **Estes Lobster House** (www.esteslobsterhouse.com; ⓒ **207/833-6340**) serves various lobster plates in relaxed, festive surroundings (closed from November to mid-May).

While close to some of Maine's larger towns (Portland is only 45 minutes away), the Harpswell Peninsula has a remote, historical feel with sudden vistas across meadows to the blue waters of northern Casco Bay. It has few hiking trails and no garish attractions—just winding roads good for country drives. (Narrow shoulders and fast cars make for poor biking, however.)

The islands are perfect for a beautiful drive back into an older Maine, and a good lobster dinner at the end of the peninsula (see above), on a good day. But if the weather's bad, skip it—you'll just find it monotonous. Note that, as in much of Maine, there is nothing at all to do on the peninsula at night besides enjoy the quiet.

Where to Stay on the Harpswell Peninsula

Toward the southern tip of the peninsula, the character changes as clusters of colorful Victorian-era summer cottages displace the farmhouses found farther inland. Some of these cottages rent by the week, but savvy families book up many of them years in advance. If you're interested, drop by any local real estate agency (or, increasingly, online rental platforms such as Airbnb and VRBO.)

Driftwood Inn ★   Dating from 1910, the oceanside Driftwood Inn is a family-run retreat at the end of a dead-end road, more or less just a compound of weathered, shingled buildings and a handful of cottages. The rooms of time-aged pine have a simple turn-of-the-last-century flavor that hasn't been gentrified in the least. Most rooms share bathrooms along the hallways, but some do have private sinks and toilets. (The inn also has seven rooms for solo travelers, a rarity these days.) Cottages on a small, private cove are furnished in budget style: Expect plastic shower stalls and pretty dated furniture, but where else in Maine can you sleep at water's edge this cheaply? The inn maintains an old saltwater pool and porches with wicker furniture to while away the afternoons, as well. From Route 24 in Bailey Island, cross the bridge and turn left onto Washington Avenue and proceed to the end.

81 Washington Ave., Bailey Island. www.thedriftwoodinnmaine.com. ⓒ **207/833-5461**. 30 rooms (many share hallway bathrooms) and 4 cottages. $105–$130 double;

$720–$785 weekly cottage; some units $115–$125 per day off season. No credit cards. Closed Nov–mid-May; dining room closed Labor Day–late June. **Amenities:** Restaurant; saltwater pool.

Where to Eat on the Harpswell Peninsula

Dolphin Marina and Restaurant ★ TRADITIONAL NEW ENGLAND One of the premier places for chowder in the state is the down-home Dolphin Marina at Basin Point. Wander inside this Midcoast institution to find a long dining room with a full wall of windows looking out over Casco Bay. Renovated in 2011, this formerly humble shack lost a little character, but it did gain a relaxed bar with TVs (Patriots football is big here) and a pretty gorgeous deck. The legendary fish chowder and lobster stew live up to the hype; they're reasonably priced ($9–$12) and absolutely delicious, and the blueberry muffins that accompany them, by tradition, are warm and capped with a crispy crown. If you're more in the mood for steak or pasta or something, it's your loss, but at least you get the muffin with the rest of the entrees, too. To find it, drive 12 miles south of Brunswick on Route 123, turn right at Ash Point Road near the West Harpswell School, and then take the next right on Basin Point Road and continue to the end.

515 Basin Point Rd. (off Rte. 123), South Harpswell. www.dolphinmarinaandrestaurant. com. **② 207/833-6000.** Sandwiches $9–$14; dinner entrees $18–$36. Memorial Day–Oct daily 11:30am–9pm; Apr–Memorial Day Thurs–Sun 11:30am–8pm. Closed Nov–early Apr.

Exploring the Harpswell Peninsula

There's no set itinerary for exploring the area. Just drive south from Brunswick on Route 24 or Route 123 until you can't go any farther, and then backtrack for a bit and strike south again.

Among the "attractions" worth looking for are the wonderful ocean and island views from **South Harpswell** at the tip of the westernmost peninsula (park and wander around for a bit), and the clever **Cribstone Bridge ★★** connecting Bailey and Orrs islands. The hump-backed bridge was built in 1928 of granite blocks stacked in such a way that the strong tides could come and go and not drag the bridge out with it. No cement was used in its construction.

A little more than a mile past the bridge, hang a left on Washington Avenue to reach the **Giant's Stairs Trail ★**, a dramatic, half-mile seaside hike with a bunch of great cliffs to clamber around on.

WISCASSET ★★ & THE BOOTHBAYS ★

Wiscasset is 11 miles NE of Bath; The Boothbays begin 11 miles S of Wiscasset

Wiscasset is a cute riverside town just inland from the Atlantic (no views), and it's not shy about letting you know: THE PRETTIEST VILLAGE IN MAINE, boasts a sign at the edge of town and on many brochures. Whether or not you agree with this self-assessment (and not all locals do), the town is attractive, even if

Eagle Island was the summer home of famed Arctic explorer and Portland native Robert E. Peary, who claimed in 1909 to be the first person to reach the North Pole. (We're still not sure if he did; his accomplishments have been the subject of exhaustive debates among Arctic scholars, some of whom insist he inflated his claims.) Regardless, in 1904 Peary built a simple, shingled home on a remote, 17-acre island at the edge of Casco Bay; in 1912, he added flourishes in the form of two low stone towers. After his death in 1920, his family kept up the home; they later donated it to the state, which has since managed it as a state park, and in 2015, it became a National Historic Landmark. The home is open to the public, maintained much as it was when Peary lived here. **Atlantic Seal Cruises** (www. atlanticsealcruises.com; ✆ 207/865-6112) leads two 3-hour trips a day from Freeport in the summer, with up to 28 passengers aboard (adults $35, kids 5–12 $25; kids 1–5 $20). **Marie L Cruises** (www. marielcruises.com; ✆ 207/833-5343) runs out to the island in a cozy former mailboat, with two trips Friday–Sunday in summers from the Dolphin Marina in South Harpswell (adults $30, kids $15). The trip includes a brief coastal tour and 2 hours to wander the island.

the persistent line of traffic snaking through the center town through the summer diminishes its charm somewhat. Still, it makes a good stop for stretching one's legs and grabbing a bite to eat en route to other coastal destinations.

South of Route 1 on Route 27, you'll pass through the Boothbays, a string of several small, scenic villages down a peninsula—East Boothbay, Boothbay Harbor, and Boothbay—set so close to the ocean that, in some cases, they actually provide frontal views of it. Bland, boxy motels hem in the harbor, where side-by-side boutiques hawk T-shirts emblazoned with puffins (and it is a ghost town in the off-season); still, there's some charm to be found here among the clutter and cheese, especially on days when foghorns bleat mournfully at the harbor's mouth.

Essentials

GETTING THERE
Wiscasset is right on U.S. Route 1, between Bath and Damariscotta. Boothbay Harbor is off Route 1, southeast down a peninsula on Route 27; coming from the south, turn right shortly after crossing the bridge in Wiscasset. Both **Greyhound** (www.greyhound.com; ✆ 800/231-2222) and **Concord Coach** (www. concordcoachlines.com; ✆ 800/639-3317) buses stop in Wiscasset.

VISITOR INFORMATION
As befits a place where tourism is a major industry, the Boothbay region has *three* visitor information centers in and around town. On U.S. Route 1, at the Route 27 turnoff, there's an info center open seasonally, a good place to stock up on initial brochures. A mile before you reach the villages is the also-seasonal **Boothbay Information Center** (open June through October). If you zoom past that one or it's closed, don't fret: the year-round **Boothbay Harbor**

Region Chamber of Commerce (www.boothbayharbor.com; ☎ 207/633-2353) is at the intersection of routes 27 and 96.

SPECIAL EVENTS

Summer hasn't truly kicked off in the Boothbay region until the midcoast's fleet of windjammers—old-school, tall-masted sailing ships (see p. 152) docks in Boothbay Harbor for **Windjammer Days** (www.windjammerdays. org; ☎ 207/633-2353). From the end of June through Fourth of July weekend, as many as a dozen historic ships offer tours and day sails. There's live music all over town nearly every night of the week, plus a staged pirate invasion, oyster-shucking contests, a race across lobster traps bobbing the bay, a codfish race, and other types of marine tomfoolery.

Where to Stay in The Boothbays

Nothing in the way of budget chains and a lot in the way of seaside resorts and mom-and-pop inns—that's the lodging scene in the Boothbay region. Make July and August reservations the winter before to count on first-choice lodging in this heavily touristed corner of the state. You can save a little money by snagging a room farther up the peninsula—like the clean, cottage-style doubles at **White Anchor Inn** (609 Wiscassett Rd., Boothbay; www.white anchorinnboothbay.com; ☎ 207/633-3788), 3 miles north of Boothbay Harbor on Route 27. Still, since driving around and parking in Boothbay Harbor itself is a bear, it may be worth the extra scratch to enjoy the walkability of lodging in-town. A lot of year-round Boothbanians skip town during the busiest months, so Airbnb-style rentals are plentiful.

Five Gables Inn ★ The handsome Five Gables was built in 1896 and painstakingly restored in the late 1980s; it sits proudly amid a small colony of summer homes on a quiet road above a peaceful cove. It's nicely isolated from the confusion and hubbub of Boothbay Harbor. Rooms are pleasantly appointed, nearly all of them look out onto the water, and five have fireplaces burning manufactured logs; some also sport four-poster beds. Don't come expecting televisions or phones—it's a quiet place lacking both. Room no. 8 is a corner room with morning light and coastal views; room no. 14 is the biggest unit, with more watery views and a fireplace with a marble mantel. Some first-floor rooms open onto a common deck, which means little privacy, so take that into consideration when you're booking. The inn's included breakfast buffet is a good one. You'll find it by driving through East Boothbay on Route 96; turn right at the blinking light onto Murray Hill Road.

Murray Hill Rd., East Boothbay. www.fivegablesinn.com. ☎ **207/633-4551.** 16 units. $145–$265 double. Rates include breakfast. Closed mid-Oct to May. Children 12 and older welcome. **Amenities:** Afternoon tea; free Wi-Fi.

Newagen Seaside Inn ★★ Newagen is a good, small, low-key resort with stunning ocean views amid a fragrant spruce forest, and there's been a new push here to renovate everything from rooms to amenities; a spa is said to be on the way. The inn is housed in a low, white-shingled building with cruise ship–like hallways sporting pine wainscoting and a cozy lobby. The 30 guest rooms have polished wood floors, Amish-style quilts, and country-themed decor—but *no* televisions. Air-conditioning was added to most rooms in 2015, and the bathroom fixtures got a handsome upgrade then, too. Downstairs, adults can relax in a pub or shoot some pool while kids try out the two candlepin lanes. (This may be the only inn in New England with its own bowling alley. If you're not from New England, know this: Candlepins are maddening. Deal with it.) The 85-acre grounds are filled with decks, gazebos, a handsome in-ground pool, and walkways with magnificent water views. Five cottages with names like "Starfish" and "Spruce" offer additional privacy, eat-in kitchens, and one to three bedrooms each. Take Route 27 south from Boothbay Harbor across the Southport Island bridge, continuing to the south tip of the island.

60 Newagen Colony Rd., Southport. www.newagenseasideinn.com. ⓒ **800/654-5242** or 207/633-5242. 35 units. $175–$245 double; $255–$345 suite; $375–$425 cottage (week minimum late June–Aug, 3-night minimum spring and fall). Rates include breakfast (inn rooms only). Packages available. Closed mid-Oct–mid-May. **Amenities:** Dining room; pub; bikes; boat tours; bowling alley; Jacuzzi; heated outdoor pool; saltwater pool; free rowboats; tennis courts; free Wi-Fi.

Spruce Point Inn Resort ★   On a rocky point facing west across the harbor, this inn was built as a hunting and fishing lodge in the 1890s and evolved into a summer resort soon thereafter; some find it a mixed-bag experience, but it has benefited greatly from a spiffing-up that's been ongoing since the late '80s, including the addition of 55 deluxe suites with modern amenities such as Jacuzzis, marble bathrooms, private decks, woodstoves, carpeting, and new furniture. Guests typically idle in Adirondack chairs admiring the 15 acres of grounds, or partake of croquet, shuffleboard, and tennis on clay courts. Although it's more of a couples' place, children's programs accommodate a growing number of kids here. The spa is a welcome addition, and the formal dining room enjoys good sunset views across the mouth of the harbor. From Boothbay Harbor, turn seaward on Union Street and continue on 2 miles to the inn.

88 Grandview Ave., Boothbay Harbor. www.sprucepointinn.com. ⓒ **800/553-0289** or 207/633-4152. 93 units. Late June–Aug $185–$395 double; spring and fall $145–$288 double; year-round $260–$870 cottages and condo. 15% resort tax additional. 3-night minimum stay in summer and some holidays. Closed mid-Oct–mid-May. Some rooms accept pets. **Amenities:** 2 restaurants; pub; babysitting; concierge; conference rooms; fitness center; Jacuzzi; 2 outdoor pools; tennis court; free bikes; private boat launch; spa; free Wi-Fi.

Get Your Kicks on Route 1? Umm . . . No.

While there's a certain retro charm in the *idea* of traveling Maine on historic Route 1, the reality is quite different. It can be congested (Wiscasset) and unattractive (Waldoboro) in this part of the state, and you're not missing anything if you take alternative routes. For memorable explorations, be sure to leave enough time for forays both inland and down the lesser roads along the coast.

Topside Inn ★   This old gray house on the hilltop, looming above the town, looks a bit spooky at first glance. Fear not: Topside has spectacular ocean views at a reasonable price from its quiet perch over downtown Boothbay Harbor. The inn—a former boardinghouse for shipyard workers—has simple, clean, comfortable rooms mostly done in whites and pastels, furnished with a mixture of antiques and contemporary furniture. At the edge of the lawn there are two outbuildings stocked with basic motel-style units; these are on the smallish side, though two end units (room nos. 9 and 14) might have the best views on the whole property. Most units allow some glimpse of the water, in fact, and many have decks or patios. Renovations in 2008 and 2013 have left the whole place feeling much fresher than you'd expect from a 19th-century sea captain's home.

60 McKown St., Boothbay Harbor. www.topsideinn.com. © **888/633-5404** or 207/633-5404. 23 units. $189–$309 double. Rates include full breakfast. 2-night minimum weekends, 3-night minimum holiday weekends. Children 6 and older welcome. Closed Dec–Apr. Packages available. **Amenities**: Shared guest kitchen; free Wi-Fi.

Where to Eat in Wiscasset and the Boothbays
THE BOOTHBAYS
More creative dining can be found in the dining room of the Spruce Point Inn (see p. 132).

The Lobster Dock ★ LOBSTER   Across the harbor footbridge from downtown Boothbay Harbor, this place offers no-frills lobster and seafood; it's the best pick from a cluster of lobster-in-the-rough places lining the waterfront nearby. Lobsters are priced to market, and there are the usual fried-food baskets and sandwiches for those who don't dig crustaceans. This is a fine place for a classic Maine outdoor meal on a sunny day (though it's admittedly less interesting in rain or fog). Beer by the pitcher is a nice touch, the lobster stew is a standout, and don't skip dessert—I'd honestly come here just for the blueberry pie.

49 Atlantic Ave., Boothbay Harbor. www.thelobsterdock.com © **207/633-7120.** Sandwiches and grilled foods $6–$25; dinners $18–$29. Memorial Day–Columbus Day daily 11:30am–8:30pm (sometimes as late as 10pm Fri–Sat). Reservations not accepted.

Lobsterman's Wharf ★ LOBSTER   On the water in East Boothbay, the Lobsterman's Wharf has the comfortable, pubby feel of a popular neighborhood bar, complete with pool table. That makes it popular with locals, but the kitchen also serves better-than-standard meals and knows how to make out-of-towners feel at home. Specials have included a mixed-seafood grill, a barbecue shrimp-and-ribs platter, grilled swordfish with béarnaise sauce, seafood fettuccine, tuna sashimi, and lobsters served at least four different ways. Blueberry pie and chocolate cake make good finishers. At lunch, there are burgers, baked haddock, lobster rolls, and steamed lobsters.

224 Ocean Pt. Rd. (Rte. 96), East Boothbay. www.lobstermanswharf.com. © **207/633-3443.** Sandwiches $8–$11; dinners $13–$28. Late May–Oct daily 11:30am–10pm (Mon until 3pm). Reservations accepted only for parties of 6 or more. Closed Nov–late May.

WISCASSET

Red's Eats ★ LOBSTER/TAKEOUT   Red's is a tiny red shack next to Route 1 smack in downtown Wiscasset—right where the traffic maddeningly backs up at the bridge—that's received more than its fair share of national ink and TV attention for its famous lobster rolls. And they are good, mostly judging by volume—so many big, fresh, moist chunks of chilled lobster, you actually can't see the toasted hot-dog roll beneath. Red's famously serves its rolls naked, with just a dish of butter and one of mayo on the side. Be aware that they're pricey—you can find less expensive, less filling versions anywhere else—and that the lines are long. On a bad day, plan to spend 45 minutes to an hour waiting to place your order. (If you're impatient—or if you happen to believe that the key to a good lobster roll is in a respectable ratio of meat to grilled, buttery bun—then head across the street to **Sprague's**, where the lines aren't nearly as long.) The few tables behind the stand fill up quickly in summer; you can also walk downhill to the public riverfront dock a minute away. Beyond the lobster rolls, very cheap fare (hot dogs, sandwiches) dominates the rest of the menu. You can also get very good ice-cream cones here.

41 Water St. (just before bridge), Wiscasset. www.redseatsmaine.com © **207/882-6128.** Most sandwiches and entrees $3–$9; lobster rolls typically $15–$25. No credit cards. Mon–Sat 11am–10pm; Sun noon–6pm. Closed Oct–Apr.

Treats ★★ BAKERY   The long dine-in table in this cool, rustic space is as likely to be occupied by gossiping locals as by vacationing folks just passing through. Baker/chef Josh DeGroot churns out outstanding pastries and perfect savory, well, treats. Don't miss the luscious cinnamon rolls or the croissants (and sometimes brioche pillows) filled with ham, local cheddar, and Dijon. There's a cooler full of great sandwiches made with local meats and produce on house-made crusty breads and baguettes and, in the adjoining room, a smart selection of wines, microbrews, and local cheeses (for carry out). Plus newspapers, magazines, some little gifty foodstuffs. Oh, and the place hosts a small indoor farmers market from time to time around harvest season. Think of Treats like a classy artisan general store.

80 Main St., Wiscasset. www.treatsofmaine.com © **207/882-6192.** Most pastries, tarts, and sandwiches $4–$10. Mon–Sat 8am–6pm, Sun 10am–4pm.

Exploring Wiscasset

Aside from enjoying the town's handsome architecture and general quaintness, you can find several quirky, low-key attractions good for a break while traveling up along the coast. You'll also find a handful of worthwhile antiques shops and eateries, as well as the excellent **Wiscasset Bay Gallery** (67 Main Street), displaying a trove of Monhegan Island landscape painters.

Castle Tucker ★ HISTORIC HOUSE   This fascinating museum at the edge of town, overlooking the river, was built in 1807 to resemble a Scottish manor house. It was then radically added onto and altered by a local cotton trader (yes, a cotton trader) named Richard Tucker who in 1858 transformed the house, adding a rather showy piazza and other additions. Thanks to a reversal of fortune, the house wasn't renovated again—to the benefit of modern visitors, who can see what life was like for high society in Maine in the mid-19th century. Tucker's daughter eventually donated the home to New England's antiquities society, which maintains it today; Castle staff give tours of the manse, which features a wonderful, long staircase and trompe-l'oeil-style plaster that looks remarkably like solid wood. Find it overlooking the river (behind Sarah's Café).

2 Lee St. (at High St.), Wiscasset. www.historicnewengland.org. © **207/882-7169.** Admission $8. Tours depart hourly Wed–Sun 11am–4pm June–mid-Oct; closed mid-Oct–May.

Nickels-Sortwell House ★ HISTORIC HOUSE   Another Historic New England property, this white cube of a Federal-style manor went up in 1807, owned by a prominent sea captain. It's loaded with antique Colonial Revival furnishing, and tours recall the heyday of Maine's maritime industry, when boatbuilders and captains were the worldly gentry bringing sophistication to tiny Maine villages .

121 Main St. (at High St.), Wiscasset. www.historicnewengland.org. © **207/882-7169.** Admission $8. Tours depart every half-hour Fri–Sun 11am–4pm June to mid-Oct; closed mid-Oct–May.

Exploring the Boothbay Region

Boothbay Harbor ★ was just another fishing village until it was "discovered" in the early 20th century by wealthy city folks who built imposing seaside homes here. Once it embraced the tourist dollar, the village never really looked back, and in recent years it has emerged as a premier destination for tourists in search of classic coastal Maine; the village is often a mandatory stop on bus tours, which have in turn attracted kitsch, but some of the outlying areas remain beautiful.

Summer parking in the town requires either great persistence or forking over a few dollars. A popular local attraction is the long, narrow **footbridge** across the harbor, built in 1901. It's more of a destination than a link—other than a few restaurants and motels, there's not much on the other side. The winding streets that weave through town are filled with souvenir shops purveying the usual trinkets. One exception is **Gleason Fine Art** (31 Townsend Avenue), with a fine selection of works by contemporary Maine artists.

Coastal Maine Botanical Gardens ★ GARDENS   This expansive complex of waterside gardens is well worth exploring—both for gardening and landscaping nuts and simply those who appreciate a sylvan place to stroll. Parts of the sprawling property still have an unmanicured feel, with pathways winding through mossy forest, past waterfalls, and in and out pocket gardens with different themes and flowers (plus a village of tiny fairy houses, made from sticks, rocks, and shells, that'll delight kids). All throughout, the walks are quiet and lush; one of the best trails runs along much of the tidal shoreline that's part of the property. Mid-November through December, the gardens are lit with hundreds of thousands of LED lights—it's something to see. From

Boothbay Harbor is overrun with summer visitors, but at nearby **Ocean Point,** you can leave most of the crowds behind by following a picturesque lane that twists along the rocky shore past a colony of vintage summer homes. Follow Route 96 southward from just outside Boothbay Harbor, and you'll pass through the sleepy village of East Boothbay before continuing on to the point. The narrow road runs through piney forests before arriving at the rocky finger. It's one of only a handful of Maine peninsulas that have a road edging its perimeter, allowing you fine ocean views. Colorful Victorian-era summer cottages bloom along the roadside like wildflowers. Ocean Point makes for a good bike loop, too; mountain-bike rentals are available from the **Tidal Transit** folks (see p. 137).

Route 27 in Boothbay Center, bear right at the monument, then make the first right onto Barters Island Road; drive 1 mile to the stone gate on the left. 132 Botanical Gardens Dr., Boothbay (near Hogdon Island). www.mainegardens.org. 📞 **207/633-8000.** $16 adults, $14 seniors, $8 children age 3–17; rest of year free admission. Mid-Apr–Oct daily 9am–5pm (until 6pm July–Aug). Closed Oct–mid-Apr except for Gardens Aglow events mid-Nov–Dec. 31.

Maine State Aquarium ★ AQUARIUM Operated by the state's Department of Marine Resources, this compact aquarium offers a context for the marine life in the Atlantic. Kids can view rare albino and blue lobsters, or get their hands wet in a 20-foot touch tank—a sort of petting zoo of the slippery and slimy. The aquarium is located on a point across the water from Boothbay Harbor, and parking is tight; visitors are urged to take the free shuttle bus from downtown that runs daily until 5pm.

194 McKown Point Rd., West Boothbay Harbor. 📞 **207/633-9559.** $5 adults, $5 seniors, $3 children age 5–12. Mid-May–Sept daily 10am–5pm; closed Oct–mid-May.

WONDERFUL WALKS

In good weather, stop by a Boothbay-region information center (see p. 130) and request a free guide to the holdings of the **Boothbay Region Land Trust** (📞 **207/633-4818**). More than a dozen of its properties dot the peninsula, most with quiet, lightly traveled trails good for a stroll or a picnic. Among the best: the **Linekin Preserve** ★, a 95-acre parcel en route to Ocean Point with 600 feet of riverfront. A hike around the loop trail (about 2 miles) occupies a pleasant hour. To find the preserve, drive south from Route 1 in Boothbay Harbor along Route 96 for about 3¾ miles, and look for the parking area on the left.

On the Water

The best way to see the Maine coast around Boothbay is on a boat tour. Nearly two dozen tour boats berth at the harbor or nearby. **Balmy Days Cruises** (www.balmydayscruises.com; 📞 **800/298-2284** or 207/633-2284), for instance, runs a half-dozen 90-minute trips daily around the harbor in summertime (mid-June to mid-September) from Pier 8 on Commercial St. for $18 per adult, $9 per child age 3 to 11. If you'd rather be sailing, ask about the five or so 90-minute harbor cruises daily from the same outfit aboard the Friendship sloop the *Bay Lady* ($30 for adults, $20 for children age 3–11). Schedules are reduced in spring and fall; call ahead for reservations. Balmy Day also runs trips out to Burnt Island ($25 for adults, $15 age 3–11), where Maine's Department of Marine Resources leads lighthouse tours and hikes around the island. It's a 15-minute boat trip that gives you 2½ hours on the island.

The most personal way to see the harbor is via sea kayak. **Tidal Transit Kayak Co.** (www.kayakboothbay.com; © **207/633-7140**) offers morning, afternoon, full-day, and sunset tours of the harbor for $55 to $100 (sunset's the best bet). Single kayaks can also be rented for $25 an hour or $55 per day; tandem kayaks and stand-up paddleboards available too. The shop is open daily in summer (except when it rains heavily), and is actually located on a dock at 18 Granary Way.

PEMAQUID PENINSULA ★★★

An irregular, rocky wedge driven deep into the Gulf of Maine, the Pemaquid Peninsula is far less commercial than Boothbay Peninsula across the Damariscotta River; it's much more suited to relaxed exploration and nature appreciation than its cousin. Rugged and rocky Pemaquid Point, at the extreme southern tip of the peninsula, is one of the most dramatic destinations in Maine, when the ocean surf pounds the shore.

Essentials

ARRIVING

The Pemaquid Peninsula is accessible from the south and west by taking U.S. Route 1 to Damariscotta, then turning south down Route 129/130. Coming from the north or northeast, take U.S. 1 through Waldoboro, then turn south down Route 32 just south of town.

VISITOR INFORMATION

The **Damariscotta Region Chamber of Commerce** (www.damariscotta region.com; © **207/563-8340**), is a good source of local information. A walk-in information center in the middle of town (at the corner of Main Street and Vine Street) is filled with literature.

Where to Stay on the Pemaquid Peninsula

Seasonal homes and cottage rentals are the dominant summer lodging around the peninsula—try **Newcastle Vacation Rentals** (www.mainecoastcottages. com; © **207/563-6500**) or the usual online rental platforms (Airbnb, Home-Away, and so on). For shorter stays, you're looking at B&Bs and small, often time-worn inns.

Bradley Inn ★ The Bradley Inn is within easy hiking or biking distance to the point, but there are plenty of reasons to lag behind at the inn, too. Wander the nicely landscaped grounds or settle in for a game of cards at the pub. The rooms are tastefully appointed with four-poster cherry beds (though no televisions). The third-floor rooms are the best despite the hike up to them, thanks to distant glimpses of John's Bay, and a high-ceilinged second-floor suite occupying the entire floor is equipped with a full kitchen and dining room. The inn is popular for summer weekend weddings, so ask in advance if you're seeking solitude and quiet. A seaside spa, opened in 2007, offers a menu of wellness services.

3063 Bristol Rd. (Route 130), New Harbor. www.bradleyinn.com. © **800/942-5560** or 207/677-2105. 16 units. $180–$255 double; $275–$475 suite and cottage. Rates include full breakfast and afternoon tea. Packages available. Closed Jan–Mar. **Amenities:** Dining room; pub; free bikes; room service; spa, free Wi-Fi.

Hotel Pemaquid ★   This 1889 coastal classic isn't directly on the water—it's about a 2-minute walk from Pemaquid Point—but the main inn has the flavor of an old-time boardinghouse. Outbuildings are a bit more modern. Though most rooms now have private bathrooms and flatscreen TVs, the inn is still old-fashioned at its core, with a no-credit-cards policy, narrow hallways, and antiques, including a great collection of old radios and phonographs. It could be better, but it is what it is, and some guests love that. The two- and three-bedroom suites—one with a sun porch and one with a kitchen—are good for families, and there are cottages and a carriage house rented by the week.

3098 Bristol Rd. (Rte. 130), Pemaquid Point. www.hotelpemaquid.com. © **207/677-2312.** 33 units (4 with shared bathroom). $115–$142 double with private bathroom; $99 double with shared bathroom; $174–$255 suite; $985–$1775 cottage weekly. 2-night minimum stay on weekends. No credit cards. Closed mid-Oct–mid-Apr. **Amenities:** Free Wi-Fi in main lobby.

Where to Eat on the Pemaquid Peninsula

Coveside Bar and Restaurant ★★ PUB   It's not much more than a small marina with a pennant-bedecked lounge and basic knotty-pine-paneled dining room, but this is a locals' favorite hangout in Christmas Cove. The food's pubby, the beer list is solid, and the views are outstanding. You might even catch a glimpse of the celebrity yachtsmen who tend to stop off here. Reservations are a good idea on summer weekends.

105 Coveside Rd., Christmas Cove (South Bristol). ww.covesiderestaurant.com. © **207/644-8282.** Entrees $11–$26. Daily 11am–9pm. Closed Nov–Apr.

Crissy's Breakfast & Coffee Bar ★ BREAKFAST/BAKERY   It's worth the short wait you'll often encounter on weekend mornings for the Latin-tinged plates and sweet treats at this bright and cute café and bakery. Specialties like huevos rancheros, pulled pork hash, and enchiladas and eggs are generous and piquant, and the lunch menu has favorites carnitas tacos and a perfectly griddled Cuban sandwich. It's the small touches that make the place, though: the little blueberry muffin bites on every table, the basket of children's books for the kids. The many-partitioned dining room (it's an old residential home) makes for an intimate feeling breakfast no matter how crowded the place gets.

212 Main St., Damariscotta. ww.cbandcb.com. © **207/563-6400.** Breakfast items and sandwiches $6–$10. Wed–Sun 8am–2pm. Reservations suggested for groups of 6 or more.

SPOTLIGHT ON maine diners, PART #2

An entire book could be written about **Moody's Diner** (℃ 207/832-7785) in Waldoboro—in fact, it has. This is *the* place to stop on Route 1 when traversing north toward Acadia and points beyond. Not because the food's amazing so much as it's simply throwback to an earlier time: sticky-sweet pies and only-in-Maine specials like boiled dinner on Thurs, haddock with egg sauce on Fri,

and of course, baked beans on Sat. The place simply serves food you can find almost nowhere else in the state, the old food ways are disappearing that fast. Finish with Indian pudding or one of those mile-high pies—walnut cream and rhubarb are two good choices, though any of them will satisfy. The prices, too, seem nearly locked in 1948, which is when Moody's first opened for business.

Shaw's Fish and Lobster Wharf ★ LOBSTER   Shaw's attracts hordes of tourists, but it's no trick to figure out why: It's one of the best-situated lobster pounds, with postcard-perfect views of the working harbor. You can stake out a seat on either the open deck or the indoor dining room (go for the deck), or order some appetizers from the raw bar. This is one of the few lobster joints in Maine with a full liquor license, and the lobster rolls are considered by experts (okay, eaters like me) to be some of Maine's best.

129 Rte. 32, New Harbor. ℃ **207/677-2200.** Lobster priced to market (typically $10 per pound), entrees $12–$25. Mid-May–mid-Oct daily 11am–8pm. Closed mid-Oct–mid-May.

Exploring the Pemaquid Peninsula

The Pemaquid Peninsula invites slow driving and frequent stops. At the head of the harbor, Damariscotta and Newcastle are twin towns with a couple of good pubs, an artisan butcher, a food co-op, and a great bookstore in **Sherman's Maine Coast Book Shop** (158 Main St.; www.shermans.com; ℃ 207/563-3207). There's even a fine organic distillery in **Split Rock Distilling** (16 Osprey Point Rd.; www.splitrockdistilling.com; ℃ 207/563-2669), and one of the coolest places you'll ever drink beer in the middle of the woods: **Oxbow Brewing Company** (274 Jones Woods Rd.; www.oxbowbeer.com; ℃ 207/315-5962). The Damariscotta River that runs through middle of town is one of the country's richest oystering grounds; paddlers can rent a boat from **Midcoast Kayak** at 47 Maine Street (www.midcoastkayak.com; ℃ 207/563-5732) to explore the estuary. Two-hour to full-day rentals $28–$50.

Head south on Route 129 (Bristol Road) and you'll first hit sleepy Walpole, where the road splits. Keep following Route 129 (the right-hand road) and you'll pass the austerely handsome Walpole Meeting House, dating from 1772. Though it's usually not open to the public, services are held here during the summer and the public is welcome. Keep going another 10 miles; at the end of the road you'll find picturesque **Christmas Cove,** so named because Captain John Smith (of Pocahontas fame) anchored here on Christmas Day in 1614.

On Route 32 at the eastern end of New Harbor, look for signs pointing to the **Rachel Carson Salt Pond Preserve ★**, a Nature Conservancy property, where noted naturalist Rachel Carson studied tide pools extensively while researching her 1956 bestseller *The Edge of the Sea*. Another couple miles up Route 32, you'll also find the **La Verna Preserve ★**, with 3 miles of trail and some great rocky beaches. Both preserves are wonderful spots for budding naturalists and experts alike. At low tide, you can see horseshoe crabs, periwinkles, barnacles, and maybe the occasional starfish in the tidal pools and among the rocks.

If instead you take the left-hand road at the Walpole split—Route 130—in 10 miles or so you'll reach the village of **New Harbor.** Look for signs west to **Colonial Pemaquid State Historic Site** (© **207/677-2423**). Open daily from Memorial Day to Labor Day, this state historic site has exhibits on the original 1625 settlement here; archaeological digs take place in the summertime. The $3 admission charge ($1 for children 5–11) includes a visit to stout **Fort William Henry,** a 1907 replica of a supposedly impregnable fortress. Nearby **Pemaquid Beach** is good for a (chilly) ocean dip or a picnic with the family.

But **Pemaquid Point ★★**, owned by the town of **Bristol,** should be your final destination; it's the place to while away an afternoon (© **207/677-2492**). The lighthouse is one of Maine's most photographed, the cluttered museum in the keeper's house is a trip, and the gnarly rock ledges stretching out in front of the lighthouse are good for an hour of climbing. Bring a picnic and a book, and find a spot on the dark, fractured rocks to settle in. The ocean views are superb, and the only distractions are the tenacious seagulls that might take a profound interest in your lunch. While you're here, **Pemaquid Beach Park** is also worth a visit; there's a small admissions charge.

Route 32, which strikes northwest out of New Harbor, is the most scenic way to leave the peninsula if you plan on continuing eastward on Route 1 to places such as Camden and Rockland (see Chapter 7).

On the Water

From New Harbor, you can get a great view of the coast from the sea by taking a boat trip. **Hardy Boat Cruises ★** (www.hardyboat.com; © **207/677-2026**) operates summertime tours aboard the 60-foot *Hardy III,* and excursions include a 1-hour seal-watch cruise ($16 for adults, $12 for children age 3–11) and a highly acclaimed 90-minute puffin tour out to Eastern Egg Rock ($30 for adults, $12 for children age 3–11). Yes, you will see puffins. Extra clothing for warmth is strongly recommended, because it gets chilly out on the sea. The company operates from mid- or late May through Labor Day. Finally, the Hardy Boat runs a ferry to **Monhegan Island** (see p. 141).

MONHEGAN ISLAND ★★★

Monhegan Island ★★★ is Maine's premier island getaway. Visited by Europeans as early as 1497, the wild, remote island was settled by fishermen attracted to the sea's bounty in offshore waters. In the 1870s, artists discovered the island and stayed for a spell, including Rockwell Kent (the artist most closely associated with the island), George Bellows, Edward Hopper, and Robert Henri.

It's not hard to figure out why artists have been attracted to this place, with its almost-mystical sense of tranquility. It's also a superb destination for hikers, since most of the island is undeveloped and laced with footpaths.

Just be aware that this is not Martha's Vineyard. There's one ATM on Monhegan, and few pay phones—heck, even electricity is scarce. That's what most visitors seem to like about it, and an overnight at one of the island's very simple inns is strongly recommended if you've got time; the island's true character doesn't emerge until the last day boat sails back to the mainland. If you just can't stomach the complete quiet and the lack of phones, TVs, and late-night takeout, day trips are also easy to arrange.

Essentials
ARRIVING

Access to Monhegan Island is via boat from New Harbor, Boothbay Harbor, or Port Clyde. The picturesque trip from **Port Clyde** is the favorite route of longtime visitors; the boat passes the Marshall Point Lighthouse and a series of spruce-clad islands before reaching the open sea and plying its way island-ward.

Several boats make the run to Monhegan from little Port Clyde. The *Laura B* is a doughty workboat (building supplies and boxes of food are loaded on first; passengers fill in the available niches on the deck and in the small cabin), and makes the run in about 1¼ hours. A newer boat—the slightly faster, passenger-oriented *Elizabeth Ann*—also makes the run, offering a large heated cabin and more seating, in about 50 minutes. You'll need to leave your car behind, so pack light and wear sturdy shoes. The fare is $35 round-trip for adults, $20 for children ages 2 to 12, and $5 for pets. They do take credit cards, but reservations are advised. Contact **Monhegan Boat Line** (www.monheganboat.com; ✆ **207/372-8848**). Parking is available just off the Port Clyde dock for $7 per day.

You can also get out here from **New Harbor** (see p. 140) by boarding a **Hardy Boat** (www.hardyboat.com; ✆ **800/278-3346**) to Monhegan. There are two departures daily in the summer and 3 days a week in the shoulder season, with round-trip fares $36 adults, $20 for children age 3–11.

Finally, if you're in coming from the **Boothbays** (see p. 129), **Balmy Days** (www.balmydayscruises.com; ✆ **800/298-2284** or 207/633-2284) also does a Monhegan run in summer, from mid-June through early October (and weekends only for a couple weeks on either side of that). The boat leaves once daily at 9:30am, drops you off, and touches the island again at 4:15pm: perfect for day-trippers. (Or day-and-a-half-trippers.) The round-trip costs $38 for adults, $19 for children age 3 to 11.

VISITOR INFORMATION

Monhegan Island has no formal visitor center, but it's small and friendly enough that you can make inquiries of just about anyone you meet on the island pathways. Clerks at the ferry dock in Port Clyde may also be helpful. Be sure to pick up the inexpensive map of the island's hiking trails at the ticket office or various shops around the island. Also, a great website maintained by island residents dispenses very complete info to first-time visitors. Find it on the web at **www.monheganwelcome.com**.

Where to Stay & Eat on Monhegan Island

Things have changed—a little—since the day when you had zero options for sleeping or dining overnight on Monhegan, and had to retreat to the mainland. There are a handful of cottages, simple inns, and plain restaurants on the island (and, at last check, at least one Airbnb rental). In a pinch, hit **L. Brackett & Son** (222 Monhegan Ave., ✆ 207/594-2222) for picnic supplies.

Monhegan House ★ The handsome Monhegan House has been accommodating guests since 1870, and it has the comfortable, worn patina of a venerable lodging house. The accommodations at this four-story walk-up are austere but comfortable, more so after recent renovations; it's a bit pricey, though, for what you get. There are no closets, and everyone uses clean dormitory-style bathrooms except those who stay in one of two newish two-bedroom suites. The downstairs lobby with fireplace is a welcome spot to sit and take the fog-induced chill out of your bones, since it can get cool on the island even in August. A dining room serves dinner nightly during the short summer season, and Monhegan's first public Wi-Fi hotspot (never thought I'd be writing *that* sentence) and ATM are in the casual eatery, the **Novelty**, behind the inn, which proudly touts its whoopee pies. Yes, if you're not a New Englander, those are a real food. Damned yummy, too.

Across the road from the church, Monhegan Island. www.monheganhouse.com. ✆ **207/594-7983.** 28 units (most with shared bathroom). $125–$179 double; $199–$229 suite. Rates include breakfast. Closed Oct to late May. **Amenities:** 2 restaurants; free Wi-Fi (with bandwidth limitations).

Trailing Yew ★ At the end of long summer afternoons, guests congregate near the flagpole in front of the main building of this simple, rustic hillside compound. They're waiting for the ringing of the bell that signals the start of the included-for-a-fee dinner, just like at summer camp. Inside, guests sit around long tables, introduce themselves to their neighbors, and wait for the family-style repast. This is a friendly, informal place popular with hikers and birders. Guest rooms are simply furnished in a pleasantly dated, summer-home style. Only one of the four guest buildings has electricity, however—guests in rooms without electricity are provided kerosene lamps and instructions for their use. Also, all rooms are unheated. Rates here are charged

You may find the tearing into a whole lobster a bit uncouth, or just intimidating. Or the monster shore dinner of a whole lobster with mussels, clams, corn, and other fixin's may just be more than you want to take on. Lucky for you, the spiraling popularity of the lobster roll has made it so you can taste Maine's quintessential shellfish basically anywhere you go. The classic Maine lobster roll is cold, fresh-picked lobster served on a buttered and lightly griddled hot dog bun (the split-top New England variety, not the side-split version found elsewhere around the country), then complemented with a touch of mayo to bind it. Some eschew mayo and go instead for drawn butter (if the lobster's served hot, this is known as "Connecticut-style"). There's much acrimony over whether a lobster roll ought to contain anything else—some fancy a bit of celery or lettuce for crunch, while purists will tell you this is an abomination. The crazy gastronomes down in Portland have taken to adding everything from wasabi powder to jalapeños to bacon.

per person: $110 for a single adult, less for groups of two or more and for children (prorated according to age).

Lobster Cove Rd. www.trailingyew.com. © **207/596-0440.** 37 units (36 with shared bathroom). $150 (2 adults) double; children's rates differ according to age. Rates include a full breakfast. No credit cards. Packages available. Closed mid-Oct–mid-May. **Amenities:** Dining room, some rooms have shared kitchens.

Exploring Port Clyde

Port Clyde is located at the tip of a long finger of land about 15 miles south of Route 1. Its charm derives from the fact that it's still just a fishing village. While some small-scale tourist enterprises have made their mark here, it caters primarily to working fishermen and the ferrymen who keep Monhegan supplied. The area also attracts a lot of artists; check out **Barbara Prey Projects** at 855 Main Street, a gallery featuring one of Maine's most successful current artists.

Head to the **Port Clyde General Store ★** on the waterfront and soak up the cracker-barrel ambience (there's actually a decent selection of wine here, attesting to encroaching upscale-ism). Order a sandwich to go, and then drive to the **Marshall Point Lighthouse Museum** (www.marshallpoint.org; © 207/372-6450)—to find it, follow the road along the harbor east and bear right to reach the point. The museum opens weekends only during May, then daily from Memorial Day until Columbus Day. Does it look somehow familiar? It is: This small lighthouse received a few moments of fame when Forrest Gump turned around here and headed back west during his cross-country walks in the movie, but it also happens to be one of the most peaceful and scenic lighthouses in the state.

Exploring Monhegan

Walking is the chief activity on Monhegan island; it's genuinely surprising how much distance you can cover on these 700 acres (about 1½ miles long and ½ mile wide). The village clusters tightly around the harbor; the rest of the island is mostly wild land, laced with 17 miles of trails.

Much of the island is ringed with high, open bluffs atop fissured cliffs; pack a picnic lunch and hike the **perimeter trail** ★★★, spending much of the day sitting, reading, and enjoying the surf rolling in against the cliffs. The inland trails are appealing in a far different way. Deep, dark **Cathedral Woods** ★★ is mossy and fragrant; sunlight only dimly filters through the evergreens to the forest floor.

Birding is also a popular spring and fall activity. The island is right on the Atlantic flyway, and a wide variety of birds stop here during annual migrations.

The sole attraction on the island is the good **Monhegan Museum** ★ (www. monheganmuseum.org; ✆ **207/596-7003**), at 1 Lighthouse Hill next to the 1824 lighthouse on a high point above the village. The museum, open for only a short season (11:30am–3:30pm daily July–Aug, 1:30–3:30pm daily late June and Sept), holds a quirky collection of historical artifacts and provides context for this rugged island's history. Nearby is a small and select art museum that opened in 1998 and features changing exhibits showcasing the works of illustrious island artists, including Rockwell Kent. There's no admission charge.

The spectacular **view** ★★ from the grassy slope in front of the lighthouse is the real prize, though. The vista sweeps across a marsh, past the historic Monhegan House Hotel (see p. 142), taking in Manana Island and across the sea beyond. Get here early if you want a good seat for the sunset; folks often congregate here after dinner for the view.

Mid-afternoon on Monhegan, before the ferries start showing up, has evolved into a sort of ritualistic happy hour ever since **Monhegan Brewing Company** (www.monheganbrewing.com) opened at 1 Boody Lane in 2013. The beer is much better than you'd expect 10 miles out to sea, based on recipes by Maine brewing pioneer Danny McGovern, the longtime brewmaster at Belfast's Marshall Wharf Brewing Company. Closed mid-October through April, it begins to open for weekends in May and is open daily throughout the summer months.

Artists are still attracted to this island in great numbers (notably Jamie Wyeth, whose home can be seen from a distance in picturesque **Lobster Cove**), and many open their **studios** to visitors during posted hours in summer. Some of the artwork runs along the lines of predictable seascapes and sunsets, but much of it rises above the banal. Look for the bulletin board along the main pathway in the village for a listing of the days and hours the studios are open.

UPPER MIDCOAST: AROUND PENOBSCOT BAY

Let's say you're traveling east on the Maine coast along Route 1, and you're the sort of person who travels with one eye on the compass or GPS heading. Somewhere around Rockland, you suddenly notice something strange: You're pointed almost due north. Huh? Yet it's true. The culprit behind this geographic quirk is Penobscot Bay, a sizable bite out of the coast that forces drivers to take a lengthy northerly detour in order to cross the head of the bay, where the Penobscot River flows into it at Bucksport.

Fear not; you'll find some of Maine's most distinctive coastal scenery in this little region, which is dotted with offshore islands and hills rising above the shore. Although the mouth of Penobscot Bay is occupied by two large islands, its waters still churn when the winds and tides are right.

Thanks to both its natural beauty and architectural cuteness, the bay's western shore sees a steady stream of tourist traffic in summer, especially along the stretch of U.S. Route 1 passing through artsy **Rockland** and affluent **Camden.** You'll need a small miracle to find a weekend bed without a reservation in summer or early fall. Nevertheless, this is a great area if you want to get a taste of the real Maine coast. Services for travelers are everywhere.

Following Route 1 around the bay, you can stop to check out the historic shipbuilding towns of **Belfast** and **Searsport;** detour south on the east side of the bay to visit the quiet tree-shaded streets of **Castine,** or get away from it all on outdoorsy **Deer Isle.** Forming the eastern boundary of Penobscot Bay, the lovely **Blue Hill Peninsula** is a sort of backroads paradise. If you came to Maine to get lost on country lanes that dead-end at the sea or loop back on themselves, this is the place. By and large, the peninsula is overlooked by the majority of Maine's tourists, especially those who like their itineraries well structured and their destinations clear. In my book, that makes it doubly worth considering for a day or two's visit.

ROCKLAND & ENVIRONS ★

185 miles NE of Boston and 78 miles NE of Portland

Located on the southwestern edge of Penobscot Bay, Rockland has long been proud of its blue-collar waterfront roots. Built around the fishing industry, the city long historically dabbled in tourism but never really waded. With the recent decline of local fisheries and the rise of Maine's tourist economy, though, that balance has shifted. Rockland is swiftly being colonized by restaurateurs, innkeepers, artisans, and other folks who are transforming the place from fish-processing center to arts-and-crafts mecca.

The waterfront has a small park from which windjammers come and go, but even more appealing is Rockland's downtown—basically, one long street lined with historic brick architecture. If you're seeking picturesque harbor towns, however, head instead for Camden (p. 145), Rockport (p. 164), Port Clyde (p. 143), or Stonington (p. 174). Rockland is best as a sensible local base for exploring a beautiful coastal region, especially if you like your towns to be a bit rough and salty around the edges.

Essentials

ARRIVING

By car, U.S. Route 1 passes directly through the center of Rockland. **Concord Coach** (www.concordcoachlines.com; © **800/639-3317**) runs one to two daily buses from Portland and Boston.

Surprisingly, Rockland's tiny local **airport** (Knox County Regional Airport, airport code RKD) is served by daily direct flights from Boston on **Cape Air** (www.capeair.com; © **866/227-3247** or 508/771-6944) that are often remarkably affordable. There's a local taxi on call, and rental car kiosks at the terminal. The airport itself is actually in Owls Head, off Route 73.

VISITOR INFORMATION

The **Penobscot Bay Regional Chamber of Commerce** (www.therealmaine.com; © **800/562-2529** or 207/596-0376) staffs an information desk on Park Drive by Harbor Park. It's open daily from Memorial Day to Labor Day, on weekdays the rest of the year.

SPECIAL EVENTS

The **Maine Lobster Festival** (www.mainelobsterfestival.com; © **800/562-2529**) takes place at Rockland's Harbor Park the first weekend in August (plus the preceding Thursday–Friday). Entertainers and vendors of all sorts of Maine products—especially, of course, the famous Maine crustaceans—fill the waterfront parking lot for thousands of festivalgoers who enjoy the pleasantly buttery atmosphere. The event includes the Maine Sea Goddess

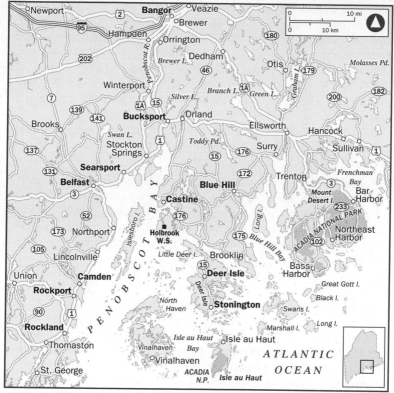

Coronation Pageant. Admission is \$5–\$10 per day for adults, \$2 for children; food, of course, costs extra. Four-day passes are also available.

During the last 2 weeks of October, Rockland celebrates the changing of colors—though with a unique twist: a scarecrow-making contest. It's part of the city's Festival of Scarecrows and **Harvest Day** celebrations.

Later, in late November, Rockland's **Festival of Lights** kicks off with Santa arriving not by reindeer but by Coast Guard boat—make of that what you will—then moves on to a program of caroling, horse-drawn carriage rides, a parade, and interesting tours of some of the area's most historic inns. Call © **207/596-0376** for more information.

Where to Stay in Rockland

As Rockland's star has risen as an arts and culture destination, a few stylish new hotel options have popped up, while old classics have gotten a "boutique" rebrand. New in 2016, the **Rockland Harbor Hotel** (520 Main St.; www. rocklandharborhotel.com; © **207/594-2131**) transformed a run-down old motor inn into a fresh, attractive 82-room property with seaside color schemes and balconies overlooking the ferry terminal. With doubles hovering around $200 night in peak season, it's within walking distance to everything downtown. If you're craving that "old Maine" seaside inn feel, you can still find it, especially farther down the peninsula. Try the **East Wind Inn** in Tenant's Harbor (www.eastwindinn.com; Ⓒ 800/241-8439 or 207/372-6366), at 21 Mechanic Street. It's a former sail loft converted to lodgings, perfectly situated beside the harbor with water views from all rooms and a long wraparound porch. Doubles with private bathrooms start around $175 during the summer.

The city of Rockland has made an effort to regulate rampant seasonal Airbnb rentals, but you won't want for options on that or other online rental platforms, and there are deals to be had.

250 Maine Hotel ★ This boutique hotel has a high-design, industrial-chic feel that calls to mind urban condos—which is just what the building was initially intended to be, although it eventually became a hotel for lack of demand. The developer's loss is travelers' gain. Running with Rockland's revived identity as an arts destination, the hotel hasn't found a wall that it couldn't decorate with local art, from crisp landscape photography to watercolors to reimagined 1950s tourism propaganda—there's even artist-designed wallpaper. Rooms are individually designed/decorated, and both they and the common areas are filled with midcentury modern furniture in bright colors and lots of showy reclaimed wood. If none of that is mod enough for you, each room has a complimentary concierge tablet to play around on. On a summer evening, the rooftop deck overlooking the harbor is a pretty unbeatable place to unwind (and they pour wine up there).

250 Maine St., Rockland. www.250mainhotel.com. Ⓒ **207/594-5994.** 26 units. Memorial Day–Columbus Day $315–$489 double; rest of year $173–$250 double. Packages available. **Amenities:** free Wi-Fi.

Berry Manor Inn ★ A stalwart midcoast B&B, Berry Manor goes for classic luxury with just a bit of quirk. On the one hand, expect poster beds, floral wallpaper, rich draperies and bedding, pillows piled up like an opium den—all the over-the-top trappings of Victorian comfort. On the other hand, there's co-owner Mike LaPosta showing off his collection of dancing toy hamsters, and there's the three Pie Moms—two moms of the owners plus a third tag-along, who have enjoyed some local celebrity after cable TV appearances alongside Bobby Flay and Mike Rowe. The daffy trio cracks wise while baking knockout fruit pies from scratch—and these are available to guests, along with vanilla ice cream, in a 24/7 pantry. Yum.

81 Talbot Ave. www.berrymanorinn.com. Ⓒ **207/596-7696.** 12 units. June–mid-Oct $140–$315 double; late Oct–May $125–$285 double. Rates include breakfast. Packages available. **Amenities:** Free Wi-Fi.

LimeRock Inn ★ This turreted, Queen Anne–style inn sits sleepily on a quiet side street just 2 blocks off Rockland's main drag. Attention has been paid to detail throughout, from the kingly choices of country Victorian furniture to the Egyptian cotton bed sheets. All eight guest rooms are welcoming and colorful, bordering on whimsical; among the best are the Island Cottage Room, a bright and airy south-of-France-like chamber wonderfully converted from an old shed (it has a private deck and a Jacuzzi); the Turret Room, with a canopy bed, cherry daybed, and French doors leading into a bathroom with a claw-foot tub and shower; and the elegant Grand Manan Room, with a big four-poster mahogany king bed, fireplace, and double Jacuzzi that puts one in mind of a southern plantation home.

96 Limerock St., Rockland. www.limerockinn.com. © **800/546-3762.** 8 units. $125–$249 double. Rates include full breakfast. **Amenities:** Free Wi-Fi.

Samoset Resort ★★ Established in 1889 on a scenic hill just outside Rockland (technically it's in Rockport), the Samoset was meant as a grown-up summer camp for the wealthy. Even the cathedral-ceilinged lobby, constructed of massive timbers salvaged from an old grain silo in Portland, is worth photographing. This is not the original building—the original was shuttered, auctioned off, and destroyed by fire decades ago. But the place has bounced back big-time as a noted golf resort and luxury property, thanks to a number of exciting recent upgrades. A few years back, a new heated pool and hot tub were added on the hill's highest point, with sweeping views of the bay, plus a tiki bar serving frozen drinks and light meals. Rooms vary in position and view, but many have balconies or porches with grand Penobscot Bay views; all have rich wood-and-leather headboards, flatscreen TVs, and marble vanities. Bathrooms are extra-big, some with whirlpool tubs. The golf course remains one of the most scenic in New England, while the quiet local roads are perfect for strolling, and there's even a mini-lighthouse adjacent to the property. Check out the good health club, then head to dinner—your options include seasonal **Marcel's,** serving excellent resort fare, and the **Breakwater Grill,** serving lighter fare year-round. All in all, a great luxury comeback.

220 Warrenton St., Rockport. www.samoset.com. © **800/341-1650** or 207/594-2511. 178 units. Early July–late Aug $299–$339 double, $409–629 suite; May–early July and late Aug–Nov $159–$299 double, $259–$589 suite; $619–$1,849 cottages year-round. MAP rates available. **Amenities:** 3 restaurants; babysitting; children's programs; concierge; fitness center; golf course; golf school; health club; Jacuzzi; indoor pool; heated outdoor pool; room service; sauna; 4 tennis courts; free Wi-Fi.

Where to Eat in Rockland

A good choice for the family in downtown Rockland is the Italian eatery **Rustica Cucina Italians** (www.rusticamaine.com; © 207/594-0015), serving standard Italian favorites. It's open for lunch and dinner Monday through Saturday in high season; call for off-season hours. For a night on the town, don't miss **Fog** on Main Street (© 207/593-9371). With high ceilings, hand built blond-wood furniture, and classic movies screening on the back wall, the vibe (and clientele) pretty nicely encapsulates the "new midcoast": hip, not flashy, a little rustic. The American brasserie chow fits the same description—great burgers, fish tacos, and truffle mac and cheese. Terrific beer list at the long bar.

Cafe Miranda ★★ ECLECTIC A midcoast institution, Café Miranda has one of the longest, craziest menus in New England. Hidden on a side street, it's a tiny, contemporary restaurant with a huge ever-morphing menu of big flavors and hip attitude. "We do not serve the food of cowards," owner-chef Kerry Altiero is quoted right on top of the menu, and he's right. I could write a whole book on the regularly changing menu here, but Altiero already did in 2014—*Adventures in Comfort Food*, which pretty well sums it up. Small plates and entrees could include things like grilled lamb patties with parsley and garlic; "50 MPH tomatoes" deep-fried and served with spicy ranch dressing; a "squash-o'-rama" (roasted squash with cheese); fire-roasted feta with sweet peppers, tomatoes, "really good" olives, and herbs; a Portuguese seafood combo of mussels, shrimp, clams, fish, and sausage steamed in wine and pummeled with parsley; "Aunt Fluffy's Pasta" (penne with veggies, caramelized onions, and Romano); the "Polish hippie" (grilled sausage with horseradish, arugula, and beets!); "Old Bleu" (handmade pasta tossed in blue cheese and basil cream); chicken paprikash; steaks; or, of course, the immortal "Pitch a Tent": sausage, gravy, onions, garlic, and mushrooms beneath a "tent" of pasta. Share everything with your fellow diners, because you'll never eat at a place this original again. Altiero again: "It's comfort food for whatever planet you're from." Amen.

15 Oak St., Rockland. www.cafemiranda.com. ℂ **207/594-2034.** Lunch $11–$20, small plates $12–$19, entrees $15–$27. Mon–Thurs 11:30am–2pm and 5–8:30pm, Fri–Sat 11:30am–2pm and 5–9pm, Sun 10:30am–2pm and 5–8:30pm. Reservations strongly recommended.

Suzuki's ★★ JAPANESE Keiko Suzuki Steinberger started surprising diners in Rockland with her distinctive brand of sushi back in 2006. The mostly self-taught sushi chef (she did a brief stint at Tokyo's Sushi Academy) relies heavily on the local catch, so expect to find exquisitely plated and unconventional sashimi, maki, and nigiri made with halibut, herring, mackerel, tuna, whelks, or clams. Chef Keiko was a 2016 James Beard Foundation semifinalist; more than a decade in, her kitchen staff (all women) are at the top of their game.

419 Main St., Rockland. www.suzukissushi.com. ℂ **207/596-7447.** Sushi $3–$11, noodle dishes $14–$25. Tues–Sat 5–9pm.

Yardbird Canteen ★ SEAFOOD Discovering a great meal at an unassuming seafood shack on a quiet coastal road is why you came to Maine, right? Yardbird's "dining room" is a set of picnic tables under an awning in what is actually someone's backyard (with little buckets full of citronella and bug spray because, duh, Maine summer). Yardbird has a limited barbecue menu, but what it really excels at is fried fish. Magic batter and a perfect fry makes for light and golden fish and chips, fried clams, and more, served in a basket lined with faux newspaper. Big yard for the kiddos to play in. To get

CRAFTING A vacation

The Maine coast has been a haven for visual artists, jewelers, sculptors, photographers, potters, and other creative types for as long as I can remember. Studios, galleries, arts centers, and museums of surprising quality crop up nearly everywhere, even in the tiniest coastal villages.

While cruising the coast, you'd do well to drop in to some of these crafts studios—and the best way to find them quickly is to contact the **Maine Crafts Association** (www.mainecrafts.org; © **207/205-0791**), which publishes a comprehensive annual guidebook to its member artists, which maintains a database of its members online, searchable both by media and region. You'll find everything from glassblowers to sculptors to fiber artists to basketmakers.

It's recommended you call ahead to get studio hours before making the trek to an out-of-the-way crafts studio or gallery. They *are* artists, after all—hours are likely to be a little whimsical.

here, head west out of Rockland on Route 1 to Thomaston (3 miles), then go south on Route 131 another 14 miles.

686 Port Clyde Rd., Tenant's Harbor. © **207/372-1068.** Sandwiches $6–$14, seafood baskets $10–$23. Mid-May–mid-Sept Thurs–Sat 11am–7pm, Sun 11am–5pm.

Primo ★★★ MEDITERRANEAN/NEW AMERICAN Primo opened in 2000 and quickly developed a buzz as one of northern New England's top eats; it still is. The restaurant occupies two nicely decorated floors of a century-old home, a short drive south of Rockland's downtown. Owner/chef Melissa Kelly graduated first in her class at the Culinary Institute of America and won a James Beard Foundation award for "best chef in the Northeast" in the 1990s and again in 2013. Her Italian-inflected menu reflects the seasons and draws from local products wherever available (much of the meat and produce the kitchen's working with comes off the restaurant's expansive farm). Start with an appetizer such as wood-fired pizza with artisanal mushrooms, planked octopus with chickpea salad, seared *foie gras* over poached strawberries, antipasti, or fried and roasted local oysters paired with rémoulade sauce and house-cured Tasso ham. Entrees might run to seared diver scallops with fettuccine, local halibut over a white bean puree, monkfish medallions with peekytoe crab-risotto cakes, grilled steak or duck, tuna au poivre, or chicken with lavender-and-honey roasted figs and a sweet ricotta gnocchi. Finish with one of co-owner/pastry chef Price Kushner's inventive desserts: warm Belgian chocolate cake, an espresso float, a rhubarb-strawberry tartlet with vanilla gelato and strawberry sauce, homemade cannoli, a bowl of hot zeppole (small Italian doughnuts) tossed in cinnamon and sugar, or an apple *crostata* sided with pine-nut-and-caramel ice cream. The wine list is outstanding. It's hard to get a last-minute table here during summer; failing that, order off the menu from the cozy upstairs bar.

2 S. Main St. (Rte. 173), Rockland. www.primorestaurant.com. © **207/596-0770.** Appetizers $13–$18, entrees $33–$48. Summer daily 5:30–9:30pm; call for dates and hours in off season; closed Jan–early May. Reservations highly recommended.

windjammers ON THE WATER

During the transition from sail to steam, captains of fancy new steamships belittled old-fashioned sailing ships as "windjammers." The term stuck; through a curious metamorphosis, the name evolved into one of adventure and romance.

Maine is the windjammer cruising capital of the U.S., and the two most active Maine harbors are **Rockland** and **Camden** on Penobscot Bay. Cruises last from 3 days to a week, during which these handsome, creaky vessels poke around tidal inlets and small coves that ring the beautiful bay. It's a superb way to explore the coast the way it's historically always been explored—from out on the water, looking in. Rates run between about $110 and $180 per day per person (which is $300–$1,200 per person for an entire trip); the best rates are offered early and late in the season.

Maine boasts a sizable fleet of sailing ships both vintage and modern that offer private cabins, meals, entertainment, and adventure. The ships range in size from 50 to 130 feet, and accommodations range from cramped and rustic to reasonably spacious and well appointed. Most are berthed in the region between Boothbay Harbor and Belfast—they cruise the Penobscot Bay region during summer, and some migrate south to the Caribbean for the winter.

Cruise schedules and amenities vary widely from ship to ship, even from week to week, depending on the inclinations of captains and the vagaries of Maine weather. You choose your adventure: An array of excursions is available, from simple overnights to weeklong expeditions gunkholing among Maine's thousands of scenic islands and coves. A "standard" cruise often features a stop at one or more of the myriad spruce-studded Maine islands (perhaps with a lobster bake on shore). Breakfasts are served at tables below decks (or perched cross-legged on the deck), and you absorb a palpable sense of maritime history as the ships scud through frothy waters.

Ideally, you'll have a chance to look at a couple of ships to find one that suits you before signing up. Several windjammer festivals and races are held along the Maine coast throughout the summer; these are perfect events to shop for a ship on which to spend a few days. Among the more notable events are **Windjammer Days** in Boothbay Harbor (late June; see p. 131) and the **Camden Windjammer Weekend** in early September (see p. 156). If you can't do that, contact the **Maine Windjammer Association** (www.sailmainecoast.com; ☏ **800/807-9463**) for a packet of brochures or simply check its good website of member ships and comparison-shop. If you're trying to book a *last-minute* windjammer cruise on a whim, stop by the chamber of commerce office on the Rockland waterfront (see above) and inquire about open berths.

Exploring Rockland

Rockland's walkable Main Street, close enough to the harbor that you can catch a whiff at low tide, is lined with restaurants, boutiques, art galleries, and two of Maine's most impressive museums in the **Center for Maine Contemporary Art** and the **Farnsworth Museum.** You may also want to check out the contemporary art at the **Dowling Walsh Gallery,** 365 Main Street. Not so long ago, a lot of these storefronts were empty, but comparatively cheap real estate has attracted creative types, entrepreneurs, and younger folks and families who can afford this still-rough-around-the-edges harbor town better than Camden and Rockport. When the CMCA opened in 2016, it seemed like confirmation of Rockland's new direction, and a handful of sleek new Main Street restaurants opened on its heels.

Artists have long been drawn to Rockland's coastal surroundings (and the islands nearby). A trip to nearby **Cushing**, 12 miles southwest of Rockland, shows off scenery that's been captured on canvas by the likes of Edward Hopper and Andrew Wyeth (including the farmhouse made famous in *Christina's World*—see below). It's worth a call to the Georges River Land Trust at ✆ **207/594-5166** to ask about the **Langlais Sculpture Preserve** at 576 River Road; as of this writing, it is slated to open in fall 2017. When it's open, the pastoral property will feature a self-guided walk among the site-specific sculptures of the late Bernard Langlais, a much-admired, somewhat whimsical sculptor whose preferred medium was scrap wood. Highlights include his geometric, 13-foot *Horse* and a model of Richard Nixon standing in a pond.

Center for Maine Contemporary Art ★★★ MUSEUM

The sleek new headquarters of the CMA opened in 2016 to much fanfare, and the architecturally striking building on the old waterfront (its spiky roofline is meant to recall the waves) has been drawing crowds since to its three galleries filled with cutting edge (often sculptural or multimedia) contemporary art. In the courtyard outside, a piece from Maine artist Jonathan Barofsky's 24-foot *Human Structures* series (he has similar sculptures permanently installed in San Francisco and Beijing) gives you a pretty good idea what you're in for: work that's modern, a little abstract, and a little whimsical.

21 Winter St., Rockland. www.cmcanow.org. ✆ **207/701-5005.** $6 adults, kids 12 and under free. June–Oct Tues–Sat 10am–6pm, Sun 1–6pm; Nov–May Wed–Sat 10am–5pm, Sun 1–5pm; first Friday of every month 10am–8pm with free admission.

Farnsworth Museum ★★ MUSEUM

Rockland, for all its rough edges, has long and historic ties to the arts. Noted sculptor Louise Nevelson grew up in Rockland, and in 1935 philanthropist Lucy Farnsworth bequeathed a fortune to establish the Farnsworth Museum, which has since become one of the most respected little art museums in New England. Located right downtown, the Farnsworth has a superb collection of paintings and sculptures by renowned American artists with connections to Maine—not only Nevelson, but also three generations of Wyeths (N. C., Andrew, and Jamie), plus Rockwell Kent, Childe Hassam, and Maurice Prendergast. The exhibit halls are modern, spacious, and well designed, and shows are professionally prepared. Equally interesting is the museum-owned **Olson House ★**, a 25-minute drive southwest from Rockland, in the village of Cushing; it's perhaps Maine's most well-known home, immortalized in Andrew Wyeth's famous painting *Christina's World.*

356 Main St., Rockland. www.farnsworthmuseum.org. ✆ **207/596-6457.** Museum $15 adults, $13 seniors, $10 students 17 and older, free for children under 17; add $5 for admission to Olson House. June–Oct daily 10am–5pm; Nov–Dec Tues–Sun 10am–5pm; Jan–March Wed–Sun 10am–4pm; April–May Tues–Sun 10am–5pm.

Owls Head Transportation Museum ★ MUSEUM   You don't need to be a car or plane buff to enjoy this museum, though it helps. Founded in 1974 and located 3 miles south of Rockland on Route 73, the museum has an extraordinary collection of cars, motorcycles, bicycles, and planes, nicely displayed in a tidy, hangarlike building at the edge of the Knox County Airport. Look for an early Harley Davidson motorcycle and a sleek Rolls-Royce Phantom dating from the roaring '20s.

117 Museum St., Owls Head. www.ohtm.org. (℗ **207/594-4418.** $14 adults, $10 seniors, under 18 free. Daily 10am–5pm.

Strand Theatre ★ THEATER   The social hub of Main Street on any given Friday or Saturday night is the sidewalk outside the Strand, where theatergoers gather underneath the bright vertical marquee that's kind of a totem of Rockland's downtown. Restored in 2004, the nearly century-old theater hosts first-run indie movies and documentaries, concerts by national touring bands like BeauSoleil and Patty Griffin (the schedule is Americana-heavy), and the occasional local theater performance.

345 Main St. www.rocklandstrand.com. (℗ **207/594-0070.** Shows nightly.

CAMDEN ★★

8 miles N of Rockland

A quintessential coastal Maine town at the foot of wooded Camden Hills, the affluent village of Camden sits on a picturesque harbor that no Hollywood movie set could improve on. It has been attracting the gentry of the eastern seaboard for more than a century. The mansions of the moneyed set still dominate the town's shady side streets (many have been converted into bed-and-breakfasts), and Camden is possessed of a grace and sophistication that eludes many other coastal towns.

On the downside, some longtime visitors say that all this attention (and Camden's growing appeal to bus tours) is having a deleterious impact on the atmosphere; yes, there are T-shirt shops here. And there are occasional cries raised about the increasing snootiness of the place. As long as you don't expect a pristine, undiscovered fishing village, you'll be in good shape to enjoy it.

Essentials
ARRIVING

By car, Camden is right on U.S. Route 1. Coming from the south, you can shave a few minutes off the trip here by turning left onto state Route 90 about 6 miles past Waldoboro, bypassing the downtown streets of the city of Rockland. **Concord Coach** (www.concordcoachlines.com; (℗ **800/639-3317**) runs bus service (one or two trips daily) from Boston and Portland; buses stop at the Maritime Farms grocery store on Route 1 in Rockport, a little more than a mile's walk from either downtown Camden or Rockport harbor. (For more on Rockport, see p. 164).

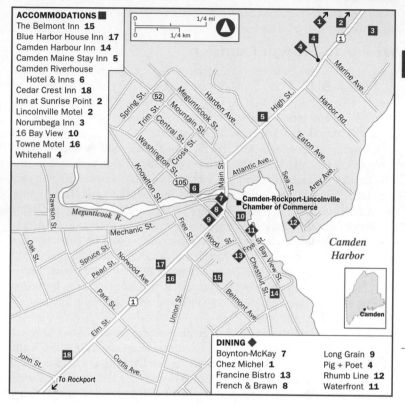

ACCOMMODATIONS ■
The Belmont Inn **15**
Blue Harbor House Inn **17**
Camden Harbour Inn **14**
Camden Maine Stay Inn **5**
Camden Riverhouse
  Hotel & Inns **6**
Cedar Crest Inn **18**
Inn at Sunrise Point **2**
Lincolnville Motel **2**
Norumbega Inn **3**
16 Bay View **10**
Towne Motel **16**
Whitehall **4**

Camden-Rockport-Lincolnville
Chamber of Commerce

*Camden
Harbor*

DINING ◆

Boynton-McKay **7**	Long Grain **9**
Chez Michel **1**	Pig + Poet **4**
Francine Bistro **13**	Rhumb Line **12**
French & Brawn **8**	Waterfront **11**

VISITOR INFORMATION

The **Penobscot Bay Regional Chamber of Commerce** (www.camdenrock land.org; © **800/562-2529** or 207/236-4404), dispenses helpful information from its center at the **Public Landing** (waterfront) in Camden, where there's also free parking—though spaces are pretty scarce in summer. The chamber is open daily year-round.

In need of a hotel room? **Camden Accommodations and Reservations** (www.camdenac.com; © **800/344-4830** or 207/236-6090) provides assistance with everything from booking rooms at local B&Bs to finding cottages for seasonal rentals.

SPECIAL EVENTS

Humanities types will enjoy Camden's annual **Harbor Arts and Books Fairs** (© **800/223-5459** or 207/236-4404), two weekends of local artworks displayed against the stunningly scenic backdrop of the Camden Hills' changing colors, along with a giant, tented used book sale. One happens in July, the other early in October. In between, over Labor Day weekend, the **Camden**

Windjammer Festival (see box p. 152) sees the region's tall-ship fleet parade through the harbor, along with food, music, and games like the annual lobster crate race, with kids (and the occasional brave adult) bounding across bobbing wooden crates in the harbor).

Where to Stay in Camden

Camden vies with Kennebunkport, Maine, and Manchester, Vermont, for the title of "bed-and-breakfast capital of New England." They're everywhere. The stretch of Route 1 just north of the village center—called High Street here—is a virtual bed-and-breakfast alley, with many handsome homes converted to lodgings. Others are tucked away on side streets.

Despite the preponderance of B&Bs, though, the total number of guest rooms in town is still too small to accommodate the crush of peak-season visitors, and during summer or fall, the lodging is tight. It's best to reserve well in advance. You might also try **Camden Accommodations and Reservations** (www.camdenac.com; ℰ **800/344-4830** or 207/236-6090) for help in finding anything from overnight rooms to seasonal rentals. In the name of keeping these folks in business, Camden has recently cracked down a bit on townsfolk offering private rentals through Airbnb and VRBO, prohibiting standalone properties (as compared to spare rooms) from renting for any duration shorter than a week. Further permitting and inspection regulations may be forthcoming, but for now, there are still plenty of properties available in summer via these online rental platforms.

If the inns and B&Bs listed below are unavailable or out of your budget, a handful of area motels and hotels might be able to accommodate you. South of the village center on Route 1 are the **Cedar Crest Inn,** 115 Elm Street (www.cedarcrestinnmaine.com; ℰ **207/236-4839**), a handsome seasonal motel (peak-season rates $159–$169, spring and fall cheaper), and the long-time mainstay **Towne Motel,** 68 Elm Street (www.camdenmotel.com; ℰ **207/236-3377**), within walking distance of the village (open year-round; peak season rates $124–$139 double, cheaper off-season). Also right in town, just across the footbridge, is the modern, if generic, **Camden Riverhouse Hotel and Inns,** 11 Tannery Lane (www.camdenmaine.com; ℰ **207/236-0500**), with an indoor pool, fitness center, and Wi-Fi. It's open year-round; peak season rates range from $209 to $269 for a double room or suite, while the off-season is far cheaper.

16 Bay View ★★ Until this boutique hotel opened in late 2015, Camden strangely lacked any true waterfront hotel lodging. A former moviehouse and restaurant, 16 Bay View is just steps from the harbor, with views of the waves and the tall-masted ships from the top-floor accommodations and the rooftop terrace. You'll pay for it, of course—the hotel pitches to a luxury crowd, and the fireplaces, free-standing pedestal tubs, and Cuddledown bedding give the rooms a pretty genteel feel. Continental breakfast (good pastries and quiches) is delivered in-room each morning. The clubby bistro/bar/lounge feels like a world away from the busy Camden street scene in midsummer (and the tapas plates are pretty yum).

16 Bay View St., Camden. www.16bayview.com. © **844/213-7990.** 21 units. July–Oct $329–$379 double, $449–$649 suite; May–June and Nov-Dec $209–$299 double, $349–$499 suite; Jan–April $149–$239 double, $259–$399 suite. Rates include a full breakfast. Some rooms accommodate pets ($35 per night fee). Packages available. **Amenities:** Restaurant; lounge; rooftop bar; free Wi-Fi.

The Belmont Inn ★   A handsome, shingle-style 1890s home with a wrap-around porch, the Belmont is set in a quiet residential neighborhood of unpretentious homes away from Route 1. The inn has an understated, Victorian sort of theme throughout, featuring numerous floral prints by Maine artist Jo Spiller for instance (there's also a guest room with great morning light named after Spiller). All units have polished wood floors and are furnished simply with eclectic antiques and country touches such as cast-iron stoves, sleigh beds, writing desks, and wingback chairs. Downstairs, there's an elegant common room with a fireplace alcove and built-in benches. One room, the Allen Room, magically becomes a suite (and costs more) when the owners open a little door connecting it to a sitting room.

6 Belmont Ave., Camden. www.thebelmontinn.com. © **207/236-8053.** 6 units. $169–$259 double; $259–$299 suite. Rates include full breakfast. No children 11 and under. Packages available. **Amenities:** Free Wi-Fi.

Blue Harbor House Inn ★   On busy Route 1 just south of town, this pale-blue 1810 farmhouse has been an inn since 1978. It's decorated throughout with a floral, country look. Rooms and suites vary in size; some are smallish, with slanting angles and low ceilings, but you can expect touches such as four-poster beds, claw-foot tubs, wicker furniture, Jacuzzis, triptych mirrors, writing desks, and slipper chairs in various configurations. And the exposed wood floors are absolutely lovely. The best rooms are the carriage-house suites, with their private entrances and extra amenities—two, Captains Quarters and Compass Rose, share a private outdoor patio. The early evening hours feature a nice cocktail service, with cocktails made to order and lovely hors d'oeuvre for a small extra charge. (Fun fact: One of the owners used to work as a cocktail bartender on the real "Love Boat" cruise ship; Gopher, Isaac, and Julie would be proud.)

67 Elm St., Camden. www.blueharborhouse.com. © **800/248-3196** or 207/236-3196. 11 units. $125–$189 double; $159–$199 suite. Rates include full breakfast. Packages available. **Amenities:** Dining room; shared refrigerator; library; free Wi-Fi.

Camden Harbour Inn ★★★   This 1871 mansion sits in a quiet neighborhood on a rise with a view of the sea and mountains beyond, on the way to Rockport—think of it as Camden's "quiet side." This had been just another fusty, Victorian-era hotel until 2007, when it got a complete makeover from the two Dutchmen who bought it. No longer a creaky place of floral wallpaper and simple antiques, it's now one of the region's more renowned luxury inns, a member of the Relais & Chateaux collection, with a spa, gourmet restaurant, even a wine refrigerator in every room. The place is all about modern design. All rooms have private bathrooms and flatscreen TVs, of course, but most also feature water views, fireplaces, and/or terraces. The New Amsterdam Suite is one of the poshest in town, with its king-size featherbed and two private decks; other suites are designed in Taiwanese, Thai, and Mauritian themes. The inn's within walking distance of downtown, and there's an excellent French-influenced, farm-to-table restaurant, **Natalie's ★**, as well.

83 Bayview St., Camden. www.camdenharbourinn.com. ℂ **800/236-4266** or 866/626-1504 20 units. Mid-June–mid-Oct $399–$475 double, $499–$1,490 suite; late Oct–early June $225–$295 double, $325–$699 suite. Rates include full breakfast. 2-night minimum on weekends in peak season. Packages available. **Amenities:** Restaurant; bar; spa; free Wi-Fi.

Camden Maine Stay Inn ★

The Maine Stay is one of Camden's friendliest bed-and-breakfasts. In a home dating from 1802 (later expanded in Greek Revival style in 1840), it's your classic slate-roofed New England manse in a shady yard within walking distance of both downtown *and* Camden Hills State Park. Guest rooms, spaced out over three floors, have ceiling fans (only a few have televisions). Each is distinctively furnished in antiques; expect lots of frilly and floral things, handsome exposed wooden floors, and wicker furniture. Note that top-floor rooms have foreshortened ceilings with intriguing angles. The downstairs Carriage House Room unit, away from the buzz of Route 1, is popular: Its French doors lead to a private stone patio, while a Vermont Castings stove keeps things toasty inside. Interesting tidbit: The inn's owned by two Italian innkeepers—one from the south of Italy, one from Milan (the north).

22 High St., Camden. www.mainestay.com. ℂ **207/236-9636.** 8 units. $110–$250 double and suite. Rates include full breakfast. Packages available. Children 12 and older welcome. **Amenities:** Dining room; 2 parlors; sun porch; free Wi-Fi.

Inn at Sunrise Point ★

This peaceful, private sanctuary 4 miles north of Camden's bustling main drag, in the quieter village of Lincolnville, seems a world apart. Service is crisp and helpful, and the setting can't be beat: the edge of Penobscot Bay, down a long, tree-lined gravel road. The property is a cluster of contemporary, yet classic, shingled buildings; a granite bench and Adirondack chairs on the lawn allow guests to enjoy the views. Guest rooms and suites—each named for a different Maine writer or artist—are spacious, comfortable, and packed with amenities such as fireplaces, TVs with VCRs, individual heat controls, and stunning views from the plentiful windows. Breakfasts are served in a sunny conservatory. The inn's four cottages are even more luxe and private, featuring double Jacuzzis, fireplaces, wet bars, and private decks; the Fitz Hugh Lane cottage almost feels like it's *in* the bay.

55 Sunrise Point Rd., Lincolnville. www.sunrisepoint.com. ℂ **207/236-7716.** 12 units. $335–$525 double and suite; $395–$685 cottage Rates include full breakfast. 5% inn service charge and 7% state sales tax. 2-night minimum stay Memorial Day–Columbus Day. Closed Jan–Apr. No children 13 and under. Packages available. **Amenities:** Bar service; library; free Wi-Fi.

Lincolnville Motel ★★★   It's far from the most opulent lodging on the Maine Coast, but it might be the most fun. Built as a motor-court motel in the 1950s, this set of six cabins and a four-room motel got a lighthearted, minimalist refresh when Alice Amory reopened the place in 2015. The outdoor pool is full of goofy inflatable animals; the comfy little housekeeping cabins are appointed with mini-fridges, fresh flowers, and record players. Each has its own little deck, and the common spaces (a big shared yard and library) have a social vibe when the place is filled up. Not the place to stay if you want seclusion; terrific if you'd like to make friends (and enjoy one of the region's best values).

4 Sea View Dr., Camden. www.lincolnvillemotel.com. ✆ **207/236-3195**. 10 units. $85–$165 double; $105–$175 two-room cabin. Closed mid-Oct–mid-May. **Amenities**: Outdoor pool; library; free Wi-Fi in common area.

Norumbega Inn ★   You'll have no problem at all finding the Norumbega: just head north out of town and look for the castle on the right. Well, it's actually a mansion (built of stone in 1886 by telegraph system inventor Joseph Stearns), but it *looks* like a castle. Wonderfully eccentric and full of curves, turrets, angles, and rich materials, this hotel's on the National Historic Registry. There's extravagant carved-oak woodwork in the lobby, a stunning oak-and-mahogany inlaid floor, and a roomy solarium. When Sue Walser and Phil Crispo took it over in 2013, the stunning building had sat empty a couple years after some ups-and-downs with previous owners. They replaced a lot of dated furnishings and bedding, made some structural repairs, added heated bathroom floors, and rebuilt the awesome decks out back, which overlook a sprawling lawn and glittery sea. In short, the place is feeling much fresher than its 130 years. The two suites here rank among the finest in northern New England: the bright and airy Library Suite, in the original two-story library (so big it has an *interior* balcony, surrounded by books and a sliding ladder), and the sprawling Penthouse with its superlative bay views, king-size bed, and huge oval tub. Phil's Culinary Institute of America training pays off at breakfast, and multi-course tasting dinners are an option as well.

63 High St., Camden. www.norumbegainn.com. ✆ **877/363-4646** or 207/236-4646. 11 units. June–Oct $269–$629 double and suite; Nov–May $199–$449 double and suite. All rates include full breakfast. 2-night minimum in summer, Sat–Sun, and holidays. Packages available. **Amenities:** Lounge; library; free Wi-Fi.

Whitehall ★★   Set at the edge of town on busy Route 1, Whitehall is a venerable Camden institution, thanks partly to its association with local poet Edna St. Vincent Millay, who was "discovered" here by a guest who went on to fund Edna's college education. But with new ownership and a $1.7-million, bottom-to-top renovation in 2015, the place feels a lot less like a musty historic tribute to an obscure poet. You'll still find grand columns, gables, a long roofline, and atmospherically winding staircases, but gone are the antique furnishings and Oriental carpets, which have been replaced by bright patterned upholstery, a whole lot of upcycled barnwood, iPads and Apple TVs in every room, and accents of grasscloth and highly patinaed metal. No longer a country inn, Whitehall has a splashy boutique feel through and through (though a few rooms still share a hallway bathroom), complete with a hip restaurant up front (**The Pig + Poet**—see p. 161). The patio, with its firepit, is a terrific respite on cooler evenings.

52 High St., Camden. www.whitehall-inn.com. © **800/789-6565** or 207/236-3391. 40 units, some with shared bathroom. July–Oct $279–$349 double; mid-May to June $109–$169 double. Rates include full breakfast. Closed Nov–mid-May. Packages available. **Amenities:** Restaurant; bar; concierge; free Wi-Fi.

CAMPING

Seasonally open **Camden Hills State Park** (© **207/236-3109**), about a mile north of the village center on Route 1, has 107 campsites, which cost $35 to $45 per night for non-Maine residents in summer ($10 discount for residents), depending on whether you snag one of the new water-and-electrical hookup sites or not. There's a discount from mid-September until the park closes.

Where to Eat in Camden

In addition to its fine-dining options, downtown Camden has a wealth of places to nosh, snack, lunch, and brunch. Some unbeatable breakfast skillets, for instance, are served up at busy **Boynton-McKay,** 30 Main Street (© **207/236-2465**), a former pharmacy that's now a locals' favorite breakfast stop (and a great place for picking up picnic supplies, should you be so inclined.) Note that it's closed on Mondays. Just up the street, pick up a bag of gourmet groceries at **French & Brawn** (© **207/236-3361**) on Main Street at the corner of Elm.

Chez Michel ★ FRENCH/SEAFOOD   This French-and-seafood restaurant, right across the road from the Isleboro ferry (about 6 miles north of downtown Camden), has had a devoted local following since 1992 when chef Jean Michel Hetuin opened it. That's because it offers good value amid a sea of higher-priced area options, though the dining room has way more of a no-frills family-restaurant vibe than one might expect from the name. Instead, the menu blends elements of French, Maine, and American cooking. You might begin with mussels steamed in wine or locally smoked salmon, then move on to duck au poivre, steak Oscar, or haddock in meunière sauce . . . or you might get plunked down next to a local family enjoying a feed of lobsters, scallops, pasta, or fried oysters, and decide to join in the fun. Specials on the chalkboard could be anything from salmon Béarnaise to pan-fried haddock or tenderloin brochette—or could be a simple chicken parm.

Rte. 1, Lincolnville Beach. © **207/789-5600.** Entrees $19–$29. Tues–Sun 4–9:30pm (closed Tues until July). Closed mid-Oct–early May.

Francine Bistro ★★ FRENCH   This place feels more like a French brasserie in Manhattan's Meatpacking District than a coastal seafood joint—and that's a good thing. A meal from chef/owner Brian Hill (long-ago of the seminal Boston alternative-rock band Heretix, but I digress) might begin with sweet corn and chanterelle soup; a seviche of halibut, Serrano chilies, and red onions; mussels in Bordeaux and shallots; or skewers of grilled lamb with white pesto, orange, and endive. Entrees might run to roast chicken with a chèvre gratin or a cauliflower-cheese hash; duck à l'orange; a crispy skate wing with Jerusalem artichokes; slow-braised local pork with chili verde; mussels with lime and black butter; a haddock stuffed with scallops; or some always-reliable steak frites. Hill cut his teeth in some truly great kitchens around the country, and he was one of the pioneers of the last couple decades, nudging the state beyond the fried fish and lobster that so long characterized Maine dining.

55 Chestnut St., Camden. www.francinebistro.com. *C* **207/230-0083.** Entrees $15–$30. Tues–Sat 5:30–10pm. Reservations recommended.

Long Grain ★★★ THAI   If you'd have told me WASPy little Camden had some of the county's best Thai food, I wouldn't have believed you, but here's Long Grain. The glossy food mags have all sung its praises (the restaurant's Chicken Khao Soi soup was even a *Bon Appétit* cover girl in 2013), and the impossibility of a walk-in table most summer nights is a pretty good vote of confidence. With just a handful of tables and bar seats (it's rumored to be expanding soon), the dining room is cozy, but chefs Paula Palakawong and Ravin Nakjaroen turn out fragrant and flavorful dishes of ramen, pad seaw, and pad kemao (all with house-made noodles), along with terrific curries, pork dumplings, lemongrass mussels, and more. Call way ahead for takeout.

31 Elm St., Camden. www.longgraincamden.com. *C* **207/236-9001.** Entrees $9.50–$12.50. Tues–Sat 11:30am–2:45pm, 4:30–9pm. Reservations highly recommended.

Pig + Poet ★ NEW AMERICAN   At the house restaurant at **Whitehall** (see p. 159), chef Justin Perdue somehow pulls off a menu that's an unlikely combination of Southern comfort food and Maine farm/sea-to-table. It's maybe the only menu I can think of where lobster mac-and-cheese makes thematic sense (and is actually quite good). Pork, as the name implies, is also central to the menu, popping up in the shrimp and grits, the gnocchi, and the clam chowder. Wisely, chef Perdue has kept it out of the lobster roll, though he's added an unconventional filler of avocado, greens, and leeks that adds some brightness and crunch to that classic buttery Maine treat. The room is rustic-funky as can be, and clever cocktail names like The Bearded Hipster (local rye whiskey, Fernet-Branca, green Chartreuse) are a self-conscious nod to the milieu.

52 High St., Camden. www.pigandpoetmaine.com. *C* **207/236-3391.** Entrees $14–$24. Mid-May–Oct Wed–Sun 5–10pm (bar opens at 3pm). Closed Nov–mid-May. Reservations recommended.

Rhumb Line ★★ SEAFOOD   Way-fresh seafood served at picnic tables, right on the dock, in a building shared with a boatbuilder and overlooking the harbor. No place filled with so many yachties should feel this welcoming and unpretentious, and yet Rhumb Line does. There's some indoor seating too, but it has to be blowing pretty hard outside for that to be more appealing. Go fancy with gorgeously plated oysters or chilled lobster off the raw bar, or else make like the dockworkers and dig into a basket of perfectly fried whole belly clams, a terrific lobster roll, blackened haddock tacos, and other coastal proletarian faves.

59 Sea St., Camden. www.rhumblinecamden.com. © **207/230-8495.** Raw bar $12–$19; baskets and entrees $12–$26. Mid-May–mid-Oct Wed–Mon 11:30am–9:30pm. Closed rest of year.

Waterfront ★ ECLECTIC It's not the most glamorous place to dine in greater Camden, but that might be why locals like to lunch here so much. That and the view. The wide deck out back is maybe the best al fresco dining on the midcoast, with the waves lapping at pilings right beneath you and the green hump of Mount Battie looming behind. Find a little bit of everything on the menu, from steaks to a chicken enchilada to really nicely executed Maine seafood classics. I highly recommend the mussels in white wine appetizer, and all the salads are substantial enough to be meals. Service is unfussy, and there's certainly no dress code.

48 Bayview St., Camden. www.waterfrontcamden.com. © **207/236-3747.** Lunch entrees $10–$18; dinner entrees $14–$30. Daily 11:30am–9pm.

Exploring Camden

The best way to enjoy Camden is to park your car—which may require driving a block or two off U.S. Route 1, which unfortunately runs right up through the center of town. The village is of a perfect scale to explore on foot, with plenty of boutiques and galleries. Don't miss the hidden **town park ★** (look behind the library on upper Main Street and Atlantic Avenue): It was designed by none other than the firm of Frederick Law Olmsted, the famed landscape architect who designed New York City's Central Park. It's a good spot for a picnic: grassy, ideal for people-watching, and possessed of outstanding bay views.

The Camden-Rockport Historical Society has prepared a 9-mile bike or car tour with brief descriptions of some of the historic properties around the two adjacent towns. The brochure describing the tour is free; check for it at the Penobscot Bay Chamber visitor center (see p. 155). The brochure also includes a 2-mile walking tour of downtown Camden.

Camden Hills State Park ★★ (© **207/236-3109**), about a mile north of the village center on Route 1, covers 6,500 acres that ranges from an seaside lower section to an upper section with fine bay views. There's an oceanside picnic area, camping at 107 sites (see p. 160), a variety of well-marked hiking trails, and a winding toll road up 800-foot Mount Battie with spectacular views from the summit. The day-use fee is $6 for non-Maine resident adults, $2 for nonresident seniors, and $1 for children ages 5 to 11. The fee's only charged mid-May to mid-October.

WONDERFUL WALKS

If hikes and mild heights don't bother you, I definitely recommend an ascent to the ledges of **Mount Megunticook ★★** in Camden Hills State Park. The best time for this hike is early in the morning, before the crowds have amassed (and while mists still linger in the valleys). Leave from near the park's campground—

the trail head is clearly marked—and follow the well-maintained path to open ledges. The hike takes only 30 to 45 minutes; spectacular views of the harbor await, plus glimpses of smaller hills and valleys. Depending on your stamina level, you can keep walking on the park's trail network to Mount Battie, or into lesser-traveled woodlands on the east side of the Camden Hills.

On the Water

Several sailing ships make Camden their home base, and it's a rare treat to come and go from this harbor, which is considered by many to be the most beautiful in the state.

The 57-foot windjammer *Surprise* (www.schoonersurprise.com), first launched in 1918, has been based in Camden Harbor for decades now. Captain and First Mate Ramiro and Nicole de Acevedo Ramos take a maximum of 18 passengers on 2-hour, nonsmoking sailing trips from the town's Public Landing. Four daytime excursions ($43 adults, $33 children under 12) are offered daily from mid-June to mid-August, and three are run daily in May, and from mid-August through mid-October. There are sunset and full moon trips too, both with homemade desserts and acoustic music. Reserve ahead online, or else show up at the ticket table on the waterfront and cross your fingers for a cancellation.

Modeled after the Gloucester fishing schooners of the late 19th century, the *Schooner Lazy Jack II* (www.schoonerlazyjack.com; ✆ 207/230-0602) has been plying the waters since 1947. The ship goes out on four 2-hour cruises per day on weekends from May through mid-September, then three per day through October. The tours cost $40 per adult, $27 per child under age 12; BYO wine, beer, and snacks.

For a more intimate view of the harbor, **Maine Sport Outfitters** (www. mainesport.com; ✆ 800/722-0826 or 207/236-8797) daily offers three sea-kayaking tours of Camden's scenic harbor, from June through August (but no tours Mondays in June); the tour lasts 2 hours, costs $40 for adults ($35 for children 10–15), and takes paddlers out to Curtis Island at the outer edge of the harbor. It's an easy, delightful way to get a taste of the area's maritime culture. On Tuesdays in midsummer, for a little more money ($85 adults, $75 kids) and effort, you can take the same trip on a stand-up paddleboard (and if you'd like to avoid busy Camden harbor, there's also a 2½-hour stand-up paddleboard tour of Lake Megunticook, just west of town). Longer trips and instruction are also available. The shop, located on Route 1 in Rockport (a few minutes' drive south of Camden), has a great selection of outdoor gear and is worth a stop if you're gearing up for some local adventures or heading up to Acadia next. Sign up for the tours either at the store or at the Camden boat-house, which is located at the head of the harbor near the town park.

SPORTS & OUTDOOR ACTIVITIES AROUND CAMDEN

BIKING The Camden area is great for exploring by bike. A nice loop several miles long takes you from Camden into the cute little village of **Rockport ★★** (see p. 164), which has an equally scenic harbor and fewer tourists. Bike rentals, maps, and riding advice are available in town at **Maine Sport Outfitters** on Route 1 in Rockport (www.mainesport.com; ✆ **888/236-8797** or 207/236-7120). They're open year-round.

GOLF The golf course at the **Samoset Resort,** just west of Camden in Rockport (www.samoset.com; ✆ **800/341-1650** or 207/594-2511) is among the state's most dramatically scenic and challenging. It's also among the priciest, with greens fees running as high as $145 during peak season—if you can get a reservation. Six of the 18 holes literally hug the lapping edge of Penobscot Bay (don't shank one here!), and the place has got history: It dates from 1902. The course is hard enough as it is, but things become even more challenging once you hit the shifting sea breezes (worst in the afternoon, believe me). There's a golf school here, with lessons available. Remember that this is a championship-caliber course and it gets busy in peak season, so reserve ahead. Serious golfers will want to play it at least once, but beginners may feel intimidated.

HIKING A good destination for hilly coastal hiking is **Camden Hills State Park,** on the west shore of Penobscot Bay. *Fifty Hikes in Southern and Coastal Maine,* by John Gibson (The Countryman Press, 2016), is a reliable directory to trails in the Camden Hills area. **L.L. Bean's Outdoor Discovery Schools** (www.llbean.com; ✆ **888/270-2326**) offers weeklong guided hiking adventures along the midcoast, with days spent wandering the Camden Hills and Acadia National Park, evenings spent lounging at local inns, with the occasional wine tasting thrown in for good measure.

SKIING The only ski mountain of any significance along the coast is the **Camden Snow Bowl ★** (www.camdensnowbowl.com; ✆ **207/236-3438**), just outside of town on Hosmer's Pond Road. This small, family-oriented ski area has a handful of trails and a modest vertical drop of 950 feet (full-day lift tickets cost $33–$43), but it's the rare opportunity to downhill ski within sight of the ocean. Maybe best of all, it also has an exhilarating **toboggan run ★★**, open weekends only. Toboggans are available for rent, or you can bring your own; it's $10 per person per hour if you rent, $5 with your own ride to zip down the slope. If you'd like to detour inland a bit for some higher slopes, get a pamphlet with basic information about Maine skiing from the **Ski Maine Association** (www.skimaine.com; ✆ **207/773-7669**). The association's website also offers up-to-date reports on ski conditions during the winter.

A Side Trip to Rockport ★

Rockport is absolutely worth a few hours during any trip to Camden. Try this route, either by bike or by car: Take Bayview Street from the center of Camden out along the bay, passing by opulent seaside estates. The road soon narrows and becomes quiet and pastoral, overarched by leafy trees. At the stop sign just past the cemetery, turn left and continue into Rockport. (Along the way, you might pass happily grazing cows.)

In Rockport, stroll downstairs to the water and snoop around the historic **harbor ★★★**, with its walking trail and outstanding photo opportunities. There's a scenic public park by the boat landing with a great view of the boats in the harbor. (Check out the knockout, eclectic food truck **Fox on the Run ★**, which is known for its Cuban sandwiches and fish tacos). **Walker Park** and **Mary Lea Park,** just uphill, also offer grassy expanses and nice views.

Then re-mount the hill and drop by the **Peter Ralson Gallery,** 23 Central Street (www.ralstongallery.com; ℂ **207/230-7225**), a small gallery showing the work (often coastal in nature) of one of Maine's most accomplished living photographers. When you're through, cross the street and grab some oysters and one of the delicious, esoteric cocktails at **18 Central** (you can guess the address, www.18central.com; ℂ **207/466-9055**). Try the Small Craft Advisory cocktail, a daily special which the bartender dreams up each day based on the marine weather report.

BELFAST TO BUCKSPORT ★

Belfast is 18 miles N of Camden; Bucksport is 19 miles NE of Belfast

The northerly stretch of Penobscot Bay is rich in history, especially maritime history. In the mid–19th century, Belfast and Searsport produced more than their share of ships, along with the captains to pilot them on trading ventures around the globe. In 1856 alone, 24 ships of more than 1,000 tons were launched from Belfast. The now-sleepy village of Searsport once had 17 active shipyards, which turned out some 200 ships over the years.

When shipbuilding died out, the Belfast area was sustained by a thriving poultry industry, and after that left, credit card giant MBNA ushered in a white-collar shift and a huge economic boost. Alas, they've all moved on, but the legacy of each era—along with that of the crunchy back-to-the-landers who found cheap property nearby around the turn of the 1970s—combine into the funky stew that is modern-day Belfast.

These days, the town's alive with artisans and entrepreneurs of various stripes who've set up shop downtown. Boatbuilding is big again, and the city has invested in its riverfront, cleaning up the mess of the poultry area (imagine a river slick with chicken grease) and putting in terrific stretch of parks and trail. Tourists tend to pass through the region quickly, en route from the tourist enclave of Camden (p. 154) to the tourist enclave of Bar Harbor (p. 207), but Mainers know it as one of Maine's hippest little coastal towns. Well worth slowing down for.

Essentials

ARRIVING

Route 1 connects Belfast, Searsport, and Bucksport.

VISITOR INFORMATION

The **Belfast Area Chamber of Commerce** (www.belfastmaine.org; ℂ **207/338-5900**), staffs an information booth at 15 Main Street, near the waterfront park, that's open daily from June through September, Monday to Friday 10am to 4pm.

Where to Stay in Belfast

If you're stuck for a bed along this stretch of the coast and don't mind the chain-hotel ambience for a night, the **Fireside Inn & Suites,** 159 Searsport Ave. (U.S. 1) (www.belfastmainehotel.com; ℭ **207/338-2090**), is a very good backup option. Some rooms have kitchenettes and/or whirlpools; there's a pool; a small breakfast is served; and some rooms come with sublime views of the bay (if there's no fog, that is). However, check as soon as possible—the place sometimes fills up early. High season double rooms run from $145 to $219 per night; suites are more expensive.

The Jeweled Turrett Inn ★★   A hotshot attorney built this Victorian grand dame in 1898, and it's been hosting guests since the '80s. Interested in history? Because this place is full of it. Like, literally, chock full of antiques and 19th-century bric-a-brac and running out of space on some walls to hang old photos and paintings. The shared den downstairs is centered on a huge, gnarly fireplace said to have been built with stone from every state in the union (there were only 45 states in 1898, but still). Guest rooms are classic B&B style: Expect four-poster beds, lots of lace and wicker, antique mahogany, the works. All have private bathrooms. Not one, but two breezy verandas wrap around the house, spots to unwind with an iced tea or a lemonade (served in the afternoon on hot days).

40 Pearl St., Belfast. www.jeweledturrett.com. ℭ **888/696-2304** or 207/338-2304. 7 units. $129–$179 double. Rates include full breakfast. 2-night minimum on weekends July–mid-Oct. **Amenities:** Free Wi-Fi.

Where to Eat in Belfast

Anchoring the Belfast waterfront, the locals' favorite pub **three tides** (2 Pinchy Lane; www.3tides.com; ℭ **207/338-1707**) sits right next to the boats—walk all the way to the end of Main Street. The bar menu is eclectic—quesadillas, salads, panini, local oysters, and mussels—but the real draw is a huge list of beers from **Marshall Wharf Brewing Company** next door, known for "big" beers not subtle on flavor or low on ABV (if you're there in fall, try the oyster stout, a meal of a beer brewed with ten dozen live oysters in every batch). The outdoor deck is a good spot to relax while the sun goes down.

Chase's Daily Restaurant ★★ VEGETARIAN   This place is special. A vegetarian restaurant that doesn't make any point at all of being virtuous or preachy, Chase's was formed by a local farm family (the Chases) with a simple philosophy: Cook superlocal foods, as freshly as possible, based on the things being grown at the farm. It maintains a balance between simple, hearty food and more sophisticated offerings—so good that a line often stretches out the door, even on weekdays, even at lunch. Breakfast (Saturdays only) ranges from oatmeal to breakfast burritos to healthy fruit smoothies; lunch segues nicely into a menu of very popular pizzas, sandwiches, soups, and salads with an emphasis on Asian, Latin American, and European themes. Dinner happens just once a week, on Friday nights, and might feature anything from grilled polenta to Indian food. The whole room is very inviting and light-filled, with

PACKING A picnic IN BELFAST AND SEARSPORT

Searsport has an outstanding little pocket park, **Mosman Park,** just off the hustle of busy Route 1; look for the post office in the center of the village, then walk downhill one block along Water Street to the water. It makes for a great quick picnic, and there's a pretty good playground—plus bay views—and it's free. Pick up rudimentary snacking foods and beverages at **Tozier's Market**

(ℰ **207/548-6220**), a convenience store on Route 1 just south of the Maritime Museum. Or if you're in Belfast, one of Maine's oldest, biggest, and best natural-foods stores, the **Belfast Co-op ★** (www.belfast.coop; ℰ **207/338-2532**), is at 123 High St. The selection of imported beers and the cuts of organic beef are excellent; the co-op also features a deli. It's open from 7:30am to 8pm daily.

wooden floorboards, lots of local art, and a pressed-tin ceiling, and Sunday brunches are highly regarded—you'll occasionally meet some road-tripping Portland foodies. From June through November or so, there's a daily farmer's market in back. Absolutely call ahead about table availability if you're serious about eating here in high season.

96 Main St., Belfast. www.chasesdaily.me. ℰ **207/338-0555.** Breakfast/lunch entrees $8–$13, dinner entrees $17–$22. Tues–Thurs 11am–2:30pm; Fri 11am–2:30pm and 5:30–9pm; Sat 7–10am and 11am–2:30pm; Sun 8am–1pm. Reservations accepted for dinner only.

Darby's ★ AMERICAN/ECLECTIC   Located in a Civil War–era pub with stamped tin ceilings and a back bar with Corinthian columns, Darby's is a popular local hangout. You can order a Maine microbrew or a single-malt whiskey while you read the menu, which is more creative than you might expect given the surroundings. The kitchen serves not only bar favorites (burgers on bulky rolls), but also attempts more inventive dishes such as mahogany duck, pad Thai, and big salads; these are hit-or-miss, and nothing is out of this world, but the pubby atmosphere is pretty authentic. Desserts are homemade and basic: think cheesecake, pies, and an interesting "Russian cream."

155 High St., Belfast. ℰ **207/338-2339.** Entrees $10–$15 lunch, $11–$23 dinner. Mon–Thurs 11:30am–8:30pm; Fri–Sat 11:30am–9:00pm; Sun 11:30am–8:00pm. Reservations suggested after 7pm.

Meanwhile in Belfast ★ PIZZA   An unexpected ethnic gem, Meanwhile in Belfast serves arguably the best Neapolitan pizza in all of New England (there are plaques on the walls from various magazines and websites attesting to this). Proprietors Alessandro Scelsi and Clementina Senatore were both born and raised in Italy, and they top their wood-fired pies with local meats, produce, and cheeses—even fish, with their go-for-broke *frutti di mare* pie called The Harbor Master.

2 Cross St., Belfast. www.meanwhile-in-belfast.com. ℰ **207/218-1288.** Pizzas $10–$20, sandwiches (lunch only) $12–$18, salads $12–$24. Thurs–Fri 4:30–8:30pm; Sat–Mon 11:30am–2:30pm and 4:30–8:30pm.

Seng Thai ★ THAI   Just south of Belfast on Route 1, this is one of many Thai restaurants you'll be surprised to find as you cruise up and down the Maine coast. It serves up well-spiced classic dishes such as pad Thai and various curries, but also has a uniquely creative take on more upscale fare such as lobster and fish. Top off your meal with a potent Thai tea or coffee.

139 Searsport Ave. (Rte. 1). http://sengthaime.weebly.com. ✆ **207/338-0010.** Entrees $11–$20. June–Sept Tues–Sun 11am–10pm; Oct–May Tues–Sun 11am–8:30pm.

Young's Lobster Pound ★★ LOBSTER   This is one of my favorite lobster shacks in Maine—although calling it a "shack" might even be a euphemism. Beyond the driveway you'll find a hangar-size door; fear not, for behind it sits a counter of friendly folks taking your order. Guys in slickers and boots do all the dirty work, plucking lobsters from long lobster tanks gurgling seawater. Eat upstairs, where picnic tables are arrayed in an open, barnlike area, or out on the deck with views across the river to Belfast. Remember: Don't wear your finest threads, and get *lots* of napkins. The lobsters, served on paper plates with butter and corn on the cob, are tasty and fairly inexpensive. It's across the Route 1 bridge from downtown Belfast; after the bridge, look for signs (Mitchell Street is the fourth street on your right— follow the road to the water).

4 Mitchell St. youngslobsterpound.webs.com. ✆ **207/338-1160.** Lobster prices seasonal. Daily 7:30am–8pm (shorter hours in winter and spring). Reservations not accepted.

Exploring the Belfast/Bucksport Region

When approaching the Belfast area from the south, you can view some splendid historic homes by veering off Route 1 and entering downtown Belfast via High Street (look for the first DOWNTOWN BELFAST sign). The **Primrose Hill District** along High Street was the most fashionable place for prosperous merchants to settle during the early and mid-19th century, and their stately homes reflect an era when stature was equal to both the size of one's home and the care one took in designing and embellishing it. Downtown Belfast also has some superb examples of historic brick commercial architecture, including the elaborate High Victorian Gothic–style building on Main Street that formerly housed the Belfast National Bank.

Alamo Theater ★ THEATER   In the paper-mill town of Bucksport, the organization **Northeast Historic Film** was founded in 1986 to preserve and show early films related to New England. In 1992 the group bought Bucksport's vintage Alamo Theatre, which was built in 1916 and closed (the last showing was *Godzilla*) in 1956. Films are now shown on weekends in the renovated theater; call or check the group's website to see what's coming up—even first-run popcorn flicks usually are accompanied by a few minutes of archival film from the organization's collection before the show starts. Visitors can also stop by the museum at the front of the theater (open Monday through Friday 9am to 4pm) to browse videos and other items.

85 Main St., Bucksport. www.oldfilm.org. ✆ **800/639-1636** or 207/469-0924.

A Hot Museum

If you enjoy kitsch and uniquely American things, on a rainy day in Belfast you could do worse than making the 30-minute detour inland through the hills to little Thorndike to browse through the **Bryant Stove Museum** (www.bryant stove.com; ✆ **207/568-3665**), a nothing-if-not-entertaining experience. Joe and Bea Bryant exhibit, refurbish, and sell gorgeous cast-iron woodstoves. But looking these over is only part of the fun: The premises also house a huge selection of vintage dolls, toys, antique cars, player pianos, calliopes, concertinas, and oodles of other musical instruments and mechanical contraptions. Entering the rooms where the goodies are stored is like opening a door into an alternate universe—one presided over by suspender-wearing Joe, who sings lustily along with the pianos while puppets (rigged to the instruments) bob along in time. Get there by taking Waldo Avenue (Route 137) west out of Belfast for about 15 miles, then turning right onto Route 200 and continuing a bit farther onto Stovepipe Alley. Really. A shop attached to the museum is open 8am to 4:30pm Monday to Saturday. Admission is $5 for adults, free for kids 10 and under.

Fort Knox State Park ★ HISTORIC SITE   Across the river from Bucksport and adjacent to the **Penobscot Narrows Observatory** (see p. 170), this historic granite fort was strategically located at an easily defended narrows in the Penobscot River. Built in the 1840s to defend against possible British naval invasion, the solid and imposing fort was never attacked, although it was manned during the Civil War and Spanish-American War. It's an impressive edifice to explore, with graceful granite staircases and subterranean chambers that produce wonderful echoes.

740 Fort Knox Rd. (Rte. 174), Prospect. http://fortknox.maineguide.com. ✆ **207/469-7719.** Admission to park $4.50 adult, $1.50 senior, $1 children 5–11 (park plus observatory $7 adult, $4 senior, $1 children 5–11). May–Oct daily am–sunset; closed Nov–Apr.

Penobscot Marine Museum ★★★ MUSEUM   The Penobscot Marine Museum is one of the best small museums in New England—and relatively unsung. Housed in a cluster of historic buildings atop a gentle rise in tiny downtown Searsport, the museum does a great job of educating visitors about the vitality of the local shipbuilding industry, the essential role of international trade to daily life in the 19th century, and the hazards of life at sea. Exhibits (such as "The Art of Lobstering") are uncommonly well organized, and wandering from building to building induces a keen sense of wonderment at the vast enterprise that was Maine's maritime trade. Also on display is the landscape art of Thomas and James Buttersworth and Robert Salmon. Among the most intriguing exhibits are a wide selection of dramatic marine paintings, black-and-white photographs of many of the 286 weathered sea captains who once called Searsport home, an exquisite collection of scrimshaw, and an early home decorated in the style of a sea captain, complete with lacquered furniture and accessories hauled back from trade missions to the Orient. The museum's photo archive is also uncommonly rich, with knockout photo exhibits that often veer away from the maritime theme (recent examples on the history of the postcard and Maine's early women photographers wouldn't have been out of place at a landlocked institution).

2 Church St. (at corner of U.S. Rte. 1), Searsport. www.penobscotmarinemuseum.org. © **207/548-0334.** $12 adults, $8 children 8–15, $30 families. Memorial Day–mid-Oct Mon–Sat 10am–5pm; Sun noon–5pm. Last tickets sold at 4pm. Closed rest of year.

Penobscot Narrows Observatory ★ VIEWS   At the northern tip of Penobscot Bay, where the Penobscot River squeezes through a dramatic gorge near Verona Island, Route 1 spans the gorge on an attractive modern suspension bridge, opened in 2006. Sitting high atop one of the bridge's pylons is the world's tallest public bridge observatory, perched 437 feet above the river (it's taller than the Statue of Liberty), offering panoramic views of the mountains, lakes, and even Penobscot Bay downriver. The elevator ride to the glassed-in viewing area takes just 1 minute, and placards help you interpret the landscape features you're looking at.

Rte. 1, Stockton Springs. www.maine.gov/mdot/pnbo. © **207/469-6553.** Admission (includes entry to Fort Knox State Park, see p. 169) $7 adults, $4 seniors, $3 children 5–11. Jul–Aug 9am–6pm, May–June and Sept–Oct 9am–5pm. Closed Nov–Apr.

On the Water

If you'd like to explore the northern Penobscot area by water, call **Water Walker Sea Kayaks** (www.touringkayaks.com; © 207/338-6424). Though their shop is a few miles inland, in nearby Monroe, the Water Walker team leads a 2-hour evening tour of the Belfast harbor from the beach near the town dock. Trips cost $35 per person and include snacks and some instruction; they also rent kayaks and stand-up paddleboards, and if you can't make it to Monroe, they'll deliver them to your launch of choice for a small fee.

BEACHES

Swan Lake State Park (© 207/525-4404), 6 miles north of Belfast, is a worthy beach, albeit a small one, open June through Columbus Day. Admission is $7 per non-Maine resident adult, $2 per nonresident senior, and $1 for children.

CASTINE & ENVIRONS ★★

Quiet little Castine, off the beaten track, must be one of the most gracious villages in Maine. It's not so much the handsome, meticulously maintained mid-19th-century homes that fill the side streets. Nor is it the location on a quiet peninsula, 16 miles south of tourist-clotted Route 1. No, what lends Castine most of its charm are the splendid, towering elm trees that still overarch many of the village's streets. Before Dutch elm disease ravaged the nation's elms, much of America once looked like this. Through perseverance and a measure of good luck, Castine has managed to keep several hundred of its elms alive, and it's worth the drive here to see them.

But Castine offers more than trees. It's enduringly quiet, which is probably what you're seeking in your Maine vacation. And it's full of history. This outpost served as a strategic town during various battles among the British, Dutch, French, and colonists in the centuries following its settlement in 1613 (yes, 7 years before Plymouth Rock). Castine was occupied by each of those groups at some point; and historical personages such as Miles Standish and Paul Revere passed through town. It was a very important place—strange, because now it seems almost thoroughly forgotten, except for the maritime academy at one end of the village, which still trains young sailors and cadets. Castine still looks and feels as if it has it not changed much since the locals welcomed British soldiers with open arms during the American Revolution.

You'll have to work (which means drive significant distances) to find much nightlife or dining, but if you like your towns quiet, you'll love it here.

Essentials

ARRIVING

Castine is 16 miles south of U.S. Route 1. Turn south on Route 175 in Orland (east of Bucksport) and follow it to Route 166, which winds its way to Castine. Route 166A offers another, alternate route along Penobscot Bay.

VISITOR INFORMATION

For phone inquiries, try the **town office** (www.visitcastine.com; ✆ **207/326-4502**), where clerkes are often helpful with local information. (Don't abuse this privilege, though, since they have actual work to do running the town.) The town office is normally open weekdays from 11am to 3pm. Volunteers staff a postage-stamp visitor center at the entrance to the harbor, on the corner of Water St. and Main St., open Mon–Sat from 10am to 4pm, Sun noon–4pm from Memorial Day weekend until the end of September. For wider regional inquiries, the **Blue Hill Peninsula Chamber of Commerce** (see p. 180) can also help you.

Where to Stay in Castine

Castine Inn ★   The Castine Inn is a Maine rarity: a hotel with historic cred that was originally built *as* a hotel, not a private residence. The handsome, cream-colored inn, designed in an eclectic Georgian Federal Revival style and built in 1898, has a great wraparound porch and attractive gardens. The lobby is filled with wingback chairs, love seats, and a fireplace in the parlor. Guest rooms on the two upper floors are attractively (though sometimes unevenly) furnished in Early American style with graceful prints, pastel walls, pencil-poster beds, and sofas; three suites have views of the inn's well-kept gardens.

41 Main St., Castine. www.castineinn.com ✆ **207/326-4365.** 19 units. June–Oct $120–$245 double and suite; rates lower Nov–May. Rates include continental breakfast. 2-night minimum July–Aug. May, open weekends only; closed mid-Oct–Apr. Children 8 and older are welcome. **Amenities:** Dining room; sauna; free Wi-Fi.

Pentagöet Inn ★★   At the Pentagöet, "activities" consist of sitting on the wraparound front porch on cane-seated rockers watching the everyday goings-on along Main Street. This quirky, yellow-and-green (ca. 1894) inn with the prominent turret is tastefully, sturdily built. The lobby features hardwood floors, oval braided rugs, and a woodstove; it's all comfortable without being prissy, professional without being chilly. Most units sport king-size beds with heavy, ornate headboards and lacy white coverlets—some have claw-foot bathtubs and/or fireplaces, and one even includes a balcony with flowers. Rooms on the upper two floors of the main house are furnished eclectically in a mix of antiques and collectibles, as are five units in the adjacent Perkins Street building (an austere, Federal-era house), where the recently revamped bathrooms are all done up in marble. Quite a collection of ornate wooden headboards in this place. The **pub** ★ (charmingly decorated with the globetrotter bric-a-brac of a Victorian-era chevalier) and the offerings in the **dining room** ★ are both excellent.

26 Main St., Castine. www.pentagoet.com. ⓒ **207/326-8616**. 16 units (2 with private hallway bathrooms). May–Oct $135–$295 double. Rates include full breakfast. Closed Nov–Apr. Some rooms accommodate pets (by reservation only, $25 fee). Suitable for older children only. **Amenities:** Dining room; pub; bikes; free Wi-Fi

Where to Eat in Castine

Dennett's Wharf ★ SEAFOOD   In a soaring waterfront sail loft with dollar bills tacked all over the high ceiling, Dennett's Wharf serves upscale bar food in a lively setting leavened by a good selection of microbrews. This is a quintessential Maine fishing-village experience. When the weather is decent, there's outside dining beneath a bright (really bright) yellow awning with superb harbor views. It's all about pub grub and seafood here. Look for sandwiches, salads, and fried clams at lunch; dinner includes local lobsters, baby back ribs, pad Thai, and hanger steak. An oyster bar serves oysters on the half-shell. But, say, how did all those bills get on the ceiling, anyway? Ask your server; it will cost you exactly $1 to find out.

15 Sea St. (next to the town dock), Castine. www.dennettswharf.net. ⓒ **207/326-9045.** Reservations recommended in summer and for parties of 6 or more. Lunch items $10–$18; dinner items $14–$29. Daily 11am–9pm (bar open later). Closed Nov–Apr.

Dudley's Refresher ★★ SEAFOOD/BURGERS   The playful folks who own Mexican restaurant **El El Frijoles** (get it? L.L. Bean) down the road in Sargentville (also worth a stop) opened this equally playfood take-out seafood shack on the Castine town dock in 2015. Chef Kara van Emmerik makes a fish and chips—in the British style, with smashed peas and all—that's worth a drive up the coast for. The lobster roll's a winner too, with freshly picked meat and the option of an adventurous curried mayo. Everything's made from scratch, so the wait might be a bit longer than you expect from a no-frills waterfront stand; it's worth it. Locally churned ice cream seals the deal.

5 Sea St. (next to the town dock), Castine. www.dudleysrefresher.com. ⓒ **207/812-3800.** Sandwiches and baskets $3–$15. Tues–Sun 11am–7pm. Closed Labor Day–Memorial Day.

Exploring Castine

A seaside hamlet with stately brick architecture and elm shady streets, Castine is a quiet town that attracts visitors looking for a bit of colonial history (the town once marked the southern boundary of the French province of Acadia) or a lunch stop while exploring the pastoral Blue Hill peninsula. On the western edge of the village, you'll find the campus of the **Maine Maritime Academy** (© **207/326-4311**), which trains sailors for the rigors of life at sea with the merchant marine. The academy's 500-foot T.S. (for Training Ship) *State of Maine* ★, a hulking black-and-white vessel, is often docked here, all but overwhelming the village. (It's off cruising to places such as Odessa, Germany, and Gibraltar when it's not here.) You can call to schedule a free half-hour tour of the ship, offered on summer weekdays whenever the ship is in port.

Wilson Museum & John Perkins House ★ MUSEUM/HISTORIC HOME   One of Castine's more intriguing attractions is this appealing and quirky anthropological museum constructed in 1921 to display the collections of John Howard Wilson, an archaeologist and collector of prehistoric artifacts from around the globe. His gleanings are neatly arranged in a staid, classical arrangement of the sort that proliferated in the late 19th and early 20th centuries. Next door, but open only 2 afternoons a week and only in summer, the affiliated **John Perkins House** is Castine's oldest home. It was occupied by the British during the Revolution and the War of 1812; a guided tour features demonstrations of old-fashioned cooking techniques. Two additional attractions in the Wilson-Perkins complex (it's almost like a little historical campus, really) include a cool **blacksmith shop** and the **Hearse House** (where sleighlike wooden hearses of old were made, and are now archived). Both are free to tour and worth a quick look; just remember, both buildings have the same limited hours—2 days a week in summer, for 3 hours each—as the Perkins House does.

120 Perkins St., Castine. www.wilsonmuseum.org. © **207/326-9247.** Museum admission free; Perkins House tour $5. Museum open late May–late Sept Mon–Fri 10am–5pm, Sat–Sun 2–5pm; closed rest of year. Perkins House and other bldgs. open only Jul–Aug Wed & Sun 2–5pm.

On the Water

This is a lovely open harbor, with open land and forest edging the watery expanse. **Castine Kayak Adventures** (www.castinekayak.com; © **207/866-3506**) offers full- ($110) and half-day ($55) sea kayak tours departing from Dennett's Wharf restaurant. Both trips are appropriate for those without experience; a brief intro will get you started with this graceful and often meditative sport. You'll often spot wildlife, such as bald eagles, harbor seals, and ospreys.

A Side Trip to Cape Rosier ★★

Across the Bagaduce River from Castine, **Cape Rosier** is one of Maine's best-kept secrets. As a dead-end peninsula, it has no through traffic, and roads suddenly turn to dirt in sections. The cape still has a wild, unkempt flavor with salty views of Penobscot Bay; it's not hard to imagine that you're back in 1940s Maine.

The bad news is, to reach the cape from downtown Castine you need to backtrack to Route 175 (take Route 166 to Route 199), head south toward Deer Isle, and then follow Route 176 to the turnoff for Cape Rosier—about 18 miles of driving to cross 1 mile of water. Follow Route 176 to West Brooksville, then take Cape Rosier Road to Goose Falls. A loop of 15 miles or so circles around the cape from here; it's suitable for travel by mountain bike or as a leisurely car trip.

The views are uncommonly beautiful, with a mix of blueberry barrens, boreal forest, farmsteads, summer estate houses, and coves dotted with yachts and lobster boats. There's virtually no commercial development of any sort. It's no accident that Helen and Scott Nearing, the late back-to-the-land gurus and authors of *Living the Good Life,* chose to settle here when Vermont became too developed for their tastes. A number of Nearing acolytes continue to live on Cape Rosier.

If the weather's agreeable, stop for a walk on the state-owned **Holbrook Island Wildlife Sanctuary,** a 1,200-acre preserve laced with trails and abandoned roads. The sanctuary is located at the northern end of the cape (look for signs). Among the choices: The Backshore Trail passes along open meadows to the shoreline, and the Summit Trail is all mossy, mushroomy, and medieval, with teasing glimpses of the water from the top

On your way back, stay on Route 176 a couple of miles past the Route 175 turn-off, to visit the lively taproom at **Strong Brewing Company** (www. strongbrewing.com; *©* **207/359-8722**) at the intersection of Routes 176 and 15, on the east side of the Bagaduce River. This is a community-supported brewery (fans buy shares, like a grocery CSA), and when the weather's nice, the community fills up the picnic tables and loiters around the firepit outside. There's often live music on summer Friday nights, and sometimes there's a noodle cart for noshing too. It's an easy half-hour's drive back to Castine from here.

DEER ISLE ★★

The island known as **Deer Isle ★★** is well off the beaten path, yet worth the long detour from Route 1. Looping, winding roads cross through forest and farmland, and travelers are rewarded with sudden glimpses of hidden coves. An occasional settlement even crops up now and again. This island doesn't cater exclusively to tourists the way many coastal towns and islands do; it's still largely occupied by fifth- or sixth-generation fishermen, farmers, second-home owners, and artists who prize their seclusion here.

The main village—**Stonington,** on the island's southern tip—is still a rough-hewn sea town. Despite serious incursions over the past 10 years by galleries and enterprises partly or wholly dependent on tourism, it remains dominated in spirit by fishermen. This village does now have a handful of inns and galleries, but its primary focus is to serve locals and summer residents, not travelers. *Outside* magazine once named this one of America's 10 best towns to live in if you're an extreme/outdoorsy type. Um . . . sure, if you don't mind living several hours removed from the nearest significant population centers and airports in Maine. Still, you could pick a worse place to avoid civilization, and the mailboat that runs visitors out to **Isle au Haut**, an island outpost of Acadia National Park, helps boost Stonington's outdoorsy cred.

Essentials

ARRIVING

Deer Isle is accessible via several winding country roads that split off of U.S. Route 1. Coming from the south or west (Portland or Camden), turn onto Route 175 in Orland, then connect to Route 15 and continue to Deer Isle. From the east (that is, Bar Harbor), head south on Route 172 to Blue Hill (see p. 180), where you can also pick up Route 15. Deer Isle is connected to the mainland via a high, narrow, and graceful **suspension bridge** built in 1938—still a bit harrowing to cross in high winds. The bridge connects to Little Deer Isle; from there it's a short drive over a causeway to the main island.

VISITOR INFORMATION

The **Deer Isle–Stonington Chamber of Commerce** (www.deerislemaine. com; ☏ **207/348-6124**), staffs a seasonal information booth just beyond the bridge on Little Deer Isle. The booth is normally open daily from May through October, its opening hours dependent on volunteer availability.

Where to Stay Around Deer Isle

Inn on the Harbor ★ This appealingly quirky waterfront inn has the best location in town—perched over Stonington harbor and right on the main street. The furniture's a little on the dated side, but comfy anyway—big over-stuffed grandma chairs—and more than half of the guest rooms overlook the harbor. The more inexpensive rooms are a bargain, in or out of season: This is a good spot for resting up before or after a kayak expedition, or as a base for day trips out to Isle au Haut. All units have in-room phones (cell service in Stonington can be spotty); the recently updated American Eagle Suite, the most expensive unit, has a glass-fronted woodstove, private kitchen, and private deck.

45 Main St. Stonington. www.innontheharbor.com. ☏ **800/942-2420** or 207/367-2420. 13 units. June–early Nov $170–$275 double and suite; early Nov–May $100–$210 double and suite. High season rates include continental breakfast. Children 12 and older welcome. **Amenities:** Spa services; free Wi-Fi.

Oakland House Cottages ★★ It doesn't get much more Maine than this: Although much-beloved fourth-generation innkeeper Jim Littlefield passed away in 2010, his wife, Sally, continues to run Oakland House as it's been run for generations. Jim's great-grandfather was the original owner, a sea captain who opened the inn in 1889 on land acquired from King George. (The original sign remains.) On the mainland just north of the bridge to Deer Isle, it's a classic coastal summer resort big on quiet and closeness to nature. The simple, wonderfully relaxing 10 cottages dotting the property are tucked among 50 acres of shoreline with extraordinary views of Eggemoggin Reach. Cottages have one to two bedrooms each and are of varying vintages—most have fireplaces (wood is delivered); televisions or phones; and a variety of other amenities, from kitchenettes to claw-foot tubs. Wood-paneled Lone Pine, the most expensive unit, is a nature writer's dream: it's set into the hillside, with a stone fireplace and an outstanding view of the reach. Crow's Nest feels like the top of the world and has a similar view. If you're on a real budget, the resort added a hostel building a few years ago, with private rooms and shared everything else ($40–$85 a night). There are few amenities: no pool, dining room, or business center: just slow Wi-Fi (sufficient for checking email), some hiking trails, a beach, and those great views.

435 Herrick Rd., Brooksville. www.oaklandhouse.com. **800/359-7352** or 207/359-8521. 10 units. Early July–early Sept $165–$397 cottage; cheaper in the early and late season; weekly rates are discounted. Closed mid-Oct–late April; no housekeeping or wood-delivery service before mid-June or after Labor Day. Packages available. Some cottages accommodate dogs ($10/day fee). **Amenities:** Beach; hiking trails; kayak rental; free Wi-Fi.

Pilgrim's Inn ★★   Set just off a town road and between an open bay and a mill pond, this is a historic, handsomely renovated inn. The inn was built in the mid-island town of Deer Isle in 1793 by Ignatius Haskell, a prosperous sawmill owner. His granddaughter opened the home to boarders, and it has housed summer guests ever since. The interior is tastefully decorated in a style that's informed by Early Americana but not beholden to it. The guest rooms are well appointed with antiques and decorated in muted colonial colors; expect lots of white, a little bit of lace, and subdued flowery prints. Especially intriguing are rooms on the top floor, showing off some impressive diagonal beams. Other accents include private staircases, cherry beds, antique tubs, gas-burning stoves, and fireplaces; breakfasts are big and fancy, running to goat-cheese pancakes, eggs Benedict, smoked salmon, and the like. Three cottages near the main building allow pets and have kitchenettes for fixing your own meals. If you're not up for that, the inn also maintains a tavern-style dining room with several intriguing spaces, the **Whale's Rib**; expect steaks, fish, lobsters, and rack of lamb.

20 Main St., Deer Isle. www.pilgrimsinn.com. **888/778-7505** or 207/348-6615. 15 units. $139–$229 double; $209–$269 cottage. Rates include full breakfast. Closed mid-Oct–mid-May. Pets allowed in cottages only ($25 fee). Children 10 and older welcome in inn, all children welcome in cottages. Packages available. **Amenities:** Restaurant; pub; library; bikes; free Wi-Fi.

Where to Eat Around Deer Isle

Aragosta ★ NEW AMERICAN/SEAFOOD   Chef Devin Finigan has worked alongside some of the best names in contemporary American cooking—Thomas Keller, Michael Leviton, and fellow Mainer Melissa Kelly, among them—so she brings a pedigree to Stonington's white-tablecloth dining mecca. Aragosta goes in big for the farm-to-table ethos: The beef and the bacon on the burger were raised locally, the oysters come out of the Bagaduce, the produce (most of it) was farmed nearby, and obviously the *aragostas* (that's "lobster" in Italian) were pulled in a few dozen yards outside the front door. Fancy as the weekly changing menu is, the cedar-shingled Aragosta maintains charmingly rustic touches, from the wide-plank wood flooring to the wooden menu covers. Sit outside on the small deck, and you can hear the chatter of the lobstermen as the offload what may become your dinner. Hours seem to get reassessed with each year and each season, so call ahead.

27 Main St., Stonington. © **207/367-5500.** Lunch entrees $12–$17; dinner entrees $25–$30. Memorial Day–Columbus Day 11am–2pm and 5–8pm; closed Columbus Day–Thanksgiving; dinner only and weekends only Thanksgiving–Memorial Day. Hours/seasons prone to change. Reservations recommended peak season and weekends.

Fisherman's Friend ★ SEAFOOD On a dock near the Isle au Haut ferry and attached to a general store, this is family dining: broiled and fried fresh fish, plus some creative uses of lobsters (try the linguini). There's also a wine list and a choice of pastas. This is a local-eats place, lively and boisterous, usually as crowded as it is unpretentious. Try ordering a bowl of the lobster stew, brimming with chunks; travelers have been known to find reasons to linger in Stonington longer just to indulge in a second bowl. Dessert selections, which include such local specialties as berry pie and shortcake, are extensive and traditional New England–style.

5 Atlantic Ave. (on the dock), Stonington. © **207/367-2442.** Lobsters market priced; lunch entrees $11–$16; dinner entrees $11–$26. May–Oct daily 11am–8pm; closed Nov–Apr. Reservations recommended peak season and weekends.

Exploring Deer Isle

Deer Isle, with its network of narrow roads to nowhere, is ideal for rambling. It's a pleasure to explore by car and is also inviting to travel by bike, although hasty and careening fishermen in pickups can make this unnerving at times. Especially tranquil is the narrow road between the town of **Deer Isle** and **Sunshine** to the east. Plan to stop and explore coves and inlets along the way. To get here, follow Route 15; south of Deer Isle, turn east toward **Stinson Neck,** continuing on this **scenic byway** ★ for about 10 miles over bridges and causeways.

Stonington ★★, at the southern end of Deer Isle, consists of one commercial street that wraps along the harbor's edge. While B&Bs and boutiques

---

Full Speed Ahead!

Worth noting: Stonington is one of those Maine fishing villages that hosts big-time **lobster-boat racing.** (There are also races in Searsport and Rockland.) Stonington's race usually occurs on a weekend in early July—drop by if you're in the area. Crowds line the waterfront and piers to cheer on their favorites. You'll either be amazed or horrified by how quickly one of these diesel-powered workhorses can get up to speed when the captain's going full throttle.

have made inroads here in recent years, it's still a slightly rough-and-tumble waterfront town with some attractive white-clapboard homes mixed in. The best thing to see here is, well, Main Street and the waterfront behind it. Walk down side streets like Seabreeze Avenue and Atlantic Avenue for a closer look at the town.

The town opera house is home to a very good summer-stock theater company called **Opera House Arts ★**; log on to **www.operahousearts.org** for a schedule and other details or call them at ℂ **207/367-2788**. The Opera House also hosts art events and first-run Hollywood movies.

On the Water

Peer southward from Stonington, and you'll see dozens of spruce-studded islands between the mainland and the dark, distant ridges of Isle au Haut. These islands, ringed with salmon-pink granite, are collectively called Merchant's Row, and they're invariably ranked by experienced coastal boaters as among the most beautiful in the state. Thanks to these exceptional islands, Stonington is among Maine's most popular destinations for sea kayaking. Many of the islands are open to day visitors and overnight camping, and one of the Nature Conservancy islands even hosts a flock of sheep. Experienced kayakers should contact the **Maine Island Trail Association** (www.mita.org; ℂ **207/761-8225**) for more information about paddling here; several of the islands are open only to association members.

Old Quarry Ocean Adventures ★ (www.oldquarry.com; ℂ **207/367-8977**), just outside the village of Stonington, offers guided kayak tours as well as kayaks for rent. (Old Quarry will rent only to those with prior experience, so it's best to call ahead to discuss your needs.) Tours range from a half-day tour ($64) to a full-day 7-hour tour ($133) that weaves out through the islands and includes a stop for a swim or a picnic at an abandoned quarry. Overnight camping trips are also offered. Other services: parking and a launch site for those who've brought their own boats, sailboat tours and lessons, hourly shuttles to Green Island (which has trails and an old quarry swimming hole; $31) charter tours aboard a 38-foot lobster boat, and camping ($41–$61 per tent site, $43 for RVs). For more information, visit the company's website.

Outfitters based *outside* the region that offer guided overnight kayak trips around Merchant's Row include the **Maine Island Kayak Co.** (www.maine islandkayak.com; ℂ **207/766-2373**) on Peaks Island (near Portland) and **Maine Sport Outfitters** (www.mainesport.com; ℂ **800/722-0826** or 207/236-8797) on Route 1 in Rockport.

A Side Trip to Isle Au Haut ★★

Rocky and remote Isle au Haut offers one of the most unusual hiking and camping experiences in northern New England. This 6×3-mile island, located 6 miles south of Stonington, was originally named Isle Haut (or High Island) in 1604 by French explorer Samuel de Champlain. The name and its pronunciation evolved—today it's generally pronounced Aisle-a-*ho*—but the island itself has remained steadfastly unchanged over the centuries.

About half of the island is owned by the National Park Service and maintained as an outpost of **Acadia National Park** (see chapter 9). A 60-passenger ferry from Deer Isle, run by the **Isle au Haut Boat Company** (see below), makes a stop in the morning and late afternoon at Duck Harbor, allowing for a solid day of hiking while still returning to Stonington by nightfall.

Note: The ferry stops at two different landings. Most of the time, they stop at the "town landing"—convenient for groceries, but a 4-mile, 2-hour hike through the island's woods along the Duck Harbor Trail to the only campsite (see below). During summer, usually twice a day, special boats run directly to the Duck Harbor landing, an easy few minutes' walk to the sites. I cannot stress enough: *Check first* where your ferry is going if you are not ready or able to walk 4 miles twice. The small harborside village, which has a few old homes, a handsome church, and a tiny schoolhouse, post office, and store, is interesting, but campers and most day-trippers are better served ferrying straight to Duck Harbor.

At Duck Harbor, the NPS maintains its cluster of five Adirondack-style lean-tos, which are available for overnight **camping ★**; cost is $25 per site, and they can be used up to 3 nights in a row (5 nights outside high season). A maximum of six campers can use each site, and there are no showers or electricity; there's a water pump about ⅓ mile away. These sites fill up fast, and advance reservations are essential (due by April 1 of the year you want to visit, though occasional cancellations merit checking afterward anyway). Contact **Acadia National Park,** Eagle Lake Road (P.O. Box 177), Bar Harbor, ME 04609; call ✆ **207/288-3338** or download a reservation form at **www.nps.gov/ acad/planyourvisit/duckharbor.htm**. Other than for camping, the park doesn't charge a fee to explore its island holdings.

Who lives here? The island is partly inhabited by some fishermen who can trace their island ancestry back 3 centuries, and partly by summer visitors whose forebears discovered the bucolic splendor of Isle au Haut in the 1880s. The summer population of the island is about 300, with about 50 die-hards remaining year-round. (One resident is writer Linda Greenlaw, the former fishing-boat captain profiled in the book and movie *The Perfect Storm;* she has also written her own book, *The Lobster Chronicles*, as well as a cookbook of recipes from the island.)

You can stroll the only-partly-paved main road that circles the island, but many hardy visitors choose to explore the excellent **island trails ★★** that penetrate and encircle the isle. Some of the more scenic ones include Western Head Trail (requiring perhaps 1¼ hour one-way) and Cliff Trail (about 45 minutes one-way), with expansive cliff and sea views. The NPS can furnish you with a trail map at the campground, and rangers sometimes ride the ferries. Be careful, however: Some of these trails are rough on the feet, and they can get wet from the sea, fog, or rain; rain, in fact, may render a few (such as Goat Trail) impassable at times.

The **Isle au Haut Boat Company** (www.isleauhaut.com; ✆ **207/367-5193**) operates the ferry run, leaving from the pier at the end of Sea Breeze Avenue in Stonington. In summer (roughly mid-June to mid-September), there are three to five daily runs to the island, with four to six runs in spring and fall; call or check the website for exact schedules. The round-trip boat fare to either the town landing or Duck Harbor is $39 for adults and $19.50 for children 11 and under. (There's also a small extra surcharge if you pay by credit card.) Bikes cost $22 round-trip, kayaks $46. The crossing takes about 45 minutes to the village landing, or 1 hour and 15 minutes to Duck Harbor. Reservations are not accepted; it's best to arrive at least a half-hour before departure.

BLUE HILL ★★

In contrast to the western shores of Penobscot Bay, the Blue Hill peninsula attracts far fewer tourists and has much more of a lost-in-time, Maine-as-it-was character. The roads here are hilly, winding, and narrow, passing through forests, past old-time saltwater farms, and ticking the edge of a blue inlet here or there.

The town of **Blue Hill ★★**, population 2,400, is easy to find—just look for the dome of Blue Hill itself, which lords over the northern end of (of course) Blue Hill Bay. Set between the mountain and the bay is the quiet and historic town, clustering along the bay's shore and a little stream. There's never much going on here, which seems to be exactly what attracts repeat summer visitors; it might also explain why two excellent bookstores are located in this dot of a town. Many old-money families maintain lovely retreats along the water or in the hills around here, but the village center offers a couple choices for lodging even if you don't have local connections. It's a good place for a quiet break.

Essentials

ARRIVING

Blue Hill is southeast of Ellsworth, at the juncture of routes 15 and 172. Coming from the south (Rockland or Belfast) on Route 1/Route 3, turn south onto Route 15 about 5 miles east of Bucksport, and drive about 12 miles. From Bar Harbor, follow Route 3 through Ellsworth, cross the bridge, then follow Route 172 about 14 miles to Blue Hill.

VISITOR INFORMATION

Blue Hill does not maintain a true staffed visitor information booth. Look for the "Blue Hill, Maine" brochure and map at state information centers, or drop by the **Blue Hill Peninsula Chamber of Commerce** (www.bluehillpeninsula.org; ✆ **207/374-3242**), located at 16 South Street. Locals are also often willing to answer questions you might have.

SPECIAL EVENTS

The **Blue Hill Fair ★★** (www.bluehillfair.com; ✆ **207/374-3701**) is a traditional country fair with livestock competitions, vegetable displays, and carnival rides. The fair takes place at the fairgrounds northwest of the village on Route 172 on Labor Day weekend. Admission costs $8 to $10 per person (it varies by day); rides are individually priced. Parking is free on the fairgrounds.

Maine's Folkiest Radio Station

When in the Blue Hill area, be sure to tune into the local community radio station, WERU, at 89.9 FM (and also at 102.9 FM). Started by partners including Noel "Paul" Stookey—the "Paul" in the folk trio Peter, Paul, and Mary—in a former chicken coop (only in Maine), the idea was to spread good local and rootsy music while also encouraging provocative, countercultural thinking. It's become a little bit slicker and more professional in recent years, but WERU still retains a pleasantly homespun quality and plays some of the best true folk, roots, Americana, Celtic, and blues music of any station in New England. There's also some from-the-left news and commentary during the dinner hour each day, rock and electronic music late at night, and reggae and spoken-word poetry during other time slots.

Where to Stay in Blue Hill

Blue Hill Inn ★   The Blue Hill Inn has been hosting travelers since 1840 on one of the village's main streets, within walking distance of everything. It's a Federal-style inn, decorated in a Colonial American motif; creaky wooden floors stamp it with authenticity. The innkeepers have pleasantly furnished all rooms with antiques and down comforters; a few units in the main house have wood-burning fireplaces (main house rooms are open only from mid-May through the end of October), while a large contemporary suite in an adjacent, free-standing building has a cathedral ceiling, fireplace, full kitchen, living room, and deck (and it's open year-round). Most rooms lack telephones. Breakfasts here are very good, maybe because the eggs are fresh from the innkeepers' own coops.

40 Union St., Blue Hill. www.bluehillinn.com. ✆ **207/374-2844**. 13 units. Late June–Sept $195–$280 double; $295–$395 suite; discounts in the spring and fall. Rates include full breakfast and afternoon pastries. 2-night minimum in summer. Packages available. Main inn closed Nov–mid-May, 1 cottage open year-round. Children 13 and older are welcome. Cottage accommodates pets. **Amenities:** Dining room; wine and cocktail service; library; free Wi-Fi.

Where to Eat in Blue Hill

The **Fish Net** (✆ **207/374-5240**), at the north end of Main Street (near the junction of routes 172 and 177), is the place where locals go for quick meals of takeout fried fish, lobster rolls, clam baskets, and ice-cream cones. It's open seasonal—figure mid-April to Columbus Day, at most. If it's a sweet fix you're after, **Black Dinah Chocolatiers** (✆ **207/374-2228**), at 5 Main Street (which they share with a terrific florist), makes unparalleled, fancy little chocolates—pear and champagne truffles, peanut butter–filled frogs, choc-covered sea salt caramels. Their tasting room (open Monday through Saturday 8:30am to 5pm, Sunday 11am to 4pm) has a vintage soda-fountain counter where you can sit and sample with an espresso—or a mug of sipping chocolate.

Arborvine ★★ SEAFOOD/FUSION The Arborvine gives sleepy Blue Hill a top-flight eatery in a beautifully renovated Cape Cod–style house. The restaurant's interior is warm and inviting, with rough-hewn timbers, polished wooden floors, and a cozy bar area. The intriguing main courses change nightly but might feature haddock Niçoise, broiled Stonington halibut with grilled polenta, roast duckling with apple-ginger compote, *gallettes* of Maine crab and shrimp, or a locally raised and wood-fired Cornish game hen. Yummy desserts could include a Grand Marnier–spiked chocolate mousse; chocolate cake with raspberry ganache; a lemon mousse napoleon; a gingery vanilla crème brûlée; or a Bartlett pear in puff pastry sided with macadamia nut-flavored cream, pomegranate sauce, and a bit of cinnamon ice cream. In 2011, the owners (their son, actually) opened the **DeepWater** brew pub in an adjacent barn, so you can actually park your car and have two restaurants to choose from. The brewpub's not as impressive, but if you're after a good burger, nachos, or sports, you have an option.

33 Tenney Hill, Blue Hill. www.arborvine.com. © **207/374-2119.** Main dining room entrees $26–$34; brewpub entrees $10–$17. Summer Tues–Sun 5–9pm; off-season Fri–Sun 5:30–8:30pm.

Exploring Blue Hill

Blue Hill has traditionally attracted more than its fair share of artists, especially potters. Family-run **Rackliffe Pottery** (www.rackliffepottery.com; © **888/631-3321**) on Route 172 (Ellsworth Road), uses native clay and lead-free glazes. Visitors are welcome to watch the potters at work. It's open year-round.

If you're an ardent antiques hunter (or collector of bizarre experiences), it *might* be worth your while to detour to the **Big Chicken Barn** (www.big chickenbarn.com; © **207/667-7308**), a sprawling antiques mall and bookstore on Route 1 between Ellsworth and Bucksport. (Look for it 9 miles west of Ellsworth or 11 miles east of Bucksport.) The place is of nearly shopping-mall proportions—more than 21,000 square feet of stuff in an old poultry barn. It's open daily from 10am to 6pm during summer, 10am to 5pm in the spring and fall, 10am to 4pm in winter.

Jonathan Fisher House ★★ HISTORIC HOME A half-mile west of the village of Blue Hill, this is the best "museum" in town. Parson Fisher, Blue Hill's first permanent minister, was a small-town Renaissance man when he settled here in 1796. Educated at Harvard, Fisher not only delivered sermons in six different languages (including Aramaic), but was also a writer, painter, and inventor of boundless energy. On a tour of this yellow clapboard house, which he built himself in 1814, you can view a clock with wooden works and a camera obscura that Fisher made, plus pictures he painted and books he wrote, published, and bound by hand. Outside, the property's owners are slowly recreating Fisher's original orchard.

44 Mines Rd. (Rte. 176), Blue Hill. www.jonathanfisherhouse.org. © **207/374-2459.** $5 suggested donation. Jul–Aug Wed–Sat 1–4pm, Sept–mid-Oct Fri–Sat 1–4pm only.

WONDERFUL WALKS

A good way to explore this region is to ascend the open summit of **Blue Hill ★★**, from which you'll gain superb views of the bay and the bald mountaintops on nearby Mount Desert Island. To reach the trail head from the center of the village, drive north on Route 172 about 1½ miles, then turn west (left) on Mountain Road at the Blue Hill Fairgrounds. Drive another ¾ mile and look for the well-marked trail; park on the shoulder of the road. The fairly easy ascent is about a mile, and takes about 45 minutes. Bring a picnic lunch.

MOUNT DESERT ISLAND

8

Mount Desert Island is home to spectacular Acadia National Park, and for many visitors, the two places are one and the same. Yet the park's holdings are only part of the appeal of this popular island, which is connected to the mainland by a short causeway. Besides the parklands, there are scenic harborside villages and remote backcountry roads aplenty, lovely B&Bs and fine restaurants, oversize 19th-century summer "cottages," and the historic tourist town of Bar Harbor.

It's not hard to understand why Acadia is one of the crown jewels of the U.S. national park system. (It draws the second-most visitors annually of any national park.) The landscape here is a rich tapestry of rugged cliffs, pounding ocean surf, fishing and leisure boats lolling in harbors, and quiet forest paths. If you look at a map, you'll see that the island is nearly split in two by a great tidal inlet, Somes Sound (see "Fjord Tough," p. 186); most of the park's land is on the eastern side of the island, though there are some vast holdings in the west, too. To help orient you, I've placed a color map of Mount Desert Island inside the front cover of this guidebook.

On the much-more-developed eastern side of the island, **Bar Harbor** is Mount Desert Island's center of commerce and entertainment, a once-charming resort now in danger of being swallowed up by T-shirt and trinket shops. It has by far the best selection of lodging, meals, supplies, and services on the isle. (If you want to shop, fine-dine, or go out at night, you pretty much *have* to stay here.)

Otherwise, if quiet is what you're seeking, consider bunking elsewhere on the island. The western side has a quieter, more settled air and teems with more wildlife than tourists; here, the villages are mostly filled with fishermen and second-homers rather than actual commerce.

The island isn't huge—it's only about 15 miles from the causeway to the southernmost tip at Bass Harbor Head—yet you can do an awful lot of adventuring in such a compact space and see many different kinds of towns and landscapes. The best plan is to take it slowly, exploring if possible by foot, bicycle, canoe, and/or kayak, giving yourself a week to do it. You'll be glad you did.

ACADIA NATIONAL PARK ★★★

Acadia's terrain, like so much of the rest of northern New England, was shaped by the cutting action of the last great glaciers moving into and then out of the region about 18,000 years ago. A mile-high ice sheet rumbled slowly over the land, scouring valleys into deep U shapes, rounding many once-jagged peaks, and depositing boulders at odd places in the landscape—including the famous 10-foot-tall Bubble Rock, which appears perched precariously on the side of South Bubble Mountain.

In the 1840s, Hudson River School painter Thomas Cole brought his sketchbooks and easels to remote Mount Desert Island, which was then home to a small number of fishermen and boat builders. His stunning renditions of the coast were displayed in New York City, triggering a tourism boom as urbanites flocked to the island to "rusticate." By 1872, national magazines were touting Eden (Bar Harbor's name until 1919) as a desirable summer getaway. It attracted the attention of wealthy industrialists, and soon became the de rigueur summer home of Carnegies, Rockefellers, Astors, and Vanderbilts, who built massive "cottages" with dozens of rooms.

By the early 1900s, the island's popularity and growing development began to concern its most ardent supporters. Boston textile heir George Dorr and Harvard president Charles Eliot, aided by the largesse of John D. Rockefeller, Jr. (see box p. 197), began acquiring and protecting large tracts of the island for the public to enjoy. These parcels were eventually donated to the U.S. government, and in 1919, the land was originally designated as Lafayette National Park—the first national park east of the Mississippi—named after the French general who assisted colonists in the American Revolution.

Renamed "Acadia National Park" in 1929, the park has now grown to encompass nearly half the island, its holdings scattered piecemeal. It is a fine, even world-class, destination for those who like coastal vacations salted with adventure. Try to allow 3 or 4 days, at a minimum, for visiting the park. If you're passing through just briefly, try to work in at least two of the big three activities (hiking, biking, driving) I've described below.

And when you set out to explore the park, bring a picnic. (See "Packing a Picnic," p. 191), for there are just about no food services whatsoever within the park.

See It, Say It

There is some debate about how to correctly pronounce the island to which I'm referring throughout this chapter. The name is of French origin; technically, it should be Mount days-*airt*, but nobody says it that way anymore. Most locals say "Mount Des-*sert*," like what you have after dinner, which is pretty close to the French way of saying things. (Notice the accent on the last syllable.) However, plenty of tourists, transplants, and locals *also* say *Dez*-ert (like the Sahara), and that's not wrong. After all, that's how it's *spelled*. As for me, I go with Des-*sert*.

Essentials

ARRIVING

Acadia National Park is near Ellsworth, reached via Route 3. Normally travelers take U.S. Route 1 to Ellsworth from southern Maine, but you can avoid coastal congestion by taking the Maine Turnpike to Bangor, then picking up I-395 to Route 1A and continuing south into Ellsworth. Though this is longer in terms of miles, it's a quicker route in summer.

From Ellsworth, bear right onto Route 3 (U.S. Route 1 doesn't go onto the island) and continue about 15 minutes to the island causeway in **Trenton.** Cross the bridge and you're on the island. Consult a map carefully to determine which route to take from here; there are three possible choices, all leading to very different destinations: routes 3 and 233 go to Bar Harbor, Route 198 goes to Northeast Harbor, and Route 102 leads to Southwest harbor.

Year-round, there are several flights daily from Boston (and, seasonally, Newark) on small planes to the **Hancock County-Bar Harbor airport** (airport code **BHB;** www.bhbairport.com) in Trenton, just across the causeway from Mount Desert Island. Contact **Cape Air** (www.capeair.com; ℂ **800/227-3247**) or **PenAir** (www.penair.com; ℂ **800/448-4226**) for Boston flights, or **Elite Airways** (www.eliteairways.net; ℂ **877/393-2510**) for Newark.

From the airport, call a taxi, rent a car, or—best of all—ride the **free shuttle bus** (see p. 188) to downtown Bar Harbor from late June through mid-October.

VISITOR CENTERS & INFORMATION

Acadia staffs two visitor centers. The **Thompson Island Information Center** (ℂ **207/288-3411**) on Route 3 is the first you'll pass as you enter Mount Desert Island. This center is maintained by the local chambers of commerce, but park personnel are often on hand to answer inquiries. Open daily at 8:30am mid-May through mid-October, it's a good first stop for general lodging and restaurant information.

If you're interested primarily in information about the park itself, continue on Route 3 to the National Park Service's **Hulls Cove Visitor Center,** about 7½ miles beyond Thompson Island. This attractive, stone-walled center has professionally prepared park-service displays, such as a large relief map of the

---

Fjord Tough?

Mount Desert Island is divided deeply right down the middle into two lobes (almost like a brain) by **Somes Sound,** a tidal inlet that's often called the Lower 48's only true fjord—that is, a valley carved out by a glacier and then subsequently filled in with rising ocean water. As many a Mainer will tell you, however, the feature is more properly classified as a fjard, a close hydrogeological cousin, which is less steep and shallower, the result of a flooded glacial lowland but not a truly scoured glacial trough. You'll find that many around MDI leave the finer distinctions to the geologists (and the Scandinavians, who take this stuff quite seriously) and simply refer to Somes Sound as a fjord. Whatever vowel you prefer, it's no less dramatic to gaze upon.

Mount Desert Island/Acadia National Park

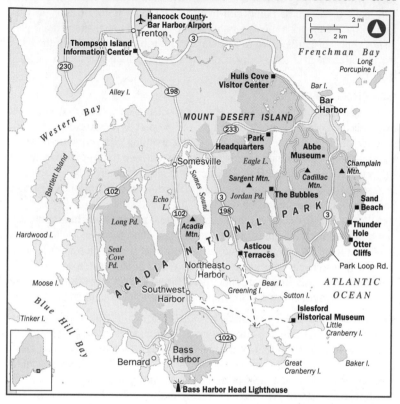

island, natural history exhibits, and a short introductory film. You can also request free brochures about hiking trails and the carriage roads, or purchase postcards and more detailed guidebooks. The center is open daily from mid-April through the end of October.

Information is also available year-round, by phone or in person, at the **park headquarters** (© **207/288-3338**), on Route 233 between Bar Harbor and Somesville, open daily (except closed weekends in summer). You can also make inquiries online at **www.nps.gov/acad**.

ENTRY POINTS & FEES

Entrance fees to the park are collected at several gates and points from May through October; the rest of the year, entrance is free—one of this nation's great outdoor bargains either way. A 1-week pass, which includes unlimited trips on the Park Loop Road (closed in winter), costs $25 per car from May through early October; there's no additional charge per passenger once you've bought the pass. Hikers, cyclists, and anyone else traveling without a vehicle (that is, motorcyclists or boaters) must pay a $12-per-person fee.

You can enter the park at several points in the interwoven network of park and town roads—a glance at a park map, available free at the visitor center, will make these access points self-evident. The main point of entry to Park Loop Road, the park's most popular scenic byway, is near the official park visitor center at **Hulls Cove** (on Route 3 just north of Bar Harbor); the entry fee is collected at a tollbooth on the loop road, a half-mile north of Sand Beach.

GETTING AROUND

A **free summer shuttle bus service** ★★ known as the *Island Explorer* (www.exploreacadia.com) was inaugurated in 1999 as part of an effort to reduce the number of cars on the island's roads. It's working; the propane-powered buses—equipped with racks for bikes—serve multiple routes covering nearly the entire island, and will stop anywhere you request outside the village centers, including trailheads, ferries, small villages, and campgrounds. (Bring a book, though; there are lots of stops.)

All routes begin or end at the central **Village Green** in Bar Harbor, but you can hop onto the bus almost anywhere else—a handy way to avoid parking hassles in town. Route no. 3, which runs from Bar Harbor along much of the Park Loop, offers easy free access to some of the park's best hiking trails.

The buses operate from late June through mid-October; ask for a schedule at island information centers, in shops, or at any hotel or campground.

GUIDED TOURS

Acadia National Park Tours (www.acadiatours.com; ✆ **207/288-0300**) offers 2½-hour park tours from mid-May through October, departing twice daily (10am and 2pm) from downtown Bar Harbor. The bus tour includes three stops (Sieur De Monts Springs, Thunder Hole, and Cadillac Mountain) and imparts plenty of park trivia, courtesy of the driver. This is an easy way for first-time visitors to get a quick introduction to the park before setting out on their own side trips. Tickets are available at Testa's Restaurant (at 53 Main St.) in Bar Harbor; the cost is $30 for adults, $17.50 for children 12 and under.

RANGER PROGRAMS

Frequent ranger programs are offered throughout the year at Acadia. These include talks at campground amphitheaters and tours of various island locales and attractions. Examples include an Otter Point nature hike, walks across the carriage roads' stone bridges, cruises on Frenchman Bay (rangers provide commentary on many trips), and discussions of the changes in Acadia's

Cost-Effective Acadia	
No daily pass to Acadia is available, so if you'll be here more than 2 weeks, purchase a $50 annual Acadia pass for your car instead of several $25 weekly passes. Or, if you really travel a lot, consider	buying an $80 "America the Beautiful" national parks pass—it gets you and your vehicle and your passengers into nearly all properties managed by the National Park Service for an entire calendar year.

AVOIDING crowds IN THE PARK

Early fall is the best time to miss the mobs yet still enjoy the weather here. If you come midsummer, try to venture out in early morning or early evening to the most popular spots, such as Thunder Hole or the summit of Cadillac Mountain. Setting off into the woods at every opportunity is also a good strategy. Probably four out of every five visitors restrict their tours to the loop road and a handful of other major attractions, leaving most of the gorgeous trail system to the more adventurous.

The best guarantee of solitude is to head to the most remote outposts managed by Acadia, such as **Isle au Haut** and **Schoodic Peninsula,** across the bay to the east. Ask for more information about these areas at the visitor centers (see p. 175 and 231).

landscape—there was even a small earthquake here in October 2006, causing rock slides that still keep a few trails closed. Ask for a schedule of park events and more information at any visitor center or campground.

WHEN TO GO

While spring is forgettable in Acadia—often intensely foggy or rainy—summer is the peak tourist season. The weather in July and August is perfect for just about any outdoor activity. Most days are warm (in the 70s or 80s/low to mid-20s Celsius), with afternoons frequently cooler than mornings owing to the sea breezes. Light fogs occasionally roll in from the southeast on a hot day, which gives a magical quality to the landscape. Sunny days are the norm, but come prepared for rain; this is the Atlantic Coast, after all. Once or twice each summer, a heat wave somehow settles onto the island, producing temperatures in the 90s (30s Celsius), dense haze, and stifling humidity, but this rarely lasts more than a few days. August in Acadia is when both heat and traffic peaks—traffic jams on the Park Loop Road and at the top of Cadillac are, sadly, the norm, and Bar Harbor is a zoo. If you can come earlier in the summer or hold off until September, consider it.

Soon enough (sometimes even during late August), a brisk north wind will blow in from the Canadian Arctic, forcing visitors into sweaters at night. You'll smell the approach of autumn, with winter not far behind. Fall here is wonderful. Between Labor Day and the foliage season in early October, days are often warm and clear, nights have a crisp tang, and you can avoid the congestion, crowds, and pesky insects of summer. It's not that the park is empty in September; bus tours seem to proliferate at this time, and it's when the cruise ship season kicks into high gear in Bar Harbor. Not to worry: Both the cruise and tour bus crowds tend to stick to the pavement—hikers and bikers need only get a minute or two off the road to find relative solitude on the trails and carriage roads.

Winter is an increasingly popular time to travel to Acadia, especially among those who enjoy cross-country skiing the carriage roads. Be aware, though, that snow along the coast is inconsistent, and services—including most restaurants and many inns—are often closed down outright in winter. Expect to stay in either a really cheap motel or an expensive resort, and to often eat what locals do: pizza, burgers, and sandwiches.

Camping In & Near the Park

NATIONAL PARK SERVICE CAMPGROUNDS

The National Park Service maintains four campgrounds within Acadia National Park—two on MDI; another, quite new campground on the Schoodic Peninsula, to the north (see p. 240 in chapter 9); and one on Isle au Haut (see p. 178 in chapter 7).

Both of the campgrounds on Mount Desert Island are extremely popular; during July and August, expect both of them to fill up by early to midmorning. The more popular of the two is **Blackwoods ★★** (© 207/288-3274), on the island's eastern side, with about 300 sites. To get there, follow Route 3 about 5 miles south out of Bar Harbor; the Island Explorer bus (see p. 218) stops here as well. Bikers and pedestrians have easy access to the loop road from the campground via a short trail. This campground has no public showers or electrical hookups, but an enterprising business just outside the campground entrance provides clean showers for a modest fee. Camping fees at Blackwoods are $30 per night from May through October, $15 per site in April and November.

The **Seawall ★** (© 207/244-3600) campground is located over on the quieter, western half of the island, near the tiny fishing village of Bass Harbor (one of the Island Explorer shuttle bus lines also stops here). Seawall has about 215 sites, and it's a good base for cyclists or those wishing to explore several short coastal hikes within easy striking distance. However, it's quite a ways from Bar Harbor and Sand Beach on the other side of the island. Also, many of the sites involve a walk of a few dozen to a few hundred yards from where your car's parked; wheelbarrows are available to tote your stuff, but for families, it might not be the best choice. The campground is open mid-May through September. Camping fees at Seawall are $22 to $30 per night, depending on whether you want to drive directly to your site, or can pack a tent in for a distance of up to 300 yards. There are also no electrical or water hookups here.

Advance **reservations** can be made for either campground by calling © **877/444-6777** between 10am and midnight (only until 10pm in winter), or

---

Regulations

The usual national park rules apply. Guns may not be used in the park; if you have a gun, it must be "cased, broken down, or otherwise packaged against use." Fires and camping are allowed only at designated areas. Pets must be on leashes at all times. Seat belts must be worn in the national park (this is a federal law). Don't remove anything from the park, either man-made or natural; this includes cobblestones from the shore.

PACKING A picnic FOR ACADIA

Before you set out to explore, pack a lunch and keep it handy. Once you get inside it, the park has very few places (other than the Jordan Pond House, see p. 192) to stop for lunch or snacks. Having drinks and snacks at hand will prevent you from having to backtrack into Bar Harbor or elsewhere to fend off starvation midday. The more food you bring, the more your options for a day expand, so hit up one of the charming general stores in any of the island's villages first and stock up on sandwiches, sweets, camera batteries, and hydration.

Acadia National Park is full of wonderful picnic spots. **Sand Beach** is gloriously scenic (bring a blanket, plus a sweater for sea winds). A hike up any of the smaller mountains such as **Day Mountain** or **Flying Mountain** is rewarded with ocean views and cooling winds (or, in fall, a blaze of colors). If you're too tired to hike, truck over to **Jordan Pond** or to **The Bubbles** for good views, or check out tiny **Suminsby Park** off the scenic Sargent Drive, on the eastern shore of the sound—it's an often-overlooked picnic spot that gets you right down to the water's edge.

by using the reservations system online at **www.recreation.gov**. An Acadia pass (see box, p. 188) is also required for campground entry.

OTHER CAMPGROUNDS

So what if the Park Service campgrounds are full? Private campgrounds handle the overflow. The region from Ellsworth south boasts a dozen-plus private campgrounds with more than 1,200 campsites, and each offer varying amenities. The **Thompson Island Information Center** (☎ 207/288-3411), open 8:30am to 5:30pm daily from mid-May through mid-October, posts up-to-the-minute information on which campgrounds still have vacancies; it's a good first stop for those arriving without camping reservations.

Two private campgrounds stand above the rest. **Bar Harbor Campground,** Route 3, Salisbury Cove (www.thebarharborcampground.com; ☎ 207/288-5185), on the main route between the causeway and Bar Harbor, does not take advance reservations. Still, you can often find a good selection of sites if you walk in before noon, even during peak season. Some of its 300 sites are set in piney woods; others are on an open hillside edged with blueberry barrens. The wooded sites are quite private. There's a pool for campers and uncommonly clean bathhouses, and campers always get to pick their own sites rather than be arbitrarily assigned one. Rates range from around $30 for a basic, no-services site to around $45 for those with hookups. Open Memorial Day through Columbus Day weekend—no credit cards accepted, but there's an ATM onsite.

Then, at the head of Somes Sound is **Mount Desert Campground ★**, Route 198 (☎ 207/244-3710), which is my favorite private facility on the island and is one that's especially well suited for campers—only those RVs 20 feet long or shorter are allowed. This heavily wooded campground has many lovely sites, including some walk-in sites right at the water's edge. The rate ranges from $43 to $69 per night in high season, $33 to $45 per site in the off

The secret to the **Jordan Pond House** ★★ (www.acadiajordanpond house.com;© **207/276-3316**)? Location, location, location. Located right in the park, on the Park Loop Road near Seal Harbor, the restaurant traces its roots from 1847, when a farm was established on this picturesque property at the southern tip of Jordan Pond looking north toward The Bubbles, a picturesque (some might say suggestive) pair of glacially sculpted mounds. In 1979, the original structure and its birch-bark dining room were destroyed by fire. A more modern, two-level dining room was built in its place—less charm, but it still has one of the island's best dining locations, on a nice lawn spread out before the pond. The main gustatory attraction here are the light, eggy pastries called popovers—afternoon tea with popovers and jam ($11) is a hallowed tradition here, though you can (and should) get them anytime. The lobster stew is expensive but very good. Dinners (reservations recommended) include classic entrees like New York strip steak, steamed lobster, pasta, and lobster stew. Entrees run around $14–$27 at lunch, $21–$33 at dinner. It's open mid-May to late October, daily from 11am to 9pm.

season. It's open from mid-June to about mid-September. (Do not confuse with the similar-named **Mount Desert Narrows Campground,** a bigger, more commercial campground that's much more RV-oriented. That one is located right at the end of the bridge after you arrive on the island.)

Another option is **Lamoine State Park** (© **207/667-4778**), which faces Mount Desert from the mainland across the cold waters of northernmost Frenchman Bay. This is an exceptionally pleasant, quiet park with private sites, a shower house, and a small beach about a half-hour's drive from the action at Bar Harbor. The campground has been belatedly discovered by travelers in recent years, but you can still get a site without a reservation if you arrive early. It's open from mid-May to mid-October, and sites cost $30 per night for nonresidents of Maine.

Should all these options be full, don't despair: You can find a room, especially in Bar Harbor, which is teeming with motels and inns. The rest of the island also has a good, if scattered, selection of places to spend the night. See the "Where to Stay" sections for Bar Harbor and the rest of Mount Desert Island later in this chapter on p. 208 and p. 221. Still desperate? Head off-island to Trenton (a clutch of motels along Route 3) and then Ellsworth.

DRIVING THE PARK LOOP ROAD

The 20-mile **Park Loop Road** ★★ is to Acadia what Half Dome is to Yosemite—the park's premier attraction, and a magnet for the largest crowds. This remarkable roadway starts near the Hulls Cove Visitor Center and follows the high ridges above Bar Harbor before dropping down along the rocky coast. Here, spires of spruce and fir cap dark granite ledges, making a sharp contrast with the white surf and steel-blue sea. After following the picturesque coast and touching on several coves, the road loops back inland along Jordan Pond and Eagle Lake, with a detour to the summit of the island's highest peak, Cadillac Mountain.

From about 10am until 4pm in July and especially August, anticipate big crowds along the loop road, at least on days when the sun is shining. Parking lots sometimes fill up and close their gates at some of the most popular destinations, including Sand Beach, Thunder Hole, and the Cadillac Mountain summit, so try to visit these spots early or late in a day. Alternatively, make the best of cloudy or drizzly days by letting the weather work to your advantage; you'll sometimes discover that you have the place nearly to yourself.

Ideally, visitors should try to make two circuits of the loop road. The first time, get the lay of the land. On the second-time circuit (one pass gets you all-day access), plan to stop frequently and poke around on foot, setting off on trails or scrambling along the coastline and taking photos. (Scenic pull-offs are strategically staggered at intervals.) The two-lane road is one-way along some of its coastal sections; in these cases, the right-hand lane is set aside for parking, so you can stop wherever you'd like, admire the vistas from the shoulder, and click away.

From the Hulls Cove Visitor Center, the Park Loop initially runs atop:

1 Paradise Hill

Our tour starts with sweeping views eastward over Frenchman Bay. You'll see the town of Bar Harbor far below, and just beyond it the Porcupines, a cluster of islands that look like, well, porcupines. Sort of.

Following the Park Loop Road clockwise, you'll dip into a wooded valley and come to:

2 Sieur de Monts Spring

Here you'll find a rather uninteresting natural spring, unnaturally encased, along with a botanical garden with some 300 species showcased in 12 habitats. The original **Abbe Museum** (© **207/288-3519**) is here, featuring a small but select collection of Native American artifacts. It's open daily from late May to September, 10am to 4pm; admission is $3 for adults, $1 for children ages 6 to 15. (A larger and more modern branch of the museum in Bar Harbor features more and better-curated displays; a ticket here gets you a discount there. See p. 218 in "Exploring Bar Harbor" for details.)

The Tarn is the main reason to stop here; a few hundred yards south of the springs via a footpath, it's a slightly medieval-looking and forsaken pond sandwiched between steep hills. Departing from the south end of the Tarn is the fine **Dorr Mountain Ladder Trail** (see "Hiking in the Park," p. 196).

Continue the clockwise trip on the loop road; views eastward over the bay soon resume, almost uninterrupted, until you get to:

3 The Precipice Trail

The park's most dramatic hiking track, the **Precipice Trail** ★★ ascends sheer rock faces on the eastern side of **Champlain Mountain.** It's only about half a mile to the summit, but it's nevertheless a rigorous climb that involves scrambling up iron rungs and ladders in exposed places (those with a fear of heights and those under 5 feet tall should *avoid* this trail). The trail is often closed midsummer to protect nesting peregrine falcons; at these times rangers are often on hand at the trail-head parking lot to suggest alternative hikes.

Between the Precipice Trail and Sand Beach is a tollbooth where visitors have to pay the park **entrance fee.**

Picturesquely set between the arms of a rocky cove is:

4 Sand Beach

Sand Beach ★★ is virtually the only sand beach on the island, although actually swimming in these cold waters (about 50°F/10°C) is best enjoyed only on extremely hot days or by those with hardy constitutions. When it's sunny out, the sandy strand is crowded midday with picnickers, tanners, tide pool explorers, and book readers.

Two good hikes begin near this beach, too. **The Beehive Trail** overlooks Sand Beach (see "Hiking in the Park," p. 196); it starts from a trail head across the loop road. From the east end of Sand Beach, look for the start of the **Great Head Trail,** a loop of about 2 miles that follows on the bluff overlooking the beach, then circles back along the shimmering bay before cutting through the woods back to Sand Beach.

About a mile south of Sand Beach is:

5 Thunder Hole

Thunder Hole ★ is a shallow ocean-side cave into which the ocean surges, compresses, and bursts out violently like a thick cannon shot of foam. (A roadside walking trail allows you to leave your car parked at the Sand Beach lot and hike to this point.)

If the sea is quiet—as it sometimes is on midsummer days—don't bother visiting this attraction; there'll be nothing to see. But on days when the seas are rough, and big swells are rolling in all the way from the Bay of Fundy, this is a must-see, three-star attraction; you can feel the ocean's power and force. The best viewing time is **3 hours before high tide;** check tide tables, available at local hotels, restaurants, and info kiosks, to figure out when that is.

Just before the road curves around Otter Point, you'll be driving atop:

6 Otter Cliffs

This set of 100-foot-high precipices is capped with dense stands of spruce trees. From the top, look for spouting whales in summer. In early fall, raftlike flocks of eider ducks can sometimes be seen floating just offshore. A footpath traces the edge of the crags.

At Seal Harbor, the loop road veers north and inland back toward Bar Harbor. On the route is:

7 Jordan Pond

Jordan Pond ★★ is a small but beautiful body of water encased by gentle, forested hills. A 3-mile hiking loop follows the pond's shoreline (see "Hiking in the Park," p. 196), and a network of splendid carriage roads converges at the pond. After a hike or mountain-bike excursion, spend some time at a table on the lawn of the Jordan Pond House restaurant (see box on p. 192).

Shortly before the loop road ends, you'll pass the entrance to:

8 Cadillac Mountain

Reach this **mountain** ★ by car, ascending an early carriage road. At 1,528 feet, it's the highest peak touching the Atlantic Ocean between Canada and Brazil. During much of the year, it's also the first place on U.S. soil touched by the rays of sunrise. But because this is the only mountaintop in the park accessible by car (and also because it's the island's highest point), the parking lot at the summit often gets jammed.

Biking the Carriage Roads ★★

The 57 miles of **carriage roads** built by John D. Rockefeller, Jr. (see box p. 197) are among the park's most extraordinary, somewhat hidden treasures. Though built for horse and carriage, they are ideal for cruising by mountain bike and offer some of the most scenic, relaxing biking found anywhere in the United States. No cars are permitted on these grass and gravel lanes; bikers and walkers have them all to themselves. Park your car near **Jordan Pond** (see above) then plumb the tree-shrouded lanes that lace the area, taking time to admire the stonework on the uncommonly fine bridges. Afterward, stop for tea and popovers at the **Jordan Pond House** (see box p. 192), which has been a popular island destination for over a century, although it's unlikely as much Lycra was in evidence 100 years ago.

The carriage roads were maintained by Rockefeller until his death in 1960, after which they became shaggy and overgrown. A major restoration effort was launched in 1990, and today the roads are superbly restored and maintained. With their wide hard-packed surfaces, gentle grades, and extensive directional signs, they make for very smooth biking. Note that bikes are also allowed on the island's free Island Explorer shuttle buses (see "Getting Around," p. 188).

A useful map of the roads is available free at visitor centers; more detailed guides may be purchased at area bookshops but aren't necessary. Where carriage roads cross private land (generally between Seal Harbor and Northeast Harbor), they're closed to mountain bikes, which are also banned from hiking trails.

Mountain bikes can be rented along Cottage Street in Bar Harbor, with rates generally in the neighborhood of $25 for a full day or $15 for a half-day (which is 4 hours in the bike-rental universe). High-performance and tandem bikes cost a bit more than that, children's bikes a bit less. Most bike shops include locks and helmets as basic equipment, but ask what's included before you rent. Also ask about closing times, since you'll be able to get in a couple of extra hours with a late-closing shop. The **Bar Harbor Bicycle Shop,** 141 Cottage Street (www.barharborbike.com; © **207/288-3886**), gets many people's vote for the most convenient and friendliest. You could also try **Acadia Bike & Canoe,** 48 Cottage Street (www.acadiabike.com; © **800/526-8615**).

Hiking in the Park

Hiking is the quintessential Acadia experience, and it should be experienced by everyone at least once. The park has 120 miles of hiking trails in all, plus 57 miles of carriage roads, which are great for easier walking. Some traverse the sides or faces of low "mountains" (which would be called hills anywhere else), and almost all summits have superb views of the Atlantic. Many of these pathways were crafted by stonemasons or others with aesthetic intent, so the routes aren't always the most direct—but they're often incredibly scenic, taking advantage of natural fractures in the rocks, picturesque ledges, and sudden, sweeping vistas.

The **Hulls Cove Visitor Center** has a brief chart summarizing area hikes; combined with the park map, this is all you need to find one of the well-maintained, well-marked trails and start exploring. Cobble together different loop hikes to make your trips more varied, and be sure to coordinate your hiking with the weather; if it's damp or foggy, you'll stay drier and warmer strolling the carriage roads. If it's clear and dry, head for the highest peaks (Cadillac, The Bubbles) with the best views.

One of the best trails is the **Dorr Ladder Trail** ★, which departs from Route 3 near **the Tarn** (see p. 193) just south of the Sieur de Monts entrance to the Loop Road. This trail begins with a series of massive stone steps

How the Carriage Roads Came to Be

John D. Rockefeller, Jr., *alone* purchased and donated some 11,000 acres of Acadia National Park—about one-third of the entire park's area—and he was almost singularly responsible for its extraordinary **carriage roads.**

It happened this way. Around 1905, a dispute erupted over whether to allow noisy new motorcars onto the island. Islanders wanted these new conveniences, but Rockefeller (whose fortune had been made in the oil industry) strenuously objected, preferring the tranquility of a car-free island for his summer vacations. The multimillionaire went down to defeat on the issue, though, and the island was opened to cars in 1913; in response, Rockefeller set about building an elaborate 57-mile system of private carriage roads on his holdings in the park, complete with a dozen gracefully handcrafted stone bridges.

These roads—open today to pedestrians, bicyclists, horses, and carriages, but no automobiles—are concentrated most densely around **Jordan Pond**; they also wind through wooded valleys and ascend some of the park's most scenic peaks.

ascending along the base of a vast slab of granite and then passes through crevasses (not for the wide of girth) and up ladders affixed to the granite. The views east and south are superb.

An easy lowland hike is around **Jordan Pond** (see p. 195) with the northward leg along the pond's east shore on a hiking trail and the return via carriage road. It's mostly level, with the total loop measuring just more than 3 miles. At the north end of Jordan Pond, consider heading up the prominent, oddly symmetrical mounds called **The Bubbles** ★. These detours shouldn't take much more than 20 minutes each; look for signs off the Jordan Pond Shore Trail.

On the western side of the island, an ascent of **Acadia Mountain** and return takes about 1½ hours, but hikers should schedule in some time for lingering while they enjoy the view of Somes Sound and the smaller islands off Mount Desert's southern shores. This 2.5-mile loop hike begins off Route 102 at a trail head 3 miles south of Somesville. Head eastward through rolling mixed forest, then begin an ascent over ledgey terrain. Be sure to visit both the east and west peaks (the east peak has the better views), and look for hidden clearings in the summit forest that open up to unexpected vistas.

Other Sports & Outdoor Activities

CARRIAGE RIDES ★★ Several types of carriage rides are offered by the park concessionaire **Wildwood Stables** (www.acadiahorses.com; ✆ **877/276-3622**), about a half-mile south of the Jordan Pond House (see box p. 192). The tours depart daily in season and take in sweeping ocean views from a local mountaintop, ramble over the Rockefeller bridges, or drop by the Jordan Pond House for (optional) tea and popovers (extra charge). There's a special carriage designed for passengers with disabilities, and you can even charter your own carriage for a private group. Reservations are recommended; figure to pay about $20–$36 per adult, or about $12–$14 per child, for a tour.

ROCK CLIMBING   Many of the ocean-side rock faces attract experienced rock climbers, as much for the beauty of the climbing areas as the challenge of the climbs and the high-grade quality of the rock. For novices or experienced climbers, **Acadia Mountain Guides** (www.acadiamountainguides. com; ⓒ **888/232-9559** or 207/288-8186) offers rock-climbing lessons and guide services, ranging from a half-day introduction to rock climbing to intensive workshops on self-rescue and instruction on how to lead climbs. The Bar Harbor branch (the other's in Orono) is located at 228 Main Street.

SKIING   Cross-country skiers have a glorious mix of terrain to choose from, especially within **Acadia National Park,** where skiing is allowed for free on park grounds throughout the winter. Volunteers groom more than 30 miles of Acadia's carriage roads—which were designed for maximum scenic potential, but also to be gradual enough not to tax horses pulling huge carriages, making them ideal for Nordic skiing. I'd go so far as to say it's among the best cross-country ski destinations in the country. Visit the Facebook page or Twitter feed of **Friends of Acadia** (www.facebook.com/FriendsofAcadia; www. twitter.com/FriendsofAcadia) for grooming updates in winter. For more about cross-country ski areas in Maine, visit the Nordic skiing website of the trade association **Ski Maine** (www.skimaine.com).

A NATURE GUIDE TO ACADIA NATIONAL PARK

The human history of Acadia National Park is usually thought of as beginning in the early 20th century, when preservationists banded together with wealthy philanthropists to set aside and create the park we know today. In fact, its clock winds much farther back than that—beginning thousands of years ago, when local Native American tribes fished its shores and hunted its hills. But even *that* is just a flake off the deep, deep time that has been required to create Acadia. The rocks upon which you climb, sun yourself, and picnic are old—staggeringly old.

Before arriving, then, one would do well to acquaint oneself with the natural history of the place. Armed with a respect and appreciation for the landscape before you, you just might treat it a bit more reverently while you're here and help ensure it remains for future generations to behold for many years.

The Landscape

The beginnings of Acadia National Park as we see it today are perhaps a half *billion* years old. At that time, deep wells of liquid rock known as magma were moving upward, exploding in **underground volcanoes,** then hardening—still underground, mind you—into granitelike rocks. Later, as natural forces such as wind and water wore away the upper layers of rock above these rocks, the rocks began to be exposed. Their journey was only beginning, however; soon enough (geologically speaking, that is), what is now eastern North America and most of Europe began to shove up against each other, slowly but inexorably. This "collision" (which was more like an extremely slow-motion car wreck), heated, squeezed, transformed, and thrust up the rocks that now form the backbone of **Mount Desert Island.**

Now in place, the rocks were once again changed by everything around them. Ice ages came and went, but the rocks remained; the successive waves of great glaciation and retreat scratched up the rocks like old vinyl records, and the thick tongues of pressing ice cut deep notches out of the rock. Near Somesville it nearly divided the island in two, creating the only natural fjord in the United States; farther "inland," the slowly flowing ice pushed forward and scooped out several more narrow, parallel valleys that would later be filled by rainwater to form Jordan Pond and Eagle Lake. Huge boulders were swept up and deposited by the ice in odd places, such as the tops of mountains (**Bubble Rock** is one).

When the glaciers finally retreated for the last time, tens of thousands of years ago, the water melting from the huge ice sheet covering North America swelled the level of the Atlantic high enough to submerge formerly free-flowing river valleys and give Mount Desert Island the distinctive, knuckled-fist shape we know it for today.

Onto the bones of this landscape came plants and then animals. After each **ice age,** conifers such as spruce and fir trees—alongside countless grasses and weeds—began to reform, decompose, and form soils. It was tough work: Acadia is a rocky, acidic place. Yet they persevered, and soon the spruces, firs, and hemlocks formed an impenetrable thicket covering the bedrock. Land **animals** came here, too, some of them now extinct from the island—the caribou, elk, eastern timber wolf, and sea mink among those extirpated by human presence. Many others survived, however, and there's plenty of wildlife here today; while the lynx and eastern cougar may no longer roam the woods, hills, and fields of Acadia, plenty of other creatures do.

Acadia's unique position—it is very near the warm Gulf Stream, yet possesses very cold waters; it is not far from the high, shallow undersea plateau

Rising from the Ashes

The park, though it appears to be fixed in time now, is actually in constant flux. Islanders got a lesson in nature's restorative powers in 1947, when a **huge forest fire** swept across the park and island, devastating most of it. In the ashes soon grew not more spruces and firs, but rather an entire new set of flowers, weeds, and trees better adapted to grow in bright, sunny, nutrient-poor meadows. Fireweeds, wildflowers, aspens, birch, oak, pine, and maple trees began to slowly fill in the denuded landscape and today help create the mixture of plants (and the fall foliage, and the deer, mice, and other animals that favor this mixture) in the park today. The spruces and firs may eventually take over again—but it will take generations to happen.

known as **Georges Bank**—has also brought an astonishing variety of marine life to its doorstep. Migrating whales make for a wonderful spectacle twice each year (and whale-watching tours out of Bar Harbor bring the lives of whales closer to the visitor). Seabirds make similar passages, lighting upon the rocks and lakes of the park coming and going. And the waters teem—though not as they once did—with fish large and small, lobsters, crabs, dolphins, and a great deal more (each creature with its particular habits, habitats, diets, life cycles, and seasonal migration patterns).

This is to say almost nothing of **Acadia's tide pools,** in that precarious zone where land and rock meet crashing ocean; a closer look at these pools reveals an ever-changing world of seaweed, snails, barnacles, darting water bugs, clams, shellfish, mud-burrowing worms, and other creatures. Interestingly, the type of life you'll find changes in well-marked "bands" as you get closer to water; rocks that are always submerged contain one mixture of seaweeds and marine organism, rocks that are exposed and then resubmerged each day by the tides contain another. Mostly dry surfaces of the shore rocks contain yet another mixture of living things. It's fascinating to note how each particular organism has found its niche, maintained it, and continues to live hardily and well—within its particular band. Move it up or down a foot, and it would perish.

The Flora

BALSAM FIR   The best-smelling tree in the park must be the mighty balsam fir, whose tips are harvested elsewhere to fabricate aromatic Christmas-tree wreaths. It's sometimes hard to tell a fir from a spruce or hemlock, though the balsam's flat, paddlelike needles (white underneath) are nearly unique—only a hemlock's are similar. Pull one off the twig to be sure; a fir's needle comes off clean, a hemlock's ragged. Still not sure you've got a fir tree on your hands? The long, glossy, almost purplish cones are absolutely distinctive.

Balsam Fir

RED, WHITE, AND PITCH PINE   The pines grow in Acadia's sandy soils and normally like some sunlight. **White pine** is the familiar "King's pine" prevalent throughout Maine; its trunk was prized for the masts of British ships of war, and countless huge pines were floated down Maine rivers by logger men. Sadly, very few virgin pine trees remain in Maine today. The white pine's extremely long, strong needles come five to a bunch. The **red pine,** not so common, can be distinguished by its pairs of needles and pitchy

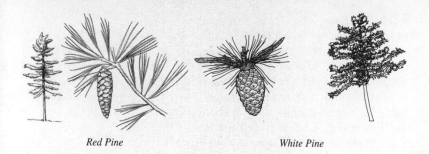

Red Pine   White Pine

trunk. The presence of a **pitch pine** indicates poor, acidic soils—this is one of the first trees to successfully rush in and take root in the wake of a fire. It can grow in the oddest places—along a cliff, on a lip of crumbling stone, in waste soil. The shorter, scrubby clumps of needles (arranged three to a group) don't look attractive but belie the tree's toughness.

RED AND SUGAR MAPLE   These two maple trees look vaguely alike when turning color in fall, but they're actually quite different—from the shapes of their leaves to the habitats they prefer. **Red maples** have skinny, gray trunks and like a swampy or wet area; often, several of the slim trunks grow together into a clump, and in fall the red maples' pointy leaves turn a brilliant scarlet color almost at once. **Sugar maples,** on the other hand, are stout-trunked trees with lovely, substantial leaves (marked with distinctive U-shaped notches), which autumn slowly changes to red and flame-orange. Sugar maples grow in or at the edges of mixed forests, often in combination with birch trees, oak trees, beech trees, hemlocks, and the like. Their sap, of course, can be collected and boiled down to make delicious maple syrup.

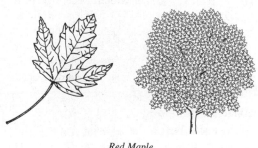

Red Maple

LOWBUSH BLUEBERRY   The lowbush blueberry, with its shrubby, tea-like leaves and hardy, thick twigging, lies low to exposed rocks on sunny hillsides or sometimes crops up in shady woods; most of the year, it's inconspicuous as anything, trailing harmlessly underfoot. Come late summer, however, it's suddenly the island's most popular plant—among bears as well as humans. The wild blueberries ripen slowly in the sun (look behind and beneath the leaves for the best bunches), and make for fine eating, pancake baking, and jam.

The Fauna
MAMMALS
Land Mammals

BEAVER   Reintroduced to Acadia in the 1920s (it had earlier nearly gone extinct from brisk world trade in beaver pelts), the beaver's lodge-building, stick-chewing, and hibernating habits are well known. You'll find it in streams, lakes, and ponds around Mount Desert Island.

Beaver

BLACK BEAR   Black bears do appear in Acadia, though in small numbers (still, you may want to keep a cover on that campfire food). The bears are mostly—emphasis on mostly—plant-eaters and docile. Though they'll eat just about anything, black bears prefer easily reached foods on the woodland floor such as berries, mushrooms, and nuts. They need them for a long winter hibernation that averages 6 months.

Black Bear

MOOSE   Nothing says Maine like a moose. The huge, skinny-legged, vegetarian moose is only sporadically seen on Mount Desert Island— it is an island, after all—but you may well run into one in the Schoodic Peninsula unit of the park (see Chapter 9, p. 240). For the most part, the moose far prefers the deep woods, lakes, ponds, and uninhabited areas of Maine's Great North Woods (see p. 33).

Moose

Marine Mammals

FINBACK WHALE   A seasonal visitor to Maine's waters twice a year when migrating between polar and equatorial waters, the finback is one of the biggest whales, and also one of the most collegial. It often travels in pairs or groups of a half-dozen or more (most whales are relatively solitary), though it does not travel close to shore or in shallow waters; you'll need a whale-watch boat to spot it. Find it by its rather triangular head and a fin that sweeps backward (like a dolphin's) rather than standing straight up like many other whales'.

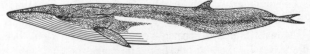

Finback Whale

HUMPBACK WHALE   Though this whale's Latin name roughly translates as "large-winged New England resident," the gentle, gigantic humpback actually isn't so often seen off the coast of Acadia. (That's mostly because they were easy targets in the heyday of whaling.) But if you do see it, you'll know it: It's huge, dark black, blows tremendous amounts of water when surfacing, and does some amazingly playful acrobatics above water. The males also sing haunting songs, sometimes for as long as 2 days at a time. The world population has shown signs of a rebound since protections went into place in the 1960s; there are maybe 12,000 individuals in the North Atlantic.

MINKE WHALE   The smallest (and most human-friendly) of the whales, the minke swims off Acadia's coast, usually moving in groups of two or three whales—but much larger groups collect in feeding areas and seasons. It has a unique habit of approaching and congregating around boats and ships, making this a whale you're quite likely to

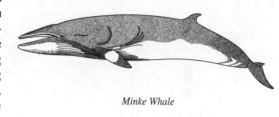

Minke Whale

see while on a whale-watching tour. The minke is dark gray on top; the throat has grooves; and each black flipper fin is marked with a conspicuous white band.

NORTH ATLANTIC RIGHT WHALE   If you see a North Atlantic right whale, you've really seen something: It's the most endangered of all the living whales—there are probably only a few hundred left—yet one has occasionally been seen off the coast of Acadia. Experts predict it will become extinct within a few more human generations, if not sooner. Huge and active as the humpback, the right is known for doing headstands (so to speak) underwater, poking its tail fins above. It can be

Northern Right Whale

spotted by its light color—often blue, brown, or even off-white—and the whitish calcium growths that often appear on its head.

PILOT WHALE   A small whale, the pilot is very rarely seen off Acadia, and very poorly understood. Its habits, world population, and diet are nearly unknown. It is

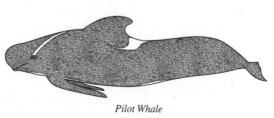

Pilot Whale

known to congregate in large groups, sometimes consisting of up to several hundred, and even to swim with other species of whale at sea. Nearly unique among the whales that pass Maine, it has teeth, and the roundish fin is swept back like a dolphin's or shark's. Sightings are possible and should be cherished.

HARBOR SEAL   Related to sea lions, the whiskered harbor seal is best seen by using one of the charter boat services that leaves from Bar Harbor and other local harbors. You can also sometimes see it basking in the sun or on the rocks of an offshore island. You'll easily recognize it: The seal's flippers have five claws, almost like a human hand; its neck is stocky and strong (as are its teeth); and then there are those whiskers and that fur.

BIRDS
Waterfowl

DUCKS   Between one and two dozen species of ducks and ducklike geese, brant, and teal seasonally visit the lakes, ponds, and tidal coves of Acadia every year, including—though hardly limited to—the **red-breasted merganser, common eider,** and the **bufflehead.** Mergansers, characterized by very white sides and very red bills (males) or reddish crests (females), occur year-round in the park but are more common in winter months. So is the eider, which inhabits offshore islands and coastal waters rather than Mount Desert Island's freshwater lakes; Maine is actually the southernmost tip of its breeding range—in winter, it forms huge rafts of birds. Males are marked with a

Common Eider

Red-Breasted Merganser

sharp black-and-white pattern. The chubby, squat bufflehead is also distinctively black and white, with a glossy green-and-purple head; it is entirely absent from the park in summer, but passes through in spring and fall, sometimes lingering for the winter. It flies much more quickly than one might imagine from its appearance.

GREAT BLUE HERON   Everyone recognizes a great blue at once by its prehistoric flapping wings, comb of feathers, and spindly legs. These magnificent hunters wade tidal rivers, fishing with lightning strikes beneath the surface, from May through around October. The smaller, stealthier green heron

Great Blue Heron

occurs less commonly, and occasional sightings of black-crowned and yellow-crowned night herons have also been recorded within the park's boundaries.

LOONS Two species of loon visit the island's lakes and tidal inlets, fishing for dinner. The **red-throated loon,** grayish with a red neck, is mostly a spring visitor and barely present at all in the heat of summer. The **common loon** is indeed more common—it can be distinguished by a black band around the neck, as well as black-and-white stripes and dots—and can be found in Acadia year-round, though it's most easily spotted in late spring and late fall. It gives the distinctive mournful, almost laughing cry for which the birds are famous. Both have been decimated by human environmental changes such as oil spills, acid rain, and airborne mercury.

Red-Throated Loon *Common Loon*

PLOVERS Plovers inhabit and breed in Acadia's muddy tidal flats, and their habitat is understandably precarious; a single human step could crush an entire generation of eggs. Only two species of plover visit the park, and they're here in significant numbers for only a relatively short time. The **black-bellied plover**—marked with a snowy black-and-white pattern—arrives in May, breeds in August and September, and is gone by Thanksgiving. The **semipalmated plover,** with its quite different brownish body and white breast, has a similar life cycle.

Semipalmated Plover

Black-Bellied Plover

SEAGULLS No bird is so closely associated with Maine as the seagull. But, in fact, there's more than one kind of gull here; three or four distinct gulls are commonly found here year-round, a few more visit seasonally, and a few more pop up occasionally. Most common is the grayish **herring gull,** which is also the gull least afraid of humans. It's found in prevalence every month of

Herring Gull

Bonaparte's Gull

the year. The aggressive **great black-backed gull** is similarly common, and is nearly all white (except for that black back and wings); it will even eat the eggs of another gull, but in general avoids humans. Less common are the glaucous, **ring-billed gull,** and even the **laughing and**

Black-Backed Gull

Bonaparte's gulls (in summer only), not to mention the related **black-legged kittiwake.** Each has a distinctive look; consult a bird guide if you're interested in telling them apart.

STORM PETRELS The tiny storm petrel is a fascinating creature. These plucky little birds fly astonishing distances in winter, eating insects on the wing, only to return to Acadia each spring like clockwork, usually in May. They spend an amazing 4 months in the nest incubating, hatching, and tending to their single, white eggs. **Wilson's storm petrel** is here for a shorter time than the **Leach's storm petrel,** which restricts its visits and nests solely to offshore rocks and islands. Both breed in the height of summer, then pack up and head south again by fall.

Wilson's Storm Petrel

Land Birds
BALD EAGLE Yes, they're here—year-round—and even breed in Acadia, though they're difficult to find and hardly conspicuous. (Their endangered status means you shouldn't really try to seek them out.) The bald eagle's black body, white head, and yellow bill make it almost impossible to confuse with any other bird. It was nearly wiped out by the 1970s, mainly due to environmental poisons such as DDT-based pesticides, which caused female eagles

Bald Eagle

to lay eggs that were too weak to sustain growing baby chicks. However, the bird has made an impressive comeback.

COMMON RAVEN The park holds jays and crows aplenty, but the raven is a breed apart—tougher, more reclusive, more ragged, more interesting. Look (or listen) for it on cliff tops, mountains, and in deep woods.

SONGBIRDS There are literally dozens of species of songbirds coming to roost in Acadia's open fields, forests, and dead snags—even in the rafters and bird boxes of houses. They are not so common on this rocky, shady island as in Maine's suburbia (Greater Portland, for instance) or in the farmlands of central and western Maine, but they are here. One thing is for certain: Songbirds love human company, thus look for them near the settled areas. The park hosts perhaps 15 or more distinct types of chirpy little **warblers,** each with unique and often liquid songs; a half-dozen **thrushes** occurring in significant numbers; winter **wrens, swallows, sparrows, vireos, finches, creepers,** and **thrashers;** the whimsical black-capped **chickadee;** and occasional (and lovely) sightings of **bluebirds, cardinals,** and **tanagers,** among many other species.

Eastern Bluebird   *Common Raven*

Black-Capped Chickadee

BAR HARBOR ★

Bar Harbor provides most of the meals and beds to travelers coming to Mount Desert Island, and it has done so since the grand resort era of the late 19th century, when wealthy vacationers first discovered this region. Sprawling hotels and boardinghouses once cluttered the shores and hillsides here, as a newly affluent middle class arrived in droves by steamboat and rail car. The tourist business continued to boom through the early 1900s, then all but collapsed when the Depression and the growing popularity of car travel doomed the era of steamship travel and extended vacations. Bar Harbor was dealt another blow in 1947, when an accidental fire spread rapidly and leveled many of the opulent cottages (see box p. 199). Some 17,000 acres burned in all, though downtown Bar Harbor and some in-town mansions on the oceanfront were spared.

In the last few decades, however, Bar Harbor has bounced back, revived and rediscovered by visitors and entrepreneurs alike. Some see the place as a tacky place of T-shirt vendors, ice-cream cones, and souvenir shops, plus crowds spilling off the sidewalks into the street and appalling traffic. That is all true. Yet the town's history, distinguished architecture, tight-knit community of year-rounders, and beautiful location on Frenchman Bay still make it a desirable base for exploring the island—and it has by far the island's best selection of lodging, meals, supplies, and services. (If you want to shop, fine-dine, or go out at night, you pretty much *have* to stay here.) Otherwise, if quiet is what you're seeking, consider bunking elsewhere on the island (see p. 221 below).

Essentials

ARRIVING

Bar Harbor is on Route 3, about 10 miles southeast of the causeway leading onto Mount Desert Island. For plane and bus access, see p. 186.

VISITOR INFORMATION

The **Bar Harbor Chamber of Commerce** (www.barharborinfo.com; ℂ **800/345-4617**) stockpiles a huge arsenal of information about local attractions, both at its offices on 2 Cottage Street (downtown, 2 blocks from the pier) and in a welcome center on Route 3 in Trenton, just before the causeway onto the island. Write, call, or e-mail in advance for a directory of area lodging and attractions. The chamber's website is full of information and helpful links, too.

Where to Stay in Bar Harbor

Bar Harbor is the bedroom community for Mount Desert Island, with hundreds of hotel, motel, and inn rooms. They're invariably filled during the busy days of summer, and even the most basic of rooms can be quite expensive in July and August. It's essential to reserve as early in advance as possible. Even the Airbnb rentals fill up well ahead of time—there are a ton of these, but MDI-dwellers know what their outbuilding/spare room is worth, so you'll find few steals.

Bar Harbor can be an expensive town, but family-owned motels have provided simple, no-frills, cheaper alternatives for decades—some rooms still remain under $100 in peak season, which is amazing. Most are on the north end of town, along or near Route 3, and almost all are open seasonally, from May through September or October. Choices in this price range include the conveniently located **Villager Motel,** 207 Main Street (www.barharbor villager.com; ℂ **888/383-3211** or 207/288-3211) and the **Highbrook Motel,** 94 Eden Street (www.highbrookmotel.com; ℂ **800/338-9688** or 207/288-3591). About 4 miles west of Bar Harbor on Route 3 is **Hanscom's Motel and Cottages** (www.hanscomsmotel.com; ℂ **207/288-3744**), an old-fashioned motor court with a dozen units (some of them with two bedrooms) that have been well maintained. Its rates range from $92 to $110 in summer, and go as low as $64 per night in the off season.

Bar Harbor

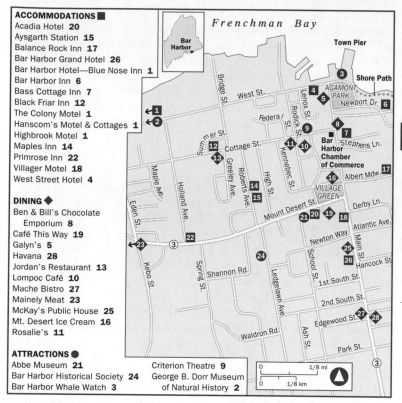

ACCOMMODATIONS ■
Acadia Hotel **20**
Aysgarth Station **15**
Balance Rock Inn **17**
Bar Harbor Grand Hotel **26**
Bar Harbor Hotel—Blue Nose Inn **1**
Bar Harbor Inn **6**
Bass Cottage Inn **7**
Black Friar Inn **12**
The Colony Motel **1**
Hanscom's Motel & Cottages **1**
Highbrook Motel **1**
Maples Inn **14**
Primrose Inn **22**
Villager Motel **18**
West Street Hotel **4**

DINING ◆
Ben & Bill's Chocolate
  Emporium **8**
Café This Way **19**
Galyn's **5**
Havana **28**
Jordan's Restaurant **13**
Lompoc Café **10**
Mache Bistro **27**
Mainely Meat **23**
McKay's Public House **25**
Mt. Desert Ice Cream **16**
Rosalie's **11**

ATTRACTIONS ●
Abbe Museum **21**
Bar Harbor Historical Society **24**
Bar Harbor Whale Watch **3**
Criterion Theatre **9**
George B. Dorr Museum
  of Natural History **2**

EXPENSIVE

Balance Rock Inn ★★★   Tucked down a quiet side alley just off Bar
Harbor's main drag, the Balance Rock (built in 1903 for a Scottish railroad
magnate) reaches for and achieves a gracefully upscale Long Island beach
house feel. The entrance alone is nearly worth the steep rack rates: You enter
a sitting room, which looks out onto the sort of azure outdoor swimming pool
you'd expect to find in a Tuscan villa, and just beyond looms the Atlantic.
Rooms are as elegant as any on the island, with a variety of layouts, some with
sea views; some have whirlpools and saunas, while the penthouse suite adds
a full kitchen. The comfortable king-size beds are adjustable using controls
and have been fitted with feather beds and quality linens. A poolside bar,
piano room, gracious staff, and fragrant flowers lining the driveway complete
the romance of the experience.

21 Albert Meadow. www.balancerockinn.com. ℂ **800/753-0494** or 207/288-2610. 27
units. July–early Sept $275–$625 double, $575–$725 suite; mid-May–June and mid-
Sept–late Oct $195–$545 double, $365–$635 suite. Rates include full breakfast. Closed

mid-Oct–early May. Some rooms accommodate pets ($40 per pet per night). Children 10 years and older welcome. Packages available. **Amenities:** Restaurant; poolside bar; fitness room; fire pit; heated outdoor pool; fitness center; free Wi-Fi.

Bar Harbor Hotel—Bluenose Inn ★ This resort-style complex—situated in two buildings—offers stunning views of the surrounding terrain. Facilities here are modern: Expect spacious carpeted rooms with huge bathrooms, small refrigerators, and balconies, as well as a good fitness center, indoor and outdoor pools, and an adjacent hilltop dining room with a bang-up view of town and Frenchman Bay. The two buildings are slightly different in character, but in either case upper-floor rooms with sea views are worth the extra cost, especially if the weather is good. The style is Euro-countryside lavish, with floral bedspreads and upholstery, cabriole-leg chairs, and the like. Staff is professional and friendly.

90 Eden St. www.barharborhotel.com. ℂ **800/445-4077** or 207/288-3348. 98 units. Mid-June–mid-Oct $159–$459 double; spring and late fall $119–$329 double. Packages available. Closed Nov–Apr. **Amenities:** Restaurant; fitness center; Jacuzzi; indoor pool; outdoor pool; spa; free Wi-Fi.

The Bar Harbor Inn ★ The Bar Harbor Inn, just off Agamont Park, nicely mixes traditional style with contemporary touches. On shady grounds just a moment's stroll from Bar Harbor's downtown, this property offers both convenience and charm. The shingled main inn, which dates from the turn of the 19th century, has a settled, old-money feel with its semicircular dining room and a buttoned-down lobby. Guest rooms, located in the main building and two outbuildings, are much more contemporary: Units in the Oceanfront Lodge and main inn both offer spectacular bay views, and many have private balconies. The third wing, the Newport Building, lacks views and its furnishings are a little dated, but you can save a little on rates here. Guests have access to a spa with Vichy showers, aromatherapy, heated-stone treatments, and facial treatments, while the somewhat formal **Reading Room** dining room serves resort meals with the best dining-room views in town.

1 Newport Dr. www.barharborinn.com. ℂ **800/248-3351** or 207/288-3351. 153 units. Mid-May–mid-Oct $255–$399 double; mid-Mar–mid-May and mid-Oct–Nov $119–$399 double. Rates include continental breakfast. 2-night minimum stay mid-June–Aug weekends. Packages available. Closed Dec–mid-Mar. **Amenities:** Dining room; lounge; fitness room; Jacuzzi; heated outdoor pool; room service; spa; free Wi-Fi.

Bass Cottage Inn ★★ This tucked-away inn gets very high marks for friendliness, service, and proximity to the water. Rooms are decked out in cast-iron beds, silk canopies, love seats, armoires, writing desks, and the like. The gentle color schemes range from ivory to sky blue to taupe, reflecting the soft light of the island, and many are decorated with nautical prints; several have Jacuzzis and/or views, as well (and the entire-top-floor suite has both). This is just a 2-minute walk from downtown, yet breakfast feasts are worthy of a gourmet restaurant: They might serve cornmeal griddle cakes with blueberries, a lobster omelet, French toast with vanilla sauce, cranberry-walnut French toast, scrambled eggs with smoked salmon, or huevos rancheros. Innkeepers Teri and Jeff Anderholm are unfailingly helpful and generous with extra flourishes such as a piano, a DVD library for anytime use, and a 24-hour guest pantry stocked with snacks. Very nice place.

14 The Field. www.basscottage.com. © **866/782-9224** or 207/288-1234. 10 units. Mid-June–early Nov $260–$400 double and suite; Mid-May–mid-June and mid-Oct–late Oct $220–$350. Rates include full breakfast. 2-night stay minimum, 3-day minimum stay holiday weekends. Closed Nov–mid-May. Children age 12 and over welcome. Packages available. **Amenities:** Wine service; free Wi-Fi.

West Street Hotel ★★   Opened in 2012, the West Street already feels as if it's always loomed over the water on the northern edge of town. Maybe that's because it's so conspicuous, its pale multicolored facade stretching the better part of a block. The theme is nautical luxe, the rooms are fairly snug, but well appointed with mahogany furnishings and leather chairs. The real genius of the place is that every room has a small private balcony with a view of the harbor—it's a terrific thing to wake up to, and you'll feel well above the bustle of the Bar Harbor street. (This is even more true when you're splashing in the rooftop pool.) Guests have access to amenities just down the road at the Bar Harbor Club sister property—another pool, tennis courts, a fitness center, and spa.

50 West St. www.theweststreethotel.com. © **877/905-4498** or 207/288-0825. 85 units. July–mid-Oct $339–$449 double, $559–$959 suite; mid-May–June and mid-Sept–late Oct $259–$399 double, $419–$635 suite. 2-night minimum stay July–Aug weekends. Closed Nov–early May. Packages available. **Amenities:** Two pools (one rooftop); restaurants; bar; tennis courts; marina; a fitness center; spa; free Wi-Fi.

MODERATE

Acadia Hotel ★★   The simple, comfy Acadia Hotel is nicely situated overlooking Bar Harbor's village green, easily accessible to in-town activities and the free shuttle buses running around the island. A handsome and none-too-large home dating from the late 19th century, the hotel gave most of its rooms the remod treatment in 2014, and the place feels fresh, with patterned upholstery, flat-screens and refrigerators in every room, new paint jobs, and a stylish new suite with a picture window looking out at Cadillac Mountain. Some rooms are slightly underground, a few steps down, but they get plenty of light. Debuting in 2017 is a new lobby and 8 more guest rooms in a brand-new building next door (still a hole in the ground when I visited). The rates have inched up from a few years back, but all things considered this is still arguably the best value in a pricey town (particularly in winter, as it's the rare MDI hotel open year-round).

20 Mt. Desert St. www.acadiahotel.com. © **888/876-2463** or 207/288-5721. 16 units. June–Labor Day $209–$349 double, $409–$429 suite; May and Columbus Day–Nov $119–$219 double, $309–$369 suite; Dec–Apr $99–$149 double, $179–$249 suite. Packages available. **Amenities:** Free bikes; outdoor hot tub; free Wi-Fi.

Bar Harbor Grand Hotel ★ Filling a gap between quaint (often expensive) inns and B&Bs and the island's family-owned motels, hotels, and cottages, this large hotel's blocky, two-tower design faithfully copies the style of the Rodick House, a now-defunct 19th-century hotel in Bar Harbor that could once boast of being Maine's largest hotel. The Grand, however, offers bigger rooms and bathrooms and, of course, all-modern fixtures. Rooms and suites are decked out in the same floral bedspreads and curtains you'd expect in any upscale business hotel, but the access to downtown Bar Harbor and the nearby ocean are big pluses. Amenities include a guest laundry, gift shop, a heated outdoor pool; not surprisingly, they're booking some tour groups in here. Expect efficiency and comfort, rather than local character.

269 Main St. www.barharborgrand.com. ✆ **888/766-2529** or 207/288-5226. 71 units. June–mid-Oct $165–$245 double; Apr–May and mid-Oct–mid-Nov $99–$155 double. Rates include continental breakfast. Packages available. Closed late Nov–Mar. **Amenities:** Fitness room; Jacuzzi; laundry; heated outdoor pool; free Wi-Fi.

Black Friar Inn ★ The seasonal Black Friar, tucked on a Bar Harbor side street overlooking a parking lot, is a yellow-shingled home with quirky pediments and an eccentric air. A former owner "collected" interiors and installed them throughout the home, including a replica of a pub in London with elaborate carved-wood paneling (it's now a common room); stamped-tin walls (look in the breakfast room); and a doctor's office (now one of the guest rooms). Rooms are carpeted and furnished in a mix of antiques; most are smallish, though the big suite features nice paneling, a sofa, wingback chair, private porch, and gas fireplace. Other rooms sport such touches as rose-tinted stained-glass windows, brass beds, and a sort of mini spiral staircase. The least expensive units are the two garret rooms on the third floor. The inn, which is also home to a small restaurant and pub, generally asks a 2-night minimum stay.

10 Summer St. www.blackfriarinn.com. ✆ **207/288-5081.** 6 units. July–mid-Oct $150–$195 double; May–June $70–$130 double. Rates include full breakfast. 2-night minimum required July–Oct. Closed late Oct–Apr. Children 12 and older welcome. **Amenities:** Restaurant; pub; free Wi-Fi..

Maples Inn ★ A modest home tucked away on a side street in a row of Bar Harbor B&Bs, the Maples is an easy walk downtown to a movie or dinner. The current innkeepers, who took over the place in 2015, are an outdoorsy young couple, and the inn tends to attract other adventuresome types; find them swapping stories about their day's exploits on the handsome front porch or lingering over breakfast to compare notes about hiking trails. Rooms are small to medium-size, but you're not likely to feel cramped—they have private bathrooms, wicker furniture, pencil poster beds, and handsome antique wooden writing desks. The two-room White Birch has a fireplace, a lacy canopy bed with a down comforter, and a bright blue-and-white decor; Red Oak has a private deck with rocking chairs. Gourmet breakfasts are served in a sunny dining room or taken on the porch; Chef Matt is big on local ingredients, even smoking his own trout.

16 Roberts Ave. www.maplesinn.com. © **207/288-3443.** 6 units. Mid-June–mid-Oct $159–$229 double and suite; May–mid-June and mid-Oct–late Oct $119–$189 double and suite. Rates include full breakfast. 2-night minimum stay in summer, 3-night minimum on holiday weekends. Closed Nov–Apr. Not appropriate for children under 12. **Amenities**: Afternoon snacks, free Wi-Fi.

Primrose Inn ★★ This handsome Victorian stick–style inn, originally built in 1878, is one of the most notable properties on the "mansion row" along Mount Desert Street. Its distinctive architecture has been preserved, and was perhaps even enhanced during a 1987 addition of rooms, private bathrooms, and balconies. This inn is comfortable, furnished with "functional antiques" and modern reproductions; many of the spacious rooms have a floral theme, thick carpets, marble vanities, canopy beds, sitting or reading rooms, and handsome day beds, wingback chairs or other furniture. (Two newer "premium" rooms also have private entrances and are stocked with king beds, gas fireplaces, and such other amenities as a porch or whirlpool tub.) Breakfasts of eggs Florentine, Belgian waffles, blueberry pancakes, and the like are a hit (and there's a fridge full of free soft drinks whenever you're parched).

73 Mount Desert St. www.primroseinn.com. © **877/846-3424** or 207/288-4031. 13 units. Mid-June–Labor Day $208–$304 double; mid-May–early June and Sept–Oct $155–$250 double. Rates include full breakfast and afternoon tea. 2-night minimum stay summer and fall. Closed late Oct–mid-May. **Amenities:** Library, free Wi-Fi.

INEXPENSIVE

Aysgarth Station ★ One of the better B&B values around Bar Harbor, little Aysgarth Station has a British countryside theme, a nod to the Yorkshire roots of proprietress Jane Holland, who runs the place with her partner, Steve Cornell, and cooks outstanding breakfasts big on farmers market ingredients. The snug living room is a cozy spot to curl up on cooler evenings (and in winter, when the B&B stays open), maybe with Jane and Steve's enormous, friendly cat. Don't worry, he (the cat) isn't allowed up into the rooms, which are mostly cozy and tastefully appointed with antique furnishings. Skipton has a regal feel, with heavy drapes, an iron-framed bed, and a Jacuzzi tub. Treefalls, on the top floor, has another Jacuzzi, an inset gas fireplace, a sitting area, and a snug sun deck with views of the MDI hills. There's nothing terribly opulent about Aysgarth, but the price is right and Steve and Jane take care of their guests.

20 Roberts Ave. www.aysgarth.com. © **207/288-9655.** 6 units. June–Oct $125–$175 double; Dec–May $85–$105. Closed Nov. Rates include full breakfast. Not recommended for children 14 and under. **Amenities:** Free Wi-Fi.

The Colony ★ Owned by the same family since 1950, Colony is a throwback motor court consisting of a handful of motel rooms plus a battery of housekeeping cottages arrayed in an oval around a longish green. It's best appreciated by those with a taste for retro motels; others might decide to look for something fancier. But the price is low, and 2016 saw a round of thorough renovations. Rest assured, the rooms are still furnished in a simple grandma's house style that won't win any awards for decor—and the plumbing may rattle a bit—but most every room and cabin is fresh and clean, with flatscreen TVs in each. There are two classes of motel room, the difference being better views and bigger beds (queens and kings instead of paired doubles). The complex is just across Route 3 from a cobblestone beach; it's about a 10-minute drive into Bar Harbor. Coolest thing about that beach? Every Saturday afternoon, The Colony pays a kilted bagpiper to stand on the rocky shoreline and blast a few tunes.

20 Rte. 3, Hulls Cove. www.colonyathullscove.com. © **207/288-3383**. 55 units. $75–$135 cottage. Closed Nov–Apr. Some cottages accommodate pets. **Amenities:** Heated outdoor pool.

Where to Eat in Bar Harbor

In addition to the selections listed below, you can get good local pizza at **Rosalie's** on Cottage Street (www.rosaliespizza.com; © **207/288-5666**); eat upstairs or down, or take out a pie to go. There's also a solid natural foods market, **A&B Naturals** (© **207/288-8480**; www.aandbnaturals.com) at 101 Cottage Street, which has prepared foods and a good little café inside.

If you're craving something sweet, head over to **Ben & Bill's Chocolate Emporium,** 66 Main Street (www.benandbills.com; © **800/806-3281** or 207/288-3281), for a big ice-cream cone. In the evenings, you may have to join a line spilling out the door. Visitors are often tempted to try the place's novelty ice cream, lobster ice cream. Like butter? Then be bold and give it a shot.

Or if you enjoy experimenting with *other* ice cream flavors, **Mt. Desert Island Ice Cream** ★, 7 Firefly Lane (www.mdiic.com; © **207/460-5515**), right beside the tourist office, is the place for you. It gives all the appearances of being just another ho-hum scoop shop of the vanilla-chocolate-strawberry ilk, but there's little conventional about a place featuring gourmet concoctions spiked with tarragon, chili, and wasabi, among other flavors. (President Barack Obama sampled a coconut cone during a surprise 2010 visit.) There's another branch at 325 Main Street (and, for your trip home, one on Exchange Street in Portland). Both locations serve coffee, tea, and yerba maté, as well.

EXPENSIVE

Havana ★★★ LATINO/FUSION Havana excited foodies all over Maine when it opened in 1999 in what was then a town of fried fish and baked haddock. The spare decor in an old storefront is as classy as anything you'll find in Boston, and the menu can hold its own against the big city, too—I've had a meal at Havana that I sometimes pause and reflect on, years later. Chef/

owner Michael Boland's menu is inspired by Latino fare, which he melds nicely with New American ideas. Appetizers are deceptively simple: appetizers of crab cakes with avocado mayo and corn salsa, duck empanadas, mussels with chorizo and sofrito. Entrees could include choices as adventurous as a lobster poached in butter served with a saffrony potato empanada; paella made with local lobsters and mussels; breast of duck with a blueberry glaze; chiles rellenos stuffed with amazing barbecue pork; or lamb shanks braised with chile and pineapple. Then desserts skew simple again (see the pattern?): apple empanadas, caramel and cream, churros with caraway chocolate ice cream. The Obamas dined here the last time they swung through Bar Harbor; I bet the President and First Lady stop to think about their meal from time to time, too.

318 Main St., Bar Harbor. www.havanamaine.com. ⌒ **207/288-2822.** Main courses $21–$35. Daily 5–10pm. Winter/spring hours generally Tues–Sat 4:30–9:30pm. Some brief seasonal closures—call ahead. Reservations recommended.

Mache Bistro ★★ NEW AMERICAN   An old Bar Harbor standby that found its way into new digs in 2014, little Mâche Bistro has developed a devoted local following The old space was ticky-tack enough that it gave the place a sort of cult appeal, masking the kitchen's sophistication; the new one is sophisticated without being any less welcoming. Like its neighbor, McKay's, a couple blocks away (see below), the new Mâche is a former residential home, and the handsome bar and copper and dark wood finishes don't make the place any less approachable than when it had plywood floors. Chef Kyle Yarborough's menu changes monthly; small plates could include crispy pork belly with fig pancetta, stuffed peppers with lobster goat cheese, or a wine-poached pear with Maytag blue cheese. Main courses, which have a little Southern flair, run to smoked duck confit, slow-roasted pork with chorizo and vegetables, grilled hanger steak with a blue cheese butter, or scallops with charred onion and caper relish.

321 Main St., Bar Harbor. www.machebistro.com. ⌒ **207/288-0447.** Small plates $13–$15; main courses $18–$32. Tues–Sun 5:30–9pm. Closed late Oct–early May. Reservations recommended.

McKay's Public House ★★ CLASSIC AMERICAN   If there were no other reason to like McKay's, the fact that it's open year-round would speak well for it. But there are plenty of other reasons, beginning with the fact that it's true to its name—this is a genuine public gathering place, and one of those spots in Bar Harbor where the line between locals and tourists pretty well dissolves. Part of that homey feel might come from the fact that it's literally an old Victorian home, with the fireplaces and wainscoting and shady porch that some family likely enjoyed back in the day. The atmosphere is somewhere between drinks-after-work and date night, the menu full of upscale pub food like a terrific lamb burger and steak frites, along with nicely trimmed rib-eyes and chops and some standby pastas. Get there early to snag a table on the beautifully landscaped patio—good Main Street people-watching from out there.

231 Main St., Bar Harbor. www.mckayspublichouse.com. (℡) **207/288-2002**. Main courses $13–$30. Daily 4:30–9:30pm. Closed Nov. Reservations recommended during peak season.

MODERATE

Cafe This Way ★★ ECLECTIC   Cafe This Way is the kind of place where they know how to do wonderful Asian and Mediterranean things with simple ingredients. It has the feel of a hip coffeehouse, yet it's much more airy and creative than that. Bookshelves line one wall, and there's a small bar tucked into a nook; oddly, they serve breakfast and dinner but no lunch. Breakfasts are excellent though mildly sinful—it's more like brunch. Go for the burritos, corned beef hash with eggs, a build-your-own benedict, or the calorific Café Monte Cristo: a French toast sandwich stuffed with fried eggs, ham, and cheddar cheese served with fries and syrup. Yikes. Dinners are equally appetizing, with tasty starters that might run to fingerling poutine with tomato-chile jam, grilled chunks of Cyprus cheese, or lobster spring rolls. The main-course offerings of the night could include anything from lobster cooked in sherry cream or stewed in spinach and Gruyere cheese to sea scallops in vinaigrette; grilled lamb and steaks; coconut Thai mussels; or tikka masala with local veggies. There's always a tasty vegetarian option, as well. Talk about eclectic.

14½ Mount Desert St., Bar Harbor. www.cafethisway.com. (℡) **207/288-4483.** Breakfast items $8–$12, dinner entrees $19–$29. Mid-Apr–Oct, Mon–Sat 7–11:30am; Sun 8am–1pm; dinner daily 5:30–9:30pm. Dinner reservations recommended.

Galyn's ★★ SEAFOOD   Normally I avoid midpriced bistros in tourist towns, because they're generally all pretty similar and almost never as special as their precious signs proclaim. But charming, unassuming Galyn's is the exception; Galyn's gets it right. From perfectly blackened and grilled Cajun shrimp, hand-cut steaks, and daily fish specials to seafood stews and penne tossed with oil, garlic, bits of feta, and all the right vegetables, everything's on point here. Finish with real Indian pudding (worth trying, and very hard to find, despite being a classic New England heritage dish) or the cappuccino sundae served in a cappuccino glass, which packs two helpful shots of espresso to fuel your sightseeing. There are nice dining rooms both upstairs and down, with art on the walls, but try to snag one of the tables out on the little street-side deck if you can: All face Agamont Park and stunning bay views beyond.

17 Main St., Bar Harbor. www.galynsbarharbor.com. (℡) **207/288-9706.** Lunch entrees $9–$19, dinner $12–$35. Daily 11:30am–10pm. Closed Dec–March. Reservations recommended.

Lompoc Café ★ AMERICAN/ECLECTIC   The Lompoc Cafe has a well-worn, neighborhood-bar feel to it—waiters and other workers from around Bar Harbor congregate here after-hours. The cafe consists of three sections: the original bar, a tidy beer garden just outside (try your hand at bocce), and

PACKING A picnic IN BAR HARBOR

Even in downtown Bar Harbor, you can have a nice picnic experience simply by settling onto a bench on the **Village Green**—that's the green, rectangular space tucked behind and between Mount Desert and Kennebec streets. People-watching abounds, and art shows and festivals sometimes come to the green. Closer to the water, at the tip of the land (at the end of West and Main streets), the pocket **Agamont Park** is superlative for its picnic spot and a view of boats and islands. There's also the quiet campus of earthy **College of the Atlantic**, back on Route 3; they surely won't mind if you plunk down a basket and graze. The great natural-foods store **A&B Naturals**, at 100 Cottage Street (www.aandbnaturals.com; ✆ **207/288-8480**), is your best bet for prepared foods, drinks, and healthy snacks. It's open Mondays through Saturdays from 8:30 to 7pm, Sundays 10am–6pm.

a small and open barnlike structure at the garden's edge to handle the overflow. Most of the beers are local (ask for a sample before ordering a full glass of blueberry ale). Bar menus are normally yawn-inducing, but this one has some surprises—terrific mussels in broth, respectable shrimp and grits, a pho-like Vietnamese noodle bowl. There's also quite a little wine list, and some house cocktails like the lemony "Blonde with an Attitude." The outdoor tables are fun, and live music acts often play here.

36 Rodick St., Bar Harbor. www.lompoccafe.com. ✆ **207/288-9392.** Sandwiches and entrees $11–$21. Daily 11:30am–1am. Closed late Oct–mid-May. No reservations.

INEXPENSIVE

Jordan's Restaurant ★ DINER   This unpretentious breakfast-and-lunch joint has been dishing up filling fare since 1976, and offers a glimpse of the old Bar Harbor. It's a popular haunt of local working folks and retirees, but staff are also friendly to tourists. Diners can settle into a pine booth or at a laminated table and order off the placemat menu, choosing from basic fare such as grilled cheese sandwiches with tomato or slim burgers. The soups and chowders are all homemade, and there are some crab dishes (the only lobster's in an omelette, on a salad, or on a roll—no shore dinner here). But breakfast is the star, with a broad selection of three-egg omelets, muffins, and pancakes made with plenty of those great wild Maine blueberries (best when they're in season). With its atmosphere of "seniors at coffee klatch" and its rock-bottom prices, this is *not* a gourmet experience, but fans of big breakfasts, Americana-style cuisine, and classic diners will enjoy it.

80 Cottage St., Bar Harbor. ✆ **207/288-3586.** Breakfast and lunch items $5–$13. Daily 5am–2pm. Closed late Nov–Mar.

Mainely Meat ★ BARBECUE/BREWPUB   West of Bar Harbor proper, in the village of Town Hill, Mainely Meat is a rough-and-tumble little barbecue shack that happens to be wedded to the taproom of Atlantic Brewing Company, one of the state's oldest craft brewers. Pitmaster Paul Douglas

---

Parking in Bar Harbor

If parking spaces are scarce downtown, head to the end of Albert Meadow (a side street across from the Village Green). At the end of the road is a small waterfront park with free parking, great views of the bay, and foot access to Shore Path. It's not well marked or publicized, so you can often find a place to park when much of the rest of town is filled up.

---

smokes up pork, chicken, ribs, and more over various Maine hardwoods in an old water tank repurposed as a smoker. You know you're at a good barbecue spot when you can get an appetizer of ribs before your entrée plate full of more meat. Needless to say, there's craft beer on draft (and Atlantic brews good sodas, too, for teetotalers). The dining room's all done up in biker paraphernalia, although most of the seating is outside, through a set of big bay doors that give the whole place an open-air feel.

15 Knox Rd., Town Hill. www.atlanticbrewing.com/mainly-meat-bbq.com. © **207/288-9200.** Sandwiches & BBQ plates $8–$20. Daily 11:30am–8pm. Closed mid-Oct–mid-May.

Exploring Bar Harbor

The best water views in town are from the foot of Main Street at grassy **Agamont Park** ★★, which overlooks the town pier and Frenchman Bay. From here, stroll past The Bar Harbor Inn on the **Shore Path** ★★, a wide, winding trail that follows the shoreline for half a mile along a public right of way. The pathway also passes in front of many elegant summer homes (some converted into inns), offering a superb vantage point from which to view the area's architecture.

Don't forget to spend an hour or two in the central **Village Green** ★, either. Bar Harbor's central park—it's at the junction of Main Street and Mount Desert Street—is a wonderful place to while away an hour or two. You might see anything from protests to marriage proposals to acoustic songwriters to kids goofing off after school, plus summer tourists snapping photos and licking ice cream cones. There's sometimes music in the bandstand, and this is the pickup point for the free **Island Explorer buses** that crisscross the entire island.

One of downtown's less obvious attractions is the **Criterion Theatre,** 35 Cottage Street (www.criteriontheatre.org; © **207/288-3441**), a movie house built in 1932 in a classic Art Deco style; so far it has avoided the degradation of multiplexification. The 900-seat theater shows first-run movies in summer and is worth the price of admission for the fantastic, if somewhat faded, interiors. As once was the case at most movie palaces, it still costs extra to sit in the more exclusive loges upstairs. Check the website or the marquee for occasional live concerts, theater, and dance events, too.

Abbe Museum ★★ MUSEUM   Opened in 2001 as an in-town extension of the smaller, simpler museum at the Sieur de Monts spring in the national park (see p. 193), the Abbe Museum showcases a top-rate collection of Native American artifacts. It's Maine's only Smithsonian affiliate and one of the best museums in the state. A new core exhibit in 2016 shows off the museum's collection of Wabanaki artifacts and contemporary art, organized around a sculpted, two-story ash tree; it incorporates interactive elements of oral history and storytelling. Temporary exhibits might focus on anything from (impressive) Wabanaki basketmaking to student art from Maine's tribes.

26 Mount Desert St., Bar Harbor. www.abbemuseum.org. © **207/288-3519.** $8 adults, $4 children 6–15, children under 6 free. May–Oct daily 10am–5pm; rest of year Thurs–Sat 10am–5pm.

Bar Harbor Historical Society ★ MUSEUM   Around the corner from the Abbe Museum (see above), the society moved into this handsome 1918 former convent in 1997, where it showcases artifacts of life in the old days—dishware and photos from those grand old hotels that once dotted the town, exhibits on the noted landscape architect Beatrix Farrand, and so forth. Scrapbooks document the devastating 1947 fire, too.

33 Ledgelawn Ave., Bar Harbor. www.barharborhistorical.org. © **207/288-0000** or 288-3807. Admission free. Mid-June–Oct Mon–Fri 1–4pm. Off-season, entrance by appointment only.

George B. Dorr Museum of Natural History ★ MUSEUM   At the northern edge of town on Route 3, this museum is on the campus of the **College of the Atlantic** (www.coa.edu; © 207/288-5015), a school founded in 1969 with a strong emphasis on environmental education. The museum occupies the national park's original HQ (who knew?), and features exhibits that focus on interactions among island residents, from the two-legged to the four-legged, finny, and furry. Check the museum's summer program: in summer, you just might stumble across a nature walk, art project, or scavenger hunt. At the very least, swing by to see the 13-foot, 1,800-pound skull of a fin whale that sits outside, a campus landmark.

105 Eden St., Bar Harbor. www.coa.edu/dorr-museum. © **207/288-5395.** Admission by donation. Mid-June–Thanksgiving, Tues–Sat 10am–5pm; rest of year, open by appointment only.

On the Water

Bar Harbor is a base for several ocean endeavors, including whale-watching tours. Operators offer excursions in search of humpbacks, finbacks, minkes, and the infrequently seen endangered right whale. The best in the area is the **Bar Harbor Whale Watch Company** (www.barharborwhales.com; © **888/942-5374** or 207/288-2386), which operates off the municipal pier at 1 West Street in downtown Bar Harbor, next to Agamont Park. Tours are on a fast, twin-hulled three-level excursion boat that can hold 200 passengers in two heated cabins. The tours run 3 hours or more. There are also puffin- and whale-watching tours; a scenic lighthouse excursion; a shorter (2-hour) nature cruise, in search of seals and birds of prey; and more. Tickets cost $32 to $64 per adult, $18 to $33 per child age 6 to 14. There's free on-site parking and a money-back *guarantee* that you'll see whales—how can you go wrong? The daily tours begin each season in late May and run through late October.

Sports and Outdoor Activities

GOLF   There are several good golf courses on Mount Desert Island. The **Kebo Valley Golf Club** (www.kebovalleyclub.com; ✆ **207/288-3000**) at 136 Eagle Lake Road in Bar Harbor (a short walk or drive from downtown) is one of the oldest in America, open in some form or another since 1888; it's a beauty. (*Golf Digest* awarded it four stars.) Greens fees run from $49 to $99 per person for 18 holes (they're highest in summer), and it can get very busy on peak summer weekends—try to reserve well ahead.

SEA KAYAKING   Sea kayaking has boomed around Mount Desert Island during the past decade. Experienced kayakers arrive in droves with their own boats. Novices sign up for guided tours that are offered by several outfitters. Many new paddlers have found their inaugural experiences gratifying; others have complained that the quantity of paddlers on quick tours in peak season makes the experience a little too much like a cattle drive to truly enjoy. A variety of options can be found on the island, ranging from a 2½-hour harbor tour to a 7-hour excursion; plenty of outfitters in Bar Harbor and the other towns offer guided excursions. Check out **Coastal Kayaking Tours,** 48 Cottage Street (www.acadiafun.com; ✆ **800/526-8615** or 207/288-9605) or **National Park Sea Kayak Tours,** 39 Cottage Street (www.acadiakayak.com; ✆ **800/347-0940**). Rates range from $50 to $60 per person for a 2- to 3-hour harbor, sunset, or half-day tour, up to perhaps $80 for a full-day excursion. **Aquaterra Adventures,** 1 West Street, Bar Harbor (www.aquaterra-adventures.com; ✆ **877/386-4124** or 207/288-0007) offers both guided tours and sea-kayak rentals; with unpredictable weather and squirrelly tides, however, kayakers are advised to have some prior experience before attempting to set out on their own.

Bar Harbor Shopping

Bar Harbor is full of boutiques and souvenir shops along two intersecting commercial streets, Main Street and Cottage Street. Most sell the usual tourist tack, but look a little harder and you can find some original items for sale at places like these.

Bar Harbor Hemporium ★   The Hemporium is dedicated to promoting products made from hemp such as paper, clothing, and more. Surprisingly, there's some interesting stuff here. 116 Main St., Bar Harbor. www.barharborhemp.com. ✆ **207/288-3014.**

Cadillac Mountain Sports ★   Sleeping bags, backpacks, outdoor clothing, and hiking boots are found at this shop, which caters to the ragged-wool and fleece set. There's a good selection of hiking and travel guides to the island, too. 26 Cottage St., Bar Harbor. www.cadillacsports.com. ✆ **207/288-4532.**

Island Artisans ★   This is the place to browse for products made by local craftspeople, such as tiles, sweetgrass baskets, pottery, jewelry, and soaps. 99 Main St., Bar Harbor. www.islandartisans.com. ✆ **207/288-4214.**

Sherman's Books & Stationery ★　The original location of Maine's beloved book chain. Wide selection of new and used books, plus Maine calendars, gifty and writerly things, and some tchotchkes. Occasional cool author events. 25 Federal St., Bar Harbor. www.shermans.com. ℂ **207/288-3161.**

ELSEWHERE ON MOUNT DESERT ISLAND ★★

You'll find plenty to explore outside of Acadia National Park and Bar Harbor. Quiet fishing villages, deep woodlands, and unexpected ocean views are among the jewels you can turn up once you get beyond Bar Harbor town limits.

Essentials

GETTING AROUND

The eastern half of the island is best navigated using Route 3, which forms a rough loop from Bar Harbor through **Seal Harbor** and past **Northeast Harbor**, then runs up along the eastern shore of Somes Sound. Route 102 and Route 102A provide access to the island's western half. Without a car, use the free **Island Explorer shuttle** (see p. 188).

VISITOR INFORMATION

The **Thompson Island Information Center**, on the right as you are about to cross onto the island, is your single best info source. It's open daily from mid-May through mid-October. Acadia National Park information is available daily, year-round, at the **park headquarters** (ℂ **207/288-3338**) on Route 233 between Bar Harbor and Somesville. Locally, the **Southwest Harbor-Tremont Chamber of Commerce** (www.acadiachamber.com; ℂ **800/423-9264** or 207/244-9264), and the **Mount Desert Chamber of Commerce** (www.mountdesertchamber.com; ℂ **207/276-5040**), can also help you.

Where to Stay Around Mount Desert Island

Acadia Yurts ★　You're not going to find a quieter stretch of what MDIers call "the quiet side." And you won't find more idiosyncratic accommodations than the six giant round tents on this 5-acre stretch of woods. They're fitted with queen beds, full kitchens, showers, air conditioning—all the comforts of home. They're also as light and open as can be (what with the built-in skylight), and plenty sturdy (the walls are wooden; only the ceiling is fabric). A community barn and a seasonal spa yurtlet make for gathering spaces, as do the firepits outside each yurt. They're spaced out enough that you can maintain privacy, but as all rentals are weekly, you're likely to make friends. The proprietors are a 30-something couple with deep MDI roots. One of their sweet touches: All the artwork was made by students from Mount Desert Island High School.

200 Seal Cove Rd., Southwest Harbor. www.acadiayurts.com. ℂ **800/307-5335** or 207/244-5335. 6 units. Late June–early Sept $1050 per week. Mid-Apr–mid-June and mid-Sept–Nov $750–$950 per week. Rates include full breakfast. Pets welcome ($100 weekly fee). **Amenities:** Yoga and spa tent; library; grills; fire pits; free Wi-Fi.

Asticou Inn ★   The once-grand Asticou Inn, which dates from 1883, occupies a prime location at the head of Northeast Harbor. It was once one of those "must-see" hotels on the island, but then slid slowly into a state of neglect. New ownership in 2010 really turned the place around; since 2015, when the company that formerly ran the park's beloved Jordan Pond House (see p. 192) started managing the inn and its restaurant, reviews have been overwhelmingly positive. The rooms are furnished in a simple summer-home style; some have claw-foot tubs, others have fireplaces or kitchenettes, but none have phones or TVs. (Also, importantly, less than half have ocean views.) There are four outbuildings scattered about the property, containing 17 cottagelike units, and these might be my first choice: they're more secluded, a bit more luxurious. Dinner in the airy, wooden-floored main dining room focuses on seafood—and now they also have the popovers that attract park visitors to Jordan Pond House. It's good to see the Asticou reclaiming its former glory, because this part of the island is magical.

15 Peabody Dr., Northeast Harbor. www.asticou.com. ℂ **207/276-3344**. 48 units. Main inn July–Aug $190–$350 double; May–June and Sept–Oct $130–$250 double; "cottage" units July–Aug $270–$390, May–June and Sept–Oct $195–$330. Rates include continental breakfast. Closed late Oct–mid-May. Some rooms accommodate pets. **Amenities:** Dining room; outdoor pool; concierge; room service; tennis court; free Wi-Fi.

The Claremont ★★   Early prints of the venerable Claremont show an austere, four-story wooden building overlooking Somes Sound from a grassy rise; it hasn't changed much since. The place offers classic New England grace. (It's somehow appropriate that one of New England's largest croquet tournaments is held here each August.) Common areas are pleasantly appointed in country style—the library with its fireplace is popular. Most guest rooms are bright and airy, outfitted in antiques, old furniture, and modern bathrooms. There's also a set of 14 cottages of varied vintages and styles in the woods and on the water, all with fireplaces and kitchenettes; they sleep from 2 to 7 people each. Aim for the four Wentworth cottages, all renovated in the last few years into clean, contemporary studios with woodstoves or inset gas fireplaces and lovely porch views of the sound. The dining room, **Xanthus ★**, offers fabulous views and a menu of lobster, crab cakes, fish, scallops, pork, and steaks.

22 Claremont Rd., Southwest Harbor. (From Southwest Harbor center, follow Clark Point Rd. to Claremont Rd. and turn left.) www.theclaremonthotel.com. ℂ **800/244-5036**. 44 units. July–Aug $312–$444 double and cottage; late May–June and Sept–mid-Oct $150–$312 double and cottage. Hotel room rates include breakfast (not cottages). Packages available. 3-night minimum in cottages. Closed mid-Oct–late May. **Amenities:** Dining room; lounge; babysitting; free bikes; library; croquet; rowboats; tennis court; free Wi-Fi.

Inn at Southwest ★   There's a late-19th-century feel to this mansard-roofed Victorian home, which thankfully stays spare rather than frilly. All guest rooms, named for Maine lighthouses, are outfitted simply in contemporary and antique furniture; all have ceiling fans and down comforters. Among the most pleasant rooms is Blue Hill Bay on the third floor, with its yellow-and-blue color scheme, big bathroom, sturdy oak bed and bureau, and glimpses of the harbor. The Winter Harbor has a pencil-poster canopy bed, French doors, and a gas-log fireplace. The snug Owls Head room has a cool headboard made from a sturdy old door. Breakfasts give you good incentive to rise early: entrees could include Belgian waffles with raspberry sauce, poached pears, or blueberry French toast.

371 Main St., Southwest Harbor. www.innatsouthwest.com. © **207/244-3835.** 7 units. $110–$225 double. Rates include full breakfast. Closed Nov–mid-May. **Amenities:** Fire pit; free Wi-Fi.

Kingsleigh Inn ★★ In a 1904 Queen Anne–style home on Southwest Harbor's bustling Main Street, the Kingsleigh has long been a reliable place to bunk down in the area. Its living room features a wood-burning fireplace and fine art, while sitting and breakfast rooms offer further refuge. All units are outfitted with thoughtful touches like sound machines (to drown out the ambient "noise"), fresh flowers, wine glasses, heated bathroom floors, and thick robes. Flowery prints and wallpapers bedeck the rooms, most of which are small to moderate size, though a few have private decks. The huge third-floor penthouse suite—by far the most expensive room here—has a fireplace, a king-size bed, the inn's only TV (with VCR and DVD players), and outstanding views (plus a telescope to see them better with). Three-course breakfasts are genuinely artistic—expect choices like asparagus frittata, local-spinach eggs Florentine, raspberry-stuffed French toast—always preceded by a shot of an esoteric juice (watermelon? celery, anyone?) and followed by dessert, believe it or not.

373 Main St., Southwest Harbor. www.kingsleighinn.com. © **207/244-5302.** 8 units. $145–$205 double; $255–$315 suite. Rates include full breakfast. 2-night minimum stay. Closed Nov–Mar. Children over 12 welcome. **Amenities:** Wine service; library; free Wi-Fi.

Seawall Motel ★ At this family-run motel, the rooms are simple, spare, and fairly dated, but the location, just across the street from the water at the Seawall entrance to Acadia, is hard to beat. This is the closest you'll come to feeling like you've gotten away from it all, short of sleeping in a tent. Ask for a room on the second floor, which offers better views of the water. The staff here is exceptional—be sure to get their input if you're planning to explore Mount Desert Island beyond the park, as they've got fantastic suggestions for hikes and nature walks.

566 Seawall Rd., Southwest Harbor. www.seawallmotel.com. © **800/248-9250** or 207/244-3020. 20 units. Late June–Labor Day $125; mid Sept–early June $70–$90. Rates include continental breakfast. **Amenities:** Coin-op laundry; free Wi-Fi.

Where to Eat Around Mount Desert Island

Twenty years ago, there were virtually no serious dining options anywhere on the quiet side of Mount Desert Island. Things have definitely changed. In addition to the choices listed below, you can find plenty of good restaurants in **Southwest Harbor** and several in **Northeast Harbor.** There are even decent options in tiny, one-dock fishing villages such as **Manset** and **Bernard.** Or just pack a picnic at either of the excellent local markets in Southwest Harbor and Northeast Harbor.

Southwest Harbor's **Common Good Soup Kitchen & Café** (www.common goodsoupkitchen.org; © **207/266-2733**) at 19 Clark's Point Road (next to the post office), is arguably the best spot to get MDI's signature pastry, the light and buttery popover. From June to Columbus Day, stop by between 7:30 and 11:30am, help yourself to all the coffee, oatmeal, and terrific popovers (with locally made jam) that you care to eat. Grab a seat on the patio, enjoy the live music, then leave whatever sort of donation you'd like on the way out—it all goes to fund a soup kitchen in the winter. Also in Southwest Harbor, **Quietside,** 360 Main St. (© **207/244-9444**), serves inexpensive club sandwiches and ice-cream cones. The **Little Notch Bakery and Cafe,** 340 Main Street (www.littlenotch.wixsite.com/my-cafe; © **207/244-3357**) makes great pizzas with its own dough, plus gourmet sandwiches in the vein of grilled chicken in focaccia with onions and aioli, prosciutto with Asiago and roasted peppers on an onion roll, and grilled flank steak on a baguette. It gets crowded and convivial on summer weekend evenings. **Eat-A-Pita,** 326 Main Street (www. eatapitasouthwestharbor.com; © **207/244-4344**), serves pitas, salads, and egg dishes. **Sips**, 4 Clark Point Road (www.sipsmdi.com; ©**207/244-4550**) is a wine bar that also happens to have great breakfast crepes, sandwiches, and comfort food-y dinners (great meatloaf).

In Northeast Harbor, don't overlook the informal **Docksider Restaurant,** hidden a block off the main commercial drag at 14 Sea Street (© **207/276-3965**). The crab rolls and lobster rolls are outstanding, made simply and perfectly. The small restaurant also features a host of other fare, including lobster dinners, sandwiches, chowder, fried seafood, and grilled salmon.

Beal's Lobster Pound ★★ SEAFOOD Some says Beal's is among the best lobster shacks in Maine, and it's certainly got the right atmosphere: Creaky picnic tables sit on a plain concrete pier overlooking a working-class harbor, right next to a Coast Guard base. (Don't wear a jacket and tie.) You go inside to pick out lobster from a tank, pay by the pound, choose some side dishes (corn on the cob, slaw, steamed clams), then pop coins into a soda machine outside while you wait for your number to be called. The food will arrive on Styrofoam and paper plates, as it should. There's also a takeout window across the deck serving fries, fried clams, and fried fish (sensing a theme?), plus ice cream.

182 Clark Point Rd., Southwest Harbor. www.bealslobster.com. © **207/244-3202.** Lobsters market priced. Summer daily 11am–8pm; after Labor Day 9am–5pm. Closed Columbus Day–Memorial Day.

PIER, BEER & lobster

The best lobster restaurants are those right on the water, where there's no pretension or frills. The ingredients for a proper feed at a local lobster pound are a pot of boiling water, a tank of lobsters, some well-worn picnic tables, a good view, and a six-pack of Maine beer. Some of the best are concentrated on Mount Desert Island, including the famous **Beal's Lobster Pier** (see p. 224) in Southwest Harbor, one of the oldest pounds in the area. **Thurston's Lobster Pound** (see p. 226) in tiny Bernard (across the water from Bass Harbor) is atmospheric enough to have been used as a backdrop for the Stephen King miniseries *Storm of the Century*; it's a fine place to linger toward dusk, with great water views from the upstairs level. **Abel's Lobster Pound** (✆ 207/276-5827) on Route 198, 5 miles north of Northeast Harbor, overlooks the deep blue waters of Somes Sound; eat at picnic tables under the pines or indoors at the restaurant. It's quite a bit pricier than other lobster restaurants at first glance, but they don't charge for the extras that many other lobster joints do—and some visitors claim that lobsters here are more succulent. Then there's **Trenton Bridge Lobster Pound** ★ (www.trentonbridgelobster. com; ✆ 207/667-2977) on Route 3 in Trenton (on the mainland) just before the bridge across to the Island, a personal favorite of mine where the lobsters are boiled in seawater. It's salty and unpretentious as all get-out. A container of their smoky lobster stew and a slice of homemade blueberry pie make for ideal takeout.

The Burning Tree ★★ SEAFOOD   Located on a busy straightaway of Route 3 between Bar Harbor and Otter Creek, The Burning Tree is an easy restaurant to blow right past; that would be a mistake. This low-key and surprisingly elegant place serves some of the best and freshest seafood dinners on the island, with New American twists. Some of the produce and herbs comes from the restaurant's own gardens, while the rest of the ingredients are bought locally whenever possible. Everything's prepared with imagination and skill—expect unusual preparations like a New Orleans–style lobster, lobster fritters (great idea), sage and almond flounder, and Swiss chard leaves stuffed with scallop mousse, plus old standards like grilled salmon and halibut (served with inventive and tasty sauces). Don't miss the house cocktails, which use local fruits and berries when possible.

69 Otter Creek Dr., Otter Creek. ✆ **207/288-9331.** Entrees $19–$26. Mid-June–Columbus Day Wed–Mon 5–10pm. Closed Columbus Day–mid-May. Reservations recommended.

Coda ★★ NEW AMERICAN/TAPAS   Southwest Harbor's newest restaurant was built from the ground up in 2015 and has an idiosyncratic mission: to be the live-music mecca of this town of 1,800 people, in addition to serving farm-to-table shareable plates. So the few tables and long bar in the rustic, barnlike room are oriented towards a small stage (there's a great patio, too). The music skews rootsy and globally influenced, and so does the menu. You might share a spaetzle and cheese, braised beef cheeks with bourbon jelly, or an inspired pairing of lobster and grits. Chef Carter Light takes the DIY ethos seriously: smokes his own sausages, makes head cheese from the head of a locally reared pig, that sort of thing. Somebody behind the bar takes the whiskey list seriously. All in all, a fun and tasty hangout that wouldn't feel out of place in some western mountain town.

18 Village Green Way, Southwest Harbor. www.codasouthwestharbor.com. © **207/244-8133.** Small plates $7–$16. Tues–Sat 5–9pm; Sun 6–9:30pm. Closed late Oct–late May. Reservations recommended weekends.

Red Sky ★★ NEW AMERICAN   Red Sky has anchored the fine-dining scene on "the quiet side" for well over a decade now. Meals take New England ingredients to creative heights, using French and other Continental techniques and accents. Begin with intriguing starters such as organic chicken liver pâté, baked oysters stuffed with crab and bacon, duck-pork sausage, or a crispy, layered polenta. Salads here are excellent; main courses could include a coriander-crusted piece of seared tuna, a chicken raised down the road and served with cranberry sauce, a round of grilled lamb bathed in Dijon mustard, citrusy scallops over Basmati rice, a pan-roasted breast of duck with a wine sauce, or maple-glazed baby back ribs. Finish with a house standard: toasted gingerbread with caramel sauce and brandied whipped cream, or else one of the sorbets or ice creams.

14 Clark Point Rd., Southwest Harbor. www.redskyrestaurant.com. © **207/244-0476.** Entrees $22–$33. July–Sept Thurs–Sun 5:30–9:30pm; rest of year closed Sun. Closed Dec–mid-Feb.

Thurston's Lobster Pound ★ SEAFOOD   Right off the end of a dock (the same place where they load the lobsters), Thurston's possesses all three key requirements of a great Maine lobster shack: a great view of Bass Harbor and its fishing boats; tasty lobster and side dishes at reasonable prices; and an unpretentious vibe blended with a dash of friendly sass. It's like a place out of the movies. The lobsters come quickly, their claws precracked for easier access; corn on the cob is perfectly cooked; scallop chowder, crunchy crab cakes, and bags of steamed mussels and clams all provide toothsome sides; and the "plain dinner" option ($5 extra) finishes with a wonderfully eggy cinnamon-blueberry cake. Start with the bubbly and unexpectedly yummy lobster-and-cream-cheese dip. There are two decks, upstairs and down; a convivial atmosphere pervades at both. This place is a true Maine classic, one of my favorite lobster shacks in the whole state.

9 Thurston Rd. (at the docks), Bernard. © **207/244-7600.** Lobsters market price. Memorial Day–Columbus Day daily 11am–8:00pm.

XYZ ★★ MEXICAN   This place is a true "foodie find." You'd be forgiven for doubting the authenticity of the Mexican food served in this shacklike bungalow a stone's throw from the crashing north Atlantic off Seawall Lane—yet it serves *very* authentic Mexican cuisine. Owners Janet Strong and Bob Hoyt are well-traveled in the Mexican states of Xalapa, Yucatán, and Zacatecas (thus the restaurant's acronym). No burritos here; this is campesino chow, a bit elevated. Expect lots of pork and chicken dishes and mole sauces, with a pile of local lettuce and corn tortillas on the side. The *sopa de aguacate*, chilled avocado soup with just a hint of tequila and chiles, is a must as an appetizer. Reservations are a must, too, as the place only seats a few dozen.

411 Main St., Southwest Harbor. www.xyzmaine.com. © **207/244-5221.** Entrees $26. Mon–Sat 5:30–9pm. Closed Columbus Day–late June. Late season hours can be unpredictable (call ahead). Reservations recommended.

Exploring Around Mount Desert Island

Down one peninsula of the eastern lobe of the island is the staid, prosperous village of **Northeast Harbor** ★★, long a favorite retreat of well-heeled folks. You can see shingled palaces poking out from the forest and shore, but the village itself (which consists of just one short main street and a marina) is also worth investigating for its art galleries, restaurants, and general store. One of the best, least-publicized places for enjoying views of the harbor is from the understated, wonderful **Asticou Terraces** ★★ (www.gardenpreserve.org; © 207/276-3727.). Finding the parking lot can be tricky: Head a half-mile east (toward Seal Harbor) on Route 3 from the junction with Route 198, and look for the small gravel lot on the water side of the road with a sign reading ASTICOU TERRACES. Park here, cross the road on foot, and set off up a magnificent path of local stone that ascends the sheer hillside, with expanding views of the harbor and the town.

Continue on the trail at the top of the hillside, and you'll soon arrive at Curtis's cabin (open to the public daily in summer), behind which lies the formal **Thuya Garden** ★★, which is as manicured as the terraces are natural. This wonderfully maintained garden, designed by noted landscape architect Charles K. Savage (he summered here) in what was once an apple orchard, attracts flower enthusiasts, students of landscape architecture, and local folks looking for a quiet place to rest. The lawns lead to a pavilion and reflecting pool; the gates were hand-carved of cedar. It's well worth the trip.

Finally, don't miss the wonderful **azalea garden** ★★ 100 yards down Route 3 (toward Somesville). Run by the same organization as Thuya Garden and the Asticou Terraces, it's a groomed, Japanese-style wonder of water and plant life—one of my favorite places on the island to wander without getting a cardio workout. There's no admission charge to any of these three lovely stops, but donations are requested—drop a few bucks in. There's limited free parking in a lot at both the terraces and the azalea garden.

When leaving Northeast Harbor, think about a quick detour out to **Sargent Drive**. This one-way route runs through Acadia National Park along the shore of Somes Sound, affording superb views of the glacially carved inlet. On the

From Northeast Harbor, visitors can depart on a seaward trip to the beguilingly remote **Cranberry Islands** ★. You have a couple of options: Either travel with a national park guide to Baker Island, the most distant of this small cluster of low islands, and explore the natural terrain; or hop one of the ferries to either Great or Little Cranberry Island and explore on your own. On Little Cranberry there's a small historical **museum** ★ run by the National Park Service that's worth a few minutes. Both islands feature a sense of being well away from it all, but neither offers much in the way of shelter or tourist amenities; travelers should head out prepared for the possibility of shifting weather. **Beal & Bunker** (© 207/244-3575) runs mail boats to the islands from Northeast Harbor, while **Cranberry Cove Boating Co.** (www.downeastwind jammer.com; © **207/244-5882** or 207/460-1981) runs a regular ferry schedule from Southwest Harbor and Manset. Figure on $25 to $32 round-trip per adult, $15–$20 for children. Be sure to check boat schedules carefully before setting off to the Cranberries to ensure that you don't miss the last ferries back to Mount Desert; there are very limited accommodations out here.

far side of Somes Sound, there's good hiking (see p. 196) and the towns of Southwest Harbor and Bass Harbor, both home to fishermen and boat-builders. Though the character of these towns is changing, they're still far more humble than Northeast and Seal harbors.

In **Southwest Harbor** look for the intriguing **Wendell Gilley Museum of Bird Carving** (www.wendellgilleymuseum.org; © 207/244-7555), on Route 102 just north of town. Housed in a new building constructed specifically to display the woodcarvings, the museum contains the masterwork of Wendell Gilley, a plumber who took up carving birds as a hobby in 1930. His creations, ranging from regal bald eagles to delicate chickadees, are startlingly lifelike and beautiful. The museum offers woodcarving classes for those inspired by the displays, and a gift shop sells fine woodcarvings. It's open Tuesday to Sunday from 10am to 4pm June to October, Friday and Saturday from 10am to 4pm in late May, November, and December. The museum is closed January to April, when it offers craft workshops. Admission is $5 for adults, $2 for children 5 to 12—but free Saturday mornings in July and August, and all day on Wendell Gilley's birthday (Aug 21).

Sports & Outdoor Activities

CANOEING Mount Desert's ponds offer scenic if limited canoeing; most have public boat access. Canoe rentals are available at the north end of **Long Pond** (the largest pond on the island, at 3 miles long) in Somesville from **National Park Canoe & Kayak Rental** (www.nationalparkcanoerental.com; © 207/244-5854). The cost is about $37 for 3 hours, $22 if you go out for sunset, or $61 for the whole day.

GOLF   The **Northeast Harbor Golf Club** (www.nehgc.com; $\textcircled{c}$ **207/276-5335**) is an attractive choice for golfers. Greens fees range from $45 to $85 per person for 18 holes; to find the course, drive all the way through the small downtown, then turn right on Manchester Drive, which takes you to the course. Alternately, a few miles north of town as you come south on Route 3/198, exit right onto Sargent Drive and continue ¹/₂ miles to the course.

THE DOWNEAST COAST

The term Downeast, as in "Downeast Maine," comes from the days when ships were still powered by sail. East Coast ships heading north and east along this coastline had strong prevailing winds at their backs—making it an easy "downhill" run to the farthest eastern ports. (Returning took more skill and determination.)

Today it's a rare traveler who gets Downeast to explore the rugged coastline of Washington County. Very few tourists venture beyond the turnoff to Mount Desert Isle, discouraged by a lack of services and high-marquee attractions. Yet Downeast Maine does have appeal—so long as you're not looking for luxury. There's an authenticity here that's been lost in much of the rest of Maine. Many long-time visitors say this is how all of Maine used to look in the 1940s and 1950s, when writers and artists first arrived in earnest. Thai food, the *New York Times,* and designer coffee have yet to make serious inroads into Washington County, where a rugged, hardscrabble way of life and tough interdependence among neighbors still predominates. And yet, just when you think you have the Downeast coast pegged, you encounter some oddball little pocket of artsy wonder or creative-class entrepreneurship with a salty tinge.

Many residents here still get by as their forebears did—scratching a living from the land and sea. Scalloping, lobstering, and fishing remain the major sources of income, as do blueberrying, logging, and other forest work. Grubbing for bloodworms in spring, picking berries in the barrens in late summer, climbing fir trees to get the fragrant tips for Christmas wreaths in the fall—that's not a vacation around here, that's what people do to make ends meet. In recent years aquaculture has also become an important part of the economy around Passamaquoddy and Cobscook bays; travelers can sometimes see vast floating pens, especially around Eastport and Lubec, where salmon are farmed for gourmet diners worldwide.

The geographical isolation of this region ensures that you'll have these back roads and tiny towns to yourself—most of your fellow travelers have been waylaid by the charms of Kennebunkport, Portland, Camden, or Acadia. But if you're hoping to get a peek at the Maine that rarely shows up on the tourist brochures, you'd be wise to make a trip here for a day or two. You might never see Maine the same way again.

At the end of your coastal exploration, you can also take a bridge to another country—and another time zone—by visiting New Brunswick, Canada, even if only for a few hours. You'll need a valid passport for that.

ESSENTIALS
Arriving
Downeast Maine is usually reached via U.S. Route 1, coming northeast from Ellsworth. You can also take a more direct, less congested route via Route 9 from Brewer (across the river from Bangor), connecting to Route 1 via Route 193 or Route 192.

Visitor Information
For information on the Machias area and other parts of Downeast Maine, contact the **Machias Bay Area Chamber of Commerce,** 85 Main St., suite 2 (www.machiaschamber.org; © **207/255-4402**), on Route 1. It's open 10am to 3pm on weekdays. For more information on the Eastport area, contact the **Eastport Chamber of Commerce** (www.eastport.net; © **207/853-4644**).

Special Events
Eastport celebrates the **Fourth of July** in extravagant fashion each year, a tradition that began in 1820 after the British gave up possession of the city (they captured it during the War of 1812). Some 15,000 New Englanders pour into this little city of 1,900 for the 4-day event, which includes pie-eating competitions, codfish racing (that's a relay while holding a dead fish, in case you didn't know), a flotilla of boats and ships in the harbor, a huge torch-lit parade (Maine's largest), parachutes, pipe bands, and the like. They go over-the-top, culminating in impressive (for the town's size) fireworks.

The popular **Machias Wild Blueberry Festival ★**, operated by the local Congregation Church, celebrates the local cash crop each summer. Washington County claims to produce an astonishing 85% of the world's wild blueberry harvest, so there's bound to be some for the tasting when you show up. The festivities typically begin with a children's parade and fish fry, continue with a Saturday blueberry pancake breakfast (of course) and road race, then move on to lobster feeds, the raffling of a blueberry quilt, a book sale, a masquerade ball in an old Grange Hall, and (of course) a blueberry-pie-eating contest. There are also performances and the sales of blueberry-theme gift items. Stamp collectors should plan to drop by the local post office for special-issue cancellation stamps, uniquely themed to blueberries each year. Check the festival website (www.machiasblueberry.com) or contact the Machias chamber of commerce (see above) for the exact dates of the festival; it's usually in mid- to late August.

The **Eastport Salmon Festival** (www.eastportsalmonfestival.com; © **207/853-6122**) takes over town each year during the first weekend after Labor Day, with a very full weekend of arts, crafts, a road race, a sailboat race, a walking tour, and plenty of seafood.

WHERE TO STAY & EAT ON THE DOWNEAST COAST

Where to Stay In Downeast Maine

Small motels, inns, and B&Bs abound along this part of the Maine coast, and resorts are almost nonexistent. The message: Prepare to rusticate. Your main bases for the region are Machias and Lubec/Eastport.

Budget travelers can do well here. Lower-end offerings on Route 1 in Machias include the **Machias River Inn**, with 35 air-conditioned riverside rooms (www.machiasriverinn.com; © 207/255-4861), and the **Bluebird Motel** (www.bluebirdmotelmaine.com; © 207/255-3333), with 40 air-conditioned units. There are also budget options in Jonesboro, Lubec, and Eastport.

You might also consider renting a cottage or farmhouse by the week or month; there are plenty to choose from on this stretch of coast in summer, and finding them is increasingly easy, as Downeast Maine gradually adopts Airbnb and other online rental platforms. Among the offerings, check out the unique **Quoddy Head Station** (www.quoddyvacation.com; © 877/535-4714), on West Quoddy Head Road in Lubec. It's a former Coast Guard lifesaving station, built in 1918, with five bedrooms; there are also five other units, all with terrific coastal views. Rentals in July and August are $120 to $330 per night or $800 to $2,200 per week—rates are lowest during the shoulder seasons.

Black Duck Inn ★   There isn't much to the little village of Corea—mostly just a clutch of fishing boats and some island views—but there is a year-round bed-and-breakfast if you care to stay the night. The new 30-something owners of the Black Duck have freshened up the two no-frills rooms (which share a bathroom, while the others have private facilities), one suite, and one waterfront cottage. It's a simple place set among quiet scenery. The first floor is a gallery for local art, and the rooms feature a mix of antique and vintage furnishings; three, including the cottage, have excellent vistas of the picturesque harbor and the lupine-strewn headland.

36 Crowley Island Rd., Corea. www.blackduck.com. © 207/963-2689. 4 units (2 with shared bathroom). $135–$300 double. Full breakfast included. **Amenities:** Free Wi-Fi.

Crocker House Country Inn ★   Built in 1884, this handsome shingled inn is off the beaten track on picturesque Hancock Point, across Frenchman Bay from Mount Desert Island. It's a cozy retreat, good for rest, relaxation, and quiet walks; it's only about a 4-minute walk from the water's edge. Rooms are tastefully decorated in country decor; there's nothing lavish here, but they're way comfortable. The common areas are more relaxed than fussy. The inn has a few bikes for guests to explore the point, visit the second-smallest post office in the U.S., or drop by the nearby clay tennis courts. **Dinner** ★ is a highlight: it's served in a fun atmosphere. Open daily May through October (weekends in several other months), the kitchen serves mostly

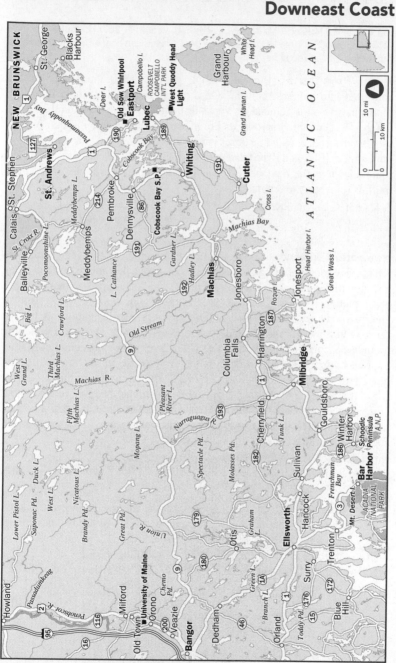

traditional favorites, such as oysters Rockefeller, scallops, fish, pasta, steak au poivre, and lamb.

967 Point Rd., Hancock Point. www.crockerhouse.com. © **207/422-6806.** 11 units. $100–$165 double. Rates include full breakfast. Closed Jan–mid-April. Pets welcome. **Amenities:** Dining room; free bikes, free Wi-Fi.

Home Port Inn ★ Built as a family home in 1880, the Home Port was converted into lodgings in 1982. On a quiet street in downtown Lubec, its rooms mostly offer tremendous views of both Cobscook Bay and the Bay of Fundy. The central living room and fireplace are the focal points; comfy guest rooms vary in size, with one occupying a former library and another a former dining room. Best bed? The Garden Overlook's king-size bed. Best view? The room known as the Bay View, of course. Breakfasts are simple, granola and muffins (blueberry, of course).

45 Main St., Lubec. © **800/457-2077** or 207/733-2077. 7 units. $99–$135 double. Rates include continental breakfast. Closed mid-Oct–mid-May. **Amenities:** Restaurant; free Wi-Fi.

Ironbound ★ Located on Route 1 about 10 minutes east of Ellsworth, this inn has five rooms above an occasionally boisterous pub and restaurant, along a stretch of Route 1 that can be a bit noisy. The landscaped garden out back offers plenty of serenity, though, as does the second-floor deck reserved for guests. Rooms are comfortable and tastefully appointed without being pretentious, with a mix of antique and contemporary furnishings. A shared sitting room has a crackling fireplace and a small library with a collection of Maine-focused books. But the real draw is the **restaurant ★**, serving comforting bistro fare with a lot of local fish and forage, all in a handsome space of pine-wood floors and a big fireplace. Meals run to finnan haddie (haddock with cream sauce, a classic Downeast treat), a big rib-eye in wine-shallot sauce, lamb sliders, and the ubiquitous lobster mac and cheese. They mix a mean cocktail behind the big bar.

1513 U.S. Rte. 1, Hancock. www.ironboundinn.com. © **207/422-3395.** 5 units. June–Oct $145 double; $185 suite. Rates include full breakfast and dinner. Closed Nov–May. **Amenities:** Restaurant; bar; free Wi-Fi.

Kilby House ★ An unassuming Queen Anne built in 1887 by one Herbert Kilby, 19th century mariner and town father, the Kilby House is today run by retired teacher Greg Noyes, who tends the place lovingly. The small rooms get a lot of light and are furnished with antiques recalling the inn's late Victorian era. No air-conditioning, but crack a window on a warm day to enjoy the sea breeze—you can see the water right across the quiet, residential street. Common spaces include a downstairs drawing room with a fireplace, a formal dining room, and a music room with a grand piano—if you ask your inn-keeper nicely, he might just play it.

122 Water St., Eastport. www.kilbyhouseinn.com. © **207/853-0989** or 800/853-4557. 4 units (all with shared bathroom). $90–$105 double. Rates include full breakfast. No children. **Amenities:** Free Wi-Fi.

Margaretta Inn ★★ New ownership in 2014 turned this formerly tired roadside motorlodge (formerly the Margaretta Motel) into a really lovely and up-to-date boutique inn with a throwback vibe. Top-to-bottom renovations gave the rooms handsome hardwood floors, all-new bathroom fixtures, heated bathroom floors, nice mattresses with thick duvet covers, flat-screen TVs in every room, keyless entry, Keurig coffee machines, mini-fridges, and microwaves. Real Maine maple syrup and fresh berries are nice touches on the continental breakfast. In general, the inn displays a level of cleanliness and attention to detail not commonly found in Downeast roadside lodging.

330 Main St, Machias. www.margarettainn.com. ℂ 207/255-6671. 12 units. $89–$120 double. Rates include continental breakfast. Closed Jan–May. **Amenities:** Free Wi-Fi.

Micmac Farm ★ Based in a 1763 home with intriguing history (the founder's family is buried in a cemetery on the premises), quiet Micmac Farm consists of just three units in a peaceful riverside setting: two rustic wood-paneled "guesthouses" in the woods (each furnished with two double beds and a kitchenette) and a more luxurious guest room located inside the main house with a big deck, king-size bed, television, and Jacuzzi tub. This third room also adjoins the home's library, which guests are welcome to use. An outdoor deck overlooks the Machias River, and it's a good spot for watching the water.

47 Micmac Lane (Rte. 92), Machiasport. www.rnicmacfarm.com. ℂ **207/255-3008.** 3 units. $125 main house double; $105 daily or $650 weekly cottage double. Pets and children welcome in cottages. **Amenities:** Free Wi-Fi.

Milliken House B&B ★ Guests at this friendly B&B are greeted with glasses of port or sherry in a big living room sporting two fireplaces. It's a nice welcome, and the five rooms are equally nice, done up in marble-top furnishings and outfitted with the original owner's collection of books. (Benjamin Milliken had made a small fortune building a dock and outfitting the big ships passing in and out of this once-busy port during Eastport's 19th-century heyday.) Expect small touches such as pillow-side chocolates and fresh flowers. All rooms feature televisions and fireplaces, something of a surprise given the low, low price. The house is located only 2 blocks from Eastport's historic district, making it ideal for local explorations. Breakfast might run to buttermilk pancakes served with a berry sauce, crepes, or a quiche Lorraine, sided with homemade bread.

29 Washington St., Eastport. www.eastport-inn.com. ℂ **207/853-2955.** 6 units. $90–$100 double. Rates include full breakfast. Well-trained pets welcome. **Amenities:** Free Wi-Fi in common areas.

Peacock House Bed & Breakfast ★ Built in out-of-the-way Lubec by an English sea captain in 1860, the Peacock House has over the years hosted prominent Mainers including U.S. senators Margaret Chase Smith and Edmund Muskie. The three second-floor rooms are queen-size-bedded and simple; the Margaret Chase Smith Suite has a queen-size bed, while the king-size-bedded Meadow Suite has the inn's largest bathroom and a sitting area. (It's accessible for guests with limited mobility.) The Peacock Suite is the most romantic choice, with a gas fireplace, four-poster queen-size bed, wet bar, refrigerator, and TV with DVD player. Tinkle the keys of the living room's baby grand piano, if you like: It's allowed and even encouraged.

27 Summer St., Lubec. www.peacockhouse.com. ℂ **888/305-0036** or 207/733-2403. 7 units. $105–$150 double. Rates include full breakfast. 2-night minimum on June–Sept weekends. No children 9 and under. **Amenities:** Library; free Wi-Fi.

Redclyffe Shore Motor Inn ★

I don't recommend many motor inns or motels in this book, but this one packs a great deal more historic and scenic punch than most. The complex, consisting of a Gothic Revival main house dating from the 1860s (note the steep gables) and a cluster of motel units, perches on a cliff with awesome views of Passamaquoddy Bay and the St. Croix River. Book one of the so-called "patio rooms" with a private balcony for maximum gazing access. Whether in the main house or the motel section, all the quite dated double- and king-size-bedded rooms and suites here sport the basics: phones, televisions, and coffeemakers. The balcony rooms are a steal considering the views, and the glassed-in **restaurant**—open every night, including to non-guests, serving standard American meals—features yet another knockout ocean view. Remember, however, that there's no breakfast service here—you'll need to head elsewhere for that.

Rte. 1, Robbinston. www.redclyffeshoremotorinn.com. ℂ **207/454-3270.** 16 units. $85–$125 double. Closed Nov to mid-May. **Amenities:** Restaurant; free Wi-Fi.

Riverside Inn ★

This far downeast, it isn't easy to find a frilly place, but the four-room Riverside Inn outside of Machias offers more than the usual motel in these parts does. The second-floor Mrs. Chase Room, named for the former captain's wife, has a claw-foot tub and skylight. The two-bedroom Lower Coach Suite features a wraparound deck overlooking the river and the inn's garden, while the popular Upper Coach Suite has even better views—from a private balcony—plus a small kitchen. Rooms are uniformly attractive and clean. The **restaurant ★** serves surprisingly fancy dinner entrees such as lobster and scallops in champagne sauce, almond-crusted fish filets, beef Wellington, pistachio-crusted pork medallions with a cranberry-plum chutney, and the like. (The restaurant is closed in winter, though the inn remains open year-round.)

622 Rte. 1, E. Machias. www.riversideinn-maine.com. ℂ **207/255-4134.** 4 units. $89–$135 double. Rates include breakfast. **Amenities:** Restaurant; free Wi-Fi.

Todd House Bed & Breakfast ★

A bright yellow house out on Todd's Head overlooking Cobscook and Passamaquoddy bays, this 1775 Cape features classic New England architectural touches such as a huge center chimney and a fireplace with bake oven. It has served as everything from a former Mason's Hall to temporary military barracks; today, the six inn rooms come in various configurations. Two rooms have kitchenettes. The ocean views are a draw, as are proprietor Ruth McInnis's collection of artifacts, from Revolutionary War items to Wabanki arrowheads. The inn is only about a .75-mile walk from Eastport's burgeoning downtown district.

1 Capen Ave., Eastport. www.toddhousemaine.com. ℂ **207/853-2328.** 6 units (3 with shared bathroom). $80–$110 double. Rates include self-service breakfast (no breakfast in winter). No credit cards. Pets welcome. **Amenities:** Free Wi-Fi.

CAMPING

Those with RVs can camp out at Pleasant River RV Park at 11 W. Side Road in Addison (www.pleasantriverrv.com; © 207/483-4083). It's open May through October, though it only has a half-dozen sites from which to choose. **Schoodic Peninsula**, part of Acadia National Park (see p. 185) also has a number of good campsites. Over the Canadian border in New Brunswick, there's camping at **Herring Cove Provincial Park** (© 506/752-7010) for C$20 to C$25 (US$15–$19), with discounts for seniors. The campground has 76 sites in all, some for tents, some with electrical hookups (some on the beach).

Where To Eat In Downeast Maine

Good places to eat are thin on the ground up here. If you're lucky, your hotel has a dining room (see reviews for the **Crocker House Country Inn,** p. 232; **Ironbound,** p. 234; **Redclyffe Shore Motor Inn,** p. 236; and **Riverside Inn,** p. 236).

If you're simply looking to fuel up on fast food or family style fare, Ellsworth is your main supply depot; expect the usual franchise chains along Route 1, especially near the point where routes 1 and 3 diverge.

To stock up for a picnic at Quoddy Head, stop by **Bold Coast Smokehouse** (www.boldcoastsmokehouse.com; © 888/733-0807 or 207/733-8912) on Route 189 in Lubec. Vinny Gartmayer smokes hot salmon, gravlax, kabobs, and trout pâté, among other products. (Another Downeast smokehouse, **Sullivan Harbor Farm,** is covered in fuller detail below.)

Helen's Restaurant ★ DINER   Reopened in 2015 after a devastating fire, this is the original Helen's with some structural upgrades. It's a cut-above-the-rest diner and one of the premier places in all of Maine to eat pie. (And, yes, there was a Helen.) You can get pork chops, fried fish, burgers, meatloaf, and other American-style square meals. But better to come for breakfast, to indulge in a plate of Helen's impossibly fluffy pancakes, chock full of blueberries (the pride of Machias). And regardless of the meal, save room for the amazingly creamy and fruity pies; strawberry rhubarb or blueberry, when in season, are out of this world, but chocolate cream, banana cream, or just about anything else will satisfy the sweet tooth. Check for daily specials. There's another Helen's on the strip just north of Ellsworth.

111 Main St., Machias. © **207/255-8423.** Entrees $4–$15. Mon–Sat 6am–8pm, Sun 7am–2pm.

Serendib ★ INDIAN/SRI LANKAN   On Ellsworth's main drag, you can find surprisingly excellent Indian and Sri Lankan food at this tiny, bright new restaurant. The menu's offerings include fragrant curries, vindaloo, and fresh, house-made paneer. It's popular enough that you might even run into a line on busy summer weekends.

2 State St., Ellsworth. © **207/664-1030.** Entrees $12–$18. Daily 10:30am–7:30pm.

Sullivan Harbor Farm & Smokehouse ★ SMOKEHOUSE   After a nasty run-in with the FDA, this legacy smokehouse reopened a revamped store and tasting room on Route 1 dedicated to one-stop shopping for Maine food (and drink products). Grab a six-pack from a nice selection of Maine craft beers, choose from stacks of locally tinned fish, pick up a few (Maine-made) Stonewall Kitchens jams and sauces. In the tasting room, you can sample a few excellent Maine-made cheeses or nosh, grab a cup of chowder or a baguette, or nosh a lobster roll. The one thing you can't get, as of press time? Sullivan-smoked salmon. As of late 2016, the company was clearing final regulatory hurdles and expected to begin smoking again come summer 2017.

1545 U.S. Rte. 1 Hancock. www.sullivanharborfarm.com. © **800/422-4014** or 207/422-2268. Tasting room plates $4–$12. Mon–Fri 10am–5:30pm, Sat 11–4.

Union River Lobster Pot ★ LOBSTER   More typical coastal dining is found in Ellsworth at this laidback gray frame lobster shack with walls of windows and a lawn overlooking the Union River, across the bridge from downtown Ellsworth. Besides featuring lobster dinners, it also serves a basic menu of Maine seafood, steaks, chicken, and sandwiches. Their chowder is a perennial favorite, as is the blueberry pie.

8 South St., Ellsworth. www.lobsterpot.com. © **207/667-5077.** Entrees $16–$25, lobsters market price. Jul–Aug daily 4-9pm, June and Sept-Oct daily 5–8:30pm. Open June–Columbus Day.

WaCo Diner ★   A touchstone in Eastport for more than 90 years, this diner has evolved somewhat from the lunch wagon that it began life as. But the WaCo still serves big breakfasts of eggs and coffee plus sandwiches at lunch and dinners of beef and fried fish. Setting itself apart from other diners of its type: a great waterfront deck and quite decent cocktails.

47 Water St., Eastport. © **207/853-4046.** Entrees $4–$20. Daily 6am–closing (varies).

EXPLORING DOWNEAST MAINE

The best way to see this area—the only way, really—is to simply drive along U.S. Route 1 and a few associated back roads and shortcuts north from Ellsworth all the way to the Canadian border . . . and beyond, if you brought your passport. The driving time direct from Ellsworth to Lubec via routes 1 and 189 is about 2 hours with no stops. Allow considerably more time for visiting the sites detailed below, and for just plain snooping around.

Set on Route 1, inland from Mount Desert Island, the friendly, artsy town of **Ellsworth** (27 miles southeast of Bangor) is our starting point. You'll swing east through the quiet fishing village of **Sullivan,** overlooking Frenchman Bay, then through **Gouldsboro,** which is actually a series of five villages. From here you may want to detour south off Route 1 down Route 186 to drive through Winter Harbor, Prospect Harbor, and Corea—don't expect anything fancy here—to **Schoodic Peninsula,** a bonus sliver of Acadia National Park.

From Gouldsboro, Route 1 angles northeast 10 more miles to **Milbridge,** jumping-off point for the Maine Coastal Islands National Wildlife Refuge. From Milbridge, there's a handy shortcut northeast along Route 1A, but if you have time, stay on Route 1 to visit quaint **Cherryfield.** Northeast of Cherryfield, you'll roll through tiny **Columbia Falls;** from here, you can either detour south on Route 187 to Jonesport and the Great Wass Island Wildlife Refuge, or stay east on Route 1 for Jonesboro, from where you can detour down Great Cove Road to scenic Roque Bluffs State Park.

From Jonesboro, it's only another 7.5 miles on Route 1 to the trim market town of **Machias.** You have two great options from here: East of town, detour southeast on Route 191 to the former shipbuilding village of **Cutler,** a prime place to shove off on a whale-watching cruise; or stay on Route 1 another 17 miles from Machias to find **Whiting**—nondescript in its own right, but a fine entry point to Moosehorn National Wildlife Refuge, the easternmost national wildlife refuge on the Atlantic migration corridor.

From Whiting, you have 2 options: Shoot east on Route 189 to visit scenic **Lubec,** the northeasternmost town in the United States, connected by bridge to Canada; or follow Route 1 north to cross Cobscook Bay at **Pembroke,** where you'll find an unusual reversing falls (the direction of the falls reverses twice each day, depending on prevailing tides). Six miles past Pembroke, at **Perry**, you have two choices: Angle southeast down Route 190 to charming **Eastport,** or head another 20 miles or so along the St. Croix River to French-inflected **Calais** (pronounced just like *callous,* unfortunately), connected by bridge to St. Stephen, New Brunswick, Canada (see p. 273).

Ellsworth

Ellsworth doesn't get much due from travelers hell-bent on making it to Mount Desert Island before dinner, but those in the know stop here to sample the town's growing cultural offerings, capitalizing on a concentration of artists and musicians. Though parts overdeveloped and commercialized—you'll pass through a stretch of Route 1 dominated by big box stores—the downtown is vibrant and pedestrian-friendly.

The town was first settled by Passamaquoddy and Penobscot tribes; later, French woodsmen explored the area, and the British inevitably followed with bridges, sawmills, and ships on the Union River. By the late 19th century, Ellsworth had become a significant port of departure for lumber cut from the big Maine woods, as well as an important shipbuilding center. After those industries faded, Ellsworth reinvented itself as a tourist jumping-off point—playing off its proximity to Mount Desert Island—and arts center.

The Telephone Museum ★ MUSEUM   It's not exactly comprehensive, but this tiny museum in a barn about 10 miles outside Ellsworth makes for a rainy Saturday afternoon diversion. You'll explore the ins and outs of the hand-crank system that first made it possible to reach out and touch some-one—talk to a switchboard operator (the early heroines of the system) and learn about telephone poles, line, linesmen, switching stations, and how they kept it all running smoothly back in the day. Tours are available. From Route 1 in Ellsworth, go 7 miles south to Happytown Road, turn right, and continue 6 miles to crossroads. Turn right onto Winkumpaugh Road.

166 Winkumpaugh Rd., Ellsworth. www.thetelephonemuseum.org. © **207/667-9491.** $10 adults, $5 children. July–Sept Sat 1–4pm; May–June and Oct by appointment only. Closed Nov–Apr.

MAINE COASTAL ISLANDS wildlife REFUGE

Stringing along the length of the Maine coast, this complex of several refuges protects a collection of uninhabited islands and parcels of land, habitat for nesting seabirds and birds of prey. The entire refuge now includes about 50 islands, three onshore areas, and more than 8,000 acres in all. It's home to terns, plovers, bald eagles, puffins, razorbills, storm petrels, and eiders, among other birds.

About 2.5 miles west of Milbridge, turn down Pigeon Hill Road and drive south 5.5 miles to the **Petit Manan Point Refuge**, which has a couple of excellent walking trails—the 1.5-mile Hollingsworth Loop and the 4-mile Birch Point Trail. Please respect the rules protecting these delicate ecosystems. Tread lightly, and light no open fires or unleash any dogs.

Another excellent way to explore the refuge is by boat. Two excellent charter boat operators, both sailing out of Bar Harbor (see p. 207 in chapter 8), run personalized tours to various islands of the refuge: **Bar Harbor Whale Watch Co.** (www.whalesrus.com; ✆ **888/942-5374** or 207/288-2386), or, for groups of up to 6, captain Winston Shaw's **Sea Venture** (www.svboattours.com; ✆ **207/288-3355**). (Captain Shaw ties up at the Atlantic Oceanside Motel, on Route 3 just north of downtown Bar Harbor.) From Cutler, a few miles up the coast, the popular **Bold Coast Charter Company** (see p. 243) also runs trips out to the refuge's Seal Island.

For more information on the refuge, go to **www.mainecoastislands.org.**

Schoodic Peninsula

7 miles S of W. Gouldsboro via Rte. 186

Schoodic Peninsula ★★ Overlooked by many travelers, this is a fine spot for dramatic photographs of surf crashing over the big rocks. It's remote, however—although it's just 7 miles from Mount Desert Island across Frenchman Bay, it's a 50-mile drive to get here. The National Park Service gave this region an overhaul during the later Obama years, installing a fine new campground and substantially expanded trail system. A pleasing one-way loop road hooks around the point (no park entry pass or fee required), winding along the water and through forests of spruce and fir. Good views of the mountains of Acadia open up across Frenchman Bay; you can also see part of a historic naval station housed on the point. Park near Schoodic Point, the tip of the peninsula, and explore salmon-colored rocks that plunge into the ocean. **Schoodic Woods Campground** ★, a pristine, 94-site campground at the top of the peninsula, has an amphitheater, ranger programs, and a handful of secluded walk-in sites (some with terrific views of MDI's peaks across the water). Camping fees range from $22 for the hike-in sites to $40 for full electric/water RV hookups (open late May to early September, reservations necessary in midsummer). Schoodic Woods is at the heart of the trail system, with new footpaths that extend all the way down the peninsula (via the bald-topped Buck Cove Mountain and 440-foot Schoodic Head), as well as an 8-mile network of smooth, occasionally hilly bike paths.

Acadia National Park, Winter Harbor. www.nps.gov/acad. ✆ **207/288-3338.** Free admission.

Milbridge

32 miles E of Ellsworth on Rte. 1

The former shipbuilding town of Milbridge is a handy base for exploring the **Maine Coastal Islands National Wildlife Refuge** (see box p. 240). The town has its own charms as well, celebrated in the town history museum; as recently as 1983 a boat was built and launched here.

Milbridge Historical Museum ★ MUSEUM This low-key museum focuses mostly on shipbuilding and fishing as a local way of life, with exhibits such as *Getting Through the Long Winter, Old Ways of Fishing*, and *Rusticators* (about summer tourists seeking to escape to a more basic way of life here). The displays include vintage photos, shipbuilding tools, and a time capsule filled with items from Downeast Maine.

Main St. (Rte. 1), Milbridge. www.milbridgehistoricalsociety.org. ☎ **207/546-4471.** Free admission. July–Aug Tues and Sat–Sun 1–4pm; June and Sept Sat–Sun 1–4pm. Oct–May by appointment only.

Cherryfield & Columbia Falls

Cherryfield is 6 miles N of Milbridge on Rte. 1. Columbia Falls is 11 miles E of Cherryfield on Rte. 1.

North of Milbridge on Route 1, you'll pass through lovely little **Cherryfield**, the self-proclaimed Blueberry Capital of the World, and **Columbia Falls**, with a town center that has retained its longtime charm thanks to the good fortune of having been bypassed by Route 1.

From Columbia Falls, detour south along Route 187 (which makes a complete loop of its peninsula) to **Jonesport,** a photogenic, lost-in-time fishing village dominated by lobstermen and boat work. Jonesport is the jumping-off point for the nature preserve on **Great Wass Island.** Or stay on Route 1 to **Jonesboro** and detour 6 miles on Great Cove Road to **Roque Bluffs State Park.**

Cherryfield-Narraguargus Historical Society ★ MUSEUM If you're lucky, you'll hit town when this small museum is open. Exhibits display tools, photographs, and other 19th-century items. Look through preserved milk bottles, flasks, and boxes from a general store, wooden trunks, washboards, period clothing, and a hand-loom, among other items.

88 River Rd., Cherryfield. www.cherryfieldhistorical.com. ☎ **207/546-2076.** $5 suggested donation. Jul–Aug Sat 1–4pm; other times by appointment.

Columbia Falls Pottery ★ SHOP In a restored schoolhouse next door to the Ruggles House, April Adams's excellent shop features nature-inspired designs such as Lupine, Blueberry, Flag Iris, and Lady's-Slipper. They even take credit cards.

150 Main St., Columbia Falls. www.columbiafallspottery.com. ☎ **877/211-2457.**

Roque Bluffs State Park ★ PARK A day-use-only park, Roque Bluffs features impressive coastal scenery plus the added attraction of both freshwater and saltwater swimming areas. Jasper Beach is particularly noteworthy for the uniformly smooth jasper stones that make it up. There are family friendly amenities here such as grills, changing areas, a playground, and a lifeguard.

145 Schoppee Point Rd. (6 miles off Rte. 1), Roque Bluffs. ℂ **207/255-3475.** $6 adults, $1 children ages 5–11, free for children 4 and under. Open mid-May–Sept.

Ruggles House ★ HISTORIC HOME   This Federal home dating from 1818 was built for Thomas Ruggles, a local timber merchant and civic leader. The house is grand and opulent, but in a curiously miniature sort of way. There's a flying staircase in the central hallway, pine doors hand-painted to resemble mahogany, and detailed woodcarvings in the main parlor done over the course of 3 years by an English craftsman equipped, legend has it, with just a penknife. Tours last 20 minutes to a half-hour.

146 Main St., Columbia Falls. www.ruggleshouse.org. ℂ **207/483-4637.** Tours $5 adults, $2 children ages 6–12. June–mid-Oct Mon–Sat 10am–4pm; Sun 12–4pm. Closed mid-Oct to mid-June.

Wild Blueberry Land ★ SHOP   Cheeseball though it may be, you probably shouldn't leave Columbia Falls without ducking into this emporium, which sells every product imaginable made from Maine's tart and justifiably lauded wild blueberries—jams, pies, cordials, syrup, muffins, chocolates . . . and, of course, the blueberries themselves. You'll know you're at the right place because the building is shaped like . . . wait for it . . . a giant blueberry.

1067 Rte. 1, Columbia Falls. www.wildblueberryland.com. ℂ **207/483-3884.** Open 9am–5pm June–mid-Oct (fall hours may be foreshortened).

WONDERFUL WALKS

West of Cherryfield, you may want to take a drive on Route 182, designated the **Blackwoods Scenic Byway** ★ (blackwoodsbyway.org). A rugged trail system in the neighborhood of **Tunk Lake** weaves among some great swimming and fishing ponds, beaches, and rolling hills, including the exposed 1,157-foot **Tunk Mountain**, with 360-degree views from its summit.

South of Jonesport (cross the bridge to Beals Island and continue across the causeway), the **Great Wass Island Preserve** ★ (ℂ **207/729-5181**) is an exceptional 1,524-acre island, acquired by the Nature Conservancy in 1978. An excellent 4.5-mile loop hike covers a wide cross section of native terrain, including bogs, heath, rocky coastline, and forests of twisted jack pines. Maps and a birding checklist can be found in a stand at the parking lot. Follow one fork of the trail to the rockbound shoreline; work your way along boulders to the other fork, then back to your car. From Jonesport, cross the bridge to Beals Island; continue across the causeway to Great Wass Island and bear right at the next fork. Continue past the lobster pound to a parking lot on the left.

Machias

16 miles NE of Columbia Falls on Rte. 1

The trim market town of **Machias** (pronounced Ma-*chai*-us) is the county seat of, and by far the biggest community in, Washington County—though it's not very big at all. Its year-round population of 2,400 seems positively

Manhattan-esque in these parts by comparison to the rest of the towns, and a University of Maine satellite campus has attracted a welcome clutch of coffee shops, galleries, and other trappings of culture. The town's name is a native word translating approximately to "Bad Little Falls," a tribute to the rough rapids and waterfalls formed where river and coast meet here; the town was originally settled by Native Americans, who used it as a fishing camp.

Early explorers used the same river mouth as a trade port, although true colonial settlement of the town waited until the mid–18th century. This river even became the site of the Revolutionary War's first naval battle on June 12, 1775, when locals turned back the British gunboat the *Margaretta,* a story that's told and retold for visitors at the Burnham Tavern (see below).

Downtown Machias still has a surprising number of historic structures. The **George Foster House** and **Andrew Gilson House** on North Street both display distinctive mansards, while Court Street is packed with historic structures. Machias's town offices are housed inside an Italianate former schoolhouse, the **Clark Perry House** has peaked lintels, and the granite **Porter Memorial Library** incorporates ballast and andirons from the *Margaretta* (talk about taking a war trophy). The **Carrie Albee House** at the corner of West and Court streets is a Victorian home dating from 1900.

Burnham Tavern ★ HISTORIC SITE   Gambrel-roofed Burnham Tavern, built on a rise overlooking the Machias River in 1770, is said to be the oldest existing building in eastern Maine. It occupies a unique place in local history: In June 1775, a month after the Battle of Lexington, a group of locals hatched a plan here that led to the first naval battle of the Revolutionary War. The armed schooner *Margaretta* was in Machias harbor to stock up on wood for the British barracks. Locals didn't think much of that plan, and attacked the ship with smaller boats, muskets, swords, axes, pitchforks—whatever they could grab. The Mainers prevailed, killing the captain of the *Margaretta* in the process; visitors can learn all about the episode during a tour of the tavern. On display is booty taken from the British ship, along with the original tap table and other historic furniture and ephemera. The tours last around 1 hour.

14 Colonial Way (Rte. 192), Machias. www.burnhamtavern.com. ℰ **207/733-4577.** $5 adults, $2 children. Mid-June–early Sept Mon–Fri 10am–5pm. Closed early Sept–mid-June.

Cutler

13 miles SE of East Machias via Rte. 191

The coastal scenery northeast of Cutler, known as the **Bold Coast,** makes for an impressive drive or hike.

Bold Coast Charter Company ★ (www.boldcoast.com; ℰ **207/259-4484**) operates cruises from May through August out of little Cutler harbor to Machias **Seal Island** (which is claimed by both Canada and the U.S. as territory; stay tuned). Captain Andy Patterson's 40-foot *Barbara Frost* tour boat sometimes lands ashore and sometimes doesn't, but either way viewing of puffins and razorbills is almost guaranteed. Patterson also makes occasional trips past **Libby Island** and its lighthouse, a 42-foot-tall, solar-powered

Cutler is more than a fishing village: It was once an important navy communications outpost, its proximity to Europe and northerly location making it ideal for communicating with submarines plying European waters.

Those two dozen or so big antennas poking up above the coast? They're said to make up the most powerful VLF transmitter in the world, as this quiet headland was for years considered a very high-risk target in the event of war. If you're an aficionado of things military, be sure to have a look. However, you should also know that the base's usefulness has greatly diminished in modern times, and the equipment is now operated by civilian personnel; most of the navy property, located on a scenic peninsula, is now being redeveloped.

granite lighthouse built in 1884 in an extremely foggy spot 4 miles out to sea. The 5-hour bird-watching tours leave around 7 or 8am and cost $130 per person (not recommended for kids under 8, even if you wanted to pay that rate for them). You board the boat at Cutler's boat ramp on the harbor. Tours for the whole summer fill up months in advance—Captain Andy starts taking reservations in January.

WONDERFUL WALKS

Marked by a sign in a small parking lot along Route 191, the dramatic **Cutler Trail** ★ (© 207/941-4412) passes through diverse ecosystems, including bogs, barrens, and dark and tangled spruce forests. The highlight of the trail, which traverses state-owned land, is a mile-long segment along rocky headlands high above the Atlantic. Some of the most dramatic coastal views in the state are located along this isolated stretch, which overlooks dark-gray-to-black rocks and the tumultuous sea. Visible on the horizon across the Bay of Fundy are the west-facing cliffs of the Canadian island of Grand Manan. Plan on at least 2 or 3 hours for the shortest loop, or a full 7-hour day to hike the entire loop to the point known as **Fairy Head Loop** to the south (find three primitive, first-come-first-serve campsites there).

Whiting

17 miles E of Machias on Rte. 1

There's not much happening in Whiting, but it's a gateway to some rewarding wilderness.

Cobscook Bay State Park ★★★ PARK   One of Maine's hidden jewels, this state park is an outstanding camping or day-trip destination for the family. Tides flow back and forth across cribworked rocks, exposing deep tidal pools, rocks, and clam–rich mudflats; bird life is also prodigious. There are in all some 900 acres of trails (cross-country skiable in winter), and the hundred-plus campsites include a number of waterside sites.

Rte. 1, 5 miles N of Whiting. © **207/726-4412.** Open daily year-round. $6 nonresident adult, $2 child 5–11.

Moosehorn National Wildlife Refuge ★ WILDLIFE Created in 1934 with proceeds from President Franklin D. Roosevelt's Duck Stamp program, this refuge north of Dennysville via Route 214 is one of America's oldest such refuges, and still home to eagles, osprey, and the unusual woodcock (check out its remarkable courtship flights). Cycling, skiing, hiking, and leashed pets are allowed on the refuge roads, though not in the wildlife areas; there are more than 50 miles of trails, plus observation decks for watching some of the many birds here. Tours are often given in summer. Note that the refuge consists of two disjoined chunks of land—this one here along Cobscook Bay on Route 1 between Dennysville and Whiting, the other to the southwest of Calais.

26 mi NE of Whiting via Rte. 1 and Rte. 214, or take Rte. 191 S from Rte. 1 in Baring. www.fws.gov/refuge/Moosehorn.

Lubec

11 miles NE of Whiting via Rte. 189

Lubec is the end of the line, literally: the northeasternmost community in the United States, connected by a bridge to Canada. (Locals joke that although this isn't the end of the earth, at least you can *see* the ends of it from here.) To get here, turn off Route 1 at Whiting and take Route 189 northeast for 11 miles. The tidal mixing of two bays at this point has long proven to be a popular hangout for massive schools of fish, and fish canning and packing plants once filled the town. Today Lubec is notable chiefly for its vistas of the ocean and offshore lighthouses; set a course for **Quoddy Head** (see below) if you crave high tides, early sunrises, and a view that would stretch all the way to Europe and Africa if not for the curve of the earth. En route to Eastport, the **Pleasant Point Passamoquoddy Reservation** offers some cultural diversions.

West Quoddy Head Light & Quoddy Head State Park ★★

LIGHTHOUSE This red-and-white lighthouse, which has been likened to a barbershop pole or a candy cane, marks the easternmost point of the United States and helps guide boats into the Lubec Channel. (Interestingly, it's also the nearest geographical point in the U.S. to Africa.) The light, operated by the Coast Guard, isn't open to the public, but visitors can walk the grounds near the light and along headlands at an adjacent state park. A visitor center inside the lightkeeper's house overlooks rocky shoals, pounding waves, and some of the most powerful tides on the planet. Watch for fishing boats straining against the currents and seals playing in the waves or sunning on offshore rocks. The park also includes 480 acres of coastline and bogs, with several trails winding through the forest and atop rocky cliffs; some of the most dramatic views can be found just a short walk down the path at the far end of the parking lot.

W. Quoddy Head Rd., Lubec. www.westquoddy.com. ✆ **207/733-0911** (state park) or 207/733-2180 (lighthouse). Lighthouse grounds: free admission. State park admission: $4 adults, $1 seniors and children 5–11. Lighthouse mid-May–mid-Oct daily 10am–4pm; grounds 9am–sunset. Closed mid-Oct–mid-May.

Pleasant Point Passamaquoddy Reservation ★ CULTURAL CENTER One of a handful of Maine's Native American reservations (*don't speed*), this is where the Passamaquoddy tribe secured a landmark settlement in 1981, receiving a big land-and-cash award; in exchange, the tribe agreed to drop a series of land claims that many believe would have won in court—and probably bankrupted the state in the process. (The tribe would have received more than half of the land in the state of Maine if it had won.) There are few tourist facilities here, save a couple of souvenir shops and the **Waponahki Museum & Resource Center**, upstairs in the Sipayik Youth Center, with its photographs, baskets, art, and cultural exhibits. Call ahead if you're intent on visiting—it's only open limited hours, but they might open it for you if you can't get here at those times.

SE of Perry on Rte. 190. 59 Passamaquoddy Rd. www.wabanaki.com/wabanaki_new/ Museum.html. 🕐 **207/853-2600, ext. 227.** In summer, open 1–4pm Mon–Thurs and second Sat of month.

Eastport

7 miles SE of Perry via Route 190

Situated on a small island across a causeway at the tip of America, Eastport (3 miles from Lubec by water, but 50 minutes by car) was once among the busiest ports on the entire East Coast. In the late 19th century it was home to nearly 5,000 residents and 18 sardine plants. The census now counts fewer than 1,500, and the sardine plants are gone, but Eastport's historic downtown is gradually making itself over as an artsy place of writers, musicians, and other creative types attracted to the slow pace of life and closeness to the sea. While the town perennially works to jumpstart its shipping industry, the fishing industry here has also reinvented itself: Salmon farm pens now fill the near-shore waters.

If you're into whirlpools, you've come to the right place: Just north of Eastport is the **Old Sow,** said to be the largest whirlpool in the Western Hemisphere. It's a bit finicky and is impressive only during the highest tides. **DownEast Charter Boat Tours** (www.oldsowtours.com; 🕐 **207/733-2009**) in Lubec leads daily trips out for $69 for adults and $49 for kids 12 and under. The timing each day is based on the tides, so call for details. Otherwise, you can get a look at Old Sow from the seasonal **ferry** to Deer Island in New Brunswick, Canada (see p. 273).

Eastport Historic District ★ HISTORIC DISTRICT Much of Eastport's handsome 19th-century brick architecture remains on Water Street—a compact thoroughfare that also affords lovely views of Campobello Island and Passamaquoddy Bay. The majority of the buildings between the post office and the library are on the National Register of Historic Places. You'll mostly see the work of architect Henry Black, who designed two-thirds of these Italianate buildings during a single hectic year after an 1886 fire razed the previous downtown. Look for his hand at the Eastport Savings Bank at 43 Water Street, the Shead Building at 58 Water Street, the M. Bradish Bakery at 68

Water Street, the Masonic Block at 36 Water Street, the Charles & M. A. Jackson Block at 74 Water Street, and (we think) the Hayscale Block at 49 Water Street.

Water St., Eastport.

Raye's Mustard Mill ★ FACTORY   Foodies may be delighted to discover Raye's artisanal mustard factory here in downtown Eastport, powered by one of the last stone mills in America. The Raye family has been cold-grinding mustard seeds and bottling various mustard concoctions here since 1903, when J. W. "Wes" Raye built the place to create mustards for a booming local sardine-canning trade. Now he supplies sardine plants as far away as Norway; MDI summer resident Martha Stewart is a fan. Free hourly tours of the factory are given, where new flavors are sometimes in the offing; in the gift shop, pick up gifts for the mustard-crazed back home.

83 Washington St., Eastport. www.rayesmustard.com. © **800/853-1903** or 207/853-4451. Tours Mon–Fri 10am–3pm, Sat by appointment.

Tides Institute & Museum of Art ★★ MUSEUM   The permanent collection at this eclectic museum anchoring downtown Eastport incorporates nearly any media you can imagine, with an emphasis on coastal New England history, design, and architecture. You might find vintage photographs, wildlife art, beautiful 19th-century maps, Wabanaki basketry, or old (surprisingly fascinating) sardine labels from the region's cannery days. Rotating exhibits throughout the summer skew towards contemporary painting and sculpture from Northeast artists. Check the online calendar for a list of events, including workshops with the artists who come to Eastport (from all across the world) for Tides' summer residency (you may well run into them at the bar later).

43 Water St., Eastport. www.tidesinstitute.org. © **207/853-4074.** Free admission. June–Sept Tues–Sun 10am–4pm; May and Oct Wed–Sat 10am–4pm; winter and spring by chance or appointment.

WONDERFUL WALKS

Although Eastport is pretty quiet, the 90-acre peninsula of **Shackford Head State Park** ★ (© **207/941-4014**) is even quieter; get there by following Route 190 almost into town, turn right at the gas station, and continue almost 1 mile along Deep Cove Road. There's a hiking trail here with nice views. Interestingly, at low tide you can see remains of several Civil War–era ships, brought here for salvage in the early 20th century. The entry fee is $4 for non-residents of Maine, $1 for seniors and kids 5–11. No campfires or all-terrain vehicles allowed.

Side Trip to Campobello Island

From Lubec (p. 245), it's only a short drive to Canada, a perfect international day-trip opportunity. You will need a valid passport to cross the border, of course. Lubec is the gateway to Canada's **Campobello Island**, a quiet jewel once favored by president Franklin D. Roosevelt. This compact island (about 10 miles long and 3 miles wide) at the mouth of Passamaquoddy Bay has been home to both humble fishermen and wealthy families over the years, and both have coexisted quite nicely. (Locals approved when summer folks built golf courses because it gave them a place to graze their sheep.) Today the island is a mix of elegant summer homes and less interesting tract homes of a more recent vintage.

Campobello is connected by a graceful modern bridge to Lubec—in fact, it's easier to get to from the United States than from Canada. From the Canadian mainland, you'd have to take two ferries, one of which operates only in summer. (From Letete, New Brunswick, there's a free ferry to Deer Island; at Deer Island's other end, there's a small seasonal ferry to Campobello operated by **East Coast Ferries** (www.eastcoastferriesltd.com; ℂ **506/747-2159;** fares C$16/US$12 for car and driver, C$4/US$3 for each additional passenger).

WHERE TO STAY & EAT ON CAMPOBELLO ISLAND

Owen House, A Country Inn & Gallery This three-story clapboard captain's house dates from 1835 and sits on 10 tree-filled acres at the edge of the bay. The first-floor common rooms are nicely decorated in a busy Victorian manner with Persian and braided carpets and mahogany furniture; view the water from the nautical-feeling, airy sunroom with its big stone fireplace. The guest rooms are a mixed lot, furnished with a mélange of antique and modern furniture; some are bright and airy and filled with salty air (room no. 1 is the largest, with waterfront views on two sides); others, like room no. 5, are tucked under stairs and a bit dark. Third-floor rooms share a single bathroom but also have excellent views. A filling hot breakfast is included in the room rates. Ask to see the owner's in-house watercolor gallery if you're an art buff. The sunroom is a great place to relax with a drink, as are the Adirondack chairs on the porch.

11 Welshpool St., Welshpool. www.owenhouse.ca. ℂ **506/752-2977.** 9 units (2 with shared bathroom). C$104–C$210 (US$78–US$158) double. Rates include full breakfast. Closed Nov–Apr. No children 5 and under in Aug. **Amenities:** Free Wi-Fi in common areas.

EXPLORING CAMPOBELLO ISLAND

Just after you cross the bridge from Lubec, you'll see on your right the **Campobello Welcome Center,** 44 Route 774, Welshpool (ℂ **506/752-2529**), open daily mid-May through mid-October.

Roosevelt Campobello International Park ★★ The U.S. and Canada maintain a joint national park here, celebrating the life of Franklin D. Roosevelt, who summered here with his family in the early 1900s. Like other affluent Americans, the Roosevelt family made an annual trek to the prosperous colony at Campobello Island. The island lured folks from the sultry cities with a promise of cool air and a salubrious effect on the circulatory system. ("The extensive forests of balsamic firs seem to affect the atmosphere of this region, causing a quiet of the nervous system and inviting sleep," read an 1890 real-estate brochure.) The future U.S. president came to this island every summer between 1883—the year after he was born—and 1921, when he was

Campobello on Two Wheels

The islands and peninsulas of Passama-quoddy Bay lend themselves nicely to cycling—especially pretty Campobello, which has plenty of good dirt roads perfect for mountain biking. But you'll need a guidebook to show you the way. Fortunately, Kent Thompson has written a handy one, called *Biking to Blissville*. It covers 35 lovely rides in the Maritimes, including some on the island, and costs C$20 (about US$15). Unfortunately, it was published in 1993, but there's plenty unchanged (kind of the selling point at Campobello). Try to order it through the publisher, Goose Lane Editions (www.gooselane.com; *©* **888/926-8377** or 506/450-4251), or, failing that, through an online retailer such as **Amazon** (www.amazon.ca).

suddenly stricken with polio. Franklin and his siblings spent those summers exploring the coves and sailing around the bay, and he always recalled his time here fondly. (It was his "beloved island," he said, coining a phrase that gets no rest in local promotional brochures.)

You can view a brief film at the visitor center and take a self-guided tour of the elaborate mansion, which is covered in cranberry-colored shingles, to learn about Roosevelt and his early life. For a "cottage" this huge, it is surprisingly comfortable and intimate. The park is truly an international park, run by a commission with representatives from both the U.S. and Canada, making it like none other in the world.

Leave some time to explore farther afield in the 2,800-acre park, which offers scenic coastline and 8.5 miles of walking trails. Maps and walk suggestions are available at the visitor center.

459 Rte. 774, Welshpool NB (in Canada). www.fdr.net. *©* **506/752-2922.** Free admission. Daily 10am–6pm (last tour at 5:45pm). Visitor center and Roosevelt Cottage closed mid-Oct–mid-May; grounds open year-round.

WONDERFUL WALKS

The island offers excellent shoreline walks at both **Roosevelt Campobello International Park** (see p. 248) and **Herring Cove Provincial Park** (*©* **506/752-7010**), which is open year-round. The landscapes are extraordinarily diverse. On some trails you'll enjoy a Currier and Ives tableau of white houses and church spires across the channel in Lubec and Eastport; 10 minutes later you'll be walking along a wild, rocky coast pummeled by surging waves. Herring Cove has a mile-long beach that's perfect for a slow stroll in the fog. (Herring Cove also has a very scenic golf course, open late April to October, and campsites, open late May to October.)

Campobello's mixed terrain also attracts a good mix of birds, including sharp-shinned hawk, common eider, and black guillemot. Ask for a checklist and map at the visitor center.

SIDE TRIPS FROM THE MAINE COAST

Once ensconced on the coast of Maine, you'd be easily forgiven if you didn't wish to do anything more strenuous than turn the pages of a book while lying in a hammock. But if you're a back-roads adventurer, an outdoors enthusiast, or a connoisseur of gourmet meals, there are some additional interesting places to be found just a little bit farther afield.

Portsmouth, New Hampshire, for instance, is well worth a quick detour across the bridge from Kittery for its coffee shops, inns, boutiques, and pleasing snugness. Next, just inland from the midcoast section of Maine, huge **Baxter State Park**—featuring the lofty and impressive peak of Mount Katahdin—is one of Maine's finest attractions, and a newly designated national monument is poised to become Maine's next great outdoor playground. Finally, coastal **New Brunswick**, an hour or less from Eastport, is worth seeing for its pretty seaside villages, islands, and high tides.

I have described each of these three side trips below, going in order—as does this book—from south to north.

PORTSMOUTH, NEW HAMPSHIRE ★★

Portsmouth is a civilized little seaside city of bridges, brick, and seagulls, and quite a gem. Filled with elegant architecture that's more intimate than intimidating, this bonsai-size city projects a strong, proud sense of its heritage without being overly precious. Part of the city's appeal is its variety: Upscale coffee shops and art galleries stand alongside old-fashioned barbershops and tattoo parlors. Despite a steady influx of money in recent years, the town retains an earthiness that serves as a tangy vinegar for more saccharine coastal spots. Portsmouth's humble waterfront must actually be sought out; when found, it's rather understated.

This city's history runs deep, a fact that is evident on even a quick walk through town. For the past 3 centuries, Portsmouth has been the hub of the coastal Maine/New Hampshire region's maritime

Portsmouth

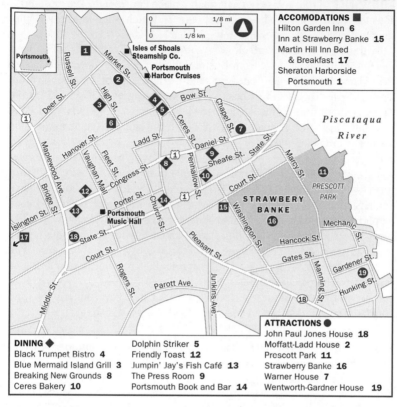

ACCOMODATIONS ■
Hilton Garden Inn **6**
Inn at Strawberry Banke **15**
Martin Hill Inn Bed
   & Breakfast **17**
Sheraton Harborside
   Portsmouth **1**

DINING ◆
Black Trumpet Bistro **4**
Blue Mermaid Island Grill **3**
Breaking New Grounds **8**
Ceres Bakery **10**
Dolphin Striker **5**
Friendly Toast **12**
Jumpin' Jay's Fish Café **13**
The Press Room **9**
Portsmouth Book and Bar **14**

ATTRACTIONS ●
John Paul Jones House **18**
Moffatt-Ladd House **2**
Prescott Park **11**
Strawbery Banke **16**
Warner House **7**
Wentworth-Gardner House **19**

trade. In the 1600s, Strawbery Banke (it wasn't called Portsmouth until 1653) was a major center for the export of wood and dried fish to Europe. Later, in the 19th century, it prospered as a center of regional trade. Just across the Piscataqua River in Maine (so important a connection that there are four bridges from Portsmouth to that state), the Portsmouth Naval Shipyard—founded way back in 1800—evolved into a prominent base for the building, outfitting, and repairing of U.S. Navy submarines. Today, Portsmouth's maritime tradition continues with a lively trade in bulk goods; look for the scrap metal and minerals stockpiled along the shores of the river on Market Street. The city's de facto symbol is the tugboat, one or two of which are almost always tied up in or near the waterfront's picturesque "tugboat alley."

Visitors to Portsmouth will discover a surprising number of experiences in such a small space, including good shopping in the boutiques that now occupy much of the historic district; good eating at many small restaurants and bakeries; and plenty of history to explore among the historic homes and museums set on almost every block of Portsmouth.

Essentials

ARRIVING   From I-95, exits 3 through 7 reach Portsmouth. The most direct downtown access is via Market Street (exit 7), which is the last New Hampshire exit, just before crossing the big bridge to Maine.

By train, it's trickier. **Amtrak** (www.amtrak.com; © **800/872-7245;**) operates four to five trains daily from Boston's North Station to downtown Dover, New Hampshire ($15–$30 one way; the trip takes about 1½ hours). From Dover, take the no. 2 **COAST** bus (www.coastbus.org; © **603/743-5777**) from Dover station to the center of downtown Portsmouth, a 45-minute trip that costs just $1.75 ($1 for seniors, free for kids 5 and under)—but be warned, the bus doesn't run on Sundays.

Bus service, for once, may be a better option. **Greyhound** (www.greyhound.com; © **800/231-2222**) runs a couple of buses daily, and **C&J Trailways** (www.ridecj.com; © **800/258-7111**) almost hourly buses from Boston's South Station to Portsmouth, plus frequent daily trips from Boston's Logan Airport. Greyhound stops at the main bus stop near Market Square, while C&J stops at a modern but distant bus station about 5 miles south at the former Pease air base (call a taxi or rent a car). Trips cost $10–$20 one way, with some student discounts. *Note:* C&J requests that passengers don't talk on cellphones while on their buses.

A one-way **Greyhound** trip from New York City's Port Authority bus station to downtown Portsmouth costs from $30 to $80, depending on how far in advance you book it, and takes about 7 to 7½ hours.

VISITOR INFORMATION   The **Greater Portsmouth Chamber of Commerce,** 500 Market Street (www.portcity.org; © **603/436-3988**), has an information center on outer Market Street as you approach the downtown off I-95's exit 7. From Memorial Day through Columbus Day, it's open Monday through Wednesday 8:30am to 5pm; Thursday and Friday 8:30am to 7pm; and normally on weekends 10am to 5pm. The rest of the year it's usually open weekdays only, from 8:30am to 5pm. During the summer, a second staffed booth opens in **Market Square**—look for the hut right in front of the Breaking New Grounds coffee shop. Hours are irregular; the info is good.

GETTING AROUND   Most of Portsmouth can be easily reconnoitered on foot, so you only need to park once. But mind the rules and signs; parking can be tight in and around the historic district in summer, and officers will ticket. The city's municipal parking garage nearly always has space and costs $1.25 per hour; it's on Hanover Street, between Market and Fleet streets. Most metered spaces are also $1.25 per hour; some are $1.75 per hour. The Strawbery Banke museum (see p. 259) also provides limited parking for visitors.

A trackless **"trolley"** (© **603/743-5777**) loops through central Portsmouth every half-hour to an hour on weekdays (less frequently on Saturday and not at all on Sunday) from about 7am to 9pm. It costs $1.50 per person to ride and covers a few blocks around Market Square and before leaving downtown for the rest of its route. A schedule is posted online at **www.coastbus.org/trolley.html**.

Where to Stay in Portsmouth

Downtown accommodations are preferable, as everything is within walking distance, but prices tend to be high. The **Courtyard Portsmouth,** 1000 Market St. (www.marriot.com; *℃* **603/436-2121**), is big and modern, with business amenities and comfortable beds right off I-95 about 2 or 3 minutes' drive from downtown. It books up fast on summer weekends or when conventions come to town, so specify and confirm your room type in advance. Since 2006, there's also a **Hilton Garden Inn** (www.hgiportsmouth.com; *℃* **603/431-1499**) in a very central downtown location with a nice indoor pool.

For more downscale, budget-priced accommodations, chain and family-owned hotels and motels cluster at the edges of town along I-95 and around the big traffic circle on the Route 1 bypass. I can't vouch for all of these; it's buyer beware.

Inn at Strawbery Banke ★ This historic little inn is tucked away in an 1814 home on Court Street, an ideal base for exploring Portsmouth: Strawbery Banke is just a block away, and Market Square (the center of the city's cafe action) is just 2 blocks. The friendly innkeepers have done a nice job of taking a cozy antique home and making it comfortable for guests. Rooms are tiny and simply furnished, yet brightened up by stenciling, pencil-poster beds, wooden shutters, and beautifully preserved pine floors; one has a private bathroom down the hall. Two sitting rooms are stocked with TVs, phones (there are none in the rooms), and lots and lots of books, and full breakfast is served in a dining room each morning.

314 Court St., Portsmouth. www.innatstrawberybanke.com. *℃* **800/428-3933** or 603/436-7242. 7 units (1 with detached bathroom). Mar–Oct $160–$170 double; Nov–Feb $100–$115 double. Rates include full breakfast. 2-night minimum stay Aug and Oct weekends. Children 10 and older welcome. **Amenities:** Free Wi-Fi.

Martin Hill Inn Bed & Breakfast ★★ This B&B in a residential neighborhood is just a short walk from downtown. The inn consists of two period buildings: a main house (built circa 1815) and a second guesthouse built 35 years later. All rooms have king or queen-size beds, writing tables, and sofas or sitting areas, and are variously appointed with distinguished wallpapers, porcelains, antiques, love seats, four-poster or brass beds, and the like. New owners took over in 2013 and have done some updates, including unearthing antique painted floorboards in the Dashing Wave room. More good stuff: A stone path from the inn leads to a small, beautiful water garden, and the included full breakfast is a highlight. It might consist of orange thyme pancakes, "sunshine" eggs, ginger waffles, and stratas with ingredients pulled from the garden during late summer.

404 Islington St., Portsmouth. www.martinhill.com. *℃* **603/436-2287.** 7 units. May–Oct $160–$240 double; rest of year $135–$180 double. Holiday rates higher. 2-night minimum stay summer and holiday weekends. Rates include full breakfast. No children 11 and under. Packages available. **Amenities:** Free Wi-Fi.

If you're driving Route 1 or I-95 south of Portsmouth, heading to or from Massachusetts, make a detour to **Seabrook** for some of the best lobsters in New Hampshire—and the amazing spectacle of two (gently) competing shacks right across the road from each other.

Brown's (www.brownslobsterpound. com; © **603/474-3331**) got here first, and it's a bit more like the typically unadorned shack you'd find in, say, Downeast Maine. (Its patio also frames a view of Seabrook's infamous nuclear power plant—and, yes, it's active.) **Markey's** (© **603/474-2851**; www.markeys lobsterpool.com) opened later and more closely resembles a small-town diner. The pounds frame both sides of state Route 286, easily reached from Portsmouth or Boston via the exits to Seabrook off both U.S. Route 1 and the New Hampshire Turnpike (I-95; drive east a few miles). From Hampton Beach, head south on coastal Route 1A a few miles and turn inland (west) on Route 286.

Sheraton Harborside Portsmouth ★★ This five-story, in-town brick hotel is nicely located on the way into town—the attractions of downtown Portsmouth are virtually at your doorstep (Strawbery Banke is about a 10-minute walk, and waterfront bars are a block or two away). Another plus: There's plenty of parking both underground and across the street. The modern building, inspired by the low brick buildings of the city, wraps around a circular courtyard; Some rooms and suites have views of the working harbor. The décor's a bit bland, but it's a well-maintained and -managed property, popular with business travelers as well as leisure travelers looking for the amenities of a larger hotel.

250 Market St., Portsmouth. www.sheratonportsmouth.com. © **888/627-7138** or 603/431-2300. 180 units. $216–$467 double and suite; off-season discounts available. Some rooms accommodate dogs. **Amenities:** Restaurant; fitness center; executive-level rooms; room service; spa; free Wi-Fi.

Three Chimneys Inn ★★★ About 20 minutes northwest of Portsmouth at the edge of the university town of Durham, this is a wonderful retreat. The main section of the inn dates to 1649, but later additions and renovations have given it more of a regal Georgian feel. All of the units are above average in size, and have been lushly decorated with four-poster or canopied beds, mahogany armoires, and cool patterned carpets. Most rooms sport chunky brick fireplaces, with either gas or Duraflame logs; these and the exposed wooden beams give the place a rustic historicity. Recent renovations uncovered a 100-year-old signature of a former owner on a previously hidden mantle; they also installed new bathroom fixtures in many rooms, painted the exterior paint job, and more—the place feels fresh. Five rooms on the ground-floor level beneath the restored barn have private entrances, Jacuzzis, and gas fireplaces; these tend to be a bit more cavelike than the other units, but luxurious and romantic. This is a popular place for weddings on summer weekends, and is always booked up long in advance of University of New Hampshire events such as graduation, football games, and homecoming weekend. Book well ahead at those times.

17 Newmarket Rd., Durham. www.threechimneysinn.com. © **888/399-9777** or 603/868-7800. 23 units. $119–$239 double. Rates include full breakfast. 2-night minimum stay on weekends Sept–Oct. Children 6 and older welcome. Some rooms accommodate pets ($50 fee). Packages available. **Amenities:** 2 restaurants; bar; free Wi-Fi.

Wentworth by the Sea ★★   The 2003 reopening of this historic resort was a major event; it's now one of the top resorts in New England. The photogenic grand hotel, which opened on New Castle Island in 1874 but later shut down, was refurbished by the owners of the Samoset (p. 149) and is operated jointly with Marriott in professional, luxurious fashion. As befits a grand old hotel, the main building's rooms vary in size, but most are spacious with good views of ocean or harbor; particularly interesting are the suites occupying the three turrets. Some rooms have gas-powered fireplaces or private balconies, while all have luxury bath amenities, new bathroom fixtures, and lovely detailing and furnishings. (Families might appreciate that many contain two queen-size beds.) Downhill, a set of luxury suites beside the marina are truly outstanding, with water views, modern kitchens, and marble bathrooms with Jacuzzis. A full-service spa offers a range of treatments and body wraps.

588 Wentworth Rd., New Castle. www.wentworth.com. © **866/384-0709** or 603/422-7322. 161 units. July–mid-Oct $460–$649 double, $499–$1,499 suite; substantial off-season discounts. Packages available. **Amenities:** 2 restaurants; bar; golf course privileges; indoor and outdoor pools; spa; free Wi-Fi.

Where to Eat in Portsmouth

Along with the dining options listed below, the **Wentworth by the Sea** resort (see p. 255) a few miles south of the city offers two choices: the **Salt Kitchen & Bar** and the more casual (and seasonal) **Latitudes** bar and grill. The fare at Salt is top-rate, served beneath a remarkable (and original) frescoed dome; entrees might include grilled swordfish, lobster with filet mignon, seared yellowfin tuna, a clambake, a lobster pie, or something more Continental. There is a moderate dress code: Men are asked to wear a collared shirt. The Latitudes grill has a simpler menu, but offers something the main inn can't—an outdoor patio of tables, softly lit at night, with lovely views overlooking the water.

Black Trumpet Bistro ★★ BISTRO/WINE BAR   When the former owners of this wine bar and restaurant space decided to sell it in early 2007, their own executive chef Evan Mallett jumped at the chance to buy it. Now he cooks exotically spiced comfort food in an intimate, two-story space carved out of a former warehouse. The menu is subtly influenced by Spain and Latin America: you partake of starters that might include quahog chowder, tomatoey octopus with chorizo, bacalao salad, local mussels and fries, or a Moroccan-spiced beet soup. Among the entrees, the mountain paella is a recent fave—incorporating chicken mole meatballs, rabbit, snails, and chorizo—as is a local trout served with frisée, celeriac, and a fried egg. The wine list is obviously strong. If the dining room's full, just sit in the bar.

29 Ceres St., Portsmouth. www.blacktrumpetbistro.com. © **603/431-0887.** Entrees $19–$32. Nightly 5–9:30pm. Reservations recommended.

Blue Mermaid Island Grill ★★ GLOBAL/ECLECTIC   The Blue Mermaid is a Portsmouth favorite for its good food, good value, and refusal to take itself too seriously. It's a short stroll from Market Square, in a historic area called the Hill, and is not pretentious—locals congregate here, Tom Waits tunes play in the background, and the service is casual but professional. The menu is adventurous in a low-key global way, leaning ever so slightly toward Mexico and the Caribbean—you might try a tortilla pizza or a salmon club sandwich for lunch, or a dinner of short ribs in guava-soy sauce, served with corn bread; Bimini-style grilled chicken with bananas and walnuts in bourbon sauce, sided with a sweet-potato hash; or beef medallions spiced up with horseradish cream and chipotle peppers. For fun, make a dinner out of small-plate offerings such as wontons, Jamaican beef patties, and the seafood-coconut wrap. They also cook seafood on a wood-fired grill; libations include local draft brews plus a full menu of coolers, mojitos, Goombay smashes, and margaritas.

409 The Hill (at Hanover and High sts.), Portsmouth. www.bluemermaid.com. © **603/427-2583.** Entrees $10–$13 lunch, $19–$24 dinner. Mon–Sat 11:30am–9pm; Sun 10am–9pm. Reservations recommended for parties of 6 or more.

Dolphin Striker ★ NEW ENGLAND   Housed in a historic brick warehouse in Portsmouth's most charming area, the Dolphin Striker tavern eschews glitz for classic oceanside-brasserie comfort. The kitchen serves traditional seafood dishes, with both New England and Continental flair—broiled haddock, mussels in Guinness, seafood fra diavolo, paella—and the execution and plating are top-notch. Seafood loathers can find refuge in a sturdy burger on a ciabatta roll, steak frites, beef Wellington, and the like. The main dining room here has a rustic, public house atmosphere with wide pine-board floors and wooden furniture; downstairs is a comfortable pub known as the Spring Hill Tavern, with quite good acoustic acts. After 10pm, the Striker shelves the heavy fare, but the kitchen stays open with a lighter "tavern" menu.

15 Bow St., Portsmouth. www.dolphinstriker.com. © **603/431-5222.** Entrees $14–$34 dinner. Mon–Sat 11am–1am; Sun 8am–1am. Reservations recommended.

Jumpin' Jay's Fish Café ★★ SEAFOOD   One of Portsmouth's best eateries, Jay's is a hopping destination, and it's especially good for those travelers who want to eat seafood that has *not* been cooked in a deep-fryer. A sleek and spare dining room is dotted with splashes of color, with an open kitchen and polished-steel bar; locals seem to have fun eating here, and the place attracts a younger, hipper clientele than most other spots in town. The

Portsmouth has one of the best cafe scenes in northern New England, nearly comparable to Cambridge's or Boston's. There are numerous places in the compact downtown alone where you can get a decent-to-very-good cup of coffee and better-than-average baked goods; new coffeehouses open all the time. There's a Starbucks (of course), but two of my favorite spots to quaff a coffee drink or pot of tea with a book are **Breaking New Grounds,** 14 Market Square (www.bngcoffee.com; *Ⓒ* **603/436-9555**), with outstanding espresso shakes, good tables for chatting out on the square, and late hours; and **Portsmouth Book & Bar,** 40 Pleasant Street (www.bookandbar.com; *Ⓒ* **603/429-9197**), which hits the trifecta: good coffee drinks, an outstanding selection of draft beers (mostly from Maine and New Hampshire), and a really

nicely curated selection of new and used books. Comfy couches, and the sandwiches aren't bad either.

If you want a bit more of a bite to go with your coffee, Portsmouth's got that covered, too. Two places leap to mind. The tie-dyed **Friendly Toast,** 121 Congress Street (www.thefriendlytoast.com; *Ⓒ* **603/430-2154**), serves a variety of eggs and other breakfast dishes all day long, plus heartier items such as burgers. The setting's eclectic, with vinyl booths and all kinds of nutty kitsch on the walls. There's a brunch rate on weekends—always a good sign. The funky little **Ceres Bakery,** 51 Penhallow St. (www.ceresbakery.com; *Ⓒ* **603/436-6518**), on a side street off the main square, has a handful of tiny interior tables; grab a sandwich, cookie, or slice of cake to go, and walk to the waterfront rose gardens nearby.

catch of the day is posted on blackboards; you pick your fish, then pair it with a sauce such as spicy orange-sesame glaze, lobster velouté, citrusy mustard sauce, or simple olive oil and herbs. Pasta dishes are also an option—you can add scallops, mussels, or even chicken.

150 Congress St., Portsmouth. www.jumpinjays.com. *Ⓒ* **603/766-3474.** Entrees $27–$34. Mon–Thurs 5–9:30pm (closes 9pm and closed Mon in winter); Fri–Sat 5–10pm; Sun 5–9pm. Reservations recommended.

The Press Room ★ PUB Locals flock here more for convivial atmosphere and easy-on-the-budget prices than for creative cuisine. An in-town favorite since 1976, the Press Room boasts that it was the first place in the area to serve Guinness beer, so it's appropriate that the place has a rustic, vaguely Gaelic charm. On cool days, a fire burns in the woodstove, and drinkers flex their elbows throwing darts in an atmosphere of brick walls, pine floors, and heavy wooden beams. Choose from a bar menu of inexpensive selections, such as burgers, fish and chips, and tacos. The jazz here is justifiably popular among locals (see p. 261).

77 Daniel St., Portsmouth. www.pressroomnh.com. *Ⓒ* **603/431-5186.** Sandwiches and Entrees $9–$13. Mon 5–11pm; Tues–Thurs & Sun 4–11pm, Fri–Sat noon–11pm. Bar open later. Reservations not accepted.

10

SIDE TRIPS FROM THE MAINE COAST

Portsmouth, New Hampshire

Exploring Portsmouth

Portsmouth's 18th-century prosperity is evident in the Georgian-style homes that dot the city. **Strawbery Banke** (see p. 259), which occupies the core of the historic area, is well worth visiting. If you don't have the budget, time, or inclination to spend half a day at Strawbery Banke, a walking tour takes you past many other significant homes, some of which are maintained by various historical or colonial societies and are open to the public. A map of the historic Portsmouth Harbor Trail is available free at information centers.

Tired from touring? Take a break at **Prescott Park ★★**, between Strawbery Banke and the water. It's one of the best municipal parks in New England. The water views, lemonade vendors, benches, grass, lovely gardens, and full card of festivals make it worth a visit. There's a full calendar of events at the park festival website, **www.prescottpark.org**. Be amazed.

John Paul Jones House ★ HISTORIC HOUSE   Scottish Revolutionary War hero John Paul ("I have not yet begun to fight") Jones is believed to have lived in this 1758 home during the war while overseeing construction of his sloop, the *Ranger,* which was likely the first ship to sail under the U.S. flag (a model is on display). He took a ragtag crew of locals to England and gave them no end of bother. The house is immaculately restored and maintained by the Portsmouth Historical Society; costumed guides lead tours.

43 Middle St., Portsmouth. www.portsmouthhistory.org. 📞 **603/436-8420.** $6 adults, children under 14 free. Late May–Oct daily 11am–5pm. Closed Nov–late May.

Moffatt-Ladd House ★★ HISTORIC HOUSE   Easy to miss as you ascend the hill into town, the Moffatt-Ladd's on the right as you begin to enter the commercial district but well before you penetrate it. It was built in 1763 by a successful merchant with a view right down onto his docks and operations. The gardens are as well known as the house's woodwork and architecture. The same family kept it for nearly 2 centuries, so most of the furnishings and artwork here are absolutely original—and that's rare.

154 Market St., Portsmouth. www.moffattladd.org. 📞 **603/436-8221.** House and gardens $7 adults, $2.50 children 11 and under; gardens only $2 per person. Mon–Sat 11am–5pm; Sun 1–5pm. Tours mid-June–mid-Oct; last tour at 4:30pm. Closed Nov–May.

Strawbery Banke ★★★ OPEN-AIR MUSEUM   In 1958, the city of Portsmouth was finalizing plans to raze this neighborhood (which was settled in 1653) to make way for urban renewal. A group of local citizens resisted the move, and they prevailed, establishing an outdoor history museum that's become one of the largest and best in New England. Here you get a true feel for the late 17th-century colonial period. Today the attraction consists of 10 acres and more than 40 historic buildings, some restored with period furnishings, situated around a big open lawn (which was once an inlet); it all has a settled, picturesque quality. One ticket gains you entry to about half the buildings—the other half, you can only view from outside. Coopers, boat builders, and potters demonstrate colonial crafts, and the Drisco House is two exhibits of Americana within one house: 1790s Portsmouth and 1950s Portsmouth. While the Banke employs staffers to assume the character of historical residents, the emphasis is more on the buildings, architecture, and history than on the costumed reenactors—as it should be.

Visitor's center at 14 Hancock St., at Marcy St., Portsmouth. www.strawberybanke.org. ℂ **603/433-1100.** Summer $19.50 adults, $10 children 5–17, $48 family; Nov rates lower. May–Oct daily 10am–5pm; Nov Sat–Sun 10am–2pm with required 90-min. guided tour. Closed Dec–April except for special events.

Warner House ★ HISTORIC HOUSE   This house, built in 1716, was the governor's mansion during the mid–18th century, when Portsmouth was the state capital. (Who knew?) After a period as a private home, it was opened to the public in the 1930s. This stately brick structure with graceful Georgian architectural elements is a favorite among architectural historians for its wall murals—said to be the oldest murals still in place in the U.S.—early wall marbleizing, and original white pine paneling.

150 Daniel St., Portsmouth. www.warnerhouse.org. ℂ **603/436-8420.** $7 adults, $6 seniors, $3 children 7–12, children 6 and under free. June–Oct Wed–Mon 11am–4pm. Closed Nov–May.

Wentworth-Gardner House ★★★ HISTORIC HOUSE   Arguably the most handsome mansion in the Seacoast region, this is considered one of the nation's best examples of Georgian architecture. The 1760 home features many period elements, including pronounced *quoins* (blocks on the building's corners), pedimented window caps, plank sheathing (to make the home appear as if made of masonry), an elaborate doorway with Corinthian pilasters, a broken scroll, and a paneled door topped with a pineapple, the symbol of hospitality. Perhaps most memorable is its scale—though a grand home of the Colonial era, it's modest in scope; some architectural circles today may not consider it much more than a pool house. Admission also gets you in to the **Tobias Lear House**, another Georgian mini-mansion on the same block.

50 Mechanic St., Portsmouth. www.wentworthlear.org. ℂ **603/436-4406.** $6 adults, $3 children 6–14, children 5 and under free. June–Oct Thurs–Mon 11am–4pm. Closed Nov–May. From rose gardens on Marcy St. across from Strawbery Banke, walk south 1 block, turn left toward bridge, make a right before crossing bridge; house is down the block on your right.

On the Water

Portsmouth is especially attractive when seen from the water. A small fleet of tour boats ties up at Portsmouth, taking scenic tours of the Piscataqua River and the historic Isle of Shoals throughout the summer and fall.

The long-established **Isles of Shoals Steamship Co.** ★★ (www.islesof shoals.com; ℂ **603/431-5500**) sails from Barker Wharf on Market Street on a variety of tours aboard the 90-foot, three-deck MV *Thomas Laighton* (a modern replica of a late-19th-century steamship). Most popular are the excursions to the Isle of Shoals, where passengers can disembark and wander about Star Island, a dramatic, rocky landmass that's part of an island cluster far out in the offshore swells. Reservations are strongly encouraged. Other popular trips include a sunset lighthouse cruise. Fares range from $18 to $35 per adult, depending on the length of the cruise; dinner cruises cost extra. Parking is an additional charge, as well.

Portsmouth Harbor Cruises ★ (www.portsmouthharbor.com; ℂ **800/776-0915** or 603/436-8084) specializes in seasonal tours of the historic Piscataqua River aboard the *Heritage,* a 60-foot, 49-passenger cruise ship with plenty of open deck space. It leaves from the Ceres Street docks, beside the tugboats. Cruise past five old forts or enjoy the picturesque tidal estuary of inland Great Bay, a scenic trip upriver from Portsmouth. Trips run daily in summer, weekend only in spring and fall; reservations are suggested. Fares are $18 to $25 for adults, $16 to $22 for seniors, and $11 to $18 for children ages 2 to 12.

Portsmouth Shopping

Portsmouth's historic district is home to dozens of boutiques offering unique items. The fine contemporary **N.W. Barrett Gallery,** 53 Market Street (www.nwbarrett.com; ℂ **603/431-4262**), features the work of area craftspeople, with a classy selection of ceramic sculptures, glassware, lustrous woodworking, and handmade jewelry. The **Robert Lincoln Levy Gallery,** operated by the New Hampshire Art Association, 136 State Street (www.nhartassociation.org; ℂ **603/431-4230**), frequently changes exhibits and is a good destination for some quality fine art produced by New Hampshire artists. **Nahcotta**, 110 Congress Street (ℂ **603/433-1705**), is a gallery purveying high-end paintings and sculptures, many of which are quietly edgy and entertaining.

The women's consignment shop **Wear House,** 74 Congress Street (www.wearhouseportsmouth.com; ℂ **603/373-8465**) has a notably hip, eclectic mix of apparel, jewelry, and accessories. Also, a whole wall full of designer shoes. Some deals here. **Hazel Boutique**, 7 Commercial Alley (www.hazelportsmouth.com; ℂ **603/766-1780**) has urban-bohemian women's fashions (great dresses especially), handbags, jewelry, and more from some 30 designers in a neat little exposed-brick alleyway nook off Market Street.

Off Piste, 37 Congress Street (ℂ **603/319-6910**), is a gift shop with a sense of humor and an indie ethos. If you need a *Top Gun* t-shirt or a Versace

Most travelers tend to visit just Strawbery Banke, do a little shopping at the downtown boutiques, grab a bite, and hustle onward to Maine. To get a fuller sense of historic Portsmouth, though, take the time to stroll a bit off the beaten track. The so-called "South End" neighborhood around the **Wentworth-Gardner House** (p. 259) and **Prescott Park** is a great area to snoop around in. You'll find lanes too narrow for SUVs to fit into, twisting roads, fish and lobster shacks, and wooden-frame houses of all shapes and sizes. It's a great taste of the early 19th century, and definitely off the beaten tourist track.

coloring book or a hardcover collection of Instagrammed cat photos, you've come to the right place. **Macro Polo,** 89 Market Street (℡ **603/436-8338**), is the original novelty shop in town (besides sporting arguably the best name of *any* shop in New Hampshire). It's a good place to find Bernie Sanders action figures, mildly lewd magnets, bandages that look like bacon, and the like.

Finally, I'd be remiss if I didn't mention **Bull Moose Music ★★**, 82–86 Congress Street (www.bullmoose.com; ℡ **603/422-9525**). It's a Maine chain, but the Portsmouth location has one of its widest selections. There's nothing glamorous about the cavelike space, but it is *the* place in northern New England to pick up vintage vinyl records and surf new and used books, graphic novels, CDs, DVDs, and games (video, tabletop, and other). I can't count the hours I've whiled away here, but I'd never call them wasted.

Portsmouth After Dark

PERFORMING ARTS

The Music Hall ★★ ARTS VENUE   This historic theater dates from 1878 and was restored to its former glory by a local arts group. A variety of shows are staged here, from film festivals and comedy revues to *The Nutcracker* and concerts by visiting symphonies and pop artists (David Crosby, Pat Metheny). Call or check the website for a current calendar. 28 Chestnut St., Portsmouth. www.themusichall.org. ℡ **603/436-2400.**

BARS & CLUBS

The Press Room ★ BAR   A popular local bar and restaurant (see p. 257), the Press Room also offers casual entertainment almost every night, either upstairs or down. It's best known locally for its live jazz; the club brings in quality performers from Boston and beyond. You might also hear beat poetry or blues. 77 Daniel St., Portsmouth. www.pressroomnh.com. ℡ **603/431-5186.**

Spring Hill Tavern ★ BAR   Quality acoustic noodling, live jazz, classical guitar, and low-key rock is offered most evenings of the week here. It's located right beneath the popular Dolphin Striker seafood restaurant (see p. 256). 15 Bow St. ℡ **603/431-5222.**

10

SIDE TRIPS FROM THE MAINE COAST

Portsmouth, New Hampshire

THE NORTH MAINE WOODS

There are two versions of the Maine Woods. There's the grand and unbroken forest, threaded with tumbling rivers, that unspools endlessly in the popular perception—and then there's the reality. It's tempting to see this region as the last outpost of big wilderness in the East, with thousands of acres of unbroken forest, miles of free-running streams, and more azure lakes than you can shake a canoe paddle at. A look at a road map seems to confirm this, with only a few roads shown here and there amid terrain pocked with lakes. Undeveloped, however, does not mean untouched. The reality is that this forestland is a massive plantation, largely owned and managed by paper and timber companies large and small. An extensive network of small timber roads feeds off major arteries and opens the region to extensive cutting. In the early 1980s, *New Yorker* writer John McPhee noted that much of northern Maine "looks like an old and badly tanned pelt. The hair is coming out in tufts." Forest management practices are somewhat improved today; clear-cutting is diminished, although technological advances in logging have encouraged more rapid timber harvesting on the part of some companies (either to "flip" lands for a quick return or to pay down debts incurred as the forest products industry has waned). Still, timber and paper are no longer the boom industries they once were (Maine's paper mills are shuttering at an impressive rate), and northern Maine has spent the last decade slowly embracing the potential of its recreation economy.

While the North Woods may not be a vast, howling wilderness, the region still has fabulously remote enclaves where moose and loon predominate, and where the turf hasn't changed all that much since Thoreau paddled through in the mid–19th century and found it all "moosey and mossy." So long as you don't arrive expecting utter wilderness (on the scale of, say, the remote Rockies), you're unlikely to be disappointed.

One piece of public land all Mainers seem to get behind is **Baxter State Park**. Owned and managed by the state, it's one of Maine's crown jewels, even more spectacular in some ways than Acadia National Park. This 200,000-plus-acre park in the remote north-central part of the state is unlike most state parks you may be accustomed to in New England—don't look for fancy bathhouses or groomed picnic areas. When you enter Baxter State Park, you're entering the closest thing to wilderness that the East has left.

Former Maine governor and philanthropist Percival Baxter single-handedly created the park, using his inheritance and investment profits to buy the property and donate it to the state in 1930. Baxter stipulated that it remain "forever wild." Caretakers have done a good job of fulfilling his wishes: You won't find paved roads, RVs, or hookups at the campgrounds. (Size restrictions keep all RVs out.) Even cellphones are banned. You will find rugged backcountry and remote lakes. You'll also find **Mount Katahdin**, a mile-high granite monolith that rises above the sparkling lakes and boreal forests.

To the north and west of Baxter State Park lie several million acres of forestland owned by timber companies and managed for timber production.

These concerns also control public recreation. If you drive on a logging road far enough, expect to run into a gate eventually; you'll be asked to pay a fee for day use or overnight camping on their lands.

To the east lies **Katahdin Woods and Waters National Monument**, established in 2016, which adds another 80,000-plus acres to the North Woods wildland recreation complex. Access to the monument is still on the hairy side—you'll want a high-clearance vehicle—but the National Park Service will continue to add infrastructure and interpretive elements (signage, campsite improvements, maybe front-country boardwalks) in the coming years. In the meantime, there's excellent hiking, paddling, and mountain biking to be had on the existing trail system (and something to be said for getting there before the crowds do).

Don't try to tour these woodlands by car. Industrial forestland is boring at best, downright depressing at its overcut worst, and even a drive along the tote road bisecting Baxter is only sporadically scenic. A better strategy is to select one pond or river for camping or fishing, then spend a couple of days getting to know the small area around it. Like a Hollywood set, buffer strips of trees have been left along the pond shores, streams, and rivers in this region, so it can feel like you're getting away from it all as you paddle along. Even better: lace up your hiking boots and head into the depths of Baxter or the new monument, where the woods are still as wild as Maine comes.

The towns of **Bangor** (pronounced *Bayn*-gore, please—not *Bang*-er), **Orono**, and **Old Town** lie along the western banks of the Penobscot River—not far inland from Ellsworth and Belfast on the coast—and serve as gateways to the North Woods. Once a thriving lumber port, Bangor is Maine's third-largest city (after Portland and Lewiston), the last major urban outpost with a full-fledged mall. It's a good destination for history buffs curious about the early North Woods economy. Orono and Old Town, two smaller towns to the north, offer an afternoon's diversion on rainy days.

Essentials

ARRIVING Bangor is located just off the Maine Turnpike. Take I-395 east, exit at Main Street (Route 1A), and follow signs for downtown. **Bangor International Airport (BGR)** (www.flybangor.com; ⓒ **207/992-4600**) mostly connects via Boston to other major cities, but there are four carriers and direct routes to New York, Philadelphia, Chicago, Washington D.C., and multiple Florida locations. It's sometimes as cheap or cheaper to fly into Bangor as Portland, and it could be a time-saver if your destination is Acadia or the Downeast coast. **Concord Coach** (www.concordcoachlines.com; ⓒ **800/639-3317**) and **Greyhound** (www.greyhound.com; ⓒ **800/231-2222**) offer bus service to Bangor from Portland and Boston—from Boston, it's a 4½- to 5½-hour ride costing $30 to $45 one-way.

VISITOR INFORMATION In summer, you can stop by the **Bangor Visitors Information Office** near the Paul Bunyan statue at the convention center on Main Street. The **Bangor Region Chamber of Commerce** is open

THE debate OVER MAINE'S NORTH WOODS

Much of Maine's outdoor recreation takes place on private lands—and that's especially true in the North Woods, 9 million acres once owned by only a handful of **timber companies**. Increasingly, this uninhabited land is at the heart of a simmering debate over land-use policies.

Hunters, fishermen, canoeists, rafters, bird-watchers, and hikers have been accustomed to having the run of much of this forest, with the tacit permission of most timber companies, many of which were founded here and have long historic ties to Maine's woodland communities. But a lot has changed in recent years. One of the biggest factors has been the increasing **value of lakefront property,** which has made this land far more valuable as second-home property than as standing timber. Several parcels of formerly open land have been sold off and closed to visitors.

At the same time, **corporate turnovers** in the paper industry have led to increased debt loads and greater pressure from shareholders to wring more profit from the woods; this, in turn, has led to accelerated timber harvesting and big land sales. New owners are often far-off investment groups with no particular ties to the land or interest in local ecology. Focused only on a speedy return on investment, such investors may opt to cut with abandon, then liquidate the property to a developer.

Environmentalists maintain this scenario is a disaster in the making. They believe that if the state continues on its present course, the forest can't continue to provide timber jobs *or* be a viable recreational destination. Many think there's a reckless amount of tree-cutting and herbicide spraying, while the timber companies insisting they're practicing responsible forestry.

Several conservation proposals in recent years have ranged from modest steps—like clear-cuttting restrictions, tax incentives to promote open access for recreation, and requiring timber companies to practice **sustainable forestry**—to sweeping ideas such as turning the entire region into a 2.6-million-acre **national park**. That initiative morphed into the establishment of the (much smaller) **Katahdin Woods and Waters National Monument**, designated by President Obama in 2016.

In the 1990s, several statewide referendums calling for a clear-cutting ban and major timber-harvesting regulations were defeated, but the land-use issue still hasn't sorted itself out. Big timber companies have negotiated exceptions to regulations in deals with the state that were less than transparent. The debate over the future of this forest isn't as volatile here as it is in the Pacific Northwest, but still, few residents around here lack opinions on the matter.

year-round at 519 Main Street (www.bangorregion.com; ℂ **207/947-0307**), from 8am to 5pm Monday through Friday. The **Greater Bangor Convention & Visitors Bureau** at 33 Harlow Street (www.bangorcvb.org; ℂ **800/916-6673** or 207/947-5205) maintains listings of local accommodations, businesses, and dining options.

Baxter State Park provides maps and information from its park headquarters at 64 Balsam Drive in Millinocket (www.baxterstateparkauthority.com; ℂ **207/723-5140**). Note that no pets are allowed into the park, and all trash you generate must be brought back out. Same rules apply at the monument.

Find maps and info at the **National Park Service welcome centers** in Milli-nocket, at 20 Penobscot Avenue (www.nps.gov/kaww; ✆ **207/456-6001**), and, in summer only, at the **Patten Lumbermen's Museum**, at 61 Shin Pond Road in Patten (www.lumbermensmuseum.org; ✆ **207/528-2650**).

For information on canoeing and camping *outside* of Baxter State Park or Katahdin Woods and Waters National Monument, contact **North Maine Woods, Inc.** (www.northmainewoods.org; ✆ **207/435-6213**), the consortium of paper companies, other landowners, and concerned individuals that con-trols and manages recreational access to private parcels of the Maine woods.

For help in finding cottages, rentals, and tour outfitters in the region, contact the **Katahdin Area Chamber of Commerce,** 1029 Central St., Millinocket (www.katahdinmaine.com; ✆ **207/723-4443**), open weekdays 9am to 1pm.

Where to Stay & Eat in the North Maine Woods
WHERE TO STAY IN BANGOR

Bangor has plenty of guest rooms, many along charmless strips near the air-port and the mall. If you're not choosy or if you're arriving late at night, these are fine. Be aware that even these can fill up during the peak summer season, so reservations are advised. Try the **Comfort Inn,** 10 Bangor Mall Rd. (www.comfortinn.com; ✆ **877/424-6423** or 207/990-0888) or the **Fairfield Inn by Marriott,** 300 Odlin Rd. (www.fairfieldinn.com; ✆ **888/236-2427** or 207/990-0001).

Other options: Connected to Bangor's airport is a **Four Points by Shera-ton,** 308 Godfrey Blvd. (www.sheraton.com; ✆ **800/368-7764** or 207/947-6721); near the Bangor Mall and other chain stores is the **Country Inn at the Mall,** 936 Stillwater Ave. (www.countryinnatthemall.net; ✆ **800/244-3961** or 207/941-0200). Downtown by the Civic Center, there's one slightly offbeat option: the **Hollywood Slots Hotel and Raceway,** 500 Main St. (www.hollywoodcasinobangor.com; ✆ **877/779-7771**). Yes, they have slot machines, plus about 150 pretty nice units, covered parking, an airport shuttle, and—why?—an on-site laundry service.

WHERE TO EAT IN BANGOR

Bangor's downtown has enjoyed a renaissance of late, and along the historic few blocks of Main Street, along Kenduskeag Stream, you'll find good bur-ritos and noodle shops, along with a few solid sit-down dining options. Try **Evenrood's** ★ (www.evenroods.com; ✆ **207/941-8800**), at 25 Broad St. in the curved Merchant's Bank Building, serving classic steak and seafood entrées in a clubby dining room designed around (and in) an impressive old vault. Around the corner, at 56 Main St., **Nocturnem Draft Haus** ★ (✆ **207/907-4380**; www.nocturnemdrafthaus.com) is arguably the state's best beer bar. As impressive as the rotating draft list is, the small menu also stands out, with comfort-y specialties like housemade spinach pie, a great cheese and charcuterie plate, soft pretzels served beer cheese, and really terrific smoked hot wings.

WHERE TO STAY & EAT IN THE KATAHDIN AREA

Lodging and dining are both pretty bare-bones around the Katahdin region, where a sprinkle of B&Bs, lodges, hunting camps, and (often pretty run-down) roadside motels make up the bulk of your lodging options. On the upside, more and more folks around greater Millinocket are availing themselves of Airbnb and other online rental platforms, where you can often find super affordable rentals and cabins. Camping is really the classic way to experience the region, but if you must have a roof, try the **Baxter Park Inn,** 935 Central Street (www.baxterparkinn.com; ℂ 866/633-9777), which has breakfast and an indoor pool, or the **Rivers Edge Motel,** closer to the highway at 2166 Medway Road in Medway (ℂ 207/746-5162), a clean if unremarkable motor lodge where the friendly owner also sells pizzas out of the front office.

On Grand Lake Road, which leads to both parks' north entrances, **Matagamon Wilderness Campground and Cabins** (www.matagamon.com; ℂ 207/446-4635) has spacious riverside campsites, six rustic cabins, a small family restaurant. and a camp store (it's a clutch beer and/or ice cream stop when leaving the park). **Shin Pond Village** (www.shinpond.com; ℂ 207/528-2900) is a similar camp-lodge-store-restaurant complex on Route 11, between Patten and the north entrances.

The only place in the Katahdin region that can fairly be described as don't-miss dining as the **Appalachian Trail Café ★** in Millinocket, at 210 Penobscot Ave. (ℂ 207/723-6720), which has less to do with the hearty breakfasts and lunches than the vibe—chatty locals mingling with jubilant thru hikers just off the Appalachian Trail (their names, in Sharpie, adorn the café's walls and ceiling). This is a great place to pick up tips on the day's hiking/fishing/exploring itinerary.

New England Outdoor Center ★   One of the region's top outfitters (see p. 273), NEOC also offers a wide range of cabins and lodges. Some have a pioneer feel, with bunk beds and wooodstoves, original to the 1960s cabin village this place evolved out of; others multi-bedroom retreats of brand new construction, with heated floors, flatscreen TVs, modern furniture and fixtures, and comfy queen beds. Some have premium Katahdin views. The NEOC's cheery, rustic-mod **River Drivers Restaurant ★** is open daily (you can prepay for dinners as part of your lodging rate) and serves great pub food along with big-feed dinner entrees like rib-eye steaks and crab-stuffed haddock roulade. The place wouldn't hold up in Portland, but it's maybe the best dinner you can get in the North Woods. The lounge in front of the big fieldstone fireplace is a pretty unbeatable spot to unwind with a beer or a cocktail, especially in winter.

30 Twin Pines Rd., Millinocket. www.neoc.com. ℂ 800/634-7238 or 207/723-5438. 21 units. $245–$641 cabins/lodges (sleep 4–14). 2-night minimum peak summer and winter weekends. Some cabins accommodate pets ($20/night fee). Packages available. Look for signs 9 miles northwest of Millinocket, on road to Baxter State Park. **Amenities:** Restaurant; lounge; free kayaks and canoes; firepits; rental snowmobiles; beach, volleyball and basketball courts; free Wi-Fi.

Mt. Chase Lodge ★   Mike and Lindsay Downing took over this classic sporting lodge in 2015 (Lindsay's parents ran it for decades before), and they've set about turning it into the most pleasant basecamp in these parts. The main lodge and its eight rooms share a definite hunting camp vibe (indeed, hunters make up a lot of the clientele), with mounted animal heads on the wall, quilted bedspreads, plank wood walls and stone accents and furnishings made out of birch stumps. Rooms are cozy and share hallway bathrooms, except for #8, which has its own bathroom. In the Maine hunting lodge style—and because meals are included—lodge rates are per person. The five cabins (plus a yurt) sleep 3 to 8 people and have the same rustic vibe. All have full bathrooms; some have full kitchens. The Downings' deep knowledge of the area is a huge selling point—they've been recreating at the adjacent national monument since before anybody even proposed a national monument. And they do a terrific job in the **dining room**, serving up family-style breakfasts and dinners. Dinners are open to non-guests by reservation and might include pan-seared salmon with blueberry chutney or roast pork loin with apples, onions and fennel, along with some of Mike's beautiful (and tasty) sourdough breads.

1517 Shin Pond Rd., Mount Chase. www.mtchaselodge.com. ✆ **207/528-2183**. 13 units. $119–$159 cabins; $59 per person (single occupancy), $69 per person (double occupancy) lodge. Rates include full breakfast and dinner. 2-night minimum stay in cabins. Cabins accommodate pets ($10/night fee). **Amenities:** Restaurant; lounge; free kayaks; free Wi-Fi in common areas.

WHERE TO CAMP IN THE KATAHDIN REGION

Baxter State Park has eight campgrounds accessible by car, and two more backcountry camping areas that must be walked into; most are open from mid-May until mid-October. Don't count on finding a spot if you show up without reservations in the summer; the park starts processing requests on a first-come, first-served basis the first week in January, and dozens of die-hard campers traditionally spend a cold night outside headquarters to secure the best spots. Call well in advance (as in, during the previous year) for the forms to mail in. The cost of camping inside the park ranges from $15 to $32 per site (a night in a bunkhouse is $12 per person per night), while entire cabins can be rented for from $57 to $135. Reservations can be made by mail, in person at the headquarters in Millinocket (see p. 266), or (sometimes) by phone, though *only* less than 14 days from arrival. Don't call them about any other dates. And remember: **they don't accept credit cards inside the park,** only when reserving by mail or online ahead of time.

   North Maine Woods, Inc. (see p. 265) maintains a small network of primitive campsites on its 2-million-acre holdings. While you may have to drive through massive clear-cuts to reach them, some are positioned on secluded coves or picturesque points. A map showing logging-road access and campsite locations is available for a small fee plus postage from the North Maine Woods headquarters. Daily camping fees are minimal, though you must also pay an access fee to the lands.

There are a few drive-in campsites (notice I'm not saying campgrounds) at the **Katahdin Woods and Waters National Monument,** but they are still underdeveloped and not for the faint of heart—little more than fire pits and, at one site, a pit latrine. They're free, though, first-come-first-served and noted on the park map.

Exploring Bangor, Orono & Old Town

In its heyday as a lumber port, Bangor shipped millions of board feet cut from the woods to the north and floated down the Penobscot River. While much of the town burned in 1911 and has since suffered from ill-considered urban-renewal schemes, visitors can still discern a robust history just below the surface.

While this is a major transportation hub, and the commercial center for much of eastern and northern Maine, Bangor isn't much of a tourist destination, nor is it as cosmopolitan as Portland. The downtown has enjoyed a renaissance in recent years, however, and now hosts things like a juice bar, a hip beer bar, a mess of new restaurants, some new condos, decent shopping, a great wine shop, and more. A new waterfront concert venue brings national touring acts all summer long, which has given Bangor tourism s shot in the arm. The same riverside hosts events like June's Tap Into Summer Beer Festival or the multi-stage American Folk Festival in August, which brings in more diverse and impressive world music acts than seems likely for this little north woods city.

Despite the city's rich history and the distinguished architecture of the commercial district, Bangor is probably best known as home to horror novelist and one-man Maine industry **Stephen King.** King's sprawling Victorian home seems a fitting place for the Maine native author; it's got an *Addams Family*-like creepiness, which is only enhanced by the wrought-iron fence with bats on it. His home isn't open to the public, but it's worth a drive by. To find the house, take the Union Street exit off I-95, head toward town for 6 blocks, then turn right on West Broadway. You'll quickly figure out which one it is, trust me.

University of Maine Museum of Art ★ MUSEUM Although UMaine's campus is up the road in Orono, its art collection is displayed here in downtown Bangor. The permanent collection includes works by heavy hitters like Andy Warhol, Roy Lichtenstein, Edward Hopper, and Pablo Picasso, plus Maine artists like Andrew Wyeth and Marsden Hartley. Maine contemporary artists get a lot of play in the temporary exhibitions: You might catch a photography show, high-concept installation art, or punky graphic illustration. Pretty nice second life for a shuttered old department store.

40 Harlow St., Bangor. http://umma.umaine.edu. ℂ **207/561-3350.** Admission free. Open Tues–Sat 10am–5pm.

Cole Land Transportation Museum ★ MUSEUM Vintage-car and early transportation buffs will enjoy a detour to this museum, which features old automobiles lined up in a warehouse-size display space, along with quirky machinery such as snow rollers, cement mixers, power shovels, and tractors. Especially well represented are early trucks, appropriate given its connection with Cole Express, a Maine trucking company founded in 1917.

405 Perry Rd., Bangor. (Off exit 45B of I-95, near intersection with I-395.) www.cole museum.org. ℂ **207/990-3600**. $7 adults, $5 seniors, ages 18 and under free. Daily May–mid-Nov 9am–5pm.

University of Maine ★ UNIVERSITY   Spread out on a riverside plain in the town of Orono, the main campus of the University of Maine (founded in 1868) features a pleasing mix of historic and contemporary buildings. The campus was originally designed by noted landscape architect Frederick Law Olmsted, but its early look has been obscured by later additions. On campus in the Collins Center for the Arts, the modern and spacious **Hudson Museum** ★ (www.umaine.edu/hudsonmuseum; ℂ **207/581-1901**) features exhibits on anthropology and native culture. While it's full of crafts and artwork from native cultures around the world, it's especially strong in North American displays—there's even a wigwam on view. It's open Monday to Friday from 9am to 4pm and Saturday from 11am to 4pm. Admission is free.

Orono, 8 miles N of Bangor on Rte. 2. www.umaine.edu.

Old Town Canoe Visitor Center and Factory Outlet Store ★ STORE   A few minutes north of Orono on Route 178 is the riverside community of Old Town, famous for the classic canoes made by hand here since the turn of the 20th century. The company's now owned by Johnson Outdoors of Wisconsin, but it's a point of Maine pride that the original factory is still here, cranking out top-quality watercraft. Next door to the headquarters, this is more store than visitor center, but there are some deals—plus a big pool where you can try out a few models.

100 Gilman Falls Ave., Old Town. www.oldtowncanoefactoryoutlet.com. ℂ **207/827-1530.** Tues–Sat 9am–5pm, Sun 10am–3pm; closed Sun and Mon in fall and winter.

Exploring Baxter State Park, Katahdin Woods and Waters National Monument & Environs

Most hikers coming to Baxter State Park are intent on ascending **Mount Katahdin**, Maine's highest peak. An ascent up this rugged, glacially scoured mountain is a trip you'll not soon forget. The raw drama and grandeur of the rocky, windswept summit is equal to anything you'll find in the White

Grinning & Bearing It in Baxter

There are a few dozen black bears in Baxter State Park, and while they are not out to eat you, they do get ornery when disturbed, and they do get hungry at night. The park has published these tips to help you keep a safe distance:

o Put all food and anything else with an odor (toothpaste, repellent, soap, deodorant, and perfume) in a sealed bag or container and keep it in the car.

o If you're camping in the backcountry without a car, put all your food, dinner leftovers, and other "smell-able" things in a bag and hang it between two trees (far from your tent) so that a bear can't reach it easily. Never keep any food in your tent.

o Take all your trash with you from the campsite when you leave.

o Do not feed bears or any other animals in the park. They may bite that hand that feeds them! And don't toss any food on the trail.

Mountains. Dozens of other peaks are well worth scaling as well, and simply walking through the deep woods here is a sublime experience in stretches; you will hear no chainsaws.

Baxter State Park lies 85 miles north of Bangor. Take I-95 to Medway (exit 244), then head west 11 miles on Route 11/157 to the mill town of Millinocket, the last major stop for supplies. Go through town and follow signs to Baxter State Park. There's also another, less-used entrance in the park's northeast corner. Follow I-95 to exit 259, then take Route 11 north through Patten and west on Route 159, which becomes Grand Lake Road, into the park. Speed limit in the park is 20 mph; motorcycles and ATVs are not allowed here. **Park entry** is free to Maine residents; visitors driving cars with out-of-state license plates are charged a per-day fee of $14 per car. This fee is charged only once per stay if you're coming to camp; otherwise, you need to repay each day you enter the park. *Tip:* A season pass costs $39 per car for out-of-staters. If you'll be in the park more than 3 days during any given year, buy the pass instead.

To reach nearby Katahdin Woods and Waters National Monument, leave I-95 at Sherman (exit 264), 20 miles north of Medway. The south entrance, which leads to the scenic driving loop and some dayhiking trailheads, is 13 miles west along Staceyville Road; the north entrance is along the same Grand Lake Road that accesses Baxter's north entrance (see above). As of this writing, a fee infrastructure is not yet in place at the new national monument, nor have entrance booths been erected, so the monument is a fee-free area.

SPORTS & OUTDOOR ACTIVITIES

BACKPACKING   Baxter maintains about 180 miles of backcountry hiking trails and more than 25 backcountry campsites, some of them accessible only by canoe. Reservations are required for backcountry camping; many of the best spots fill up quickly in early January when reservations open for a calendar year (see "Where to Stay & Eat in the Katahdin area," p. 266).

CANOEING The state's premier canoe trip is the **Allagash River ★★**, starting west of Baxter State Park and running northward for nearly 100 miles, finishing at the village of Allagash. The **Allagash Wilderness Waterway** (www.maine.gov/allagashwildernesswaterway; ℂ **207/941-4014**) was the first state-designated wild and scenic river in the country, protected from development since 1970. Most travelers spend between 7 and 10 days making the trip from Chamberlain Lake to Allagash. The trip begins on a chain of lakes involving light portaging. At Churchill Dam, a stretch of Class I–II white water runs for about 9 miles, then it's back to lakes and a mix of flatwater and mild rapids. Toward the end, there's a longish portage (about 450 ft.) around picturesque Allagash Falls before finishing up above the village of Allagash.

About 80 simple campsites are scattered along the route; most have outhouses, fire rings, and picnic tables. The camping fee is $12 per night, $6 for Maine residents (no fee for kids under 15 and seniors 70 and older).

The **East Branch of the Penobscot ★**, along the eastern edge of the Katahdin Woods and Waters National Monument, is another of Maine's classic river trips—and a fine shorter alternative to the Allagash. It's a 3-day paddle (26 river miles) from Grand Lake Matagamon near the north entrance to where the river meets the monument's south entrance ford at Whetstone Falls. The first day involves multiple short portages over wild-tumbling rapids and falls; after that, the river smooths out for a mellow 2-day float and chance to spot moose, deer, eagles, and maybe even an elusive lynx. Great fishing for native brook trout, too. About a dozen riverside campsites (free, first-come-first-serve) allow you to break up the trip in a bunch of different ways. Nearby **Bowlin Camps** (www.bowlincamps.com; ℂ **207/267-0884**) offers guided trips and shuttles.

HIKING With 180 miles of maintained backcountry trails and 46 peaks (including 18 that are higher than 3,000 feet), Baxter State Park is a serious destination for serious hikers. The most imposing peak is 5,267-foot **Mount Katahdin ★★★**, the northern terminus of the **Appalachian Trail**

The Appalachian Trail and More

En route to Mount Katahdin, the Appalachian Trail winds through the "100-Mile Wilderness," a remote stretch where the trail crosses few roads and passes no settlements. It's the quiet habitat of loons and moose. Trail descriptions are available from the **Appalachian Trail Conservancy,** 799 Washington Street, Harpers Ferry, West Virginia (www.appalachiantrail. org; ℂ **304/535-6331**). Where the Appalachian Trail ends at Katahdin,

the **International Appalachian Trail** begins. It's a still-in-progress footback that winds up to the Gaspe country in Quebec, but 35 of its best miles pass through Katahdin Woods and Waters National Monument, with rather nicely maintained lean-tos available to backpackers on a first-come-first-served basis. Detailed information is available at monument welcome centers (see p. 275) and at **www.international atmaine.org**.

Allow at least 8 hours for the round trip ascent up Mount Katahdin, and abandon your plans if the weather takes a turn for the worse while you're en route. The most popular route departs from **Roaring Brook Campground.** In fact, it's popular enough that it's often closed to day hikers—when the parking lot fills, hikers are shunted off to other trails. You ascend first to dramatic **Chimney Pond,** which is set like a jewel in a glacial cirque, then continue upward toward Katahdin's summit via one of two trails. (The **Saddle Trail** is the most forgiving, the **Cathedral Trail** ★ the most dramatic.) From here, descent begins along the aptly named **Knife Edge,** a narrow, rocky spine between Baxter Peak and Pamola Peak. Do not take this trail if you are afraid of heights: In spots, the trail narrows to 2 or 3 feet with a drop of hundreds of feet on either side. Obviously, it's also not the spot to be if high winds move in or thunderstorms are threatening. From the Knife Edge, the trail follows a long and gentle ridge back down to Roaring Brook.

(see "Climbing Katahdin," above). Katahdin draws the biggest crowds, but the park also maintains numerous other trails where you'll find more solitude and wildlife than on the main peak. One pleasant day hike is to the summit of **South Turner Mountain,** which offers wonderful views across to Mount Katahdin and blueberries for picking (in late summer). This trail departs from Roaring Brook Campground, and requires about 3 to 4 hours for a round trip. To the north, more good hikes begin at the **South Branch Pond Campground.** My advice? Talk to rangers and buy a trail map at park headquarters first.

Shorter day hikes are the order of the day at the national monument. Two of the best spur off of the scenic **Katahdin Loop Road** in the southwest corner of the monument. A 4-mile out-and-back hike up the little granite hump of **Barnard Mountain** shows off some pretty exposed ledges as you ascend the switchbacks. The 9-mile out-and-back hike to the 1,964-foot summit of **Deasey Mountain** begins an easy ford off the Loop Road, climbs steeply past a massive erratic boulder and through some old-growth woods, then culminates with terrific views of Katahdin's eastern face.

MOUNTAIN BIKING Head for the north entrance of the national monument to reach a 5-mile stretch of the International Appalachian Trail called **Old Telos Tote Road,** ideal for mountain bikes. The route follows the west bank of the East Branch of the Penobscot River, passing five different stretches of cascading whitewater. Highlights include a gnarly 20-foot rock formation called **Haskell Rock** and the dramatic **Grand Pitch,** a roaring 30-foot falls that stretches across the river. In winter, the trail is groomed for **cross-country skiing.** You'll have to bring your own ride, alas, as there's no place yet to rent mountain bikes nearby—as people start showing up to the new monument, I expect some entrepreneur in Patten will get on top of this.

WHITEWATER RAFTING One unique way to view Mount Katahdin is by rafting the west branch of the Penobscot River. Flowing along the park's southern border, this wild river has some of the most technically challenging white water in the East. At least a dozen rafting companies take trips on the Penobscot, with prices around $90 to $115 per person, including a lunch. The trade group **Raft Maine** (www.raftmaine.com; © **800/723-8633**) can connect you to one of its member outfitters. Among the better-run outfitters in the area is **New England Outdoor Center** (www.neoc.com; © **800/766-7238**), on the river southeast of Millinocket. An anchor of the region's outdoor-recreation ecosystem, NEOC offers trips and experiences of every kind in all seasons—guided fishing, moose-spotting, and photography tours, rafting trips, even its own groomed ski trails come winter—and has a good restaurant and a range of lodgings (see p. 266).

MARITIME CANADA

Once you've reached the northernmost limits of coastal Maine, it's just a skip onward to the pleasures of maritime Canada. If you're not hurting for vacation time, it's worth packing your passport to spend a couple of nights in genteel, historic St. Andrews or the windswept world apart that is Grand Manan Island. Whereas Campobello Island (see p. 247) is essentially an afternoon jaunt from adjacent Lubec, the New Brunswick side of the Passamaquoddy region rewards deeper exploration, and it's easy to reach by crossing the bridge over the St. Croix River at Calais, Maine, about a 40-minute drive north from Eastport (p. 246).

The heart of the Passamaquoddy region is the briny **Bay of Fundy,** which is rich with plankton, and therefore rich with whales. Some 15 types of whales can be spotted in the bay, including finback, minke, humpback, the infrequent orca, and the endangered right whale. Whale-watching expeditions sail throughout the summer from Grand Manan, St. Andrews, and St. George. Any visitor information center can point you in the right direction.

St. Stephen

Directly across the river from Calais, Maine, St. Stephen is the gateway to Canada for many travelers arriving from the United States. The two towns have a symbiotic relationship—it's a local call across the international border

---

Time Has Come Today

Remember that New Brunswick is in the *Atlantic* Standard Time (AST) zone, also known as ADT (Atlantic Daylight Time) during the summer, and that it's 1 hour *ahead* of Maine, Boston, and New York time (Eastern Standard Time). Let's just call it New Brunswick time, for now. That means if it's 9am in Maine, when you cross the border, it's 10:01am in New Brunswick when you get across. And if you step right back across, it's 9:02am. You get the idea: reset your watch—or at least make a mental note—when crossing the border, and again when coming back. I have expressed all opening and closings times for New Brunswick attractions and restaurants in ADT; in other words, in New Brunswick time.

from one town to the other, fire engines from one country will respond to fires in the other, and during an annual summer parade, bands and floats have sometimes marched right through Customs. Though downtown St. Stephen is hardly a destination itself, it is a handy pit stop—and the smell of chocolate (see below) does sneakily attempt to entice you into a longer stay. The **Provincial Visitor Information Centre** (© 506/466-7390), located at Milltown Boulevard and King Street, is open daily from 9am to 8pm June through early October.

St. Stephen is a town in transition. The lumber industry and wood trade that were responsible for those handsome brick-and-stone buildings that line the main street have mostly dried up. The town now depends largely on the pulp industry, the large **Ganong chocolate factory**, and pass-through tourists like yourself for its economic mainstays. (For the cocoa bean–obsessed, there's also a small Chocolate Festival in summer.) As a regional commercial center, it has a gritty feel to it, though not much in the way of stylish shopping or restaurants.

You can learn about the region's history with a brief stop at the **Charlotte County Museum,** 443 Milltown Blvd. (© 506/466-3295), open June through August (and by appointment only in September); it's quite close to the tourist office described above. There's no charge for admission.

The Chocolate Museum ★ MUSEUM   Chocolate is so integral to this town's history, of course there's a museum to the cacao bean. Here you can view an 11-minute video about the history of local chocolates. Displays and exhibits explain 19th-century chocolate boxes, and there are interactive multimedia displays about the making of candy and games for young children (such as "Guess the Centers"). One highlight is watching the expert hand-dippers make chocolates the old-fashioned way; samples, of course, are available afterward. Want more? **Ganong's Chocolatier**, the company's candy shop, is located in the storefront adjacent to the museum. (Don't miss the budget bags of factory seconds.) There's also a **Heritage Chocolate Walk**

The Sweet Truth About St. Stephen's Sweet Tooth

St. Stephen's claim to fame is that it's purported to be the home of the chocolate bar—the first place where somebody thought to wrap chocolate pieces in foil and sell them individually. In 1910, they say. At least that's according to local lore. Chocolate is big around here—not as big as in Hershey, Pennsylvania, but still a big part of the local psyche and economy. The Ganong brothers began selling chocolate from their general store here in 1873, and

from that an empire was built, employing some 700 people by the 1930s. Ganong was also the first place to package chocolates in heart-shaped boxes for Valentine's Day, and still holds 30% of the Canadian market for heart-box chocolates. The modern new plant on the outskirts of town isn't open to the public, but there's a museum in one of the company's early factories, a large brick structure on the main street.

offered, which combines a factory tour with a walk through the downtown's historic areas. Plan to spend about an hour here altogether.

73 Milltown Blvd. www.chocolatemuseum.ca. © **506/466-7848.** Admission C$10 (US$7.50) adults, C$8.50 (US$6.50) students and seniors, free for children under 5, C$30 (US$22.50) families. Downtown tour plus museum C$15 (US$11) adults, C$13.50 (US$10) seniors, free for children 5 and under, C$45 (US$34) families. July–Aug Mon–Sat 9am–6pm, Sun 10am–5pm; always at least Mon–Sat 10am–5pm in shoulder seasons and winter.

St. Andrews ★★

The lovely village of St. Andrews—or St. Andrews By-the-Sea, as the chamber of commerce persists in calling it—traces its roots back to the days of the Loyalists. After the American Revolution, New Englanders who had supported the British were made to feel unwelcome. They decamped first to Castine, Maine, which they presumed was safely on British soil. But it wasn't; the St. Croix River was later determined to be the border between Canada and the United States. Forced to uproot again, the Loyalists dismantled their new homes, loaded the pieces aboard ships, and rebuilt them on the welcoming peninsula of St. Andrews, a short sail away. Some of these remarkably resilient saltbox houses still stand in town today.

In the late 19th century, this community emerged as a fashionable summer resort, as many of Canada's affluent and well-connected built homes and gathered annually here for social activities. The Tudor-style **Algonquin Hotel** (now known as The Algonquin Resort) was built on a low rise overlooking the town in 1889, and quickly became the town's social hub and defining landmark.

St. Andrews is beautifully sited at the tip of a long, wedge-shaped peninsula. Thanks to its off-the-beaten-track location, the village hasn't been spoiled much by modern development, and walking the wide, shady streets—especially those around the Algonquin—invokes a more genteel era. Some 250 homes around the village are more than a century old. A number of appealing boutiques and shops are spread along Water Street, which stretches for some distance along the town's shoreline. It's easy to grab a boat tour from the waterfront, and on Thursday mornings in summer, don't miss the weekly farmer's market on the waterfront. I definitely recommend this town if you're seeking a tame, easy tourism dip into New Brunswick.

ESSENTIALS

ARRIVING After crossing the bridge into Canada from Calais, Maine, take Route 1 east to Route 127 and head southward 16 km (29 miles).

VISITOR INFORMATION St. Andrews' seasonal **Welcome Centre** (© 506/529-3556) is located at 24 Reed Avenue, on your left as you enter the village. It's open daily from 8am to 8pm in July and August, from 9am to 5pm in May, June, and from September until it closes in early October. The rest of the year, visit or contact the **Chamber of Commerce** (www.standrewsbythe sea.ca; © 506/529-3555) at 252 Water St., St. Andrews.

WHERE TO STAY IN ST. ANDREWS

Those traveling on a budget might head for the **Picket Fence Motel,** 102 Reed Avenue (www.picketfencenb.com; *Ⓒ* **506/529-8985**). This trim and tidy property is near the handsome Algonquin golf course (see p. 281) and within walking distance of St. Andrews' village center. Rooms cost C$80 to C$100 (US$60–US$75) double. For something slightly more upscale yet unlikely to break your bank, consider the **Europa Inn ★** (see restaurant listing p. 277). Small, basic rooms with Wi-Fi and breakfast go for C$139 to C$149 double (US$104–US$112); some suites and apartment have kitchenettes.

The Algonquin Resort ★★

The Algonquin dates from 1889. The original structure was destroyed by fire in 1914, but the surviving annexes were rebuilt in Tudor style; in 1993 an addition was built across the road, linked by a gatehouse-inspired bridge, and in 2012, the whole place got a C$30 million renovation. The red-tile–roofed resort commands one's attention through its sheer size and aristocratic bearing (not to mention the kilt-wearing, bagpipe-playing staff). The inn is several long blocks, affording panoramic bay views from a second-floor roof garden and many rooms. The rooms have been refreshed, and are comfortable and tasteful. In addition to the outstanding seaside golf course (see p. 281), there's a full spa. Note that the hotel markets itself to bus tours and conferences; if one of those is here when you're year, you might feel a bit overwhelmed.

184 Adolphus St., St. Andrews. www.fairmont.com. *Ⓒ* **855/529-8693** or 506/529-8823. 234 units. C$244–C$329 (US$183–US$247) double; C$429–C$479 (US$322–US$360) suite; lower rates in winter and spring. Rates include continental breakfast. Valet parking. Small cats and dogs C$35 (US$26) per night. **Amenities:** 2 restaurants; 2 bars; babysitting; bike rentals; children's programs; concierge; game room; golf course; health club; Jacuzzi; outdoor heated pool; sauna; spa; 2 tennis courts; free Wi-Fi.

Kingsbrae Arms Relais & Châteaux ★★★

Kingsbrae Arms, part of the Relais & Châteaux network, is a five-star inn informed by an upscale European feel. The inn occupies an 1897 manor house built by prosperous jade merchants in 1897, and features a heated pool amid rose gardens at the foot of a lawn. Immediately next door are the 11-hectare (27-acre) Kingsbrae Horticultural Gardens; some rooms have wonderful views of the gardens, while others offer a panorama of the bay. Guests will feel pampered, with amenities including high-thread-count sheets, plush robes, and a guest-services suite stocked with snacks and refreshments. Some rooms have Jacuzzis; all have gas fireplaces. Guests can also enjoy a five-course meal in the dining room during peak season. (This dining room is not open to the public.) Entrees on a given visit might

> ### It Costs How Much?
>
> A word to the wise: New Brunswick's combined provincial and federal sales tax of 15% can prompt some sticker shock, particularly when ringing up your lodging totals. Some restaurants may roll this "harmonized sales tax" right into their menu pricing, so check out the fine print.

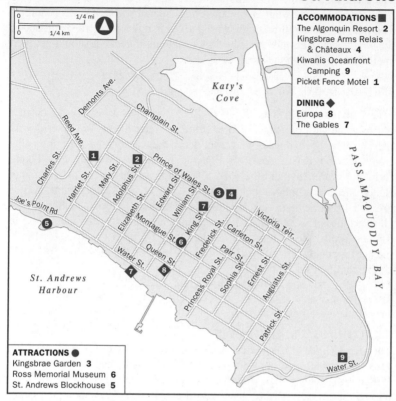

St. Andrews

ACCOMMODATIONS ■
The Algonquin Resort **2**
Kingsbrae Arms Relais
& Châteaux **4**
Kiwanis Oceanfront
Camping **9**
Picket Fence Motel **1**

DINING ◆
Europa **8**
The Gables **7**

Katy's
Cove

PASSAMAQUODDY BAY

Demonts Ave.

Reed Ave.

Champlain St.

Charles St.

Joe's Point Rd

Harriet St.

Mary St.

Adolphus St.

Prince of Wales St.

Elizabeth St.

Edward St.

William St.

Montague St.

Queen St.

Water St.

King St.

Frederick St.

Carleton St.

Victoria Terr.

Parr St.

Sophia St.

Ernest St.

Augustus St.

Princess Royal St.

Patrick St.

St. Andrews
Harbour

Water St.

10

SIDE TRIPS FROM THE MAINE COAST

Maritime Canada

ATTRACTIONS ●
Kingsbrae Garden **3**
Ross Memorial Museum **6**
St. Andrews Blockhouse **5**

include Fundy salmon, PEI mussels, roasted guinea hen, goat cheese in a hazelnut glacé, New Zealand rack of lamb, or Alberta steaks.

219 King St.. St. Andrews. www.kingsbrae.com. © **506/529-1897.** 8 units. C$153–C$339 (US$115–US$254) double; C$419–C$639 (US$315–US$480) suites. 2-night minimum; 3-night minimum July–Aug weekends. Closed Nov–Apr. Pets allowed with advance permission. **Amenities:** Children's programs; library; free Wi-Fi.

WHERE TO EAT IN ST. ANDREWS

Europa Inn ★★ CONTINENTAL   In an intriguing cedar shake building that once housed a movie theater and dance hall, Bavarian husband-and-wife transplants Markus and Simone Ritter whip up great French-, Swiss- and German-accented Continental cuisine for a dining room with just a dozen or so tables. Starters include smoked salmon with rösti and capers; a house specialty of seared scallops in Mornay sauce, baked with cheese; French onion soup; and escargot. Main courses run to several versions of schnitzel (grilled pork or veal steak), each with distinct fillings, toppings, and sauces; beef stroganoff; lobster thermidor; rack of lamb; haddock in lemon butter or champagne sauce; steak in béarnaise sauce; and tiger shrimp in mango-curry sauce. All are prepared with skill and restraint. Finish with chocolate mousse, homemade almond parfait, or one of several homemade ice creams or sorbets. The wine list is also surprisingly strong given that this is such a small, out-of-the-way town. All in all, consider this restaurant a gem—a should-get-there spot if you're at all in the area.

48 King St., St. Andrews. www.europainn.com. ℃ **506/529-3818.** Entrees C$23–C$28 (US$17–US$21). Daily 5–9pm. Reservations recommended.

The Gables ★ SEAFOOD/PUB FARE   This informal eatery is located in a trim home with prominent gables fronting Water Street. You enter down a narrow alley; sky and water views suddenly break through a soaring window from a spacious outside deck. It's all about maritime decor and plastic-porch–furniture informality, and the food matches that—this is not a foodie spot. Lunch and dinner options include burgers, steaks, and seafood items such as breaded haddock, daily catches, and sometimes a lobster "clubhouse"—a chopped lobster salad with cheese, cucumber, lettuce, and tomato mixed in. There's a kids' menu, too, and margaritas and sangria are available by the pitcher for adults. The view definitely pulls rank on the menu, but if you like simple family restaurants, it's an option.

143 Water St., St. Andrews. ℃ **506/529-3440.** Sandwiches and burgers C$8–C$18 (US$6–US$14), entrees C$12–C$24 (US$9–US$18). Daily 11am–9pm; offseason hours are variable year-to-year—call ahead.

EXPLORING ST. ANDREWS

Look for *A Guide to Historic St. Andrews,* produced by the St. Andrews Civic Trust (or download a copy to your phone at www.standrewscivictrust.ca). With this in hand you'll be able to launch your own mini history tour. To make it even easier, many of the private dwellings in St. Andrews feature plaques with information on their origins. Look in particular for the saltbox-style homes, some of which are thought to be the original Loyalist structures that traveled here by barge.

The village's compact and handsome downtown flanks Water Street, a lengthy commercial street that parallels the bay. You'll find low, understated commercial architecture, much of it from the turn of the 20th century, that encompasses a gamut of styles. Allow an hour or so for browsing at boutiques and art galleries. There's also a mix of restaurants and inns.

At the west end, where Water Street becomes Joe's Point Road, a stout wooden **blockhouse** sits just off the water behind low grass-covered earthworks; it was built by townspeople during the War of 1812, when the British colonials anticipated a U.S. attack that never came. This structure is all that remains of the scattered fortifications created around town during that war. Across the street from the blockhouse, the peaceful **Centennial Gardens** were established in 1967 to mark the centenary of Canadian confederation. The compact, tidy park has views of the bay and makes a pleasant spot for a picnic.

At its east end, Water Street curves around the open space of **Indian Point** and the Kiwanis Oceanfront campground. The views of the bay are panoramic; somehow it's even dramatic on foggy days, and swimming in these icy waters will earn you definite bragging rights. Look for history right at your feet when exploring the park's rocky beaches: You'll sometimes turn up worn and rounded flint and coral that has washed ashore. It's not native, but rather imported—early traders sailing here from afar loaded up their holds with flint from Dover, England, and coral from the Caribbean to serve as ballast on their crossings. When they arrived, the ballast was just dumped offshore, and today it still churns up from the depths.

For a more protected swimming spot, wander down Acadia Drive, which runs downhill behind the Algonquin. You'll come to popular **Katy's Cove**, where floating docks form a sort of natural saltwater swimming pool along a lovely inlet. You'll find a snack bar, a playground, and an affable sense of gracious ease here, and it's a fine place for families to while away an afternoon. There's a small fee.

Kingsbrae Garden ★ PARK This 11-hectare (27-acre) public garden opened in 1998, using the former grounds of a long-gone estate. The designers incorporated the existing high hedges and trees, and have ambitiously planted open space around the mature plants. The entire project is very promising, and as the plantings take root and mature, it's certain to become a noted stop for garden lovers. The grounds include almost 2,000 varieties of trees (including old-growth forest), shrubs, and plants. Among the notable features: a day lily collection, an extensive rose garden, a small maze, a fully functional Dutch windmill that circulates water through the two duck ponds, and a children's garden with an elaborate Victorian-mansion playhouse. With views over the lush lawns to the bay below, the on-site Garden Cafe is a pleasant place to stop for lunch. (Try the thick, creamy seafood chowder and one of the focaccia bread sandwiches.) There's also a gift shop and art gallery. Those with a horticultural bent should plan to spend at least a few hours here.

220 King St., St. Andrews. www.kingsbraegarden.com. ⓒ **866/566-8687** or 506/529-3335. C$16 (US$12) adults, C$12 (US$9) students and seniors, C$38 (US$29) family, free for ages 5 and under. Daily 9am–8pm (until 6pm Sept–mid-Oct). Closed mid-Oct–mid-May.

Ministers Island Historic Site/Covenhoven ★★ HISTORIC HOME This rugged, 200-plus-hectare (500-acre) island is linked to the mainland by a sandbar at low tide, and the 2-hour tours are scheduled around the tides. (Call for upcoming times.) You'll meet your tour guide on the mainland side, then drive your car out convoy-style across the ocean floor to the magical island estate created in 1890 by Sir William Van Horne. As president of the Canadian Pacific Railway, Van Horne was the person behind the extension of the rail line to St. Andrews. He then built a sandstone mansion (Covenhoven) with some 50 rooms (including 17 bedrooms), a circular bathhouse (where he indulged his passion for landscape painting), and one of Canada's largest and most impressive barns. The estate also features heated greenhouses, which produced grapes and mushrooms, along with peaches that weighed up to 2 pounds each. When Van Horne was home in Montreal, he had fresh dairy products and vegetables shipped daily (by rail, of course) so that he could enjoy fresh produce year-round. You'll learn all this, and more, on the tours.

199 Carriage Rd. (off Rte. 127, northeast of St. Andrews), Chamcook.. www.ministersisland. net. ⓒ **506/529-5081.** Tours C$10 (US$7.50) adults, kids under 8 free. Closed Nov–Apr.

Ross Memorial Museum ★ HISTORIC HOUSE   For a dose of local history, stop by this historic home, which was built in 1824; in 1945 the home was left to the town by Rev. Henry Phipps Ross and Sarah Juliette Ross, complete with their eclectic and intriguing collection of period furniture, carpets, and paintings.

188 Montague St., St. Andrews. www.rossmemorialmuseum.ca. ⓒ **506/529-5124.** Suggested donation C$4 (US$3) per person. June–early October, Tues–Sat 10am–4:30pm (Jul–Aug Mon also).

Wild Salmon Nature Centre ★ NATURE CENTER   The splashy visitor center of the Atlantic Salmon Federation is dedicated to educating the public about the increasingly rare and surprisingly intriguing Atlantic salmon. Located in a bright and airy post-and-beam facility, the center allows visitors to get oriented through exhibits, presentations, and viewing salmon through underwater windows or strolling the outdoor walkways along Chamcook Stream. Plan to spend about a half-hour here.

24 Chamcook Rd. (6.5km/4 miles from St. Andrews via Rte. 127). www.salarstream.ca. ⓒ **506/529-1384.** C$6.80 (US$5) adults, C$3.40 (US$2.50) students, C$17 (US$13) families. Mon–Sat 9am–5pm; Sun noon–5pm. Closed Sept–mid-May.

ON THE WATER

St. Andrews is an excellent spot to launch an exploration of the bay, which is very much alive, biologically speaking. On the water you'll look for whales, porpoises, seals, and bald eagles, no matter which trip you select. Two to 3-hour tours generally run C$60 to C$70 (US$45–US$52) per adult, less for children.

Quoddy Link Marine (www.quoddylinkmarine.com; ⓒ **877/688-2600** or 506/529-2600) offers seasonal (late June to early Oct) whale-watching tours on a 17m (55-ft.) power catamaran, and the tour includes seafood snacks and use of binoculars; the tours take 2½ to 3 hours. Two-hour tours in search of wildlife aboard 7.2m (24-ft.) rigid-hull Zodiacs are offered by **Fundy Tide Runners** (www.fundytiderunners.com; ⓒ **506/529-4481**); passengers wear flotation suits as they zip around the bay. This outfitter is open for a slightly longer season than many others, from mid-May to mid-October.

For a more traditional experience, sign up for a trip aboard the 22m (72-ft.) square-rigged cutter the *Jolly Breeze of St. Andrews* ★ with **Tall Ship Whale Adventures** (www.jollybreeze.com; ⓒ **866/529-8116** or 506/529-8116). The outfit offers 3-hour tours, three times daily, from mid-June through mid-October; tickets cost C$60 (US$45) per adult, C$40 (US$30) for children age 4 to 14. A discount for families of four or more is available. Watch for seals, dolphins, and eagles—all have been sighted from the ship's deck.

GOLF

In St. Andrews, **The Algonquin Resort**'s Thomas McBroom–designed golf course has long been a beauty—easily among Eastern Canada's top 10, right behind the bigger-name stars on Cape Breton Island and Prince Edward Island. Among its draws: a set of seaside holes that become increasingly spectacular as you approach the point of land separating New Brunswick from Maine. The course reopened in 2017 following a thorough redesign (still in progress at press time) by golf architect Rod Whitman, who set out to maximize views of the Bay. Service and upkeep are impeccable here, and there are both a snack bar on premises and a roving club car with sandwiches and drinks. Greens fees are C$39 to C$105 (US$29–US$79) for 18 holes (carts cost extra; fees are lowest after 3pm). You can also rent clubs and take lessons, and there's a short-game practice area in addition to a driving range; call ✆ **888/529-8693** or 506/529-8168 for tee times.

Grand Manan Island ★

Geologically rugged, profoundly peaceable, and indisputably remote, this handsome island of 2,800 year-round residents is a 90-minute ferry ride from the port of Blacks Harbour, which is just southeast of St. George in New Brunswick. Even though it is located incredibly close to Maine (you can see it from Quoddy Head near Lubec), you can't get there from Maine directly.

Grand Manan is a much-prized destination for adventurous travelers—sometimes a highlight of their vacation. Yet the island remains a mystifying puzzle for others, who somehow or other fail to be smitten by its rough-edged charm. Either this is your kind of place, or it isn't. The only way to find out is to visit.

Grand Manan is a special favorite among serious **birdwatchers**. Hiking the island's trails, don't be surprised to come across knots of very quiet people peering intently through their binoculars. Nearly 300 different species of birds either nest here or stop by the island during their long migrations; if you come at the right season, it's a good place to add mightily to your "life list," if you're into such a pursuit. With birds ranging from bald eagles to puffins (though you'll need to sign up for a boat tour to catch a glimpse of those sea-nesting puffins), you're just about guaranteed to see something with wings you've never seen before except in books.

It's also a favorite spot for devotees of Pulitzer Prize–winning novelist **Willa Cather**, who found her way from Nebraska and New York to a summer cottage here. Cather wrote some of her books while staying on the island. Her die-hard fans are as easy to spot as the birders, say locals, and something of a wild breed themselves; during one Cather conference some years ago, several dozen got up, wrapped themselves in sheets, and danced around a bonfire during the summer solstice.

ESSENTIALS

ARRIVING   Grand Manan is connected to Blacks Harbour on the mainland via frequent ferry service in summer. **Coastal Transport ferries** (www.coastaltransport.ca; *©* **506/642-0520**), each capable of hauling 60 cars, depart from the mainland and the island every 2 hours between 7:30am and 5:30pm during July and August; a ferry makes 3 to 4 daily trips the rest of the year. The round-trip fare is C$12 (US$9) per passenger (C$6/US$4.50 for ages 5 to 12), plus C$36 (US$27) for your car if you're bringing one. **Note**: Boarding the ferry on the mainland is free; you purchase the tickets when you *leave* the island. The ferry arrives in the village of North Head at the northern end of Grand Manan Island.

A couple of tips: Reserve your return boat at least a day ahead to avoid getting stranded on the island an extra night, and get in line early to secure a spot. A good strategy for departing from Blacks Harbour is to bring a picnic lunch, arrive an hour or two early, put your car in line, and head to the grassy waterfront park adjacent to the wharf. It's an attractive spot; there's even an island to explore at low tide.

VISITOR INFORMATION   The island's **Visitor Information Centre,** at 130 Route 776 in Grand Harbour (*©* **888/525-1655** or 506/662-3442), is usually open daily in summer. It's closed from mid-September through early June, though; if you're coming and it's not open, ask at island stores or inns for a free island map published by the **Grand Manan Tourism Association** (www.grandmanannb.com), which has a listing of key island phone numbers and spots.

WHERE TO STAY & EAT ON GRAND MANAN ISLAND

Options for dining out aren't exactly extravagant on Grand Manan. The inns listed here offer good meals, however, and you'll encounter a few more family restaurants and grocers along the road.

If you're here on Saturday morning, late June through mid-September, check out the weekly **farmer's market** in North Head.

Inn at Whale Cove CottagesInn at Whale Cove Cottages ★★

A delightful family-run compound, the Inn at Whale Cove is set in a grassy meadow overlooking a quiet and picturesque cove. The original building, a cozy 1816 farmhouse, has been restored rustically with a nice selection of country antiques. The three guest rooms in the main house are comfortable (Sally's Attic has a small deck and a big view). There are also five cottages scattered about the property, varying in size from one to four bedrooms. One of the older units was author Willa Cather's famous cottage—reason enough to stay here, for devotees of her writing--while the newer John's Flat and Cove View cottages are the most modern, with extra bedrooms, dining rooms, decks, televisions, and so forth. The grounds, especially the path down to the quiet beach, are wonderful. Innkeeper Laura Buckley received her culinary training in Toronto, and the **dining room ★** demonstrates a deft touch with local ingredients. From

June through mid-October, dinner is served nightly. Some cottages are only rented by the week; nearly all units are pet-friendly.

120 Whistle Rd., North Head. www.whalecovecottages.ca. © **506/662-3181.** 9 units. Inn rooms and select cottages C$140–C$150 (US$105–US$113) double; C$1000–C$1200 (US$750–US$900) weekly cottage. Rates include full breakfast. All but 1 unit closed Nov–Apr. Pets accepted for C$10/day (US$7.50/day). **Amenities:** Dining room; library; free Wi-Fi.

Marathon Inn ★   A short walk from the ferry terminal, this former sea captain's home overlooks glittering Flagg Cove. Rooms exude a certain old-timey farmhouse opulence, with floral bedspreads, antique furnishings, ornate wooden headboards, and clawfoot tubs. The floors are a little creaky and the walls a little thin in this aging place, but the house definitely has character—and, moreover, it has a terrific deck and beer and wine service, so you'll mostl likely spend any down time enjoying an Adirondack chair and the ocean view. The adjacent dining room serves breakfast daily and sometimes, with a reservation, dinner.

19 Marathon Inn, North Head. www.marathoninn.com. © **888/660-8488** or 506/662-8488. 24 units. C$89–C$139 (US$67–US$104) double and suite. Closed Nov–May. **Amenities:** Dining room; lounge; heated outdoor pool; free Wi-Fi.

CAMPING ON GRAND MANAN ISLAND

Anchorage Provincial Park ★ (© **800/561-0123** or 506/662-7022) has about 100 campsites scattered about forest and field, available late May to late September. There's a small beach and a hiking trail on the property, and it's well situated for exploring the southern part of the island. It's very popular midsummer; call before you board the ferry to ask about campsite availability. Sites run from about C$25 to C$39 (US$19–US$29), some with hookups for RVs and some better suited for a simple tent.

EXPLORING GRAND MANAN ISLAND

Start your explorations before you arrive. As you come abreast of the island aboard the ferry, head to the starboard side. You'll soon see **Seven Day's Work** in the rocky cliffs of Whale's Cove, where seven layers of hardened lava and sill (intrusive igneous rock) have come together in a sort of geological Dagwood sandwich.

From the Island to Another Island

Quiet as Grand Manan is, you can find even more solitude (and cross one more island off your life list) with an excursion to **White Head Island.** To get there, drive to Ingalls Head (follow Ingalls Head Road from Grand Harbour) and catch the half-hour ferry to this rocky island, home to about 200 locals. On the island, you can walk alongshore to the lighthouse guarding the way between Battle Beach and Sandy Cove. The ferry holds 12 cars, is free of charge, and sails up to 10 times daily in summer.

Once you've landed, you can begin to open the puzzle box that is local geology at the **Grand Manan Museum** (www.grandmananmuseum.ca; © **506/662-3524**) at 1141 Route 776 in Grand Harbour, one of three villages on the island's eastern shore. The museum's geology exhibit, located in the basement, offers pointers about what to look for as you roam the island. Birders will enjoy the Allan Moses collection upstairs, which features more than 300 stuffed and mounted birds in glass cases. The museum also has a fair amount of paraphernalia related to novelist Willa Cather, who summered on the island for many years, and an intriguingly random collection of stuff that's washed ashore over the years from the frequent shipwrecks., The museum is open from June to mid-September, Monday through Friday 9am to 4pm; it's also open on Saturdays during July and August. The requested admission is C$5 (US$3.75) for adults, C$3 (US$2.25) for seniors and students, and free for children ages 11 and under.

SPORTS & OUTDOOR ACTIVITIES ON GRAND MANAN ISLAND

This relatively flat and compact island is perfect for exploring by bike; the only stretches to avoid are some of the faster, less scenic segments of Route 776. All the side roads offer **superb biking.** Especially nice is the **cross-island road** ★★ (paved) to **Dark Harbour,** where you'll find a few cabins, dories, and salmon pens. The route is wild and hilly at times but offers a memorable descent to the ocean on the island's west side.

Bike rentals are available at **Adventure High** ★ (www.adventurehigh.com; © **800/732-5492** or 506/662-3563) in North Head, not far from the ferry. (Day-trippers who are fit enough should consider leaving their cars at Blacks Harbour and exploring the island by bike alone, then returning on the last ferry.) Bikes rent for C$25 (US$19) per day, C$18 (US$13) for a half-day.

Adventure High also offers **sea kayak tours** of the island's shores for those who prefer a cormorant's-eye view of the impressive cliffs. Kayak tours run from C$45 (US$34) for a 2-hour sunset tour to C$110 (US$82) for a full-day's excursion. Adventure High also rents out cabins and offers multiday tours.

WONDERFUL WALKS

Numerous hiking trails lace Grand Manan Island, and they offer a popular diversion throughout the summer. Trails can be found just about everywhere, but most are a matter of local knowledge. Don't hesitate to ask for advice at your inn or the tourist information center, or even to ask anyone you meet on the street.

The invaluable guidebook *Hiking Trails of New Brunswick* (Goose Lane Editions; www.gooselane.com; © **506/450-4251**) lists 12 hikes with maps. Look for a copy at **Of Time and Tides**, 1217 Route 776 in Grand Harbor (© **506/662-3327**), a cute crafts and gifts store with a small selection of local guidebooks.

The most accessible clusters of trails are at the island's northern and southern tips. Head north up Whistle Road to Whistle Beach, and you'll find both the **Northwestern Coastal Trail** ★ and the **Seven Day's Work Trail** ★, a pair of marked trails that track along the rocky shoreline with marvelous sea views. Near the low lighthouse and towering radio antennae at Southwest Head (follow Route 776 to the end), trails radiate out along cliffs topped with scrappy forest; the views are remarkable when the fog's not in.

ON THE WATER

A fine way to experience island ecology is to leave dry land behind and mosey offshore. Several outfitters on the island offer complete nature tours, providing a nice sampling of the world above and beneath the sea. On a boating excursion you might see minke, finback, or humpback whales, along with exotic birds including puffins and phalaropes.

Sea Watch Tours (www.seawatchtours.com; ℂ **877/662-8552** or 506/662-8552), run by Peter and Kenda Wilcox, operates a series of 5-hour excursions in season from July to late September, aboard a 13-meter (42-foot) vessel with sun canopy. Whale sightings are guaranteed or your money back. The rate is C\$66 (US\$49) for adults and C\$46 (US\$34) for children ages 12 and younger.

11

PLANNING YOUR TRIP TO THE MAINE COAST

This chapter provides the nuts-and-bolts travel information you'll need before setting off for coastal Maine. Browse through this section before hitting the road to ensure you've touched all the bases.

ARRIVING

BY PLANE

Several commercial carriers serve the coast of Maine, though airlines commonly connect to Maine's airports after stops in New York or Boston; direct connections from other cities, such as Chicago and Philadelphia, are available. Remember that some scheduled flights to Maine from Boston are aboard small propeller-driven ("prop") planes; ask the airline or your travel agent if this is an issue for you.

Portland International Jetport (airport code PWM), is the largest airport in Maine. It's served by flights from American Airlines (www.aa.com; ✆ 800/433-7300), Delta (www.delta.com; ✆ 800/221-1212), Elite Airways (www.eliteairways.net; ✆ 800/393-2510), JetBlue (www.jetblue.com; ✆ 800/538-2583), Southwest Airlines (www.southwest.com; ✆ 800/435-9792), and United Express (www.united.com; ✆ 800/864-8331). The airport got a significant expansion in 2011, and there are plans in place for further upgrades in 2018. For general airport information, see the airport's website, www.portlandjetport.org, or call ✆ 207/874-8877.

Some savvy visitors to northern New England find cheaper fares and a wider choice of flight times by flying into **Boston's Logan Airport** (code: BOS), then renting a car to drive north (or taking a connecting bus or train). Boston is about 2 hours by car from Portland, and 5 hours from Bar Harbor. Almost every major airline in the U.S. (and many others worldwide) flies into Boston daily, so the fare competition can result in a better ticket price. Note that

From Memorial Day through Labor Day, sometimes longer, I-95 from Boston to Maine becomes sluggish (even stopped-to-a-standstill) on Friday afternoons and evenings as weekend traffic backs up at the toll gates for miles. Sunday nights bring a reverse-repeat of this scene. It might sound comical that you could be stuck in gridlock in a tidal flat in the middle of nowhere; trust me, it's not nearly so funny once you're ensnared in it. U.S. Route 1 along the coast seems like an escape route—but it's not. Instead, it bottlenecks at the same times of day and week, especially in spots where two-lane bridges span the local tidal rivers. There's really no cure for this condition; you can, however, do a few things to prevent getting stuck. Try to stay put on weekends and during the big summer holidays—travel midweek or midday instead, if at all possible. Or simply take an extra day off work and head back after the holiday crush. It'll pay handsome dividends in lowered blood pressure—and you'll save a few hours you would have wasted idling your engine going nowhere.

Boston's airport can become congested, especially at check-in and security; delayed flights are common; and traffic can snarl. But the fare savings can be large.

When researching fares, also check flights going into **Manchester Airport** (airport code: MHT) in New Hampshire, a regional hub for **Southwest Airlines** (see above). The airport is less than 2 hours from Portland by car (1 hour to York or Kittery), and you can sometimes find deep discounts on routes from Southwest hub cities such as Chicago, Dallas, Orlando, Los Angeles, or Houston that don't already have direct flights to Portland.

Travelers to Downeast Maine might check on rates to the **Saint John, New Brunswick** (airport code: YSJ) airport, about 2 hours from Eastport by car—just remember to budget additional time for the border crossing.

Finally, if you need a quick connection directly to Midcoast Maine, check with the regional airline **Cape Air** (www.capeair.com; ✆ **866/227-3247** or 508/771-6944), which operates three to six daily flights from Boston to the **Knox County Regional Airport** in the Camden-Rockland region, using small nine-seat twin-engine business jets. If you book well ahead, an off-peak round-trip fare from Boston can cost as little as $85 per person. Cape Air can also get you from Boston to the **Hancock County-Bar Harbor airport** in Trenton, just across the causeway from Mount Desert Island, as can **PenAir** (www.penair.com; ✆ **800/448-4226**). Elite Airways (see above) runs flights to Bar Harbor from the New York City area's Newark airport in New Jersey.

BY CAR

From Boston, New York, and points farther beyond, the interstate highway **I-95** is by far the quickest way to get to the coast of Maine. Note that I-95 is a toll road for stretches through New Hampshire, as well as in stretches of

Maine, where I-95 is called the **Maine Turnpike.** To reach Portland, exit the Turnpike at Exit 44 and follow I-295 (a free highway) into the city. To get to the Midcoast or Downeast Maine, continue north to Exit 52 and take the Falmouth Spur to connect with coastal **U.S. Route 1 North**.

Note: From New York City, I-95 can sometimes be congested for much of its length, particularly on summer weekends. It's often quicker to take **I-91** north from New Haven, Connecticut, cut north on **I-84** toward Boston, and circumvent Beantown via **I-495** north, which joins **I-95** near Portsmouth, New Hampshire.

Road maps can sometimes be deceptive—keep in mind that Maine is much **bigger than it looks** on a one-page road map. Budget accordingly for drive time. I have noted driving distances or driving times in this book wherever possible, but a good rule of thumb to follow is that 50 miles of rural driving takes about 1 hour if there's little traffic. In summer, passing through a string of busy towns, it might take up to twice that long.

BY TRAIN

Train service to coastal Maine is very limited, but it does exist. **Amtrak** (www.amtrak.com; ℭ 800/872-7245) re-launched rail service to Maine in late 2001, restoring a line that had been idle since the 1960s. In 2012, service was extended from Portland to Brunswick. Amtrak's **Downeaster** service operates four to five times daily between Boston's North Station and Portland. If you're coming from elsewhere on the East Coast, you will need to change train stations in Boston—a slightly frustrating exercise requiring either a taxi ride through congested streets or a ride and transfer on Boston's aging subway system. The train stops in **Wells, Saco**, and **Old Orchard Beach** before arriving in Portland, then on to **Freeport** and **Brunswick**.

Total travel time is about 2½ hours from Boston to Portland. Bikes can be loaded or off-loaded at Boston, Portland, and Brunswick. The one-way fare from Boston to Portland is $20–$34 (with a discount for same-day round-trips). The line has its own website, located at **www.amtrakdowneaster.com**, with fares, schedules, and other useful information.

International visitors can buy a **USA Rail Pass**, good for 15, 30, or 45 days of unlimited travel on **Amtrak** (www.amtrak.com; ℭ **800/USA-RAIL** [872-7245]). The pass is available online or through many overseas travel agents. Reservations are generally required and should be made as early as possible. Regional passes are also available.

BY BUS

Express bus service is well run, but spotty, in coastal Maine. You'll be able to reach the major cities and tourist destinations, but only a few of the smaller towns or villages. Tickets from Boston to Portland usually cost between $15 and $30 per person, one-way, depending on such factors as day of week, time of day, and how far in advance you purchase the tickets. Taking the bus

BEWARE: MOOSE x-ing

Driving across the northern tier of Maine, you'll often see MOOSE CROSSING signs, complete with silhouettes of the gangly herbivores. These are not placed here to amuse the tourists. In Maine, the state with the most moose (an estimated 30,000, at last count), crashes between moose and cars are increasingly common.

These encounters are usually more dramatic than deer-car collisions. For starters, the large eyes of moose don't reflect in headlights like those of deer, so you often come upon them with less warning when driving late at night. Also, moose can weigh up to 1,000 pounds, with almost all of that weight placed high atop spindly legs—when a car strikes a moose broadside in the road, it usually knocks the legs out and sends a half-ton of hapless beast right through the windshield. Need we dwell on the results of such an encounter? I thought not. In 1998 alone, the state of Maine recorded 859 crashes involving moose, with 247 injuries and five fatalities. When in moose country, drive slowly and carefully.

requires no advance planning or reservations, but in summer it's still a good idea to buy as early as possible; often you can also save money this way. Two major bus lines serve coastal Maine from Boston and New York City. **Greyhound** (www.greyound.com; ℂ **800/231-2222**) serves Portsmouth, New Hampshire; Portland; Bangor; and points in between with frequent departures from Boston's South Station or New York's Port Authority. **Concord Coach Lines** (www.concordcoachlines.com; ℂ **800/639-3317** or 603/228-3300) serves Portsmouth, New Hampshire; Portland; and Bangor from Boston, and it also connects a few key smaller towns such as **Belfast**, **Camden**, **Rockport**, **Brunswick**, and **Damariscotta**. Sadly, neither line goes anymore to Bar Harbor.

GETTING AROUND

Maine is like much of the rest of America: A set of small cities and suburbs, strung together by transportation corridors, with a whole bunch of small towns and rural areas filling in the rest of the map. Bus, train, and regional plane services are sporadic at best. This all means you will almost certainly need to travel by car (yours, or one you have rented) if you really want to see the coast of Maine in any detail.

BY CAR

Mark my words: You'll need a car. Portland's airport (see p. 84) has plenty of rental options, from all the multi-national rental agencies.

Traffic in Maine is generally light compared with that in urban and suburban areas of the East Coast, but the Maine Turnpike and U.S. Route 1 can get heavily congested, especially when entering Maine on a summer Friday evening or departing it on a Sunday night. Expect **delays** at peak times, and try to travel off-peak if possible.

North-south travel is fairly straightforward in Maine, thanks to **I-95 and Route 1**. Don't underestimate the length of the Maine coast, though—from Kittery to Eastport (the easternmost city in the United States) is 293 miles, much of it winding slowly through coastal villages or sitting at stoplights. Driving times can be longer than you'd expect due to narrow roads and zig-zagging peninsulas.

Here are some representative distances between points:

NEW YORK CITY TO	
Bar Harbor, Maine	493 miles
Portland, Maine	319 miles
PORTLAND, MAINE, TO	
Eastport, Maine	250 miles
Bar Harbor, Maine	174 miles
Camden, Maine	85 miles
York, Maine	45 miles
Kennebunk, Maine	27 miles
Manchester, New Hampshire	95 miles
North Conway, New Hampshire	65 miles
Burlington, Vermont	232 miles

BY BUS

As I have already mentioned, express bus service *into* the region is pretty good, but there is really no non-car means of traveling *within*. Quirky schedules and routes may send you well out of your way, and what may seem like a simple trip could take hours. Traveling north-south between towns along a single bus route (for example, Portland to Bangor) is feasible, but east-west travel across Maine is, by and large, impractical. For information on bus travel within Maine, contact either **Greyhound** or **Concord Coach Lines** (see p. 289).

BY PLANE

Service between airports in Maine is sketchy at best. You can find limited direct flights between some cities (such as Portland to Bangor), but for the most part, you'll have to backtrack to Boston and fly out again to your final destination. Convenient, it's not. See p. 286 for details

BY TRAIN

Amtrak (www.amtrak.com; © **800/872-7245**) provides limited rail travel on the southernmost coast of Maine (see p. 288 for details). There is talk here and there of expanding passenger rail lines west to Lewiston and beyond, to Montreal, but I wouldn't start planning a trip around it anytime soon.

WHAT THINGS WILL COST

EXCHANGE RATES

US$	Can$	UK£	Euro (€)	Aus$	NZ$
1	C$1.32	£.79	€.95	A$1.30	NZ$1.40

Frommer's lists exact prices in the local currency. The currency conversions quoted above were correct at press time. However, rates fluctuate, so before departing, consult a currency exchange website, such as **www.oanda.com/convert/classic**, to check up-to-the-minute rates.

Costs

Here's a scene I've seen repeated dozens of times in Maine. It's late Saturday afternoon, maybe early in July. A young (or not-so-young) couple has driven up from the city by car or motorcycle, "just for the day," in sparkling clear weather. But something magical has happened. They've fallen in love with each other all over again, and with the quaint lovely Maine-ness of (insert town here). They've decided to stay for the night in a feather bed, eat a nice meal, and maybe watch the sun set over the (ocean/mountains/lake) and have a beer, and head home tomorrow morning fully assured that all is right with the world.

Except that here they stand, before a tourist information center staff member, looking despondent (or even desperate) as the staffer holds a phone in one hand, waiting for an answer.

WHAT THINGS COST ON THE MAINE COAST	US$
Taxi from Portland airport to downtown Portland	25 + tip
Double room, moderate	130
Double room, inexpensive	85
Three-course dinner for one, moderate, no wine	25–35
Bottle of domestic beer	2
Bottle of Coca-Cola	1.29
Cup of coffee	2–3
1 gallon of gas	2.35
Admission to Ogunquit Museum of American Art	9–10 per person
Admission to Acadia National Park, May–Oct	12–25 per vehicle
Admission to Acadia National Park, Nov–Apr	Free

"Isn't there anything cheaper?" pleads one of the lovebirds. "No, and that's a good price," responds the person behind the desk as kindly as possible. "You won't find anything better. Now, do you want me to book it, or not?"

Yes, travelers are in for a little sticker shock on the coast of Maine, at least during peak travel seasons. In midsummer, there's simply no such thing as a cheap motel room in places such as Portland, Camden, or Bar Harbor. Even no-frills mom-and-pop motels can and do sometimes happily charge $100 a night or more for a bed that could fairly be described as a notch above car-camping. Blander-than-bland chain hotels demand even more.

To be fair, innkeepers in some of these tourist areas must reap nearly all their annual profits in what amounts to just a 2- or 3-month season each year, so that's one reason for the approaching-bank-stickup rates. It's not like they enjoy your misery (I don't think).

Anyhow, take heart. *Outside* of peak foliage season and holidays, the cost of rooms, meals, and day-to-day expenses is generally a lot less here than you'd pay in a major non-New England city. You can find excellent entrees at upscale, creative restaurants for around $20, comparing favorably with similar dishes at big-city restaurants that would top $30.

Still, lodging here is more expensive than in almost any other rural part of the United States, and planning can prove tricky for budget travelers.

It's highly recommended that you travel with at least one major credit card. You must have one to rent a car, and hotels and airlines usually require a credit card imprint as a deposit against expenses.

WHEN TO GO

The well-worn joke about the climate in coastal Maine is that it has just two seasons: winter and August. There's a kernel of truth in this, but it's also probably a ploy to keep outsiders from moving here. In fact, the ever-shifting seasons make Maine distinctive, and with one exception, the seasons are well defined.

SUMMER The peak summer season runs from July 4th to Labor Day (although increasingly, businesses report that summer traffic lasts solidly until the end of September). Vast crowds surge up the Maine coast during and between the two holiday weekends, swelling traffic on the turnpike and Route 1, and causing countless motels and inns to hang "No Vacancy" signs. Expect to pay premium prices at hotels and restaurants along the coast in midseason. This should be no surprise: Summers are exquisite, in spite of the occasional stretches of fog or rain. (In Portland it tops 90°F/32°C only 4 or 5 days a year, on average.)

Maine's coastal weather is largely determined by whatever breezes are prevailing. Southerly winds bring haze, heat, humidity, fog (thick fogs occasionally linger for days), and even thunderstorms. Northwesterly winds bring cool weather and knife-sharp vistas. (Northeasters bring wind and storms, though these are rare in summer.) These systems tend to alternate during summer, with the heat arriving stealthily and slowly, then getting exiled by stiff, cool winds a few days later. Along the immediate coast it's often warmest in the late morning; sea breezes typically kick up around lunchtime, pushing temperatures back down for the rest of the afternoons. Rain is rarely far away—some days it's an afternoon thunderstorm, sometimes it's a steady drizzle that brings a 4-day soaking. On average, about 1 day in 3 will bring at least a little rain. Travelers should come prepared for some.

Also be aware that early summer brings out black flies and mosquitoes in multitudes, a state of affairs that has ruined many a camping and hiking trip. While this is especially true inland, it applies along the coastline and on islands as well. Outdoors enthusiasts are best advised to wait until July 4 or later for long camping-out adventures unless they want to end up resembling human pincushions.

AUTUMN Fall is to Maine what the Grand Canyon is to the Southwest: It's one of the great natural spectacles of the place. The rolling hills become saturated in brilliant reds and stunning oranges (every year's foliage is different); the season is almost garish. Even hardened locals still get dewy-eyed at the sight of the annual colors year after year.

Don't be surprised if you sense fall approaching as early as mid-August, when a first few leaves turn orange on the maples at the edges of wetlands. Fall comes early to Maine, puts its feet up on the couch, and hangs around for some time. The foliage season begins in earnest in the northern part of the region by the third week in September; in the south, it reaches its peak around mid-October. Happily, thanks to Maine's low elevation and the moderating influences of ocean temperatures along the coast, foliage season tends to run longer along the coast than it does inland; sometimes the tart colors even linger into the first few days of November.

Keep in mind that this is also a hugely popular time of year for other travelers, however—bus tours flock like migrating geese to all parts of New England in early October. As a result, hotels are often booked solid, and advance reservations are essential. Don't be surprised if you're assessed a foliage surcharge of $10 to $50 per night at some inns. Pay it and be glad you're here.

Maine maintains a recorded **foliage hot line** and **website** to let you know where and when the leaves are at their brightest peaks. Call © **888/624-6345** for the latest updates, or log onto the state's foliage website at **www.maine foliage.com**.

WINTER Maine winters are like wine; some years are good, some are lousy. During a good season, mounds of light, fluffy snow blanket the deep woods and fill the ski slopes. The muffling qualities of fresh snow bring a great silence to the region, and the hiss and pop of a wood fire at a country inn can sound like a heavenly symphony. During these winters, exploring the powdery forest floors on snowshoes or cross-country skis is an experience bordering on the magical.

AN ONLINE TRAVELER'S toolbox

Savvy travelers know that it's a great idea to use online resources when planning a trip to the coast of Maine. Here are a few websites I keep bookmarked:

www.pressherald.com
Portland Press Herald, Maine's largest newspaper

www.maine.gov
Maine state government website

www.nps.gov/acad
Acadia National Park

www.visitmaine.com

During those other winters, though (the lousy ones), the weather gods bring a nasty melange of rain, freezing rain, and sleet. The woods become filled with dirty crusty snow; the sky seems perpetually cottony and bleak. In 1998, a destructive ice storm wreaked so much havoc on the woods that you can still see evidence (fallen trees) today. During times like this, even the stoutest residents wish they'd been born in the Caribbean.

Beach towns such as York Beach and Ogunquit and tourist destinations such as Boothbay Harbor shut down almost entirely and become almost depressing in winter. Skip those. Winter visitors are better off heading for places with more substantial year-round communities and a good selection of year-round lodging and cultural attractions, such as the Kennebunks, Portland, and Bar Harbor. (A foray inland to Baxter State Park is also a fine idea in a cold clear winter; see p. 262.)

SPRING Maine's spring seemingly lasts only a weekend or so, often around mid-May but sometimes as late as June. One day the ground is muddy, the trees barren, and gritty snow is still collected in shady hollows. The next day it's in the 70s or 80s, trees are blooming, and kids are jumping off docks into the ocean.

Travelers need to be alert if they want to experience spring in Maine; it's also known as "mud season" in these parts, and many innkeepers and restaurateurs actually close up shop for a few weeks for repairs or to venture someplace a lot more cheery. Yet April and May can offer superb days when a blue sky arches overhead and it's warm in the sun. This might be the most peaceful time of year—a good time for taking solitary walks on the beach or sitting on rocky promontories with only seagulls for company. And here's another secret: Maine hotel rooms are never cheaper than they are in springtime. Just be aware that as soon as that sun slips behind a cloud, it'll feel like winter again; don't leave the parka or gloves far behind.

Portland's Average Monthly Temperatures

		JAN	FEB	MAR	APR	MAY	JUNE	JULY	AUG	SEPT	OCT	NOV	DEC
AVG. HIGH	(°F)	31	35	42	53	64	73	79	78	70	59	48	37
	(°C)	-1	2	6	12	18	23	26	26	21	15	9	3
AVG. LOW	(°F)	13	17	25	35	44	54	59	58	50	39	31	20
	(°C)	-11	-8	-4	2	7	12	15	14	10	4	-1	-7

CALENDAR OF EVENTS

Banks, government offices, post offices, and many stores, restaurants, and museums are closed on the following legal national holidays: January 1 (New Year's Day), the third Monday in January (Martin Luther King, Jr., Day), the third Monday in February (Presidents' Day), the last Monday in May (Memorial Day), July 4 (Independence Day), the first Monday in September (Labor Day), the second Monday in October (Columbus Day), November 11 (Veterans' Day/Armistice Day), the fourth Thursday in November (Thanksgiving Day), and December 25 (Christmas). The Tuesday after the first Monday in November is Election Day, a federal government holiday in presidential-election years (held every 4 years, and next in 2020).

Beyond this, civic festivals are a mainstay of Maine's little towns, each one clamoring to stake its claim to some obscure aspect of Maine life and culture, and its hard to keep up with all the **Whoopie Pie festivals** (in Dover-Foxcroft in June), **Potato Blossom festivals** (in Fort Fairfield in July), and **Moxie festivals** (also July, in Lisbon). Maine Office of Tourism maintains a pretty comprehensive and searchable calendar at www.visitmaine.com/events. In the late summer and early fall, various small-town and county **agricultural fairs** present a classic slice of rural Americana—midways, tractor pulls, livestock exhibits, and so on. **The Blue Hill Fair** in early August and the **Fryeburg Fair** in early October are the best of these. Check www.**mainefairs.org** for a list.

JANUARY

New Year's Portland. Ring in the New Year with a smorgasbord of events and entertainment throughout downtown Portland. Events for families are scheduled in the afternoon; adult entertainment, including loads of live music, kicks off later in the evening. One admission price buys entrance to all events. December 31 and January 1.

FEBRUARY

U.S. National Toboggan Championships, Camden. A raucous and lively athletic event where being overweight is an advantage. Held at the Camden Snow Bowl's toboggan chute (www.camdensnowbowl.com; ✆ **207/236-3438**). Early February.

MARCH

Maine Boatbuilders' Show, Portland. More than 200 exhibitors and 9,000 boat aficionados gather as winter fades to make plans for the coming summer. A great place to meet boat builders and get ideas for your dream craft (www.portlandcompany.com/boatshow; ✆ **207/774-1067**). Mid-March.

Maine Maple Sunday. Maple sugarhouses throughout the state open their doors to visitors (www.mainemapleproducers.com; ✆ **207/287-3491**). Fourth Sunday in March.

APRIL

Ogunquit Patriot's Day Festival. Commemorating the 1775 Battle of Lexington and Concord, Ogunquit's celebration is all about fife and drum bands, colonial-themed games and races, historical reenactments, and the like. Call ✆ **207/646-2939**. Weekend of the 3rd Monday in April.

MAY

All Roads Music Festival, Belfast. Dozens of Maine bands and performers converge on every available venue in Belfast for a full-day of concerts, panels, and special collaborations (www.allroadsmusicfest.org; ✆ **207/370-9197**). Late May.

JUNE

Old Port Festival, Portland. A block party in the heart of Portland's historic district with live music, food vendors, and activities for kids (www.portlandmaine.com/old-port-festival; ✆ **207/772-6828**). Mid-June.

Annual Windjammer Days, Boothbay Harbor. For nearly 4 decades, windjammers have gathered in Boothbay Harbor to kick off the summer sailing season. Expect music, food, and a parade of magnificent sailboats (www.windjammerdays.org; ✆ **207/633-2353**). Late June.

JULY

Independence Day, region-wide. Communities all along the coast celebrate with parades, greased-pole climbs, cakewalks, cookouts, road races, and fireworks. The bigger the town, the bigger the fireworks.

But many small coastal towns feature seafood and/or lobster-boat racing, an unusual and fun way to celebrate the occasion. Eastport's 4-day-long celebration is particularly impressive (see p. 231). Check local newspapers or contact chambers of commerce for details. July 4.

Portland Summer Concerts. They run all summer, but July's the peak month for big outdoor concerts at Portland's Maine State Pier and Thompson's Point, featuring everything from country acts to jam bands to Bob Dylan. Check www.waterfrontconcerts.com and www.thompsonspointmaine.com for summer schedules. June, July, and August.

York Days, York Village. Enjoy a quintessential coastal Maine celebration complete with crafts, road races, parades, dances, concerts, fireworks, and much more. Call ☎ **207/363-1040**. Late July to early August.

AUGUST

Maine Lobster Festival, Rockland. Enjoy a boiled lobster or two, and take in ample entertainment during this informal waterfront gala celebrating Maine's favorite crustacean (www.mainelobsterfestival.com; ☎ **800/576-7512**). First week of August.

Wild Blueberry Festival, Machias. A festival marking the harvest of the region's wild blueberries. Eat to your heart's content (www.machiasblueberry.com; ☎ **207/255-6665** or 207/633-2353). Mid-August.

SEPTEMBER

Camden Windjammer Festival. Come visit Maine's impressive fleet of old-time sailing ships, which host open houses throughout the weekend at this scenic harbor (www.camdenwindjammerfestival.com; ☎ **800/562-25290**). Labor Day weekend.

Blue Hill Fair, Blue Hill. A classic country fair just outside one of Maine's most elegant villages. Call ☎ **207/374-3701**. Early September.

Common Ground Country Fair, Unity. A sprawling, old-time state fair with a twist: The emphasis is on organic foods, recycling, and wholesome living. Great music and demonstrations. This is a Maine classic (www.mofga.org/thefair; ☎ **207/568-4142**). Late September.

OCTOBER

Fall Foliage Festival, Boothbay. More than 100 exhibitors display their arts and crafts at the Railroad Village; plenty of festive foodstuffs and live music, too. Call ☎ **207/633-4727**. Early October.

Damariscotta Pumpkin Fest & Regatta. Many pumpkin-themed activities; huge painted pumpkin sculptures lining Main Street. But the highlight is when local crazies hop inside giant, hollowed-out pumpkins and race them across the harbor, either with paddles or outboard motors. You have to see it to believe it (www.mainepumpkinfest.com; ☎ **207/563-8340**). Columbus Day weekend.

Mount Desert Island Marathon, Bar Harbor. A scenic 26.2-mile race through gorgeous island scenery (www.runmdi.org; ☎ **207/276-4226**). Mid-October.

OgunquitFest, Ogunquit. A 3-day pre-Halloween bash, featuring arts, crafts, costumes, and a parade. Call ☎ **207/646-2939**. Late October.

NOVEMBER

Festival of Lights, Rockland. Horse-drawn carriages, singing, shopping, and open houses of local inns. Call ☎ **207/596-0376**. Late November.

Portland Beer Week. Special brewery tours, tap takeovers, a battle of the bands, and, of course, a tricycle race (www.portlandbeerweek.org). Early November.

DECEMBER

Christmas Prelude, Kennebunkport. Santa arrives in a lobster boat, followed by a blitz of street shows, pancake breakfasts, and tours of the town's splendid inns (www.christmasprelude.com; ☎ **207/967-0857**). Early December.

Vintage Christmas, Portsmouth, New Hampshire. The streets are decked, the tree is lit, and the historic Strawbery Banke Museum dazzles with old-time decorations and more than 1,000 candles lighting the 10-acre grounds (www.vintagechristmasnh.org; ☎ **603/433-1100**). First 3 weekends in December.

York Village Festival of Lights. This beautiful festival displays an entire York Village and York Beach lit with Christmas lights, carolers, a parade, and much more. Call ☎ **207/363-1040**. Early December.

STAYING HEALTHY

Mainers by and large are a healthy bunch, something locals ascribe to clean living, brisk northern air, vigorous exercise (leaf raking, snow shoveling, and so on), and a sensible diet. Other than picking up a germ that may lead to a cold or flu, you shouldn't face any serious health risks when traveling in the region.

Exceptions? Well, yes—you may find yourself at higher risk when exploring the outdoors, particularly in the backcountry. A few things to watch for when venturing off the beaten track:

POISON IVY The shiny, three-leafed plant is common throughout the region. If touched, you may develop a nasty, itchy rash that will seriously erode the enjoyment of your vacation. The reaction tends to be worse in some people than others. It's safest to simply avoid it. If you're unfamiliar with what poison ivy looks like, ask at a ranger station or visitor information booth for more information. Many have posters or books to help with identification.

GIARDIA That crystal-clear stream coursing down a backcountry peak may seem pure, but it may be contaminated with animal feces. Gross, yes, and also dangerous. Giardia cysts may be present in some streams and rivers. When ingested by humans, the cysts can result in copious diarrhea and weight loss. Symptoms may not surface until well after you've left the backcountry and returned home. Carry your own water for day trips, or bring a small filter (available at most camping and sporting-goods shops) to treat backcountry water. Failing that, at least boil water or treat it with iodine before using it for cooking, drinking, or washing. If you detect symptoms, see a doctor immediately.

LYME DISEASE Lyme disease has been a growing problem in New England since 1975 when the disease was identified in the town of Lyme, Connecticut, and some 25,000 cases are reported nationwide annually. The disease is transmitted by tiny deer ticks—smaller than the more

---

For Those Who Love Historic Homes

Historic New England is a nonprofit foundation that owns and operates 36 historic properties around New England, ranging from places built in the 17th century to the present, including a number of properties profiled in this book. Members get into all of the organization's properties for free, and receive a number of other benefits including a subscription to *Historic New England* magazine; a guide to the group's properties; and invitations to members-only events and other perks. Memberships cost $50 per year for individuals, $60 for households. For more information on Historic New England and its properties, visit the group's website at www.historicnewengland.org, or call the organization's Boston headquarters at ✆ **617/277-3956.**

common, relatively harmless wood ticks. Look for a bull's-eye-shaped rash (3-8 in. in diameter); it may feel warm but usually doesn't itch. Symptoms include muscle and joint pain, fever, and fatigue. If left untreated, heart damage may occur. It's more easily treated in early phases than later, so seek medical attention as soon as any symptoms are noted.

RABIES Since 1989, rabies has been spreading northward from New Jersey into New England. The disease is spread by animal saliva and is especially prevalent in skunks, raccoons, bats, and foxes. It is always fatal if left untreated in humans. Infected animals tend to display erratic and aggressive behavior. The best advice is to keep a safe distance between yourself and any wild animal you may encounter. If bitten, wash the wound as soon as you can and immediately seek medical attention. Treatment is no longer as painful as it once was, but still involves a series of shots.

Those planning longer excursions into the outdoors may find a compact first-aid kit with basic salves and medicines very handy to have along. Those traveling mostly in the towns and villages should have little trouble finding a local pharmacy, Rite Aid, or Walmart to stock up on common medicines (such as calamine lotion or aspirin) to aid with any minor ailments picked up along the way.

IF YOU GET SICK

If you suffer from a chronic illness, consult your doctor before your departure. For conditions like epilepsy, diabetes, or heart problems, wear a **MedicAlert identification tag** (© **888/633-4298**; www.medicalert.org), which will immediately alert doctors to your condition and give them access to your records through MedicAlert's 24-hour hot line. Pack **prescription medications** in your carry-on luggage, and carry them in their original containers, with pharmacy labels—otherwise they won't make it through airport security.

If you get sick while in Maine, consider asking your local hotel concierge to recommend a local doctor—even his or her own. You can also try the emergency room at a local hospital. Some hospitals in Maine have walk-in clinics for emergency cases that are not life-threatening. There are large, good hospitals and clinics in the cities of Maine, as well as many small towns. Check with your hotel or the local tourism office if you're concerned about proximity to hospitals.

SPECIAL INTEREST TRIPS

One rewarding way to spend a vacation is to learn a new outdoor skill or add to your knowledge. Maine especially lends itself to outdoorsy adventures that combine fresh air and exercise with Mother Nature as your instructor in Maine's vast, beautiful classroom. You can find plenty of options in Maine, ranging from formal weeklong classes to 1-day workshops. Here are a couple of the most popular:

FLY-FISHING IN MAINE   What says Maine more than L.L.Bean? The world-famous outdoors-store's educational offerings are growing by leaps and bounds, and are highly recommended by travelers of all ages. Among the many options, the intriguing fly-fishing outings are worth a look. There's a good catalog available by mail or at the flagship store (open 24 hours a day) on Main Street in Freeport (see p. 116). L.L.Bean also offers a number of shorter workshops on various outdoor skills through its **Outdoor Discovery Program** (www.llbean.com/adventures; ✆ 888/552-3261).

ALL ABOUT BIRDS   Budding and experienced naturalists can expand their understanding of marine wildlife while residing on 333-acre Hog Island in Maine's wild and scenic Muscongus Bay through the **Maine Audubon Society**. You're brought by boat, then stay on the island for 5 nights; see the web site **hogisland.audubon.org** for more details. (Famed birder Roger Tory Peterson once taught birding classes here.) I can personally vouch for Maine Audubon's other outdoors and educational programs, too. Call or visit their lovely headquarters at 20 Gilsland Farm Road in Falmouth (see p. 102; www.maineaudubon.org; ✆ **207/781-2330**), 10 minutes north of Portland.

TIPS ON ACCOMMODATIONS

"The more we travel," said an unhappy couple one morning at a nameless New England inn, "the more we realize why we go back to our old favorites time and again." The reason for their chagrin? They had been forced to switch rooms at 2am when rain had begun dripping right onto them through the ceiling. I hasten to add that this story is not an isolated incident. Small, quaint inns here often come with their own drips, creaks, and quirks.

Maine is famous for its country inns and bed-and-breakfasts, which offer a wonderful alternative to the sort of cookie-cutter, chain-hotel rooms that line U.S. highways from coast to coast. But (as the unhappy couple learned) there are reasons why some people prefer the cookie-cutter hotels. In a chain hotel,

---

Renting a House or Cottage in Maine

Renting a house or cottage in Maine for a week is another good option, particularly outside the summer high season, though there really isn't a centralized resource for doing so. You get the comforts of having your own kitchen or kitchenette and not worrying about parking, checkout times, or untimely "room service" knocks on your door. For a nice house with an ample supply of bedrooms and an unobstructed ocean view, expect to pay anywhere from $2,000 to $10,000 per week; a simpler cottage will run you less but might still cost more than you expected. Do a Web search for Maine house or cottage rentals, or go to a nationwide rent-by-owner website such as **www.vrbo.com**. In various regional chapters, we've also listed local rental services we've found. While these certainly aren't the only choices along the Maine coast, they'll give you a good head start.

The difference between an inn and a B&B may be confusing for some travelers, since the gap between the two narrows by the day. A couple of decades ago, inns were full-service affairs, whereas B&Bs consisted of private homes with an extra bedroom or two and a homeowner looking for a little extra income. These old-style B&Bs still exist around the region. I've occupied a few evenings sitting in a well-used living room watching Tom Brokaw with the owner, as if visiting with a forgotten aunt.

Today, however, B&Bs are more commonly professionally run affairs, where guests have private bathrooms, a separate common area, and attentive service. The owners have apartments tucked away in the back, prepare sumptuous breakfasts in the morning (some

B&Bs offer "candlelight breakfasts"), and offer a high level of service. All of the B&Bs in this guide are of the more professionally run variety (although some still have shared bathrooms).

The sole difference between inns and B&Bs—at least as defined by this guide—is that inns serve dinner (and sometimes lunch). B&Bs provide breakfast only. Readers shouldn't infer that B&Bs are necessarily more informal or in any way inferior to a full-service inn. Indeed, many have the air of gracious inns that just happened to have overlooked serving dinner. That's true for many of the B&Bs listed in this guide; and with a little luck, you'll stumble into Ralph Waldo Emerson's idea of simple contentment: "Hospitality consists in a little fire, a little food, and an immense quiet," he wrote in his journal.

you can be reasonably sure that water won't drip through your ceiling in the middle of the night. Likewise, the beds will be firm, the sink will be relatively new, and you'll have a TV, telephone, and counter space next to the bathroom sink.

Every **inn** and **B&B** listed in this guide yields a decent, and often high-quality, experience. Just keep in mind that each place is different, and you need to match the personality of the place with your own personality. Some inns are more polished and fussier than others; this is a rural area, so a lot of them (even some calling themselves "resorts") lack basic amenities to which business travelers have grown accustomed in chain hotels. (In-room phones and air-conditioning lead the list.)

Saving on Your Lodging

How to save on lodgings? Let us count the ways! Here are just a few tips for those who need to pinch pennies.

o **Consider private B&B accommodations and complete home rentals.** As most travelers know, it's often cheaper to rent a room in someone's home or a complete house than it is to stay in a hotel. That's why you'll now find dozens upon dozens of options on **AirBnB.com, HomeAway.com, VRBO. com, FlipKey.com, Wimdu.com** and others. Please note that *none* of these services vet the homes they're renting for quality; these are simply clearing-houses. So look at the pictures carefully and ask a lot of questions before booking. Remember too that there are fees attached to these types of arrangements, which always include a percentage given to the website through which you've booked; and may also include a cleaning fee. So be sure to add up *all* the numbers before committing.

- **Consider the timing carefully.** Resort hotels are most crowded and therefore most expensive on weekends, so discounts are usually available for midweek stays. And in Maine, summer prices are vastly different from off-season rates.

- **Sidestep excess surcharges and hidden costs**. Many hotels have the unpleasant practice of nickel-and-diming their guests with opaque surcharges. When you book a room, ask what is included in the room rate, and what is extra. Avoid dialing direct from hotel phones, which can have exorbitant rates. And don't be tempted by the room's minibar offerings: Most hotels charge through the nose for water, soda, and snacks. Finally, ask about local taxes and service charges, which can increase the cost of a room by 15% or more

- **Know your resort fees.** There are a small handful of **all-inclusive** resorts in Maine. The term "all-inclusive" means different things at different hotels; here, it means three meals daily and use of the resort's sports equipment (such as canoes and kayaks). You should also carefully consider your hotel's **meal plan**. If you enjoy eating out and sampling the local cuisine, it makes sense to choose a Continental plan (also known as B&B), or a European plan, which doesn't include any meals and allows you maximum flexibility. If you're more interested in saving money, opt for a Modified American plan (MAP), which includes breakfast and dinner, or the American plan, which includes all three meals (quite rare in this region). If you must choose a MAP, see if you can get a free lunch at your hotel if you decide to do dinner out.

- **Ask if the hotel charges extra for additional guests** (beyond two). The room rates published in this guide are all for two people sharing one room. Most places charge $10 and up per extra guest sharing the room. Don't assume that children traveling with you can stay for free—usually they can, but ask first about extra charges—and don't assume that every room can hold more than two.

- **Ask about a minimum stay requirement and discounts for multiday stays.** Many inns now require guests to book a minimum of 2 nights or more during the busiest times (holiday weekends, peak ski season, peak fall foliage season). These policies are mentioned in the following pages if known, but check anyway. And they might not apply if you walk in off the street; innkeepers develop sudden amnesia when faced with a chance to sell an empty room on a Saturday night despite a policy against such a stay.

Service Charges

Rather than increase room rates in the face of rising competition, hotels, inns, and B&Bs are increasingly tacking on nickel-and-dime fees to their guests' bills. Most innkeepers will tell you about these fees when you reserve or check in; a few will surprise you at checkout.

The most common surcharge is an involuntary "service charge" of 10% to 15%. Coupled with state lodging taxes (even "sales-tax-free" New Hampshire hits tourists with a 9% levy), that bumps the cost of a bed up by nearly 25%. (The rates listed in this guide don't include service charges or sales tax.)

Other charges may include a pet fee ($10 or more per day extra), a foliage-season surcharge ($10—$50 per room), and a "resort fee" (of 15%—20% tax at certain resorts). Some hotels even tack on a $1 per day fee for the presence of an in-room safe, whether it is used or not.

Traveling with Pets

No surprise: Some places allow pets, some don't. I've noted inns that allow pets, but I don't recommend showing up with a pet in tow unless you've cleared it over the phone with the innkeeper. Note that many establishments have only one or two rooms (often a cottage or room with exterior entrance) set aside for guests traveling with pets, and they won't be happy to meet Fido if the pet rooms are already occupied. Also, it's increasingly common for a surcharge of $10 or $40 to be charged to pet owners to pay for the extra cleaning. On the positive side, all **Motel 6** hotels accept pets as a matter of policy, and so (surprisingly) do some upscale inns.

Keep in mind that dogs are prohibited on hiking trails and must be leashed at all times on federal lands administered by the National Park Service (this includes Acadia National Park; see chapter 8). But **no pets of any sort are allowed at any time** (leashed or unleashed) into Baxter State Park (see p. 262), a short side trip from the coast. Most other Maine state parks do allow pets on a leash, however.

[FastFACTS] COASTAL MAINE

Area Codes Maine's area code is **207** throughout.

Business Hours Shops in Maine are usually open weekdays from 9am to 6pm, Saturdays from 10am until 5 to 7pm, and Sundays from noon until 5 or 6pm. In bigger cities like Portland, and in shopping-mall and outlet-shop areas, shops stay open

as late as 9pm during peak shopping days and/or seasons.

Cellphones (Mobile Phones) Don't take a cell signal for granted on the back roads of Maine, or even at your rustic country B&B. It's a good bet that your phone will work in the region's major cities and along Route 1, at least until

you get way Downeast. The peninsulas can be a crap-shoot, though, and the same goes for heading inland. Before heading out, Look over your wireless company's coverage map on its website; T-Mobile and Sprint are particularly weak at covering rural areas.

Foreign cellphones may or may not work here due

to the poorly developed GSM network; they will probably work on the southern Maine coast, but may not on the rest of the coast. Foreign phones may or may not be able to use SMS to send text messages.

Need to rent a cellphone? Check at the airport in Boston or Portland when you arrive. Or head for a shopping mall or the central business district/main street of the town or city you're visiting.

Drinking Laws The legal age for purchase and consumption of alcoholic beverages is 21; proof of age is required and often requested at bars, nightclubs, and restaurants, so it's always a good idea to bring ID when you go out. Do not carry open containers of alcohol in your car or any public area that isn't zoned for alcohol consumption. The police can fine you on the spot. Don't even think about driving while intoxicated.

Liquor of some sort is sold at special, state-operated stores; some supermarkets; and many convenience stores in Maine. Restaurants without liquor licenses sometimes allow patrons to bring in their own—this is particularly common at lobster shacks, but ask first. Bars sell liquor until 1am in Maine.

Electricity Like Canada, the United States uses 110 to 120 volts AC (60 cycles), compared to 220 to 240 volts AC (50 cycles) in most of Europe, Australia, and New Zealand. Downward converters that change 220–240 volts to 110–120 volts are difficult to find in the United States, so bring one with you.

Embassies & Consulates All embassies are located in the nation's capital, Washington, D.C. The embassy of the **United Kingdom** is at 3100 Massachusetts Ave. NW, Washington, DC 20008 (www.britainusa.com; *℡* **202/588-6500**). Other British consulates are located in Atlanta, Chicago, Denver, Houston, Los Angeles, Miami, New York, San Francisco, and Seattle. The embassy of **Ireland** is at 2234 Massachusetts Ave. NW, Washington, DC 20008 (*℡* **202/462-3939;** www.irelandemb.org). Other Irish consulates are located in Chicago, New York, and San Francisco. The embassy of **Australia** is at 1601 Massachusetts Ave. NW, Washington, DC 20036 (*℡* **202/ 797-3000;** usa.embassy.gov. au). There are consulates in Chicago, New York, Honolulu, Houston, Los Angeles, and San Francisco. The embassy of **Canada** is at 501 Pennsylvania Ave. NW, Washington, DC 20001 (*℡* **202/682-1740;** www. canadianembassy.org). Other Canadian consulates are in Atlanta, Boston, Chicago, Dallas, Denver, Detroit, Los Angeles, Miami, Minneapolis, New York, San Francisco, and Seattle. The embassy of **New Zealand** is at 37 Observatory Circle NW, Washington, DC 20008 (*℡* **202/328-4800;** www.

mfat.gov.nz). New Zealand consulates are in Honolulu, Los Angeles, and New York.

For travelers from the British Isles, consular services are relatively close to Maine. The **British Consulate** *℡* **617/245-4500**) is at 1 Broadway in Cambridge, MA, on the campus of the Massachusetts Institute of Technology (MIT). And the **Irish Consulate** (*℡* **617/ 267-9330**) is on the 5th floor of 535 Boylston St. in Boston, near Copley Square.

Emergencies For fire, police, and ambulance, find any phone and dial *℡* **911.** If this somehow fails, dial 0 (zero) and report an emergency.

Gasoline(Petrol) Gasoline in the U.S. is sold in gallons, at stations known variously as "gas stations" or "service stations." One gallon is equal to 3.8 liters or 0.85 imperial gallons. Gas in Maine is a bit more expensive than it is in some other parts of the U.S., but still much cheaper than it is in Canada, Europe, Asia, and Australia. There are next to no full-service gas stations in Maine, meaning you can expect to pump the gas yourself.

Internet Access Many of Maine's **public libraries** maintain computer terminals with free public Internet access. It is a rare Maine inns or hotel these days that does not offer free Wi-Fi with your stay; ask when booking or checking in. Internet cafes come and go, but any reasonably hip **coffee shop** on the coast is also likely to have free Wi-Fi.

LGBTQ Travelers In 2012, Maine became one of the first three states to legalize same-sex marriage by popular vote. **Portland** hosts a sizable pride festival early each summer that includes a riotous parade and a dance on the city pier. South of Portland, **Ogunquit** is hugely popular among gay travelers, a longtime (even historic) gay resort area that features a lively beach-and-bar scene in the summer. A website, **www.gayogunquit.com**, lists information on locally gay-owned inns, restaurants, and nightclubs.

Lost Property Most bus and train stations, stores, and hotels keep lost items for a few weeks. Ask for **"lost and found."** If your credit card disappears or is stolen, contact your credit card companies immediately. (If theft was involved, also call police and get a printed police report.) Be sure to tell all of your credit card companies the minute you discover your wallet has been lost or stolen, and file a report at the nearest police precinct. Your credit card company or insurer may require a police report number or record of the loss.

Most credit card companies have an emergency toll-free number to call if your card is lost or stolen; they may be able to wire you a cash advance immediately or deliver an emergency credit card in a day or two. Visa's emergency number

is 📞 **800/847-2911;** MasterCard's is 📞 **800/627-8372;** and American Express is at 📞 **800/528-4800.**

If you need emergency cash over the weekend when all banks and American Express offices are closed, you can have money wired to you via **Western Union** (📞 **800/325-6000;** www.westernunion.com).

Mail Every town and city in Maine has a post office—in the smallest towns, it may double as a grocer or other business. At press time, domestic letters cost 47¢ (up to 1 oz.) and postcards cost 34¢. International rates are always higher. For more information on rates, go to the website **www.usps.com** and click on "Calculate a Price."

Newspapers & Magazines The *Portland Press Herald* is Portland's daily newspaper, with decent listings; the free *Portland Phoenix* and *Dispatch* are also very handy for listings of southern Maine concerts, clubs, and art shows. The biggest paper in the Downeast and Midcoast regions is the daily *Bangor Daily News*. Regional newspapers still abound in the rest of coastal Maine, too, from the *York Weekly* to the *Biddeford Journal Tribune*, *Mount Desert Islander*, *Brunswick Times-Record*, and the *Camden Herald*. There are a number of quality glossy magazines based in Maine, from longtime star *Down East* to *Portland Monthly* to *WoodenBoat*.

Police Dial 📞 **911.** You can also find the direct phone numbers for many of Maine's small-town police stations in the local phone book.

Safety Maine boasts some of the lowest crime rates in the country. The odds of anything bad happening during your visit here are very slight. But all travelers are advised to take the usual precautions against theft, robbery, and assault. The crime you're statistically most likely to encounter is theft of items from your car. Don't leave anything of value in plain view, and lock valuables in your trunk. Better still, keep them with you at all times.

Take the usual precautions against leaving cash or valuables in your hotel room when you're not present. Many hotels have safe-deposit boxes. Smaller inns and hotels often do not, but it can't hurt to ask to leave small items in the house safe.

Senior Travel Maine is well suited to older travelers, with a wide array of activities for seniors and discounts commonly available. Members of **AARP** (www.aarp.org; 📞 **888/687-2277**), get discounts on hotels, airfares, and car rentals. (But check these against the normal online discounts; the AARP price isn't always lower.) The U.S. National Park Service's **America the Beautiful Senior Pass** gives seniors 62 years or older lifetime entrance to all properties administered by the

National Park Service—national parks, monuments, historic sites, recreation areas, and national wildlife refuges—for a one-time processing fee of $10. The pass must be purchased in person at any NPS facility that charges an entrance fee. Besides free entry, the America the Beautiful Senior Pass also offers a 50% discount on some fees for camping, swimming, parking, boat launching, and tours. For more information, go to **www.nps.gov/fees_passes.htm**.

Smoking Smoking is now banned in *all* workplaces and public places (restaurants, bars, offices, hotel lobbies) in Maine.

Taxes The United States has no value-added tax (VAT) or other indirect tax at the national level. Every state, county, and city may levy its own local tax on all purchases, including hotel and restaurant checks and airline tickets. Maine has a 5.5% sales tax on most consumer goods and a 9% tax on lodging. These taxes will not appear on price tags.

Time The entire Maine coast lies within the **Eastern Standard Time zone (EST).** When it's noon in Bar Harbor and Portland, it's also noon in New York City, and it's 11am in Chicago (CST), 10am in Denver (MST), 9am in Los Angeles (PST), and 5pm in London (GMT).

Daylight saving time is in effect from 1am on the second Sunday in March to 1am on the first Sunday in November, except in

Arizona, Hawaii, the U.S. Virgin Islands, and Puerto Rico. Daylight saving time moves the clock 1 hour ahead of standard time.

Tipping Tips are a very important part of certain workers' income, and gratuities are the standard way of showing appreciation for services provided. However, tipping is certainly not compulsory if service is poor. In hotels, tip **bellhops** $2 or more per bag ($3–$5 if you have a lot of luggage) and tip **housekeeping staff** a few dollars per day (more if you have a large suite). Tip the **doorman** or **concierge** if some specific service was provided (for example, calling a cab or obtaining difficult-to-get theater tickets). Tip **valet-parking attendants** $3 to $5 each time you get your car.

In restaurants, bars, and nightclubs, tip **service staff** 15% to 20% of the check, tip **bartenders** 10% to 15%, tip **checkroom attendants** $1 per garment.

Tip **cabdrivers** 15% of your fare; tip **skycaps** at airports at least $1 per bag ($2–$3 if you have a lot of luggage).

Toilets In coastal Maine, they're called **bathrooms** or restrooms. Find them in hotel lobbies, bars, coffee shops, restaurants, fast-food places, museums, department stores, train stations, and some gas stations. (Sometimes, you will need to ask the cashier for a key, or make a purchase first.)

Travelers with Disabilities If you plan to visit

Acadia National Park, consider obtaining the **America The Beautiful National Park Access Pass,** which gives visually impaired or permanently disabled persons free lifetime entrance to sites administered by the National Park Service. This may include national parks, monuments, historic sites, recreation areas, and national wildlife refuges. The pass can only be obtained in person at any NPS facility that charges an entrance fee. You need to show proof of a medically determined disability. Besides free entry, the pass also offers a 50% discount on some fees for camping, swimming, parking, boat launching, and tours. For more information, go to **www.nps.gov/planyourvisit/passes.htm**, or call the United States Geological Survey (USGS) at © **888/275-8747**. For more on organizations that offer resources to travelers with disabilities, go to frommers.com.

Traveling with Children Families will have little trouble finding fun, low-key things to do with kids in Maine. Some recommended destinations include **York Beach** and **Acadia National Park**. Be sure to ask about family discounts when visiting attractions. Many places offer a flat family rate that costs less than paying for each ticket individually. Note that some parks and beaches charge by the carload rather than the head count.

Index

See also Accommodations and
Restaurant indexes, below.

General Index

Accommodations

Restaurants

Map List

Photo Credits

Frommer's Maine Coast 2017, 5th Edition

Published by

FROMMER MEDIA LLC

Copyright © 2017 by FrommerMedia LLC, New York City, New York. All rights reserved. No part of this publication may be reproduced, stored in a retrieval system, or transmitted in any form or by any means, electronic, mechanical, photocopying, recording, scanning or otherwise, except as permitted under Sections 107 or 108 of the 1976 United States Copyright Act, without the prior written permission of the Publisher. Requests to the Publisher for permission should be addressed to the Permissions Department, FrommerMedia LLC, 44 West 62nd Street, New York, NY 10023, or online at http://www.frommers.com/permissions.

Frommer's is a registered trademark of Arthur Frommer. FrommerMedia LLC is not associated with any product or vendor mentioned in this book.

ISBN 978-1-62887-326-9 (paper), 978-1-62887-327-6 (e-book)

Editorial Director: Pauline Frommer
Editor: Holly Hughes
Production Editor: Lindsay Conner
Cartographer: Roberta Stockwell
Photo Editor: Meghan Lamb
Cover Design: David Riedy

Front cover photo: Portland Head Lighthouse ©Scottartguy/shutterstock.com

For information on our other products or services, see www.frommers.com.

FrommerMedia LLC also publishes its books in a variety of electronic formats. Some content that appears in print may not be available in electronic formats.

Manufactured in the United States of America

5 4 3 2 1

ABOUT THE UPDATER

Brian Kevin is the managing editor of *Down East* magazine and has written for *Outside, Travel + Leisure, Men's Journal, Audubon,* and a number of other magazines. His work has been recognized or anthologized in *Best Food Writing, Best American Essays,* and *Best American Sports Writing,* and he's the author of *The Footloose American: Following the Hunter S. Thompson Trail Across South America.* He lives in Damariscotta, Maine.

ABOUT THE FROMMER TRAVEL GUIDES

For most of the past 50 years, Frommer's has been the leading series of travel guides in North America, accounting for as many as 24% of all guidebooks sold. I think I know why.

Though we hope our books are entertaining, we nevertheless deal with travel in a serious fashion. Our guidebooks have never looked on such journeys as a mere recreation, but as a far more important human function, a time of learning and introspection, an essential part of a civilized life. We stress the culture, lifestyle, history, and beliefs of the destinations we cover, and urge our readers to seek out people and new ideas as the chief rewards of travel.

We have never shied from controversy. We have, from the beginning, encouraged our authors to be intensely judgmental, critical—both pro and con—in their comments, and wholly independent. Our only clients are our readers, and we have triggered the ire of countless prominent sorts, from a tourist newspaper we called "practically worthless" (it unsuccessfully sued us) to the many rip-offs we've condemned.

And because we believe that travel should be available to everyone regardless of their incomes, we have always been cost-conscious at every level of expenditure. Though we have broadened our recommendations beyond the budget category, we insist that every lodging we include be sensibly priced. We use every form of media to assist our readers, and are particularly proud of our feisty daily website, the award-winning Frommers.com.

I have high hopes for the future of Frommer's. May these guidebooks, in all the years ahead, continue to reflect the joy of travel and the freedom that travel represents. May they always pursue a cost-conscious path, so that people of all incomes can enjoy the rewards of travel. And may they create, for both the traveler and the persons among whom we travel, a community of friends, where all human beings live in harmony and peace.

Arthur Frommer